CHILTON'S
REPAIR & TUNE-UP GUIDE
AMERICAN MOTORS 1975-82

AMX • Concord • Eagle • Gremlin • Hornet • Kammback
Matador • Pacer • Spirit • SX-4

Vice President and General Manager JOHN P. KUSHNERICK
Managing Editor KERRY A. FREEMAN, S.A.E.
Senior Editor RICHARD J. RIVELE, S.A.E.
Editor RICHARD J. RIVELE, S.A.E.

CHILTON BOOK COMPANY
Radnor, Pennsylvania
19089

SAFETY NOTICE

Proper service and repair procedures are vital to the safe, reliable operation of all motor vehicles, as well as the personal safety of those performing repairs. This book outlines procedures for servicing and repairing vehicles using safe, effective methods. The procedures contain many NOTES, CAUTIONS and WARNINGS which should be followed along with standard safety procedures to eliminate the possibility of personal injury or improper service which could damage the vehicle or compromise its safety.

It is important to note that repair procedures and techniques, tools and parts for servicing motor vehicles, as well as the skill and experience of the individual performing the work vary widely. It is not possible to anticipate all of the conceivable ways or conditions under which vehicles may be serviced, or to provide cautions as to all of the possible hazards that may result. Standard and accepted safety precautions and equipment should be used when handling toxic or flammable fluids, and safety goggles or other protection should be used during cutting, grinding, chiseling, prying, or any other process that can cause material removal or projectiles.

Some procedures require the use of tools specially designed for a specific purpose. Before substituting another tool or procedure, you must be completely satisfied that neither your personal safety, nor the performance of the vehicle will be endangered.

Although information in this guide is based on industry sources and is as complete as possible at the time of publication, the possibility exists that the manufacturer made later changes which could not be included here. While striving for total accuracy, Chilton Book Company cannot assume responsibility for any errors, changes, or omissions that may occur in the compilation of this data.

PART NUMBERS

Part numbers listed in this reference are not recommendations by Chilton for any product by brand name. They are references that can be used with interchange manuals and aftermarket supplier catalogs to locate each brand supplier's discrete part number.

ACKNOWLEDGMENTS

The Chilton Book Company expresses its appreciation to the American Motors Corporation, Detroit, Michigan for their generous assistance in the preparation of this book.

CONTENTS

Quick Reference Specifications For Your Vehicle

Fill in this chart with the most commonly used specifications for your vehicle. Specifications can be found in Chapters 1 through 3 or on the tune-up decal under the hood of the vehicle.

 Tune-Up

Firing Order_____

Spark Plugs:

Type_____

Gap (in.)_____

Point Gap (in.)_____

Dwell Angle (°)_____

Ignition Timing (°)_____

Vacuum (Connected/Disconnected)_____ _____

Valve Clearance (in.)

Intake_____ Exhaust_____

Capacities

Engine Oil (qts)

With Filter Change_____

Without Filter Change_____

Cooling System (qts)_____

Manual Transmission (pts)_____

Type_____

Automatic Transmission (pts)_____

Type_____

Front Differential (pts)_____

Type_____

Rear Differential (pts)_____

Type_____

Transfer Case (pts)_____

Type_____

FREQUENTLY REPLACED PARTS

Use these spaces to record the part numbers of frequently replaced parts.

PCV VALVE

Manufacturer_____

Part No._____

OIL FILTER

Manufacturer_____

Part No._____

AIR FILTER

Manufacturer_____

Part No._____

General Information and Maintenance

HOW TO USE THIS BOOK

Chilton's Repair & Tune-Up Guide for American Motors Cars is intended to help you learn more about the inner workings of your vehicle and save you money on its upkeep and operation.

The first two chapters will be the most used, since they contain maintenance and tune-up information and procedures. Studies have shown that a properly tuned and maintained car can get at least 10% better gas mileage than an out-of-tune car. The other chapters deal with the more complex systems of your car. Operating systems from engine through brakes are covered to the extent that the average do-it-yourselfer becomes mechanically involved. This book will not explain such things as rebuilding the differential for the simple reason that the expertise required and the investment in special tools make this task uneconomical. It will give you detailed instructions to help you change your own brake pads and shoes, replace points and plugs, and do many more jobs that will save you money, give you personal satisfaction, and help you avoid expensive problems.

A secondary purpose of this book is a reference for owners who want to understand their car and/or their mechanics better. In this case, no tools at all are required.

Before removing any bolts, read through the entire procedure. This will give you the overall view of what tools and supplies will be required. There is nothing more frustrating than having to walk to the bus stop on Monday morning because you were short one bolt on Sunday afternoon. So read ahead and plan ahead. Each operation should be approached logically and all procedures throughly understood before attempting any work.

All chapters contain adjustments, maintenance, removal and installation procedures, and repair or overhaul procedures. When repair is not considered practical, we tell you how to remove the part and then how to install the new or rebuilt replacement. In this way, you at least save the labor costs. Backyard repair of such components as the alternator is just not practical.

Two basic mechanic's rules should be mentioned here. One, whenever the left side of the car or engine is referred to, it is meant to specify the driver's side of the car. Conversely, the right side of the car means the passenger's side. Secondly, most screws and bolts are removed by turning counterclockwise, and tightened by turning clockwise.

Safety is always the most important rule. Constantly be aware of the dangers involved in working on an automobile and taking the proper precautions. (See the section in this chapter "Servicing Your Vehicle Safely" and the SAFETY NOTICE on the acknowledgement page.)

Pay attention to the instructions provided. There are 3 common mistakes in mechanical work:

1. Incorrect order of assembly, disassembly or adjustment. When taking something apart or putting it together, doing things in the wrong order usually just costs you extra time; however, it CAN break something. Read the entire procedure before beginning disassembly. Do everything in the order in which the instructions say you should do it, even if you can't immediately see a reason for it. When you're taking apart something that is very intricate (for example, a carburetor), you might want to draw a picture of how it looks when assembled at one point in order to make sure you get everything back in its proper position. (We will supply exploded views whenever possible.) When making adjustments, especially tune-up adjustments, do them in order; often, one adjustment affects another, and you cannot expect even satisfactory results unless each adjustment is made only when it cannot be changed by any other.

2. Overtorquing (or undertorquing). While it is more common for overtorquing to cause damage, undertorquing can cause a fastener to vibrate loose causing serious damage. Especially when dealing with a aluminum parts, pay attention to torque specifications and utilize a torque wrench in assembly. If a torque figure is not available, remember that if you are using the right tool to do the job, you will probably not have to strain yourself to get a fastener tight enough. The pitch of most threads is so slight that the tension you put on the wrench will be multiplied many, many times in actual force on what you are tightening. A good example of how critical torque is can be seen in the case of spark plug installation, especially where you are putting the plug into an aluminum cylinder head. Too little torque can fail to crush the gasket, causing leakage of combustion gases and consequent overheating of the plug and engine parts. Too much torque can damage the threads, or distort the plug, which changes the spark gap.

There are many commercial products available for ensuring that fasteners won't come loose, even if they are not torqued just right (a very common brand is "Loctite®"). If you're worried about getting something together tight enough to hold, but loose enough to avoid mechanical damage during assembly, one of these products might offer substantial insurance. Read the label on the package and make sure the product is compatible with the materials, fluids, etc. involved before choosing one.

3. Crossthreading. This occurs when a part such as a bolt is screwed into a nut or casting at the wrong angle and forced. Crossthreading is more likely to occur if access is difficult. It helps to clean and lubricate fasteners, and to start threading with the part to be installed going straight in. Then, start the bolt, spark plug, etc. with your fingers. If you encounter resistance, unscrew the part and start over again at a different angle until it can be inserted and turned several turns without much effort. Keep in mind that many parts, especially spark plugs, use tapered threads so that gentle turning will automatically bring the part you're threading to the proper angle if you don't force it or resist a change in angle. Don't put a wrench on the part until it's been turned a couple of turns by hand. If you suddenly encounter resistance, and the part has not seated fully, don't force it. Pull it back out and make sure it's clean and threading properly.

Always take your time and be patient; once you have some experience, working on your car will become an enjoyable hobby.

TOOLS AND EQUIPMENT

Naturally, without the proper tools and equipment it is impossible to properly service your vehicle. It would be impossible to catalog each tool that you would need to perform each or any operation in this book. It would also be unwise for the amateur to rush out and buy an expensive set of tools on the theory that he may need one or more of them at sometime.

The best approach is to proceed slowly, gathering together a good quality set of those tools that are used most frequently. Don't be misled by the low cost of bargain tools. It is far better to spend a little more for better quality. Forged wrenches, 10 or 12 point sockets and fine tooth ratchets are by far preferable to their less expensive counterparts. As any good mechanic can tell you, there are few worse experiences than trying to work on a car or truck with bad tools. Your monetary savings will be far outweighed by frustration and mangled knuckles.

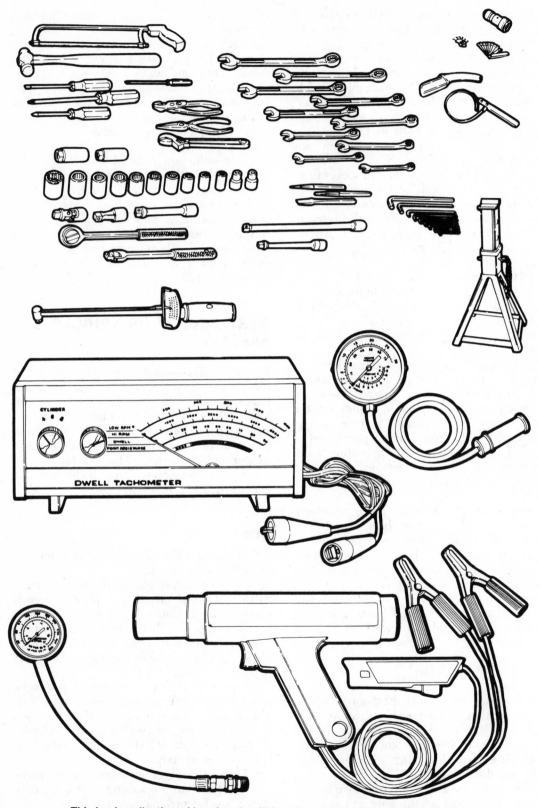

This basic collection of hand tools will handle most of your automotive needs

Begin accumulating those tools that are used most frequently; those associated with routine maintenance and tuneup.

In addition to the normal assortment of screwdrivers and pliers you should have the following tools for routine maintenance jobs (AMC uses both SAE and metric fasteners):

1. SAE/Metric wrenches—sockets and combination open end/box end wrenches in sizes from ⅛ in. (3 mm) to ¾ in. (19 mm); and a spark plug socket ($^{13}/_{16}$).

If possible, buy various length socket drive extensions. One break in this department is that the metric sockets available in the U.S. will all fit the ratchet handles and extensions you may already have (¼, ⅜, and ½ in. drive).

2. Jackstands—for support;

3. Oil filter wrench;

4. Oil filler spout—for pouring oil;

5. Grease gun—for chassis lubrication;

6. Hydrometer—for checking the battery;

7. A container for draining oil;

8. Many rags for wiping up the inevitable mess.

In addition to the above items there are several others that are not absolutely necessary, but handy to have around. These include oil dry, a transmission funnel and the usual supply of lubricants, antifreeze and fluids, although these can be purchased as needed. This is a basic list for routine maintenance, but only your personal needs and desire can accurately determine your list of tools.

The second list of tools is for tune-ups. While the tools involved here are slightly more sophisticated, they need not be outrageously expensive. There are several inexpensive tach/dwell meters on the market that are every bit as good for the average mechanic as a $100.00 professional model. Just be sure that it goes to a least 1,200–1,500 rpm on the tach scale and that it works on 4, 6 and 8 cylinder engines. A basic list of tune-up equipment could include:

1. Tach-dwell meter;

2. Spark plug wrench;

3. Timing light (a DC light that works from the car's battery is best, although an AC light that plugs into 110V house current will suffice at some sacrifice in brightness);

4. Wire spark plug gauge/adjusting tools;

5. Set of feeler blades.

Here again, be guided by your own needs. A feeler blade will set the pont gap as easily as dwell meter will read dwell, but slightly less accurately. And since you will need a ta-chometer anyway . . . well, make your own decision.

In addition to these basic tools, there are several other tools and gauges you may find useful. These include:

1. A compression gauge. the screw-in type is slower to use, but eliminates the possibility of a faulty reading due to escaping pressure;

2. A manifold vacuum gauge;

3. A test light;

4. An induction meter. This is used for determining whether or not there is current in a wire. These are handy for use if a wire is broken somewhere in a wiring harness.

As a final note, you will probably find a torque wrench necessary for all but the most basic work. The beam type models are perfectly adequate, although the newer click type are more precise.

SERVICING YOUR VEHICLE SAFELY

It is virtually impossible to anticipate all of the hazards involved with automotive maintenance and service but care and common sense will prevent most accidents.

The rules of safety for mechanics range from "don't smoke around gasoline," to "use the proper tool for the job." The trick to avoiding injuries is to develop safe work habits and take every possible precaution.

Dos

• Do keep a fire extinguisher and first aid kit within easy reach.

• Do wear safety glasses or goggles when cutting, drilling, grinding or prying, even if you have 20-20 vision. If you wear glasses for the sake of vision, then they should be made of hardened glass that can serve also as safety glasses, or wear safety gogggles over your regular glasses.

• Do shield your eyes whenever you work around the battery. Batteries contain sulphuric acid; in case of contact with the eyes or skin, flush the area with water or a mixture of water and baking soda and get medical attention immediately.

• Do use safety stands for any undercar service. Jacks are for raising vehicles; safety stands are for making sure the vehicle stays raised until you want it to come down. Whenever the vehicle is raised, block the wheels remaining on the ground and set the parking brake.

• Do use adequate ventilation when working with any chemicals. Like carbon monoxide, the asbestos dust resulting from brake lining wear can be poisonous in sufficient quantities.

• Do disconnect the negative battery cable when working on the electrical system. The primary ignition system can contain up to 40,000 volts.

• Do follow manufacturer's directions whenever working with potentially hazardous materials. Both brake fluid and antifreeze are poisonous if taken internally.

• Do properly maintain your tools. Loose hammerheads, mushroomed punches and chisels, frayed or poorly grounded electrical cords, excessively worn screwdrivers, spread wrenches (open end), cracked sockets, slipping ratchets, or faulty droplight sockets can cause accidents.

• Do use the proper size and type of tool for the job being done.

• Do when possible, pull on a wrench handle rather than push on it, and adjust your stance to prevent a fall.

• Do be sure that adjustable wrenches are tightly adjusted on the nut or bolt and pulled

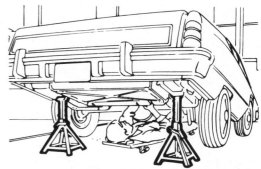

Always use jackstands when working under the car

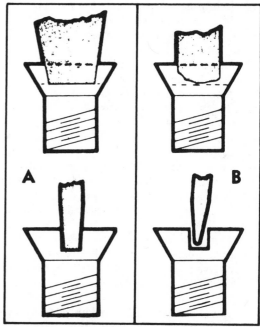

Keep screwdriver tips in good shape. They should fit the slot as shown in "A". If they look like those in "B", they need grinding or replacing

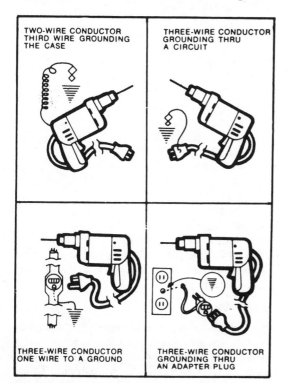

TWO-WIRE CONDUCTOR THIRD WIRE GROUNDING THE CASE

THREE-WIRE CONDUCTOR GROUNDING THRU A CIRCUIT

THREE-WIRE CONDUCTOR ONE WIRE TO A GROUND

THREE-WIRE CONDUCTOR GROUNDING THRU AN ADAPTER PLUG

When using electric tools make sure they are properly grounded

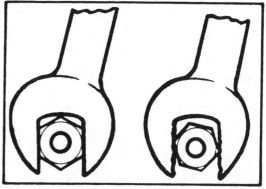

If you're using an open end wrench, use the correct size, and position it properly on the nut or bolt

so that the face is on the side of the fixed jaw.

• Do select a wrench or socket that fits the nut or bolt. The wrench or socket should sit straight, not cocked.

• Do strike squarely with a hammer—avoid glancing blows.

• Do set the parking brake and block the drive wheels if the work requires that the engine be running.

Don'ts

• Don't run an engine in a garage or anywhere else without proper ventilation—EVER! Carbon monoxide is poisonous; it takes a long time to leave the human body and you can build up a deadly supply of it in your system by simply breathing in a little every day. You may not realize you are slowly poisoning yourself. Always use power vents, windows, fans or open the garage doors.

• Don't work around moving parts while wearing a necktie or other loose clothing. Short sleeves are much safer than long, loose sleeves and hard-toed shoes with neoprene soles protect your toes and give a better grip on slippery surfaces. Jewelry such as watches, fancy belt buckles, beads or body adornment of any kind is not safe working around a car. Long hair should be hidden under a hat or cap.

• Don't use pockets for toolboxes. A fall or bump can drive a screwdrive deep into your body. Even a wiping cloth hanging from the back pocket can wrap around a spinning shaft or fan.

• Don't smoke when working around gasoline, cleaning solvent or other flammable material.

• Don't smoke when working around the battery. When the battery is being charged, it gives off explosive hydrogen gas.

• Don't use gasoline to wash your hands; there are excellent soaps available. Gasoline may contain lead, and lead can enter the body through a cut, accumulating in the body until you are very ill. Gasoline also removes all the natural oils from the skin so that bone dry hands will suck up oil and grease.

• Don't service the air conditioning system unless you are equipped with the necessary tools and training. The refrigerant, R-12, is extremely cold and when exposed to the air, will instantly freeze any surface it comes in contact with, including your eyes. Although the refrigerant is normally non-toxic, R-12 becomes a deadly poisonous gas in the presence of an open flame. One good whiff of the vapors fro burning refrigerant can be fatal.

SERIAL NUMBER IDENTIFICATION

Vehicle

The 13-digit vehicle identification number (VIN) is attached to the left top side of the instrument panel, so that it is visible through the windshield.

1975–80

First digit:
  A, for American Motors
Second digit:
  Last number of year, 5 for 1975
Third digit:
  Transmission type
    S: 3-Speed column
    F: 3-speed floor
    A: Automatic—column
    C: Automatic—floor
    M: 4-speed floor
Fourth digit:
  Series
Fifth digit:
  Body type
Sixth digit:
  Trim class
Seventh digit:
  Engine:
    A, 258-6, 1 bbl.
    B, 232-6, 1 bbl.
    C, 232-6, 2 bbl.
    E, 232-6, 1 bbl.
    G, 232-6, 2 bbl.
    H, 304-8, 2 bbl.
    N, 360-8, 2 bbl.
    P, 360-8, 4 bbl.
    Z, 401-8, 4 bbl.
Remaining digits:
  Vehicle serial number, numbering was started at 100,001 each year at the Kenosha, Wisconsin plant and at 700,001 at the Brampton, Ontario plant.

1981–82

A seventeen digit Vehicle Identification Number is embossed on a metal plate that is riveted to the upper left corner of the dash panel visible through the windshield. To decode the VIN, see the accompanying illustration

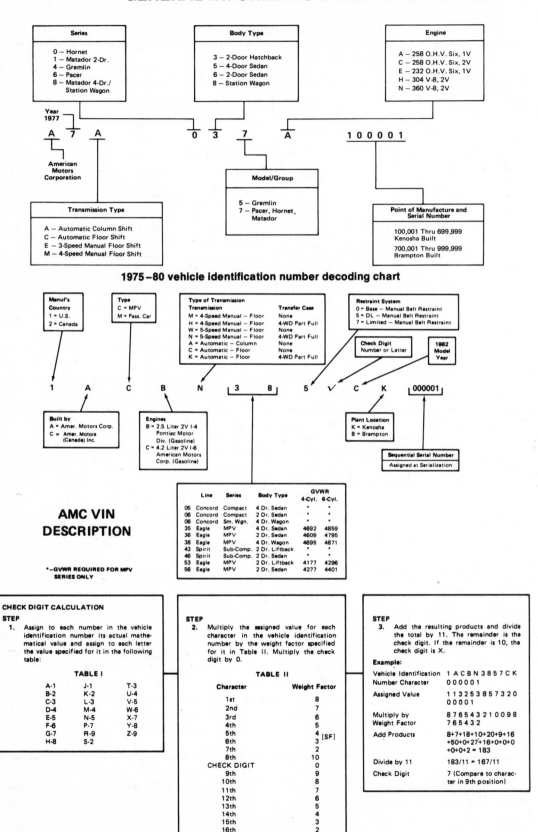

1975–80 vehicle identification number decoding chart

1981–82 vehicle identification number decoding chart

Engine Identification Chart

Displacement	Carb. No. Bbls.	■ HP	'75	'76	'77	'78	'79	'80	'81	'82
4 Cylinder Models										
121	2	80			G	G	G			
151	2	90						B	B	B
6 Cylinder Models										
199	1	128								
232	1	90		E	E	E	E			
232	1	100	E							
258	1	95		A	A					
258	1	100				A	A			
258	1	110	A							
258	2	110					C	C	C	C
258	2	120		C	C	C				
8 Cylinder Models										
304	2	120		H	H					
304	2	125					H			
304	2	130				H				
304	2	150	H							
360	2	129				N	N			
360	2	140		N						
360	2	175	N							
360	4	180		P	P					
360	4	195,220 #	P							
401	4	215		Z	Z					
401	4	225	Z							

#Dual Exhaust
■Since 1972, horsepower is given in SAE net figures. This is measured at the rear wheels with all accessories operating.

Engine

The engine code is the 4th digit of the engine build code stamped on a machined surface of the cylinder block between no. 2 and no. 3 cylinders on 6 cylinder engines, and stamped on a tag attached to the right bank valve cover on V8 engines. In addition, the engine code is the 7th digit of the 1975–80 Vehicle Iden-

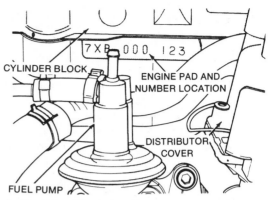

4-121 engine ID number location

tification Number (V.I.N.). On 1981–82 models, it is the 4th digit. The V.I.N. is stamped on a plate located at the left-side of the instrument panel visible through the windshield.

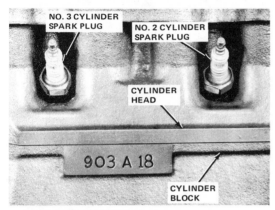

6 cylinder engine build date code location

Transmission
MANUAL

The transmission identification tag is attached to the rear of the transmission. It contains both the transmission manufacturer's and American Motors' part numbers. It is necessary to know both of these numbers when ordering replacement parts.

NOTE: *Be sure to attach the transmission identification tag in its original location when reassembling the transmission.*

8 cylinder engine build date code location

AUTOMATIC
Torque-Command

A 7-digit part number is stamped on the left-hand side of the transmission case, above the oil pan. A 4-digit number, indicating the date of manufacture, follows the part number.

NOTE: *If the date number is above 3500, add one for each day after 26 February 1971 to determine the date of manufacture. Hence, 3501 would be 27 February 1971, and 3809 would be 1 January 1972, etc.*

The final group of numbers is the transmission serial number.

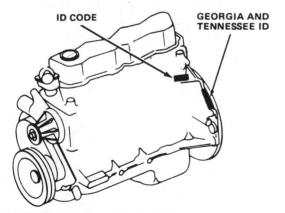

4-151 engine ID number locations

ROUTINE MAINTENANCE

Refer to the "Service Intervals" chart in this Chapter for the recommended intervals for the operations in this Section.

Air Cleaner

The air cleaner has a disposable element which should be replaced at the intervals shown in the "Service Intervals" chart. It should be checked at every oil change. To check or replace the element:

1. Remove the wing nut at the top.

2. On a 4-151 or V8, lift off the large disc under the wing nut. Remove the element.

3. On a six, detach the PCV hose at the valve cover. Don't pull the hose out of the air cleaner or you will damage it. Remove the whole top of the air cleaner and remove the element.

4. There are a couple of ways to clean the element. How well either works depends on the type of dirt trapped in the paper element. Dust and dirt can be removed by rapping the element on a flat surface or by blowing from the inside with an air hose. If the element still appears black or clogged, replace it. A clogged filter causes a rich fuel/air mixture and low gas mileage.

5. Wipe out the housing and install the new or rejuvenated element.

6. Reinstall the top of the unit and the wing nut.

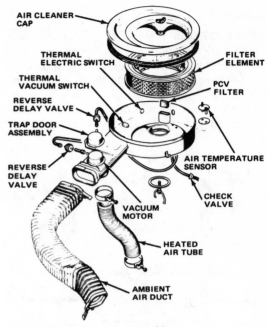

6-232, 258 air cleaner assembly

PCV System

PCV means Positive Crankcase Ventilation. This is a simple emission control system which

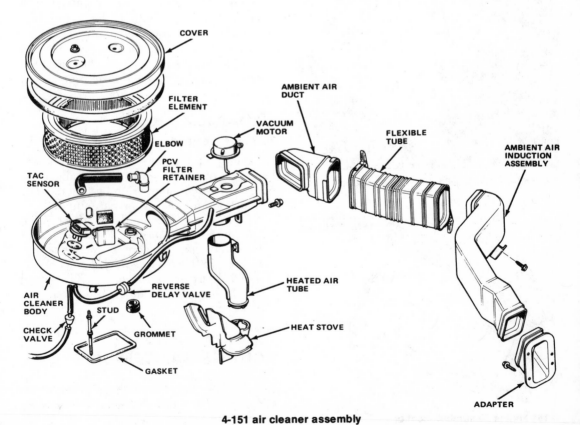

4-151 air cleaner assembly

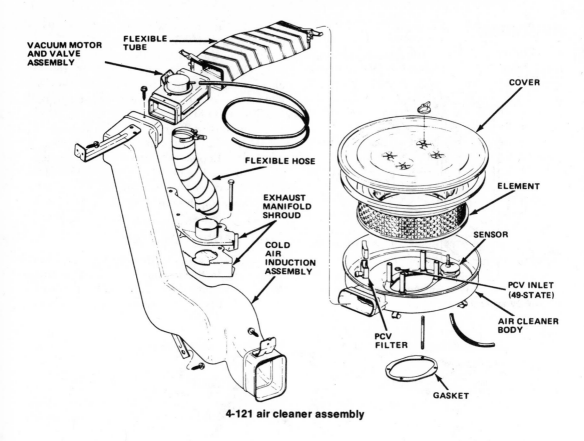

4-121 air cleaner assembly

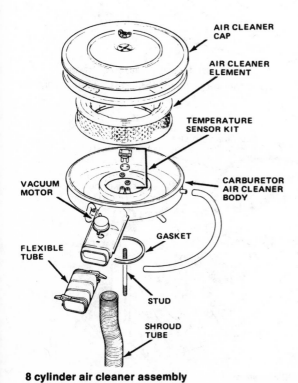

8 cylinder air cleaner assembly

routes crankcase fumes into the intake manifold or carburetor to be burned. A clogged PCV system will cause poor idle and rough running. There are two points of maintenance in this system: a valve and a filter. Maintenance intervals are shown in the "Service Intervals" chart, but remember that this system can clog pretty quickly on an older engine that is using a little oil.

On a six, the PCV valve is at the valve cover end of a hose leading from just below the carburetor to the valve cover. On a 4-151 or V8, it is at the intake manifold end of a hose leading from the carburetor to the intake manifold. To replace the PCV valve:

1. Pull the valve from its grommet in the intake manifold (V8) or valve cover (six).

2. Loosen the hose clamp and pull the valve from the hose. The valve can be washed in kerosene, but the best plan is to replace it. If the valve seems really sludged up, check the hose, too.

3. Push the new or cleaned valve into its hose. Push the valve into its grommet. The condition of this grommet is important. If it

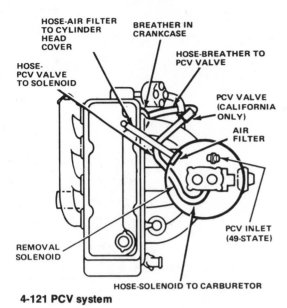

4-121 PCV system

leaks air, the engine will idle too fast because of a lean fuel/air mixture.

To clean the system filter:

1. On a six, remove the top of the air cleaner as explained previously under "Air Cleaner." Turn the top upside down and pull the filter out of the hose, inside the top. Don't pull the hose off first, or you'll damage it. Wash the filter in kerosene and replace it when dry. Replace the top of the air cleaner.

2. On a 4-151 or V8, remove the oil filter cap and wash it with kerosene. The cap contains the filter element. Replace it when dry.

Fuel Vapor Canister

The canister stores carburetor and fuel tank vapors while the engine is off, holding them to be drawn into the engine and burned when it starts. This system is on some models be-

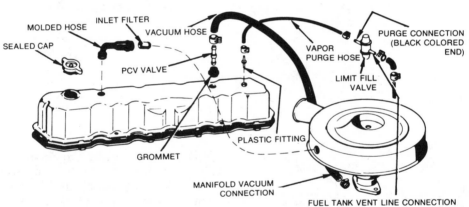

Typical 6-232, 258 PCV system; 1980–82 models don't have the purge hose. The 4-151 system is similar

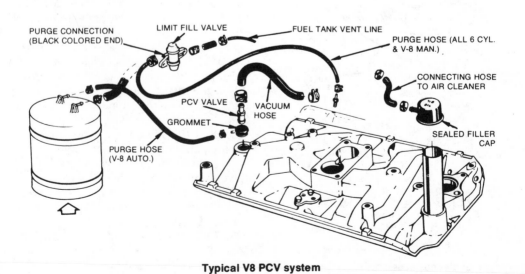

Typical V8 PCV system

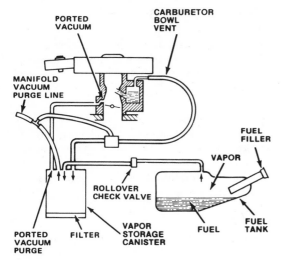

Typical fuel vapor control system

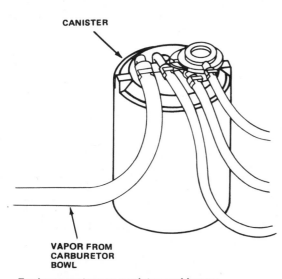

Fuel vapor storage canister and hoses

ginning 1971, and all models beginning 1973. Look for a black container about the size and shape of a coffee tin can with some hoses attached in the engine compartment. The air filter in this canister should be changed at the intervals shown in the "Service Intervals" chart. To change the filter:

1. Loosen the canister clamp screws and raise the canister enough that you can work under it. Remove it as necessary.

2. Pull out the old filter from the bottom of the canister.

3. Install a new filter, making sure that it covers the whole opening.

4. Replace the canister and tighten the clamp screws.

Exhaust Manifold Heat Valve

The exhaust manifold heat valve should be inspected and lubricated every 30,000 miles.

On six-cylinder engines, the valve is located in the center lower portion of the exhaust manifold, on the left-hand side of the engine.

CAUTION: *Be sure that the manifold is cool before carrying out inspection and lubrication.*

1. To check the heat valve operation, turn the valve shaft by hand.

2. Lubricate the heat valve with one of the special heat valve lubricants made for this purpose. Do not use grease or oil.

3. Check valve operation again.

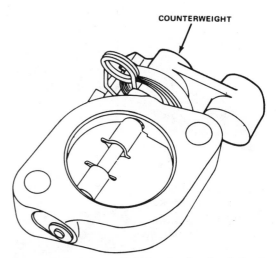

Typical exhaust manifold heat valve (heat riser); V8 shown, the others are similar

Fan Belt Tension

Check the fan belt condition and tension at least every 5,000 miles. Check the belt tension between these intervals, if a loose or worn belt is suspected.

Check the belt tension in the following manner:

1. Check belt condition. If the belt is cracked, frayed, or badly worn, replace it.

2. Check the tension at a point midway between the fan and alternator pulleys, by applying about 20 lbs finger pressure; the belt should deflect about ½ in.

3. If the deflection is greater than this; loosen, but do not remove, the alternator mounting and adjusting link bolts.

4. Apply pressure to the *front* alternator housing, with a prybar, until the proper amount of deflection is obtained.

HOW TO SPOT WORN V-BELTS

V-Belts are vital to efficient engine operation—they drive the fan, water pump and other accessories. They require little maintenance (occasional tightening) but they will not last forever. Slipping or failure of the V-belt will lead to overheating. If your V-belt looks like any of these, it should be replaced.

Cracking or weathering

This belt has deep cracks, which cause it to flex. Too much flexing leads to heat build-up and premature failure. These cracks can be caused by using the belt on a pulley that is too small. Notched belts are available for small diameter pulleys.

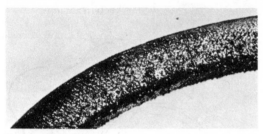

Softening (grease and oil)

Oil and grease on a belt can cause the belt's rubber compounds to soften and separate from the reinforcing cords that hold the belt together. The belt will first slip, then finally fail altogether.

Glazing

Glazing is caused by a belt that is slipping. A slipping belt can cause a run-down battery, erratic power steering, overheating or poor accessory performance. The more the belt slips, the more glazing will be built up on the surface of the belt. The more the belt is glazed, the more it will slip. If the glazing is light, tighten the belt.

Worn cover

The cover of this belt is worn off and is peeling away. The reinforcing cords will begin to wear and the belt will shortly break. When the belt cover wears in spots or has a rough jagged appearance, check the pulley grooves for roughness.

Separation

This belt is on the verge of breaking and leaving you stranded. The layers of the belt are separating and the reinforcing cords are exposed. It's just a matter of time before it breaks completely.

CAUTION: *Do not pry on the rear alternator housing, as this will damage the alternator.*

5. After obtaining the correct amount of deflection, tighten the adjusting bolt, and *then* the mounting bolt.

Fluid Level Checks

ENGINE OIL

The engine oil should be checked on a regular basis, at least at every gas stop, or more often under severe usage. If the check is made at a gas stop, wait until the tank has been filled. If the level is checked immediately after stopping, a false low reading will result. The proper level is between the FULL and ADD marks on the dipstick, preferably at FULL.

1. Pull out the dipstick on the side of the engine. Do not take a reading yet, unless the engine has been off all night.

2. Wipe off the dipstick with a clean rag.

3. Replace the dipstick, count slowly to ten or do whatever you like for ten seconds, and remove it. Check the level on the dipstick.

4. If the level is at the ADD mark, adding one full quart at the filler (usually marked OIL) will bring it to the FULL mark. Never add a full quart if the level is not down to the ADD mark, because this overfilling will result in possible damage to engine seals or rapid oil consumption. See "Oil and Fuel Recommendations" later in this chapter for the proper oils.

NOTE: *If you need to add oil when the level is down less than a full quart, you will have a problem storing partly full quart oil cans. The plastic covers that come with coffee cans are ideal for covering these cans.*

5. Replace the dipstick, seating it firmly.

TRANSMISSION

Manual 3, 4 or 5-speed

The transmission level should be checked when the oil is changed. Since your hands are apt to be pretty oily at these times, you shouldn't mind this job. To check the level, remove the filler plug in the right-side of the transmission case from under the car. There is a similar plug in the overdrive case at the rear of the transmission. With the car level, oil should drip out. If it runs out in a steady stream, let it run until it just drips. Any fluid required can be pumped in with a suction gun. All transmissions use SAE 80W–90 Gear

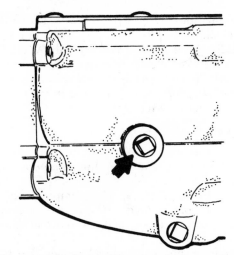

Manual transmission fill and drain plugs with the drain plug at the bottom center

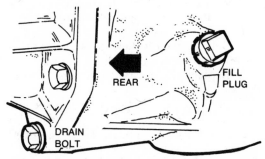

Manual transmission fill and drain plugs, using a tailshaft bolt as the drain plug

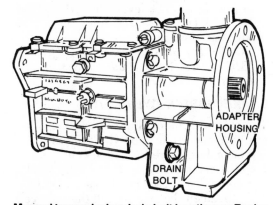

Manual transmission drain bolt location on Eagles

oil, except the 1982 T4 and T5. These use Dexron® II automatic transmission fluid.

Pacer Three-Speed with Overdrive

The overdrive unit shares a common supply of lubricant with the manual transmission. The fluid level is checked at the transmission fill plug in the same manner as for manual transmissions without overdrive. The fluid level should be checked every 5,000 miles.

If lubricant is required, use only API GL-4 SAE 80W–140 gear lubricant.

CAUTION: *Don't use antifriction or limited-slip differential lubricant in the transmission/overdrive unit.*

Automatic

Check the level at oil change intervals. With the transmission at operating temperature, proceed as follows:

1. The normal operating temperature of 175°F is not obtained until the car has been driven several miles, making frequent starts and stops.

2. Park the car on a level surface. Set the parking brake.

3. With the engine idling, shift the selector lever through all gear positions.

CAUTION: *Hold your foot on the brake.*

4. Shift into Neutral.

5. Pull out the dipstick at the right rear of the engine. Wipe it off with a clean rag.

6. Replace the dipstick and push it in all the way.

7. Pull out the dipstick after ten seconds and take a reading. The level should be between the FULL and ADD ONE PINT marks.

8. If the level is at or below the ADD ONE PINT mark, add fluid through the dipstick tube to bring the level up to the FULL mark. One pint brings the level from ADD ONE PINT to FULL. Be very cautious not to overfill the transmission.

NOTE: *The proper transmission fluid is AMC or DEXRON® II automatic transmission fluid.*

BRAKE MASTER CYLINDER

The master cylinder is in the left rear of the engine compartment, on the firewall. With power brakes, there is a round container behind the cylinder. To check the fluid level as recommended at each oil change interval:

1. Clean off the area around the cap. Very small particles of dirt can cause serious difficulties in the brake system.

2. Remove the bolt retaining the cover, or, on later models, pry the wire retaining the cap to one side with a screwdriver. Take off the cover.

3. The proper level in each of the two reservoirs is within ¼ in. of the top. Add fluid as necessary.

CAUTION: *Brake fluid dissolves paint.*

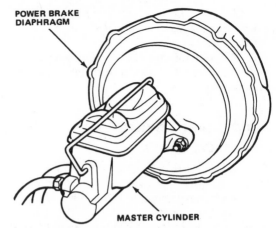

POWER BRAKE DIAPHRAGM

MASTER CYLINDER

Typical brake master cylinder; power brake models shown

4. Replace the cover. Replace the retaining bolt or snap the retaining wire back in place.

CAUTION: *Use only high-quality brake fluid designated for disc brake systems, even if you don't have discs. Lesser fluids can boil during heavy braking, causing complete loss of braking power. Make sure that brake fluid containers are sealed tightly; brake fluid can absorb moisture from the air.*

COOLANT

Since the cooling system is pressurized, the radiator cap must not be removed unless the engine has cooled. To do otherwise involves the risk of being scalded by steam. To check the coolant level:

If you have a coolant recovery system, coolant level checking is easy. The level in the plastic catch tank alongside the radiator should be between FULL and ADD with the engine at normal operating temperature. Don't add any coolant solution unless the level is at or below ADD. Add coolant only to the tank; don't remove the radiator cap. Steps 6 and 7 for "Normal Systems" apply to this type, too.

DRIVE AXLES

It is recommended that the front or rear axle lubricant level be checked at each engine oil change. The filler plug may be located either on the front or the rear of the housing, depending on the axle used. Sometimes it is an allen head plug. When the unit is warm, the level should be even with the plug hole; when cold , it may be a bit below. A finger makes a fine dip-stick. Lubricant may be added with

HOW TO SPOT BAD HOSES

Both the upper and lower radiator hoses are called upon to perform difficult jobs in an inhospitable environment. They are subject to nearly 18 psi at under hood temperatures often over 280°F., and must circulate nearly 7500 gallons of coolant an hour—3 good reasons to have good hoses.

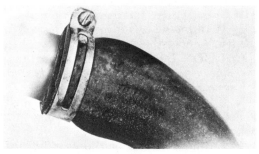

Swollen hose

A good test for any hose is to feel it for soft or spongy spots. Frequently these will appear as swollen areas of the hose. The most likely cause is oil soaking. This hose could burst at any time, when hot or under pressure.

Cracked hose

Cracked hoses can usually be seen but feel the hoses to be sure they have not hardened; a prime cause of cracking. This hose has cracked down to the reinforcing cords and could split at any of the cracks.

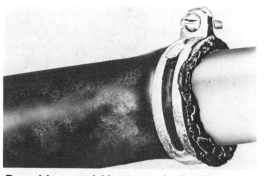

Frayed hose end (due to weak clamp)

Weakened clamps frequently are the cause of hose and cooling system failure. The connection between the pipe and hose has deteriorated enough to allow coolant to escape when the engine is hot.

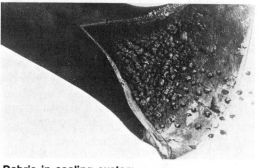

Debris in cooling system

Debris, rust and scale in the cooling system can cause the inside of a hose to weaken. This can usually be felt on the outside of the hose as soft or thinner areas.

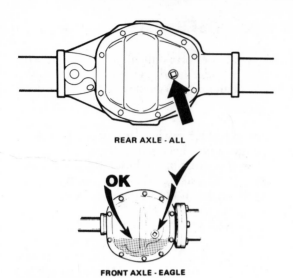

REAR AXLE - ALL

FRONT AXLE - EAGLE

Drive axle fill plugs

a suction gun. Standard differentials may use SAE 80 GL-5 gear lubricant or the special lubricant made for limited-slip differentials. Limited-slip differentials must use the special lubricant or they will be damaged. If you don't know which type of differential you have and don't want to go to the trouble of finding out, then the obvious solution is to use the special limited-slip stuff.

TRANSFER CASE

Drain and fill the transfer case at the interval recommended in the Maintenance Intervals chart. The Drain and fill plugs are on the front face of the case. Fill the case until the fluid is at the fill plug hole. Recommended fluid is:
1982: Dexron II automatic transmission fluid
1980–81: 10W-30 engine oil

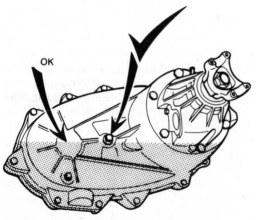

OK

Transfer case drain and fill plug locations

MANUAL STEERING GEAR

The level of lubricant in the steering gear box doesn't need to be checked unless you notice leakage. An oily film is not important, but escaping grease is. To check the level:

1. Wipe off the gearbox until you can see one cover bolt between the words CHECK LUBE. Sometimes there is a filler plug.

2. With the wheels turned all the way to the left, remove the cover bolt or filler plug.

CAUTION: *Don't remove the locknut in the center or you will mess up the gearbox adjustment. Don't take the cover off.*

3. If you can see grease, there is enough. If not, fill with chassis grease through the hole.

4. Torque the cover bolt to 25–40 ft. lbs. if you have a torque wrench. If not, just pull it down firmly but gently.

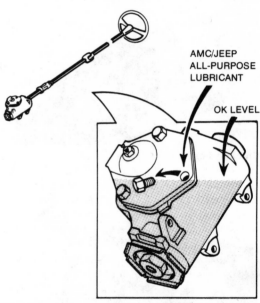

AMC/JEEP
ALL-PURPOSE
LUBRICANT

OK LEVEL

Manual steering gear fill hole location

POWER STEERING RESERVOIR

The belt driven power steering pump/reservoir is located at the front of the engine. To check the level, as recommended at oil change intervals, proceed as follows:

1. Wipe off the cap and surrounding area, after stopping the engine with the wheels straight.

CAUTION: *Very small dirt particles can cause trouble in any hydraulic system.*

2. Remove the cap.

3. If the cap has a dipstick, wipe it off with a clean rag, replace the cap, wait ten sec-

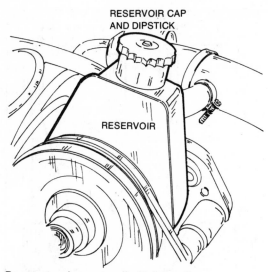

Power steering pump dipstick location

Tires and Wheels

The correct tire pressures for original equipment size tires are given on a sticker inside the glove box door on late models. Refer to the "Tire Pressure" chart if the sticker is missing. Pressures should be checked before driving, since pressure can increase as much as 6 psi due to heat. It is a good idea to have an accurate gauge and to check pressures weekly. Not all the gauges on service station air pumps are reliable. When steady speeds of 75 mph or more are planned on regular tires, the pressure should be increased 4 psi. Snow tires should not be driven this fast for any length of time; their heavy tread overheats and comes apart. All four tires should be of the same construction type; do not mix radial, bias, or bias-belted tires. Serious handling difficulties may result. It is also best not to mix tire profile series (50, 60, 70, 78).

When shopping for new tires, give some consideration to the measurements involved. If you switch to larger tires in the same series, or to another profile series be sure:

1. That the wheels are wide enough. Tire dealers have charts of tire and rim compatibility. A mismatch can cause sloppy handling and rapid wear.

2. That the height (mounted diameter) of the new tires is acceptable. This can change speedometer accuracy, engine speed at a given car speed, acceleration, and ground clearance. Tire manufacturers usually furnish full measurement specifications.

3. That the spare tire will be usable with the new tires.

4. That there won't be any body interference when loaded, on bumps, or in turning.

onds, and take a raading. The level should be at FULL.

4. If you didn't get a dipstick, the level should be 1 in. below the top.

5. The correct fluid is DEXRON® II or AMC Automatic Transmission Fluid.

BATTERY

The battery electrolyte level should be checked at least every four weeks. The correct level should be at the bottom of the well inside each cell opening. This can be seen through the case on the transparent type battery. Only colorless, odorless, preferably distilled, water should be added. It is a good idea to add the water with a squeeze bulb device to avoid having the sulfuric acid electrolyte splash out, as often happens when attempting to pour in water. If water is frequently needed, the most likely cause is overcharging, caused by an incorrect voltage regulator setting. If any acid should escape, it can be neutralized with a baking soda and water solution. When replacing a battery, it is important that the replacement have an output rating equal to or greater than original equipment.

CAUTIONS: *Avoid sparks and smoking around the battery. A battery gives off explosive hydrogen gas. If you get acid on your skin or eyes, rinse it off immediately with lots of water. See a doctor if it got in your eyes. In winter, add water only before driving to prevent the battery from freezing and cracking.*

TIRE ROTATION

See the "Service Intervals" chart fot the recommended mileage for tire rotation. Tires don't absolutely have to be rotated, but it is recommended to obtain the maximum wear. The pattern you use depends on personal preference, and whether you have a usable spare or not. Radial tires should not be cross-switched; they work better if their direction of rotation is not changed.

NOTE: *Mark your studded snow tires left and right before they are removed; they will lose their studs if their direction of rotation is changed.*

To mount the wheels on the car:

1. Place the wheel over the brake drum or disc brake hub studs.

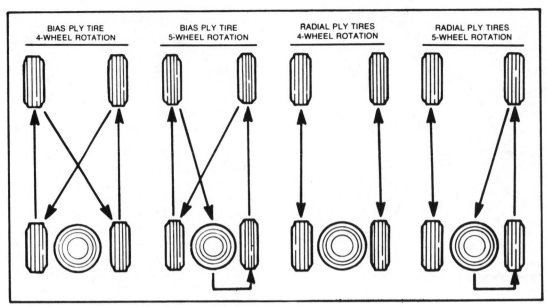

| BIAS PLY TIRE 4-WHEEL ROTATION | BIAS PLY TIRE 5-WHEEL ROTATION | RADIAL PLY TIRES 4-WHEEL ROTATION | RADIAL PLY TIRES 5-WHEEL ROTATION |

Tire rotation patterns

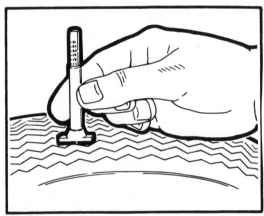

An easily acquired tool can be used to check tire tread depth

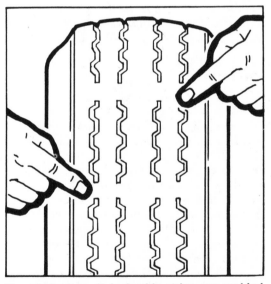

Wear indicators, ½ inch wide strips, are molded into the tires. They appear at the tread surface when tread depth is less than ¹⁄₁₆ inch

2. Install all the nuts finger-tight.

3. Tighten one nut down with the lug wrench.

4. Now tighten the opposite nut in the circular bolt pattern.

5. Repeat Steps 3 and 4 until all the nuts are tight.

CAUTION: *Avoid overtightening the lug nuts on disc brakes, or the disc will be permanently distorted. Alloy or styled wheels can also be cracked by overtightening. The proper torque is 75 ft. lbs. Use of a torque wrench is highly recommended but not essential.*

Fuel Filter

4-121, 6 and V8 models use an inline fuel filter in the line from the carburetor to the fuel pump. To replace it:

1. Remove the air cleaner as necessary.

2. Put an absorbent rag under the filter to catch spillage.

3. Remove the hose clamps.

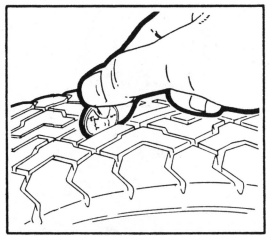

Tread depth can also be checked, roughly, using a penny. If the top of Lincoln's head is visible, replace the tire

4. Remove the filter and short attaching hoses.

5. Remove the hoses if they are to be reused.

6. Assemble the new filter and hoses.

NOTE: *The original equipment type hose clamps can't be reused with much success.*

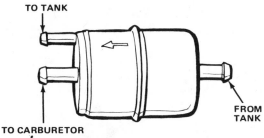

TO TANK

FROM TANK

TO CARBURETOR

Correct fuel filter installation, except 4-151

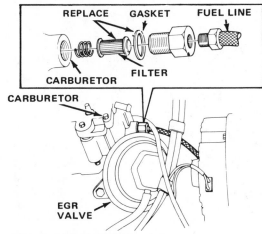

REPLACE   GASKET   FUEL LINE

CARBURETOR

FILTER

CARBURETOR

EGR VALVE

4-151 fuel filter installation

It is much better to replace them with screw type clamps.

7. Fit the filter in place, tighten the clamps, start the engine, and check for leaks. Discard the rag safely.

4-151 engines have a fuel filter located behind the fuel line inlet nut in the carburetor. See the accompanying illustration for replacement details.

Air Conditioning

This book contains no repair or maintenance procedures for the air conditioning system. It is recommended that any such repairs be left to the experts, whose personnel are well aware of the hazards and who have the proper equipment.

CAUTION: *The compressed, refrigerant used in the air conditioning system expands into the atmosphere at a temperature of −21.7°F or lower. This will freeze any surface, including your eyes, that it contacts. In addition, the refrigerant decomposes into a poisonous gas in the presence of flame. Do not open or disconnect any part of the air conditioning system.*

You can safely make a few simple checks to determine if your air conditioning system needs service. The tests work best if the temperature is warm (about 70°F).

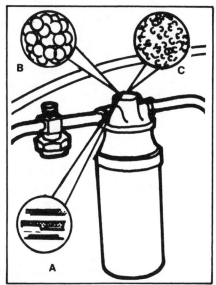

B

C

A

Oil streaks (A), constant bubbles (B), or foam (C) indicate there is not enough refrigerant in the system. Occasional bubbles during initial operation is normal. A clear sightglass indicates a proper charge or no charge at all. This can be determined by the presence of cold air at the outlets in the car. If the glass is clouded with a milky substance, have the receiver/drier checked professionally.

1. Place the automatic transmission in Park or the manual transmission in Neutral. Set the parking brake.

2. Run the engine at a fast idle (about 1500 rpm) either with the help of a friend, or by temporarily readjusting the idle speed screw.

3. Set the controls for maximum cold with the blower on high.

4. Locate the sight glass in one of the system lines. Usually it is on the left alongside the top of the radiator.

5. If you see bubbles, the system must be recharged. Very likely there is a leak at some point.

6. If there are no bubbles, there is either no refrigerant at all or the system is fully charged. Feel the two hoses going to the belt-driven compressor. If they are both at the same temperature, the system is empty and must be recharged.

7. If one hose (high-pressure) is warm and the other (low-pressure) is cold, the system may be alright. However, you are probably making these tests because you think there is something wrong, so proceed to the next Step.

8. Have an assistant in the car turn the fan control on and off to operate the compressor clutch. Watch the sight glass.

9. If bubbles appear when the clutch is disengaged and disappear, when it is engaged, the system is properly charged.

10. If the refrigerant takes more than 45 seconds to bubble when the clutch is disengaged, the system is overcharged. This usually causes poor cooling at low speeds.

CAUTION: *If it is determined that the system has a leak, it should be corrected as soon as possible. Leaks may allow moisture to enter and cause a very expensive rust problem.*

NOTE: *Exercise the air conditioner for a few minutes, every two weeks or so, during the cold months. This avoids the possibility of the compressor getting stuck from inactivity.*

Battery

Other than the maintenance of the correct electrolyte level as mentioned under "Fluid Level Checks" earlier in this Chapter, very little maintenance is required on the battery. Wipe off the top of the battery with a rag from time to time; enough dust and moisture can accumulate to cause a slight discharge. A light coat of grease on the outside of the battery

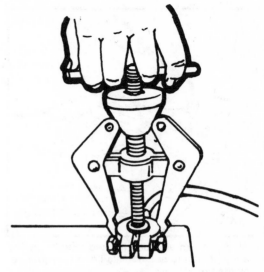

A small puller will easily remove the cables from the terminals

terminals will keep them from corroding. If they are already corroded, loosen them, then detach them from the battery, ground terminal first.

NOTE: *When working with batteries, always disconnect the ground cable first and replace it last. If you do this, you needn't fear sparks.*

CAUTION: *Don't pry the cable terminals off the battery. There is a good chance of*

Clean the inside of the terminal clamp

JUMP STARTING A DEAD BATTERY

The chemical reaction in a battery produces explosive hydrogen gas. This is the safe way to jump start a dead battery, reducing the chances of an accidental spark that could cause an explosion.

Jump Starting Precautions

1. Be sure both batteries are of the same voltage.
2. Be sure both batteries are of the same polarity (have the same grounded terminal).
3. Be sure the vehicles are not touching.
4. Be sure the vent cap holes are not obstructed.
5. Do not smoke or allow sparks around the battery.
6. In cold weather, check for frozen electrolyte in the battery.
7. Do not allow electrolyte on your skin or clothing.
8. Be sure the electrolyte is not frozen.

Jump Starting Procedure

1. Determine voltages of the two batteries; they must be the same.
2. Bring the starting vehicle close (they must not touch) so that the batteries can be reached easily.
3. Turn off all accessories and both engines. Put both cars in Neutral or Park and set the handbrake.
4. Cover the cell caps with a rag—do not cover terminals.
5. If the terminals on the run-down battery are heavily corroded, clean them.
6. Identify the positive and negative posts on both batteries and connect the cables in the order shown.
7. Start the engine of the starting vehicle and run it at fast idle. Try to start the car with the dead battery. Crank it for no more than 10 seconds at a time and let it cool off for 20 seconds in between tries.
8. If it doesn't start in 3 tries, there is something else wrong.
9. Disconnect the cables in the reverse order.
10. Replace the cell covers and dispose of the rags.

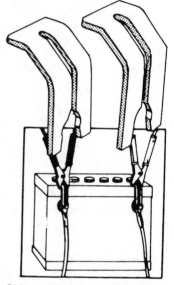

Side terminal batteries occasionally pose a problem when connecting jumper cables. There frequently isn't enough room to clamp the cables without touching sheet metal. Side terminal adaptors are available to alleviate this problem and should be removed after use.

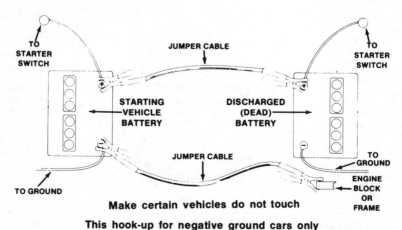

TO STARTER SWITCH

JUMPER CABLE

TO STARTER SWITCH

STARTING VEHICLE BATTERY

DISCHARGED (DEAD) BATTERY

TO GROUND

ENGINE BLOCK OR FRAME

JUMPER CABLE

TO GROUND

Make certain vehicles do not touch

This hook-up for negative ground cars only

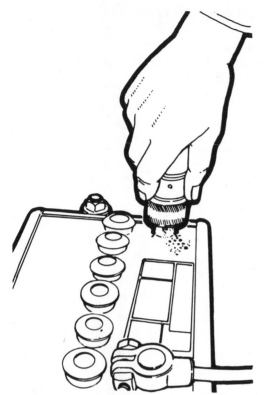

An inexpensive tool easily cleans the battery terminals

breaking the post loose or cracking the case. You can buy special pullers for battery terminals.

LUBRICATION

Fuel and Oil Recommendations

All 1975 and later models must use no-lead gasoline.

NOTE: *Be aware that your engine's fuel requirement can change with time, mainly due to carbon buildup changing the compression ratio. If your engine pings, knocks, or runs on, switch to a higher grade of fuel and check the ignition timing as soon as possible. Do not retard the timing from specifications unless you still have trouble with the higher grade fuel, and then not more than 3 degrees. Retarded timing will reduce power output and fuel mileage and increase engine temperature.*

Only oils labeled SF are approved under warranty for use. Select the viscosity rating to be used by your type of driving and the temperature range anticipated before the next oil change.

Oil Viscosity Selector

Lowest Temperature Expected (deg F)	Multi-Viscosity (SAE)	Single-Viscosity (SAE)
Above 32	10W-30 10W-40 10W-50 20W-50	20W-20
Above 0	10W-30 10W-40 10W-50	10W*
Below 0	5W-20 5W-30	10W*

*Do not run above 65 mph with SAE 10W; oil consumption will be excessive.

The multi-viscosity oils offer the important advantage of being adaptable to temperature extremes. They can allow easy starts at low temperatures, yet still give good protection at high speeds and warm temperatures. This is a decided advantage in changeable climates or in long distance touring.

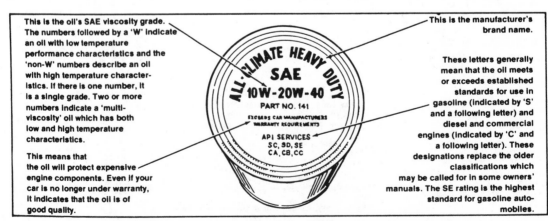

This is the oil's SAE viscosity grade. The numbers followed by a 'W' indicate an oil with low temperature performance characteristics and the 'non-W' numbers describe an oil with high temperature characteristics. If there is one number, it is a single grade. Two or more numbers indicate a 'multi-viscosity' oil which has both low and high temperature characteristics.

This means that the oil will protect expensive engine components. Even if your car is no longer under warranty, it indicates that the oil is of good quality.

This is the manufacturer's brand name.

These letters generally mean that the oil meets or exceeds established standards for use in gasoline (indicated by 'S' and a following letter) and diesel and commercial engines (indicated by 'C' and a following letter). These designations replace the older classifications which may be called for in some owners' manuals. The SE rating is the highest standard for gasoline automobiles.

ALL-CLIMATE HEAVY DUTY
SAE
10W-20W-40
PART NO. 141
EXCEEDS CAR MANUFACTURERS WARRANTY REQUIREMENTS
API SERVICES
SC, SD, SE
CA, CB, CC

The top of the oil can will tell you all you need to know about the oil

NOTE: *If your engine takes a long time in building up oil pressure after starting in warm weather, when using 10W–30 or 10W–40 oil, the problem can often be solved by switching to 20W–40. This is not specifically recommended by AMC: but it is a proven method.*

Lubricant Changes
ENGINE OIL AND FILTER

Assuming that the recommended oils are used, the oil and filter should be changed at the intervals shown in the "Service Intervals" chart. This interval should be halved under severe usage such as dusty conditions, trailer towing, prolonged high speeds, or repeated short trips in freezing temperatures.

To change the oil and filter:

1. Operate the car until the engine is at normal operating temperature. If you don't, most of the contaminants will stay in your engine. Stop the engine.

2. Slide a pan of at least five quarts capacity under the oil pan. Throw-away aluminum roasting pans work well.

3. Remove the drain plug from the engine oil pan, after wiping the plug area clean.

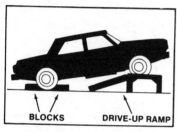

1. Warm the car up before changing your oil. Raise the front end of the car and support it on drive-on ramps or jackstands.

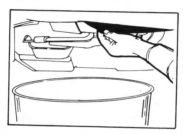

2. Locate the drain plug on the bottom of the oil pan and slide a low flat pan of sufficient capacity under the engine to catch the oil. Loosen the plug with a wrench and turn it out the last few turns by hand. Keep a steady inward pressure on the plug to avoid hot oil from running down your arm.

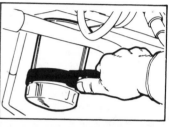

3. Remove the oil filter with a filter wrench. The filter can hold more than a quart of oil, which will be hot. Be sure the gasket comes off with the filter and clean the mounting base on the engine.

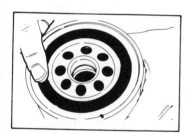

4. Lubricate the gasket on the new filter with clean engine oil. A dry gasket may not make a good seal and will allow the filter to leak.

5. Position a new filter on the mounting base and spin it on by hand. Do not use a wrench. When the gasket contacts the engine, tighten it another ½–1 turn by hand.

6. Using a rag, clean the drain plug and the area around the drain hole in the oil pan.

7. Install the drain plug and tighten it finger-tight. If you feel resistance, stop and be sure you are not cross-threading the plug. Finally, tighten the plug with a wrench.

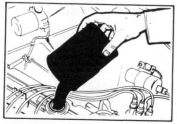

8. Locate the oil cap on the valve cover. An oil spout is the easiest way to add oil, but a funnel will do just as well.

9. Start the engine and check for leaks. The oil pressure warning light will remain on for a few seconds; when it goes out, stop the engine and check the level on the dipstick.

If this is your first attempt at oil changing, make sure that you have the engine drain plug and not the one for the transmission or something else.

CAUTION: *Watch out for that hot oil! You will probably find the plug too hot to hold, too.*

4. Allow the oil to drain into the pan. Do not replace the plug before the oil has completely stopped draining.

5. Clean off the plug, particularly the threads, and replace it.

6. The filter is on the lower right-side of the engine. Use a filter wrench to loosen it. These are available often for less than a dollar, at discount and auto supply stores. Unscrew and discard the old filter after wiping the area clean.

CAUTION: *Watch it! The filter is full of hot oil and is probably too hot to hold long, itself.*

7. If some brute has overtightened your filter, causing it to collapse when you use the filter wrench on it, drive a long punch through the cartridge as near the base as possible and use this as a lever to unscrew it.

8. Lubricate the new filter gasket with a few drops of engine oil, smeared around with a finger.

9. Screw the filter on by hand until the gasket makes contact. Then tighten the filter one half to a full turn by hand. If you overtighten the filter, you may have to resort to Step 7 to get it off next time.

10. Remove the filler cap on top of the engine, after wiping the area clean.

11. Add the oil specified under "Fuel and Oil Recommendations." If you are adding oil from a bulk container (other than 1 qt cans), keep track of the number of quarts added. Overfilling could cause damage to engine seals. Replace the cap.

12. Check the oil level on the dipstick. Start the engine and look for leaks around the drain plug and filter.

13. Stop the engine and recheck the level.

After all this is done, you note that you have a pan with foul-looking oil to dispose of. Your best bet is to funnel the stuff into plastic milk containers, bleach bottles, antifreeze jugs, or the like. If you are on good terms with a gas station man, he might let you dump it into his used oil container for recycling. Otherwise you will be forced to return it to Mother Earth by slipping the containers into your trash barrel.

TRANSMISSION
Manual

The manufacturer says that the transmission lubricant need never be changed, except for overhaul. However, if you bought your car used, or if you subject it to heavy-duty use, you may want to change the lubricant. To do this, first drive the car until it is warm, then:

1. Wipe off the area around the drain and filler plugs for the transmission and overdrive. Remove both plugs and drain the oil into a container.

2. Replace the drain plug after cleaning off the threads.

3. Use a suction gun to fill the transmission or overdrive through the filler hole. The correct level is even with the bottom of the filler hole. See "Fluid Level Checks," earlier in the Chapter, for the proper lubricants.

Automatic

The manufacturer says that the transmission fluid doesn't ever have to be changed, unless the car is used for heavy work such as trailering. In this case, the fluid is to be changed every 25,000 miles. A band adjustment is also required at the same interval for these cars.

NOTE: *See Chapter 6 for details of the band adjustment.*

1. Drive the car until it is thoroughly warm.

2. Unbolt the pan. It holds six or more quarts, so be ready.

NOTE: *If the fluid removed smells burnt, serious transmission troubles, probably due to overheating should be suspected.*

3. Unscrew and discard the filter.

4. Install a new filter. The proper torque is 28 in. lbs, though the torque wrench isn't absolutely necessary here.

5. Clean out the pan, being extremely careful not to leave any lint from rags inside.

6. Replace the pan with a new gasket. Tighten the bolts to 11 ft. lbs. in a crisscross pattern. The torque wrench isn't absolutely essential.

7. Pour six quarts of DEXRON® II or AMC automatic transmission fluid through the dipstick tube.

8. Start the engine in Neutral and let it idle for two minutes or more.

9. Hold your foot on the Brake and shift through D, 2, and R and back to N.

10. Add enough fluid to bring the level to the ADD ONE PINT mark.

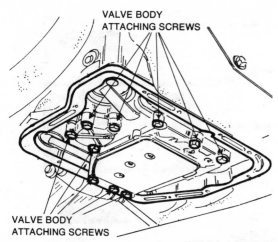

VALVE BODY
ATTACHING SCREWS

VALVE BODY
ATTACHING SCREWS

Automatic transmission filter location. Do not disturb the valve body screws when removing the filter

11. Operate the car until the transmission is thoroughly warmed up, then check the level as explained previously under "Fluid Level Checks." Add fluid as necessary.

DRIVE AXLES

The manufacturer says that the rear axle lubricant need never be changed except on models with limited-slip differentials. However, if you are buying a used vehicle, if the car is used for trailering or high speeds, or if you have driven in deep water, you may wish to change the lubricant anyway. This must be done with a suction gun inserted in the filler hole, unless your axle has a drain plug. Refer

to "Fluid Level Checks," earlier along in this Chapter for the proper lubricants and level.

Chassis Greasing

Follow the accompanying Lube charts for proper chassis greasing.

Front Wheel Bearings

The front wheel bearings should be cleaned, packed, and adjusted at the intervals shown in the "Service Intervals" chart. See Chapter 9 for details.

PUSHING AND TOWING

Cars with automatic transmission may not be started by pushing or towing. Manual transmission cars may be started by pushing. The car need not be pushed very fast to start.

To push start a manual transmission car:
1. Make sure that the bumpers of the two cars align so as not to damage either one.
2. Turn on the ignition switch in the pushed car. Place the transmission in Second or Third gear and hold down the clutch pedal.
3. Have the car pushed to a speed of 10–15 mph.
4. Ease up on the clutch and press down on the accelerator slightly at the same time. If the clutch is engaged abruptly, damage to the push vehicle may result.

The car should not be towed to start, since

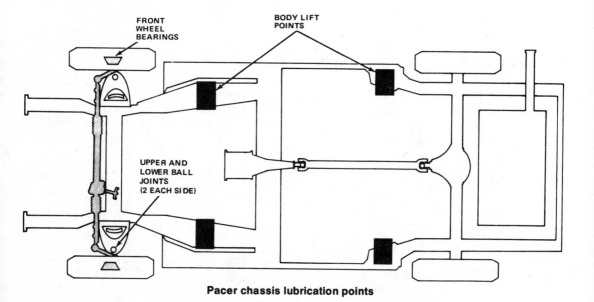

FRONT
WHEEL
BEARINGS

BODY LIFT
POINTS

UPPER AND
LOWER BALL
JOINTS
(2 EACH SIDE)

Pacer chassis lubrication points

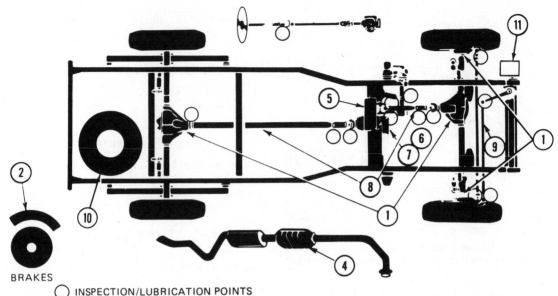

BRAKES

◯ INSPECTION/LUBRICATION POINTS

1. Check front and rear axle differential fluid level
1. Drain and change front and rear axle differential oil
2. Brake and chassis inspection lubrication ①
3. Lubricate body components ①
4. Check exhaust system ②
5. Check transfer case oil

5. Drain and change transfer case oil
6. Drain and change automatic transmission oil
7. Check manual transmission fluid level
8. Lubricate front and rear propeller shafts ③
9. Check and lubricate steering linkage ④
10. Check tire pressure in spare tire
11. Check windshield washer reservoir fluid level

Eagle chassis inspection and lubrication points

there is a chance of the towed vehicle ramming the tow car. Models with automatic should not be towed over 30 mph, for more than 15 miles. If these recommendations must be exceeded, remove the driveshaft to prevent automatic transmission damage.

JACKING AND HOISTING

The jack supplied with the car should never be used for any service operation other than tire changing. NEVER get under the car

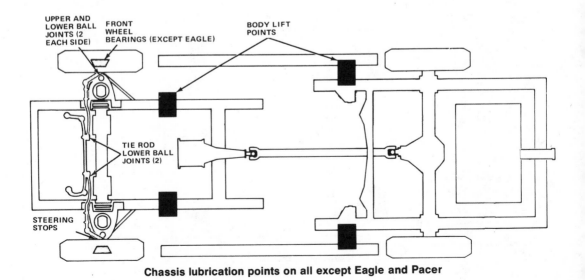

Chassis lubrication points on all except Eagle and Pacer

Capacities

Year	Engine No. Cyl. Displacement (cu. in.)	Model	Crankcase Includes Filter (qts)	Transmission Pts. to refill after draining				Drive Axle (pts)	Fuel Tank (gal)	Cooling System (qts)	
				Manual			Automatic			Non A/C	With A/C
				3-sp.	4-sp.	5-sp.					
1975	6-232	All	5.0	3.5 ②	—	—	17.0	3.0 ①	③	11.0 ④	11.5 ⑤
	6-258	All	5.0	3.5 ②	—	—	17.0	3.0 ①	③	11.0 ④	11.5 ⑤
	8-304	All	5.0	3.5	—	—	17.0	4.0	③	16.5 ⑥	16.0 ⑥⑦
	8-360	All	5.0	—	—	—	19.0	4.0	③	15.5 ⑧	15.5 ⑧
	8-401	All	5.0	—	—	—	19.0	4.0	③	15.5 ⑧	15.5 ⑧
1976	6-232	Gremlin, Hornet	5.0	2.5 ②	—	—	17.0	3.0	③	11.0	11.5
	6-232	Pacer	5.0	3.5 ②	3.5	—	17.0	3.0	③	14.0	14.0
	6-258	Gremlin, Hornet	5.0	2.5 ②	—	—	17.0	3.0	③	11.0	11.5
	6-258	Pacer	5.0	3.5 ②	3.5	—	17.0	3.0	③	14.0	14.0
	6-258	Matador Coupe	5.0	3.5	—	—	17.0	4.0	③	14.0	14.0
	6-258	Matador Sedan, SW	5.0	3.5	—	—	17.0	4.0	③	11.0	11.5 ⑨
	8-304	Gremlin, Hornet	5.0	3.5	—	—	17.0	4.0	③	16.0	16.0
	8-304	Matador Sedan, SW	5.0	3.5	—	—	17.0	4.0	③	16.5	16.5 ⑨
	8-360, 401	Matador Coupe	5.0	—	—	—	19.0	4.0	③	17.5	17.5

Capacities (cont.)

Year	Engine No. Cyl. Displacement (cu. in.)	Model	Crankcase Includes Filter (qts)	Transmission Pts. to refill after draining				Drive Axle (pts)	Fuel Tank (gal)	Cooling System (qts)	
				Manual			Automatic			Non A/C	With A/C
				3-sp.	4-sp.	5-sp.					
1976	8-360, 401	Matador Sedan, SW	5.0	—	—	—	19.0	4.0	[3]	15.5	15.5 [9]
1977–78	4-121	Gremlin	4.5	—	2.4 [10]	—	14.2	3.0	15.0	6.5	—
	6-232	Gremlin	5.0	3.5 [11]	3.5	—	17.0	3.0	21.0	11.0	14.0
	6-232	Hornet, Concord	5.0	3.5 [11]	3.5	—	17.0	3.0	22.0	11.0	11.5 [12]
	6-232	Pacer	5.0	3.5 [11]	3.5	—	17.0	3.0	22.0 [17]	14.0	14.0
	6-258	Gremlin	5.0	3.5 [11]	3.5	—	17.0	3.0	21.0	11.0	14.0
	6-258	Hornet, Concord	5.0	3.5 [11]	3.5	—	17.0	3.0	22.0	11.0	11.5 [12]
	6-258	Pacer	5.0	3.5 [11]	3.5	—	17.0	3.0	22.0 [17]	14.0	14.0
	6-258	Matador Coupe	5.0	—	—	—	17.0	4.0	24.5	13.5	13.5
	6-258	Matador Sedan, SW	5.0	—	—	—	17.0	4.0	21.0 [18]	11.5	11.5
	8-304	All exc. Matador	5.0	—	—	—	17.0	4.0	22.0	16.0 [13]	16.0 [13]
	8-304	Matador Coupe	5.0	—	—	—	17.0	4.0	24.5	18.5	18.5
	8-304	Matador Sedan, SW	5.0	—	—	—	17.0	4.0	21.0 [18]	16.5	16.5
	8-360	Matador Coupe	5.0	—	—	—	19.0 [14]	4.0	24.5	17.5	17.5

Year	Engine	Model									
	8-360	Matador Sedan, SW	5.0	—	—	—	19.0[14]	21.0[19]	4.0	15.5	15.5
1979	4-121	Spirit, Concord	3.5	2.5	2.8	—	14.2	13.0	3.0[1]	6.5	6.5
	6-232	Spirit, Concord	5.0	2.5	2.8	—	17.0	21.0	3.0[1]	11.0	14.0
	6-258	All	5.0	2.5	2.8	—	17.0	21.0	3.0[1]	11.0	14.0
	8-304	All	5.0	2.5	2.8	—	17.0	21.0	3.0[1]	18.0	18.0
1980	4-151	Spirit, Concord	4.0	—	3.3	—	17.0	21.0	3.0	6.5	6.5
	6-258	All exc. Eagle	5.0	—	3.3	—	17.0	21.0	3.0	11.0[4]	11.0[4]
	6-258	Eagle	5.0	—	3.3[15]	—	17.0[15]	22.0	3.0[16]	14.0	14.0
1981	4-151	Spirit, Concord	4.0	—	3.5	—	14.2	21.0	3.0	6.5	6.5
	4-151	Eagle	4.0	—	3.5[15]	—	14.2[15]	22.0	3.0[16]	6.5	6.5
	6-258	Spirit, Concord	5.0	—	3.5	—	17.0	21.0	3.0	11.0	14.0
	6-258	Eagle	5.0	—	3.5[15]	—	17.0[15]	22.0	3.0[19]	14.0	14.0
1982	4-151	Spirit, Concord	3.0	—	3.5	4.0	14.2	[19]	3.0	6.5	6.5
	4-151	Eagle Sedan, SW	3.0	—	3.5[20]	4.0[20]	17.0[20]	22.0	3.0[16]	6.5	6.5
	4-151	Eagle SX/4	3.0	—	3.5[20]	4.0[20]	17.0[20]	21.0	3.0[16]	6.5	6.5
	4-151	Eagle Kammback	3.0	—	3.5[20]	4.0[20]	17.0[20]	21.0	3.0[16]	6.5	6.5

Capacities (cont.)

Year	Engine No. Cyl. Displacement (cu. in.)	Model	Crankcase Includes Filter (qts)	Transmission Pts. to refill after draining				Drive Axle (pts)	Fuel Tank (gal)	Cooling System (qts)	
				Manual			Automatic			Non A/C	With A/C
				3-sp.	4-sp.	5-sp.					
1982	6-258	Spirit, Concord	5.0	—	3.5	4.0	17.0	3.0	⑲	11.0	14.5
	6-258	All Eagles	5.0	—	3.5⑳	4.0⑳	17.0⑳	3.0⑯	㉑	14.0	14.0

① 8⅞ inch ring gear: 4.0
② 4.5 with overdrive
③ Gremlin and Matador SW: 21.0
  Hornet, Concord, Pacer: 22.0
  Matador: 24.5
④ Pacer: 14.5
⑤ Matador coupe: 13.5 without coolant recovery; 15.5 with coolant recovery
  Pacer: 14.5
⑥ Matador coupe: 18.5 without coolant recovery; 20.5 with coolant recovery
  Hornet and Gremlin: 16.0
⑦ Matador sedan and SW: 16.5
⑧ Matador coupe: 17.5 without coolant recovery; 19.5 with coolant recovery
⑨ Add 2 quarts for coolant recovery
⑩ 1978: 2.8
⑪ 1978: 3.0
⑫ 1978: 14.0
⑬ 1978: 18.0
⑭ 1978: 16.4
⑮ Transfer case: before March 1980 3.0 pts; after March 1980 4.0 pts
⑯ Front axle: 2.5 pts
⑰ 1978: 20.0
⑱ Sedan: 24.5
⑲ Spirit: 21.0
  Concord: 22.0
⑳ Transfer case: 6.0 pts
㉑ SX/4, Kammback: 21.0
  Sedan, SW: 22.0

Service Intervals in Thousands of Miles*

	1975	1976	1977	1978	1979	1980	1981	1982
Replace air cleaner element	30	30	30	30	30	30	30	30
Replace PCV valve	30	30	30	30	30	30	30	30
Clean 6 cyl PCV filter	30	30	30	30	30	30	30	30
Clean 8 cyl oil filler cap	—	—	—	—	—	—	—	—
Replace fuel vapor canister filter	—	—	—	—	—	—	—	—
Change engine coolant	12	12	12	15	15	15	12.5	12.5
Rotate tires	5	5	5	5	5	5	5	5
Replace fuel filter	15	15	15	15	10	10	12.5	12.5
Change engine oil	5	5	5	5	5	7.5	5	5
Change engine oil filter	5	5	5	5	5	7.5	5	5
Change auto. trans. fluid	25 ①	25 ①	25 ①	25 ①	25 ①	25 ①	25 ①	25 ①
Adjust auto. trans.	25 ①	25 ①	25 ①	25 ①	25 ①	25 ①	25 ①	25 ①
Change limited-slip differential lubricant	30	30	30	30	30	30	30	30
Lubricate chassis	20	15	15	15	15	15	12.5	12.5
Pack front wheel bearings	25	30	30	30	30	30	30	30
Change tranfer case fluid	—	—	—	—	—	15	12.5	27.5
Change manual transmission fluid	30	30	30	30	30	30	30	30

—Not required
*Minimum intervals for a car driven 12,000 miles per year under ideal conditions. Lubricant or fluid changes can be read in months, also.
① Severe usage, such as trailering, only

while it is supported only by the jack. They very often slip or topple over. Always block the wheels when changing tires.

Some of the service operations in this book require that one or both ends of the car be raised and supported safely. The best arrangement is a grease pit or a vehicle lift. It is understood that these items are not often found in the home garage, but there are reasonable and safe substitutes. Small hydraulic, screw, or scissors jacks are satisfactory for raising the car.

Heavy wooden blocks or adjustable jack-stands should be used to support the car while it is being worked on. Drive-on trestles, or ramps, are also a handy and safe way to raise the car. These can be bought or constructed from suitable heavy timbers or steel.

In any case, it is always best to spend a little extra time to make sure that the car is lifted and supported safely.

CAUTION: *Concrete blocks are not recommended. They may break if the load is not evenly distributed. Boxes and milk crates of any description must not be used.*

Tune-Up

TUNE-UP PROCEDURES

The following are specific procedures to be used in performing each tune-up step. For a more general discussion, see the "Tune-Up" Section in Chapter 11.

Spark Plugs

1. Disconnect each spark plug wire by pulling on the rubber cap, not on the wire.

2. If the wires seem dirty or oily, wipe them clean with a cloth dampened in kerosene and then wipe them dry. If the wires are cracked, they should be replaced.

3. Blow or brush the dirt away from each of the spark plugs. This can be done by loosening the plugs and cranking the engine with the starter.

4. Remove each spark plug with a $^{13}/_{16}$ in. spark plug socket. Make sure that the socket is all the way down on the plug to prevent it from slipping and cracking the porcelain insulator.

5. Refer to the "Troubleshooting" Section at the end of the book for details on evaluating plug condition. In general, a tan or medium gray color on the business end of the plug indicates normal combustion conditions. A spark plug's useful life is about 12–15,000 miles. Thus it would make sense to throw away the plugs if it has been 12–15,000 miles or more since the last tune-up. Refer to the "Tune-Up Specifications" chart for the proper spark plug type.

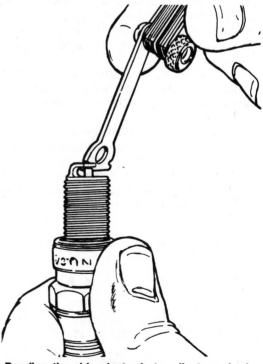

Bending the side electrode to adjust spark plug gap

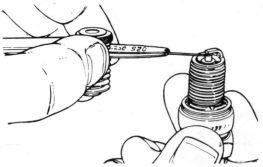

Checking spark plug gap

6. If the plugs are to be reused, file the center and side electrodes with a small, fine file. Heavy or baked on deposits can be carefully scraped off with a small knife blade or the scraper tool on a combination spark plug tool. It is often suggested that plugs be tested and cleaned on a service station sandblasting machine; however, this piece of equipment is becoming rare. Check the gap between the two electrodes with a spark plug gap gauge. The round wire type is the most accurate. If the gap is not as specified, use the adjusting device on the gap gauge to bend the outside electrode to correct.

NOTE: *Check the gap on new plugs.*

Be careful not to bend the electrode too far or too often, because excessive bending may cause it to break off and fall into the combustion chamber. This would require cylinder head removal to reach the broken piece, and could result in cylinder wall, ring, or valve damage.

7. Clean the plug threads with a wire brush. Crank the engine with the starter to blow out any dirt particles from the cylinder head threads.

8. Screw the plugs in finger-tight. Tighten them with the plug socket. If a torque wrench is available, tighten them to 25–30 ft. lbs.

9. Reinstall the wires. If there is any doubt as to their proper locations, refer to the "Firing Order" illustrations.

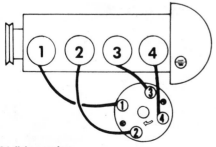

4-121 firing order

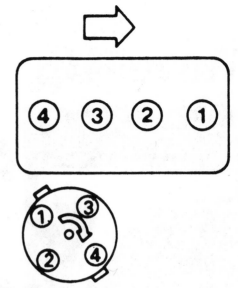

4-151 firing order

6-232, 258 firing order

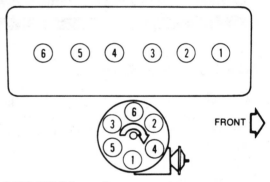

V8 firing order

Breaker Points and Condenser—Dwell Angle
4-121

The usual procedure is to replace the condenser each time the point set is replaced.

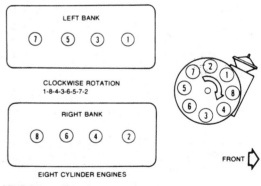

Although this is not always necessary, it is easy to do at this time and the cost is negligible. Every time you adjust or replace the breaker points, the ignition timing must be checked and, if necessary, adjusted. No special equipment other than a feeler gauge is required for point replacement or adjustment, but a dwell meter is strongly advised.

1. Push down on the spring-loaded V8 distributor cap retaining screws and give them a half-turn to release. Remove the distributor cap. You might have to unclip or detach some or all of the plug wires to remove the cap.

2. Clean the cap inside and out with a clean rag. Check for cracks and carbon paths. A carbon path shows up as a dark line, usually from one of the cap sockets or inside terminals to a ground. Check the condition of the carbon button inside the center of the cap and the inside terminals. Replace the cap as necessary.

3. Pull the rotor up and off the shaft. Clean off the metal outer tip if it is burned or corroded. Don't file it. Replace the rotor as necessary or if one came with your tune-up kit.

4. The factory says that the points don't need to be replaced if metal transfer from one contact to the other doesn't exceed 0.020 in. However, sad experience shows that it is more economical and reliable in the long run to replace the point set while the distributor is open, than to have to do this at a later (and possibly more inconvenient) time.

5. Pull off the two wire terminals from the point assembly. One wire comes from the condenser and the other comes from within

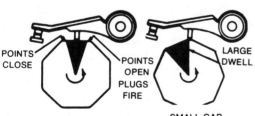

POINTS CLOSE

POINTS OPEN PLUGS FIRE

LARGE DWELL

NORMAL DWELL-NORMAL GAP

SMALL GAP EXCESSIVE DWELL

SMALL DWELL

WIDE GAP INSUFFICIENT DWELL

Dwell angle

the distributor. The terminals are usually held in place by spring tension only. There might be a clamp screw securing the terminals on some older versions. Loosen the point set hold-down screw(s). Be very careful not to drop any of these little screws inside the distributor. If this happens, the distributor will probably have to be removed to get at the screw. If the hold-down screw is lost elsewhere, it must be replaced with one that is no longer than the original to avoid inteference with the distributor workings. Remove the point set, even if it is to be reused.

6. If the points are to be reused, clean them with a few strokes of a special point file. This is done with the points removed to prevent tiny metal filings getting into the distributor.

7. Loosen the condenser hold-down screw and slide the condenser out of the clamp. This will save you a struggle with the clamp, condenser, and the tiny screw when you install the new one. If you have the type of clamp that is permanently fastened to the condenser, remove the screw and the condenser. Don't lose the screw.

8. Attend to the distributor cam lubricator. If you have the round kind, turn it around on its shaft at the first tune-up and replace it at the second. If you have the long kind, switch ends at the first tune-up and replace it at the second.

NOTE: *Don't oil or grease the lubricator. The foam is impregnated with a special lubricant.*

If you didn't get any lubricator at all, or if it looks like someone took it off, don't worry. You don't really need it. Just rub a match-head size dab of grease on the cam lobes.

9. Install the new condenser. If you left the clamp in place, just slide the new condenser into the clamp.

10. Replace the point set and leave the screw slightly loose. Replace the two wire terminals, making sure that the wires don't interfere with anything.

11. Check that the contacts meet squarely. If they don't, bend the tab supporting the fixed contact.

12. Turn the engine until a high point on the cam that opens the points contacts the rubbing block on the point arm. You can turn the engine by hand if you can get a wrench on the crankshaft pulley nut, or you can grasp the fan belt and turn the engine with the spark plugs removed.

CAUTION: *If you try turning the engine*

by hand, be very careful not to get your fingers pinched in the pulleys.

On a stick-shift car, you can push it forward in High gear. Another alternative is to bump the starter switch or use a remote starter switch.

13. There is a screwdriver slot near the contacts. Insert a screwdriver and lever the points open or closed until they appear to be at about the gap specified in the "Tune-Up Specifications."

14. Insert the correct size feeler gauge and adjust the gap until you can push the gauge in and out between the contacts with a slight drag, but without disturbing the point arm. This operation takes a bit of experience to obtain the correct feel. Check by trying the gauges 0.001–0.002 larger and smaller than the setting size. The larger one should disturb the point arm, while the smaller one should not drag at all. Tighten the point set hold-down screw. Recheck the gap, because it often changes when the screw is tightened.

15. After all the point adjustments are complete, pull a white business card through (between) the contacts to remove any traces of oil. Oil will cause rapid contact burning.

NOTE: *You can adjust dwell at this point, if you wish. Refer to Step 18.*

16. Push the rotor firmly down into place. It will only go on one way. Tighten the V8 rotor screws. If the rotor is not installed properly, it will probably break when the starter is operated.

17. Replace the distributor cap.

18. If a dwell meter is available, check the dwell. The dwell meter hookup is shown in the "Troubleshooting" Section.

NOTE: *This hookup does not apply to electronic, capacitive discharge, or other special ignition systems. Some dwell meters won't work at all with such systems.*

Dwell can be checked with the engine running or cranking. Decrease dwell by increasing the point gap; increase by decreasing the gap. Dwell angle is simply the number of degrees of distributor shaft rotation during which the points stay closed. Theoretically, if the point gap is correct, the dwell should also be correct or nearly so. Adjustment with a dwell meter produces more exact, consistent results since it is a dynamic adjustment. If dwell varies more than 3 degrees from idle speed to 1,750 engine rpm, the distributor is worn.

19. If the engine won't start, check:

a. That all the spark plug wires are in place.

b. That the rotor has been installed.

c. That the two (or three) wires inside the distributor are connected.

d. That the points open and close when the engine turns.

e. That the gap is correct and the hold-down screw is tight.

22. After the first 200 miles or so on a new set of points, the point gap often closes up due to initial rubbing block wear. For best performance, recheck the dwell (or gap) at this time.

23. Since changing the gap affects the ignition point setting, the timing should be checked and adjusted as necessary after each point replacement or adjustment.

AMC Breakerless Inductive Discharge (BID) Ignition

COMPONENTS

The AMC breakerless inductive discharge (BID) ignition system consists of five components:

- Control unit
- Coil
- Breakerless distributor
- Ignition cables
- Spark plugs

The control unit is a solid-state, epoxy-sealed module with waterproof connectors. The control unit has a built-in current regulator, so no separate ballast resistor or resistance wire is needed in the primary circuit. Battery voltage is supplied to the ignition coil positive (+) terminal when the ignition key is turned to the "ON" or "START" position; low voltage is also supplied by the control unit.

The coil used with the BID system requires no special service. It works just like the coil in a conventional ignition system.

The distributor is conventional, except for the lack of points, condenser and cam. Advance is supplied by both a vacuum unit and a centrifugal advance mechanism. A standard cap, rotor, and dust shield are used.

In place of the points, cam, and condensor, the distributor has a sensor and trigger wheel. The sensor is a small coil which generates an electromagnetic field when excited by the oscillator in the control unit.

Standard spark plugs and ignition cables are used.

OPERATION

When the ignition switch is turned on, the control unit is activated. The control unit then

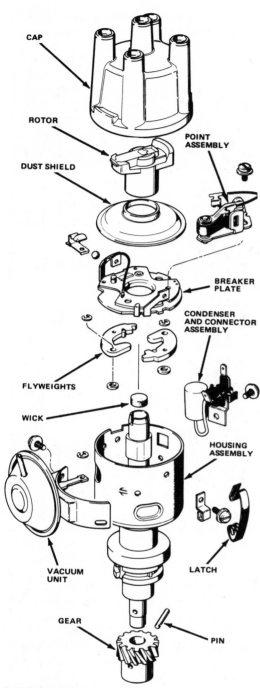

CAP

ROTOR

DUST SHIELD

POINT ASSEMBLY

BREAKER PLATE

CONDENSER AND CONNECTOR ASSEMBLY

FLYWEIGHTS

WICK

HOUSING ASSEMBLY

VACUUM UNIT

LATCH

GEAR

PIN

4-121 distributor

sends an oscillating signal to the sensor which causes the sensor to generate a magnetic field. When one of the trigger wheel teeth enters this field, the strength of the oscillation in the sensor is reduced. Once the strength drops to a predetermined level, a demodulator circuit operates the control unit's switching transistor. The switching transistor is wired in series with the coil primary circuit; it

switches the circuit off when it gets the demodulator signal.

From this point on, the BID ignition system works in the same manner as a conventional ignition system.

TROUBLESHOOTING

1. Check all of the BID ignition system electrical connections.

2. Disconnect the coil-to-distributor high tension lead.

3. Hold the end of the lead ½ in. away from a ground. Crank the engine. If there is a spark, the trouble is not in the ignition system.

4. If there was no spark in Step 3, connect a test light with a No. 57 bulb between the positive coil terminal (+) and a good ground. Have an assistant turn the ignition switch to "ON" and "START" (Do not start the engine). The bulb should light in both positions; if it doesn't, the fault lies in the battery-to-coil circuit. Check the ignition switch and related wiring.

5. If the test light lit in Step 4, disconnect the coil-to-distributor leads at the connector and connect the test light between the positive (+) and negative (−) coil terminals.

6. Turn the ignition switch on. If the test

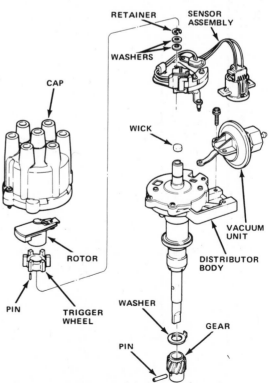

RETAINER

SENSOR ASSEMBLY

WASHERS

CAP

WICK

VACUUM UNIT

DISTRIBUTOR BODY

ROTOR

PIN

TRIGGER WHEEL

WASHER

PIN

GEAR

SSI distributor; 6 cylinder shown, the V8 is similar

Tune-Up Specifications

When analyzing compression test results, look for uniformity among cylinders rather than specific pressures.

Year	Engine No. Cyl Displacement (cu in.)	HP/carb	Spark Plugs Orig. Type•	Gap (in.)	Distributor Point Dwell (deg)	Point Gap (in.)	Ignition Timing (deg)▲ Man. Trans.•	Auto. Trans.	Valves Intake Opens (deg)▪	Fuel Pump Pressure (psi)	Idle Speed• (rpm)▲ Man Trans	Auto Trans*
'75	6-232	100	N-12Y	.035	electronic		5B	5B	12	4–5	600	550(700)
	6-258	110	N-12Y	.035	electronic		3B	3B	12	4–5	600	550(700)
	8-304	150	N-12Y	.035	electronic		5B	5B	14¾	5–6½	750	700
	8-360	175	N-12Y	.035	electronic		5B	5B	14¾	5–6½	750	700
	8-360	195	N-12Y	.035	electronic		5B	5B	14¾	5–6½	750	700
	8-401	255	N-12Y	.035	electronic		5B	5B	25½	5–6½	750	700
'76	6-232	90	N-12Y	.035	electronic		8B	8B	12	4–5	850	550(700)
	6-258	95	N-12Y	.035	electronic		6B	8B	12	4–5	850 ①	550(700)
	6-258	120	N-12Y	.035	electronic		6B	8B	12	4–5	850	550(700)
	8-304	120	N-12Y	.035	electronic		5B	10B(5B)	14¾	5–6½	750	700
	8-360	140	N-12Y	.035	electronic		—	10B(5B)	14¾	5–6½	—	700
	8-360	180	N-12Y	.035	electronic		—	10B(5B)	14¾	5–6½	—	700
	8-401	215	N-12Y	.035	electronic		—	10B(5B)	25½	5–6½	—	700
'77	4-121 ⑨	80	N-8L	.035	47	.018	12B	12B(8B)	14¾	4–6	900	800

Year	Engine	Carb/HP	Spark Plug	Gap	Dwell	Point Gap	Timing 1	Timing 2				
	6-232	88	N-12Y	.035	electronic		8B(10B)	10B	12	4–5	600(850)	550(700)
	6-258	98	N-12Y	.035	electronic		6B ③	8B ③	12	4–5	600	550(700)
	6-258	114	N-12Y	.035	electronic		6B	8B	12	4–5	600	550(700)
	8-304	121	N-12Y	.035	electronic		—	10B(5B)	14¾	5–6½	—	600(700)
	8-360	129	N-12Y	.035	electronic		—	10B(5B) ③	14¾	5–6½	—	600(700)
'78	4-121 ⑨	2 bbl	N-8L	.035	47	.018	12B	12B(8B)	41¾	4–6	900	800
	6-232	1 bbl	N-13L	.035	electronic		8B	10B	12	4–5	600	550
	6-258	1 bbl	N-13L	.035	electronic		(6B) ③	(8B) ③	12	4–5	600(850)	550(700)
	6-258	2 bbl	N-13L	.035	electronic		6B	8B	14½	4–5	600	600
	8-304	2 bbl	N-12Y	.035	electronic		—	10B(5B) ③	14¾	5–6½	—	600(700)
	8-360	2 bbl	N-12Y	.035	electronic		—	10B	14¾	5–6½	—	600(650)
'79	4-121 ⑨	2 bbl	N-8L	.035	47	.018	12B ④	12B(8B)	41¾	4–6	900	800
	6-232	1 bbl	N-13L	.035	electronic		8B	10B	12	4–5	600	550
	6-258	1 bbl	N-13L	.035	electronic		—	8B	12	4–5	—	700
	6-258	2 bbl	N-13L	.035	electronic		4B	8B	12	4–5	700	600
	8-304	2 bbl	N-12Y	.035	electronic		5B	8B	14¾	5–6½	800	600
'80	4-151	2 bbl	R44TSX	.060	electronic		10B(12B)	12B(10B)	33	6½–8	900	700
	6-258	2 bbl	N14LY ②	.035	electronic		6B	10B ⑤	14½	4–5	700	600

Tune-Up Specifications (cont.)

When analyzing compression test results, look for uniformity among cylinders rather than specific pressures.

Year	Engine No. Cyl Displacement (cu in.)	HP/carb.	Spark Plugs Orig. Type ◆	Gap (in.)	Distributor Point Dwell (deg)	Point Gap (in.)	Ignition Timing (deg)▲ Man. Trans. ●	Auto. Trans.	Valves Intake Opens (deg)■	Fuel Pump Pressure (psi)	Idle Speed ● (rpm)▲ Man Trans	Auto Trans*
'81	4-151	2 bbl	R44TSX	.060	electronic		10B ⑥	12B ⑤	25	6½-8	900	700
	6-258	2 bbl	RFN-14LY	.033	electronic		⑦	⑧	9	5-6½	700	600
'82	4-151	99	R44TSX	.060	electronic		10B ⑩	10B ⑩	25	6½-8	900	700
	6-258	110	RFN-14LY	.035	electronic		15B ⑪	15B ⑪	9	5-6½	750	650

* With transmission in Drive
◆ See the Spark Plug Replacement Chart
▲ See text for procedure
● Figure in parentheses indicates California engine
■ All figures Before Top Dead Center
B Before Top Dead Center
TDC Top Dead Center (zero degrees)
— Not applicable
① 600 rpm for Matador coupe and sedan
② N13L—Eagle
③ High Altitude—10B
④ 16B for models with code EH on upper right corner of emission information label.
⑤ 8B—Eagle for Calif. and all Pacer

⑥ Eagle except for Calif.—11B
⑦ Concord, Spirit—6B
　Eagle except Calif.—8B
　Eagle Calif.—4B　High Alt.—15B
⑧ Concord, Spirit—6B
　Eagle Except Calif.—8B
　Eagle Calif.—6B　High Alt.—15B
⑨ Mechanical valve lifter
　Clearance: intake .006–.009″; exhaust .016–.019″
⑩ 49 states Eagles: 12B
　All Calif: 8B
　All High Altitude: 15B
⑪ High Altitude except Eagle: 19B
　　　　　　　　　　Eagle: 21B

light doesn't come on, check the control unit's ground lead. If the ground lead is in good condition, replace the control unit.

7. If the bulb lights in Step 6, leave the test light in place and short the terminals on the coil-to-distributor connector together with a jumper lead, (connector separated) at the coil side of the connector. If the light stays on, replace the control unit.

8. If the test light goes out, remove it. Check for a spark, as in Step 2, each time that the coil-to-distributor connector terminals are shorted together with the jumper lead. If there is a spark, replace the control unit; if there is no spark, replace the coil.

COIL TESTING

Test the coil with a conventional coil checker or an ohmmeter. Primary resistance should be 1–2 ohms and secondary resistance should be 8–12 kilohms. The open output circuit should be more than 20 kilovolts. Replace the coil if it doesn't meet specifications.

SENSOR TESTING

Check the sensor resistance by connecting an ohmmeter to its leads. Resistance should be 1.8 ohms (±10%) at 77°F. Have the sensor replaced if it doesn't meet these specifications.

BID SYSTEM SERVICE

The BID system control unit is replaced as an assembly. If the above tests indicate a defective control unit, replace it with a new unit with the same part number. To replace the control unit, unfasten its wiring connector and remove the sheet metal screws which secure it. Install a new control unit by reversing the above.

If the tests above indicate a faulty distributor component, other than the cap or rotor, have the distributor serviced by either authorized service personel or by a shop specializing in automotive electrical system service. Do not attempt to disassemble the distributor yourself, since special tools are needed to align the trigger wheel and sensor to ensure correct operation of the BID ignition system.

The cap and rotor may be replaced just as on a conventional distributor. Remember when replacing the cap to number the spark plug leads before removing them from the old cap. Look at the firing order diagram in Chapter 3 to determine correct cap wiring.

The rotor is removed by grasping it and lifting straight up. Remember when installing the rotor, to align the rotor keyway with the key on the distributor shaft. Be sure that the rotor is not cocked on the shaft when it is installed, or damage to the cap may result.

Ignition Timing

Timing should be checked at each tune-up and any time the points are adjusted or replaced. The timing marks consist of a notch on the rim of the crankshaft pulley and a graduated scale attached to the engine front (timing) cover. A stroboscopic flash (dynamic) timing light must be used, as a static light is too inaccurate for emission controlled engines.

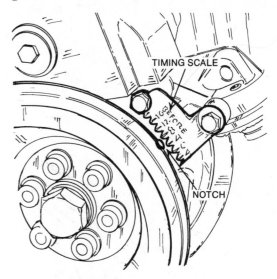

4-121 timing mark location

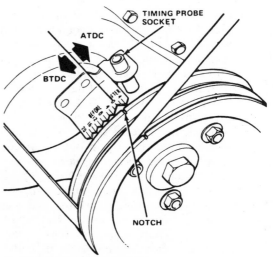

4-151 timing mark location

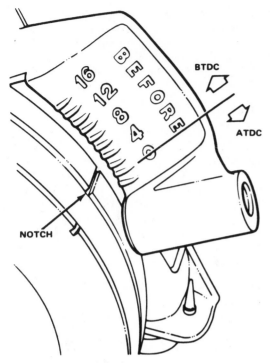

6-232, 258 timing mark location

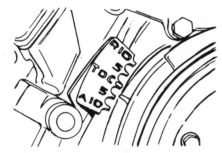

V8 timing mark location

There are three basic types of timing light available. The first is a simple neon bulb with two wire connections. One wire connects to the spark plug terminal and the other plugs into the end of the spark plug wire for the No. 1 cylinder, thus connecting the light in series with the spark plug. This type of light is pretty dim and must be held very closely to the timing marks to be seen. Sometimes a dark corner has to be sought out to see the flash at all. This type of light is very inexpensive. The second type operates from the car battery—two alligator clips connect to the battery terminals, while an adapter enables a third clip to be connected to the No. 1 spark plug and wire. This type is a bit more expensive, but it provides a nice bright flash that you can see even in bright sunlight. It is the type most often seen in professional shops. The third type replaces the battery power source with 110 volt current.

NOTE: *Connect a tachometer to the BID or SSI ignition system in the conventional way; to the negative (distributor) side of the coil and to a ground. HEI distributor caps have a "Tach" terminal. Some tachometers may not work with a BID, SSI, or HEI ignition system and there is a possibility that some could be damaged. Check with the manufacturer of the tachometer to make sure it can be used.*

To check and adjust the timing:

1. Warm up the engine to normal operating temperature. Stop the engine and connect the timing light to the No. 1 (left front on V8, front on four or six) spark plug wire. Clean off the timing marks and mark the pulley notch and timing scale with white chalk.

2. Disconnect and plug the vacuum line at the distributor. This is done to prevent any distributor vacuum advance.

3. Start the engine and adjust the idle to 500 rpm with the carburetor idle speed screw on 1975–77 cars. On 1978 and later models, set the idle speed to the figure shown on the underhood sticker. This is done to prevent any distributor centrifugal advance. If there is a throttle stop solenoid, disconnect it electrically.

4. Aim the timing light at the pointer marks. Be careful not to touch the fan, because it may appear to be standing still. If the pulley notch isn't aligned with the proper timing mark (refer to the "Tune-Up Specifications" chart), the timing will have to be adjusted.

NOTE: *TDC or Top Dead Center corresponds to 0 degrees. B, or BTDC, or Before Top Dead Center may be shown as A for Advanced on a V8 timing scale. R on a V8 timing scale means Retarded, corresponding to ATDC or After Top Dead Center.*

5. Loosen the distributor clamp locknut. You can buy trick wrenches that make this task a lot easier. Turn the distributor slowly to adjust the timing, holding it by the base and not the cap. Turn counterclockwise to advance timing (toward BTDC), and clockwise to retard (toward TDC or ATDC).

6. Tighten the locknut. Check the timing again, in case the distributor moved slightly, as you tightened it.

7. Replace the distributor vacuum line and

correct the idle speed to that specified in the "Tune-Up Specifications" chart.

8. Stop the engine and disconnect the timing light.

Idle Speed and Mixture

Some of these adjustment procedures require that the air cleaner be kept in place. A flexible screwdriver will probably be needed to reach the carburetor screws.

1975–79

Six Cylinder and V8

Beginning with the 1977 models, special carburetors, incorporating an altitude compensating circuit to increase the air flow are used on cars that are sold for use at elevations above 4,000 feet. The single barrel YF-1 is manually adjusted for altitude while the two barrel 2150-2 had an automatic compensator system, controlled by an aneroid, which is sensitive to atmospheric pressures. At high altitudes, where the atmospheric pressure is lower, the aneroid expands and opens an altitude compensating valve, allowing extra air to enter the carburetor and lean out the fuel-air mixture.

NOTE: *The aneroid is factory calibrated and is not adjustable. With a change of altitude operation, ignition timing and carburetor adjustments must be reset on all models.*

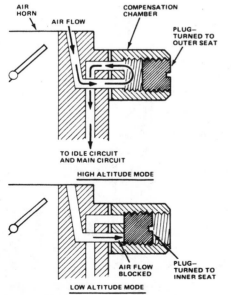

6 cylinder altitude compensator plug operation and adjustment

NOTE: *This adjustment is performed with the air cleaner installed. Do not allow the engine to idle more than three minutes at a time. If the idle/mixture adjustment is not completed by the end of three minutes, run the engine for one minute at 2,000 rpm. Return to the specified rpm and continue the adjustment.*

1. Adjust the idle screw(s) to the full rich stop(s). Note the position of the screw head slot inside the limiter cap slots.

2. Carefully remove the idle limiter cap(s) by installing a sheet metal screw in the center of the cap and turning clockwise. Discard the old caps. Return the screws to their original positions.

3. Install a tachometer on the engine.

4. Start the engine and allow it to reach normal operating temperature.

5. Adjust the idle speed to 30 rpm above the specified idle speed. See the Tune-Up Specifications chart.

NOTE: *On most engines the idle speed is adjusted with the throttle stop solenoid. Use the following procedure for idle speed adjustment. When setting idle speed, put the manual transmission in Neutral and the automatic transmission in Drive.*

a. With the solenoid wire connected, turn the nut on the solenoid plunger, idle speed adjusting screw, or the hex screw on the solenoid carriage in or out to obtain specified idle rpm.

b. Tighten the solenoid locknut, if so equipped.

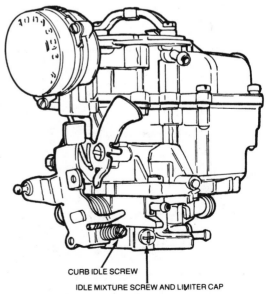

Carter YF carburetor adjustments

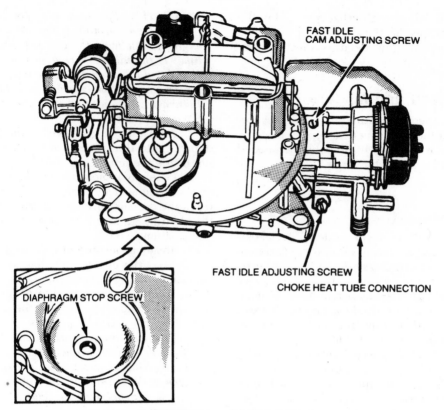

FAST IDLE CAM ADJUSTING SCREW

FAST IDLE ADJUSTING SCREW

CHOKE HEAT TUBE CONNECTION

DIAPHRAGM STOP SCREW

Autolite/Motorcraft 2100 left side

c. Disconnect the solenoid wire and adjust curb idle speed screw to obtain 500 rpm.

d. Connect the solenoid wire.

CAUTION: *On the Carter BBD 2bbl., the curb idle and fast idle screws are side by side; it is easy to get the wrong one when setting idle speed on cars without a throttle stop solenoid. The screw for idle speed is the longer of the two.*

6. Starting from the full rich stop position, as noted in step 1, turn the mixture screw(s) clockwise (leaner) until the engine loses speed.

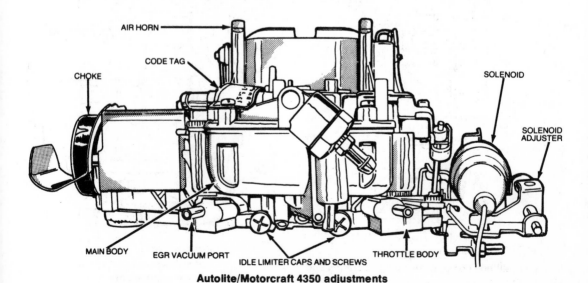

AIR HORN

CODE TAG

CHOKE

SOLENOID

SOLENOID ADJUSTER

MAIN BODY

EGR VACUUM PORT

IDLE LIMITER CAPS AND SCREWS

THROTTLE BODY

Autolite/Motorcraft 4350 adjustments

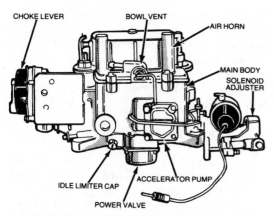

CHOKE LEVER   BOWL VENT   AIR HORN   MAIN BODY   SOLENOID ADJUSTER   IDLE LIMITER CAP   ACCELERATOR PUMP   POWER VALVE

Autolite/Motorcraft 2100 right side

7. Turn the mixture screw(s) counterclockwise until the highest rpm reading is obtained.

NOTE: *On engines with two mixture screws, turn both the screws an equal number of turns unless the engine demands otherwise.*

8. If the idle speed has changed more than 30 rpm during the mixture adjustment, reset the idle to 30 rpm above the specified idle rpm as indicated in the "Tune-Up Specifications" chart.

9. Turn the mixture adjustment screw(s) clockwise until the rpm drops as follows:

1975–76	Six cylinder automatic	25 rpm
1975	Six cylinder manual	25 rpm
1976	Six cylinder manual	50 rpm
1975	Six cylinder manual with EGR and catalytic converter	35 rpm
1976	Six cylinder manual with EGR	50 rpm
1975–76	V8 automatic	20 rpm
1975	V8 manual	40 rpm
1976	V8 manual	100 rpm
1977–79	Six cylinder manual	50 rpm
	Matador–manual	25 rpm
	automatic	25 rpm
1977–78	Six cylinder automatic Matador	175 rpm
1977–79	Six cylinder automatic, high altitude	25 rpm
1978–79	Six cylinder manual, high altitude	50 rpm
1978–79	Six cylinder two barrel automatic	25 rpm
1977–79	Six cylinder two barrel manual	50 rpm
1977–78	V8 automatic	20 rpm
1979	V8 automatic	40 rpm

10. Install new blue service idle limiter cap(s) over the idle mixture screw(s) with the limiter cap tang(s) positioned against the full rich stop(s). Be careful not to disturb the idle mixture setting while installing the cap(s). Press the cap(s) firmly into place.

4-121

The four cylinder engine uses a staged, two barrel carburetor. The primary barrel is smaller than the secondary barrel, and mechanical linkage progressively opens the secondary barrel.

Idle speed and mixture setting procedures are as follows:

NOTE: *To compensate for temperature and fuel variations, while performing idle mixture adjustments, don't idle the engine over three minutes at a time. If settings are not completed within three minutes, operate the engine at 2,000 rpm for one minute. Repeat as necessary until the proper adjustments are attained.*

1. Note position of the screw head slot in the limiter cap.

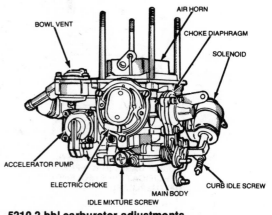

AIR HORN   BOWL VENT   CHOKE DIAPHRAGM   SOLENOID   ACCELERATOR PUMP   ELECTRIC CHOKE   MAIN BODY   CURB IDLE SCREW   IDLE MIXTURE SCREW

5210 2-bbl carburetor adjustments

2. Remove the limiter cap by installing a sheet metal screw in the center of the cap and turning the screw clockwise.

3. Reset the idle screw to its approximate original position.

4. Attach a tachometer. Start engine and warm to operating temperature.

5. A throttle stop solenoid is used to adjust curb idle. With the solenoid wire connected, turn the adjusting screw of the solenoid in or out to obtain the specified setting of 30 rpm above the specified rpm.

6. Disconnect the solenoid wire and adjust the solenoid off idle adjusting screw to obtain 500 rpm. Connect the solenoid wire.

7. Turn the mixture screw clockwise (lean) until a loss of rpm is indicated.

8. Turn the mixture screw counterclockwise until the highest rpm reading is obtained at the best lean idle setting.

9. As a final adjustment, turn the mixture screw clockwise (leaner) until the specified drop in engine rpm is obtained.

10. Install a replacement limiter cap on the idle mixture screw, with the tab positioned inside the slot on the carburetor body, while being careful not to move the mixture screw. Idle drop specifications for 1977–78 are 120 rpm, except for high altitude manual transmission models (75 rpm). For 1979 models they are 120 for manual transmissions and 45 for automatic transmissions.

1980 AND LATER

Six Cylinder

Mixture is not adjustable on 1980 and later models.

1. Connect a tachometer. Start the engine and allow it to reach normal operating temperature. The air cleaner should be installed, automatic transmissions in drive.

2. Turn the idle screw in or out to obtain the specified idle speed (see the Tune-Up Specifications chart or the car's underhood sticker).

3. If the carburetor is equipped with a solenoid:

a. Loosen the locknut on the solenoid plunger, if present. Turn the idle speed adjusting nut on the plunger, or the hex screw on the carriage to obtain the specified speed. Tighten the locknut, if present.

b. Disconnect the solenoid wire and adjust the curb idle screw to obtain 500 rpm (in Neutral). Reconnect the wire unless the carburetor has a dashpot.

4. If the carburetor has a dashpot, allow the engine to idle while fully depressing the dashpot stem. Measure the clearance be-

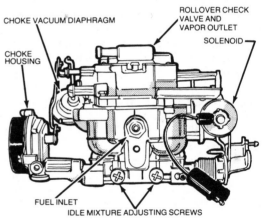

CHOKE VACUUM DIAPHRAGM

ROLLOVER CHECK VALVE AND VAPOR OUTLET

SOLENOID

CHOKE HOUSING

FUEL INLET

IDLE MIXTURE ADJUSTING SCREWS

BBD 2-bbl adjustments

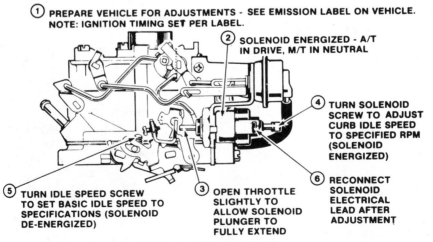

① PREPARE VEHICLE FOR ADJUSTMENTS - SEE EMISSION LABEL ON VEHICLE. NOTE: IGNITION TIMING SET PER LABEL.

② SOLENOID ENERGIZED - A/T IN DRIVE, M/T IN NEUTRAL

④ TURN SOLENOID SCREW TO ADJUST CURB IDLE SPEED TO SPECIFIED RPM (SOLENOID ENERGIZED)

⑥ RECONNECT SOLENOID ELECTRICAL LEAD AFTER ADJUSTMENT

⑤ TURN IDLE SPEED SCREW TO SET BASIC IDLE SPEED TO SPECIFICATIONS (SOLENOID DE-ENERGIZED)

③ OPEN THROTTLE SLIGHTLY TO ALLOW SOLENOID PLUNGER TO FULLY EXTEND

Rochester 2SE adjustments

tween the stem and the lever. It should be 0.093 in. Adjust by loosening the locknut and turning the dashpot. Connect the solenoid wire.

4-151

The air cleaner should be removed and associated vacuum hoses plugged, choke open, A/C compressor clutch wire disconnected (if equipped), and the deceleration valve supply hose plugged. Mixture is not adjustable.

1. Disconnect and plug the purge hose at the charcoal canister.

2. If equipped with a feedback system, connect a dwell meter to the single light blue wire which is taped to the mixture control solenoid wires at the carburetor. Set the meter on the six cylinder scale.

3. Connect a tachometer. There is a green wire above the heater fan motor for easy tachometer connection. Start the engine and allow it to reach normal operating temperature. On feedback models, the dwell meter should be fluctuating; the oscillation should be within 10 to 15 degrees of needle movement. If not, the feedback system is not operating correctly and must be repaired.

4. Set the parking brake, shift automatic transmissions to Drive; if equipped with air conditioning, turn it on. Open the throttle to extend the solenoid plunger. Set idle speed by turning the solenoid idle screw. Turn off the A/C, if equipped.

5. Disconnect the anti-dieseling solenoid wire. Use the curb idle screw to adjust idle to specifications. Connect the solenoid wire.

Engine and Engine Rebuilding

ENGINE ELECTRICAL

A conventional point-type ignition system is used on all 21-4 cylinder engines.

Starting 1975, all American Motors 6 and V8 cars are equipped with the Breakerless Inductive Discharge (BID) ignition system. The system consists of an electronic ignition control unit, a standard type ignition coil, a distributor that contains an electronic sensor and trigger wheel instead of a cam, breaker points and condenser, and the usual high tension wires and spark plugs. There are no contacting (and thus wearing) surfaces between the trigger wheel and the sensor. The dwell angle remains the same and never requires adjustment. The dwell angle is determined by the control unit and the angle between the trigger wheel spokes. In 1978 the system was modified to include a different ignition module and distributor, and was renamed Solid State Ignition (SSI). 1980 and later 4 cylinder engines use the Delco-Remy High Energy Ignition (HEI) system.

Distributor

REMOVAL

1. Detach the distributor cap.
2. Mark the position of the rotor in relation to the distributor body. Mark the position of the distributor body relative to the engine block.
3. Disconnect the distributor primary wire (the thin wire from the side of the distributor) from the coil.
4. Disconnect the distributor vacuum line.
5. Remove the hold-down bolt and lift out the distributor.
   NOTE: *Don't turn the engine while the distributor is out or the installation job will be more difficult.*
6. The procedure for installation varies depending on whether or not the engine was turned while the distributor was out.

INSTALLATION, ENGINE NOT TURNED

1. Turn the rotor about one-eighth turn past the mark indicating its original position.
2. Align the distributor locating marks on the distributor body and the block and push the unit into place. The rotor should turn back to the mark as the unit seats and the gear meshes. Wiggle the rotor slightly to start the gear in mesh as necessary.
3. Tighten the hold-down bolt and reconnect the primary wire and the vacuum line. Replace the cap.
4. Check the ignition timing as explained in Chapter 2. Theoretically, the timing shouldn't have changed if the distributor was

reinstalled exactly in its original position, but it is always best to make sure.

INSTALLATION, ENGINE TURNED

This procedure is necessary to install a new distributor or if the engine has been turned while the distributor was out.

1. Place the No. 1 cylinder in firing position by turning the engine with a finger held over the No. 1 spark plug hole. No. 1 spark plug is the left front one on a V8, and the front one on a six. When compression is felt, turn the engine to align the TDC mark on the timing pointer with the notch on the crankshaft pulley.

2. Align the metal end of the rotor with the No. 1 spark plug wire in the distributor cap.

3. Turn the distributor body counterclockwise about one-eighth turn and set it into place in the engine. Wiggle the rotor slightly to start the gear in mesh as necessary.

4. The distributor should now be positioned so that the rotor is still pointing to the No. 1 wire location on the cap.

5. Tighten the hold-down bolt and reconnect the primary wire and the vacuum line. Replace the cap.

6. Check the ignition timing as explained in Chapter 2.

American Motors Breakerless Inductive Discharge (BID) Ignition System

COMPONENTS

The AMC breakerless inductive discharge (BDI) ignition system consists of five components:
- Control unit
- Coil
- Breakerless distributor
- Ignition cables
- Spark plugs

The control unit is a solid-state, epoxy-sealed module with waterproof connectors. The control unit has a built-in current regulator, so no separate ballast resistor or resistance wire is needed in the primary circuit. Battery voltage is supplied to the ignition coil positive (+) terminal when the ignition key is turned to the "ON" or "START" position; low voltage coil primary current is also supplied by the control unit.

In place of the points, cam, and condenser, the distributor has a sensor and trigger wheel. The sensor is a small coil which generates an electromagnetic field when excited by the oscillator in the control unit.

This system was last used in 1977:

OPERATION

When the ignition switch is turned on, the control unit is activated. The control unit then sends an oscillating signal to the sensor which causes the sensor to generate a magnetic field. When one of the trigger wheel teeth enters this field, the strength of the oscillation in the sensor is reduced. Once the strength drops to a predetermined level, a demodulator circuit operates the control unit's switching transistor. The switching transistor is wired in series with the coil primary circuit; it switches the circuit off inducing high voltage in the coil secondary winding when it gets the demodulator signal.

From this point on, the BID ignition system works in the same manner as a conventional ignition system.

SYSTEM TEST

1. Check all the BID ignition system electrical connections.

2. Disconnect the coil-to-distributor high tension lead from the distributor cap.

3. Using insulated pliers and a heavy glove, hold the end of the lead ½ in. away from a ground. Crank the engine. If there is a spark, the trouble is not in the ignition system. Check the distributor cap, rotor, and wires.

4. Replace the spark plug lead. Turn the ignition switch off and disconnect the coil high tension cable from the center tower on the distributor cap. Place a paper clip around the cable ½–¾ in. from the metal end. Ground the paper clip to the engine. Crank the engine. If there is spark, the distributor cap or rotor may be at fault.

5. Turn the ignition switch off and replace the coil wire. Make the spark test of Step 3 again. If there is no spark, check the coil high tension wire with an ohmmeter. It should show 5–10,000 ohms resistance. If not replace it and repeat the spark test.

6. Detach the distributor sensor lead wire plug. Check the wire connector by trying a no. 16 (0.177 in.) drill bit for a snug fit in the female terminals. Apply a light coat of Silicone Dielectric Compound or its equivalent to the male terminals. Fill the female cavities ¼ full. Reconnect the plug.

7. Repeat the test of Step 4.

8. If there was a spark in Step 7, detach

the sensor lead plug and try a replacement sensor. Try the test again. If there is a spark, the sensor was defective.

9. Connect a voltmeter between the coil positive terminal and an engine ground. With the ignition switch on, the voltmeter should read battery voltage. If it is lower, there is a high resistance between the battery (through the ignition switch) and the coil.

10. Connect the voltmeter between the coil negative terminal and an engine ground. With the ignition switch on, the voltage should be 5-8. If not, replace the coil. If you get a battery voltage reading, crank the engine slightly to move the trigger wheel tooth away from the sensor; voltage should drop to 5-8.

11. Check the sensor resistance by connecting an ohmmeter to its leads. Resistance should be 1.6–2.4 ohms.

COIL TESTING

Test the coil with a conventional coil checker or an ohmmeter. Primary resistance should be 1.25–1.40 ohms and secondary resistance should be 9–12 kilo-ohms. The open output circuit should be more than 20 kilovolts. Replace the coil if it doesn't meet specifications.

DISTRIBUTOR OVERHAUL

NOTE: *If you must remove the sensor from the distributor for any reason, it will be necessary to have the special sensor positioning gauge in order to align it properly during installation.*

1. Scribe matchmarks on the distributor housing, rotor, and engine block. Disconnect the leads and vacuum lines from the distributor. Remove the distributor. Unless the cap is to be replaced, leave it connected to the spark plug cables and position it out of the way.

2. Remove the rotor and dust cap.

3. Place a small gear puller over the trigger wheel, so that its jaws grip the inner shoulders of the wheel and not its arms. Place a thick washer between the gear puller and the distributor shaft to act as a spacer; do not press against the smaller inner shaft.

4. Loosen the sensor hold-down screw with a small pair of needle-nosed pliers; it has a tamper-proof head. Pull the sensor lead grommet out of the distributor body and pull out the leads from around the spring pivot pin.

5. Release the sensor securing spring by lifting it. Make sure that it clears the leads.

Slide the sensor off the bracket. *Remember, a special gauge is required for sensor installation.*

6. Remove the vacuum advance unit securing screw. Slide the vacuum unit out of the distributor. Remove it only if it is to be replaced.

7. Clean the vacuum unit and sensor brackets. Lubrication of these parts is not necessary.

BID distributor assembly is as follows:

1. Install the vacuum unit, if it was removed.

2. Assemble the sensor, sensor guide, flat washer, and retaining screw. Tighten the screw only far enough to keep the assembly together; don't allow the screw to project below the bottom of the sensor.

NOTE: *Replacement sensors come with a slotted-head screw to aid in assembly. If the original sensor is being used, replace the tamper-proof screw with a conventional one. Use the original washer.*

3. Secure the sensor on the vacuum advance unit bracket, making sure that the tip of the sensor is placed in the notch on the summing bar.

4. Position the spring on the sensor and route the leads around the spring pivot pin. Fit the sensor lead grommet into the slot on the distributor body. Be sure that the lead can't get caught in the trigger wheel.

5. Place the special sensor positioning gauge over the distributor shaft, so that the flat on the shaft is against the large notch on the gauge. Move the sensor until the sensor core fits into the small notch on the gauge. Tighten the sensor securing screw with the gauge in place (through the round hole in the gauge).

6. It should be possible to remove and install the gauge without any side movement of the sensor. Check this and remove the gauge.

7. Position the trigger wheel on the shaft. Check to see that the sensor core is centered between the trigger wheel legs and that the legs don't touch the core.

8. Bend a piece of 0.050 in. gauge wire, so that it has a 90° angle and one leg ½ in. long. Use the gauge to measure the clearance between the trigger wheel legs and the sensor boss. Press the trigger wheel on the shaft until it just touches the gauge. Support the shaft during this operation.

9. Place 3 to 5 drops of SAE 20 oil on the felt lubricator wick.

10. Install the dust shield and rotor on the shaft.

11. Install the distributor on the engine using the matchmarks made during removal and adjust the timing. Use a new distributor mounting gasket.

American Motors Solid State Ignition (SSI) System

AMC introduced Solid State Ignition (SSI) as a running change on some 1977 Canadian models. It is standard equipment on all 1978 and later six and eight cylinder engines. 1980–82 four cylinder engines use the Delco HEI system, covered earlier in this section.

The system consists of a sensor and toothed trigger wheel inside the distributor, and a permanently sealed electronic control unit which determines dwell, in addition to the coil, ignition wires, and spark plugs.

The trigger wheel rotates on the distributor shaft. As one of its teeth nears the sensor magnet, the magnetic field shifts toward the tooth. When the tooth and sensor are aligned, the magnetic field is shifted to its maximum, signaling the electronic control unit to switch off the coil primary current. This starts an electronic timer inside the control unit, which allows the primary current to remain off only long enough for the spark plug to fire. The timer adjusts the amount of time primary current is off according to conditions, thus automatically adjusting dwell. There is also a special circuit within the control unit to detect and ignore spurious signals. Spark timing is adjusted by both mechanical (centrifugal) and vacuum advance.

A wire of 1.35 ohms resistance is spliced into the ignition feed to reduce voltage to the coil during running conditions. The resistance wire is by-passed when the engine is being started so that full battery voltage may be supplied to the coil. Bypass is accomplished by the I-terminal on the solenoid.

SECONDARY CIRCUIT TEST

1. Disconnect the coil wire from the center of the distributor cap.

NOTE: *Twist the rubber boot slightly in either direction, then grasp the boot and pull straight up. Do not pull on the wire, and do not use pliers.*

Hold the wire ½ in. from a ground with a pair of insulated pliers and a heavy glove. As the engine is cranked, watch for a spark.

2. If a spark appears, reconnect the coil wire. Remove the wire from one spark plug, and test for a spark as above.

CAUTION: *Do not remove the spark plug wires from cylinder 3 or 5 (1977–79) or 1 or 5 (1980 and later) on a 6 cylinder engine, or cylinders 3 or 4 of a V8 when performing this test, as sensor damage could occur.*

If a spark occurs, the problem is in the fuel system or ignition timing. If no spark occurs, check for a defective rotor, cap, or spark plug wires.

3. If no spark occurs from the coil wire in Step 2, test the coil wire resistance with an ohmmeter. It must not exceed 10,000 ohms.

COIL PRIMARY CIRCUIT TEST

1. Turn the ignition On. Connect a voltmeter to the coil positive (+) terminal and a ground. If the voltage is 5.5–6.5 volts, go to Step 2. If above 7 volts, go to Step 4. If below 5.5 volts, disconnect the condenser lead and measure. If the voltage is now 5.5–6.5 volts, replace the condenser. If not, go to Step 6.

2. With the voltmeter connected as in Step 1, read the voltage with the engine cranking. If battery voltage is indicated, the circuit is okay. If not, go to Step 3.

3. Check for a short or open in the starter solenoid I-terminal wire. Check the solenoid for proper operation.

4. Disconnect the wire from the starter solenoid 1-terminal, with the ignition On and the voltmeter connected as in Step 1. If the voltage drops to 5.5–6.5 volts, replace the solenoid. If not, connect a jumper between the coil negative (−) terminal and a ground. If the voltage drops to 5.5–6.5 volts, go to Step 5. If not, repair the resistance wire.

5. Check for continuity between the coil (−) terminal and D4, and D1 to ground. If the continuity is okay, replace the control unit. If not, check for an open wire and go back to Step 2.

6. Turn ignition Off. Connect an ohmmeter between the + coil terminal and dash connector AV. If above 1.40 ohms, repair the resistance wire.

7. With the ignition Off, connect the ohmmeter between connector AV and ignition switch terminal 11. If less than 0.1 ohm, replace the ignition switch or repair the wire, whichever is the cause. If above 0.1 ohm, check connections, and check for defective wiring.

COIL TEST

1. Check the coil for cracks, carbon tracks, etc., and replace as necessary.

2. Connect an ohmmeter across the coil + and − terminals, with the coil connector removed. If 1.13–1.23 ohms/75°F, go to Step 3. If not, replace the coil.

3. Measure the resistance across the coil center tower and either the + or − terminal. If 7700–9300 ohms at 75°F, the coil is okay. If not, replace.

CONTROL UNIT AND SENSOR TEST

1. With the ignition On, remove the coil high tension wire from the distributor cap and hold ½ in. from ground with insulated pliers. Disconnect the 4 wire connector at the control unit. If a spark occurs (normal), go to Step 2. If not, go to Step 5.

2. Connect an ohmmeter to D2 and D3. If the resistance is 400–800 ohms (normal), go to Step 6. If not, go to Step 3.

3. Disconnect and reconnect the 3 wire connector at distributor. If the reading is now 400–800 ohms, go to Step 6. If not, disconnect the 3 wire connector and go to Step 4.

4. Connect the ohmmeter across B2 and B3. If 400–800 ohms, repair the harness between the 3 wire and 4 wire connectors. If not, replace the sensor.

5. Connect the ohmmeter between D1 and the battery negative terminal. If the reading is 0 (0.002 or less), go to Step 2. If above 0.002 ohms, there is a bad ground in the cable or at the distributor. Repair the ground and re-test.

6. Connect a voltmeter across D2 and D3. Crank the engine. If the needle fluctuates, the system is okay. If not, either the trigger wheel is defective, or the distributor is not turning. Repair or replace as required.

IGNITION FEED TO CONTROL UNIT TEST

NOTE: *Do not perform this test without first performing the Coil Primary Circuit Test.*

1. With the ignition On, unplug the 2 wire connector at the module. Connect a voltmeter between F2 and ground. If the reading is battery voltage, replace the control unit and go to Step 3. If not, go to Step 2.

2. Repair the cause of the voltage reduction: either the ignition switch or a corroded dash connector. Check for a spark at the coil wire. If okay, stop. If not, replace the control unit and check for proper operation.

3. Reconnect the 2 wire connector at the control unit, and unplug the 4 wire connector at the control unit. Connect an ammeter between C1 and ground. If it reads 0.9–1.1 amps, the system is okay. If not, replace the module.

Delco-Remy High Energy (HEI) Ignition System, 4-151 Engines

The Delco-Remy High Energy Ignition (HEI) System is a breakerless, pulse triggered, transistor controlled, inductive discharge ignition system used on all 4-151 engines as standard equipment.

The ignition coil is located externally on the engine block.

OPERATION

The magnetic pick-up assembly located inside the distributor contains a permanent magnet, a pole piece with internal teeth, and a pick-up coil. When the teeth of the rotating timer core and pole piece align, an induced voltage in the pick-up coil signals the electronic module to open the coil primary circuit. As the primary current decreases, a high voltage is induced in the secondary windings of the ignition coil, directing a spark through the rotor and high voltage leads to fire the spark plugs. The dwell period is automatically controlled by the electronic module and is increased with increasing engine rpm. The HEI System features a longer spark duration which is instrumental in firing lean and EGR (Exhaust Gas Recirculation) diluted fuel/air mixtures. The condenser (capacitor) located within the HEI distributor is provided for noise (static) suppression purposes only and is not a regularly replaced ignition system component.

Beginning in 1980, three different modules are used. The original four terminal module is continued in use for most applications in 1980. Some 1980 models and most 1981 and later models are equipped with an Electronic Spark Timing (EST) distributor, which is part of the C-4 or CCC System (see the Emission Control Systems section). On these, the ignition timing is determined by the C-4 or CCC Electronic Control Module (ECM). The EST module has seven terminals. The EST distributor can be quickly identified: it has no vacuum advance diaphragm. The EST distributor can be equipped with an additional spark control, the Elec-

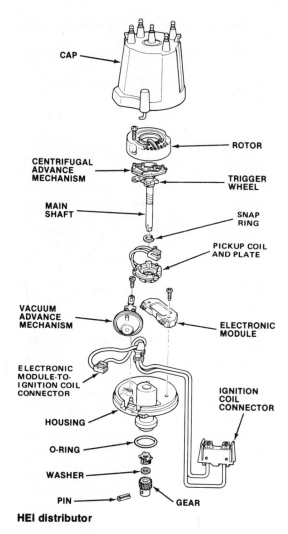

CAP

ROTOR

CENTRIFUGAL
ADVANCE
MECHANISM

TRIGGER
WHEEL

MAIN
SHAFT

SNAP
RING

PICKUP COIL
AND PLATE

VACUUM
ADVANCE
MECHANISM

ELECTRONIC
MODULE

ELECTRONIC
MODULE-TO-
IGNITION COIL
CONNECTOR

IGNITION
COIL
CONNECTOR

HOUSING

O-RING

WASHER

PIN

GEAR

HEI distributor

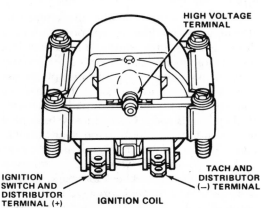

HIGH VOLTAGE
TERMINAL

IGNITION
SWITCH AND
DISTRIBUTOR
TERMINAL (+)

IGNITION COIL

TACH AND
DISTRIBUTOR
(–) TERMINAL

4-151 coil

tronic Spark Control (ESC) system. This is a closed loop system that controls engine detonation by retarding the spark timing. The ESC is usually used on turbocharged engines. Some models are equipped with Elec-

tronic Module Retard (EMR). This system uses a five terminal module which retards ignition timing a calibrated number of crankshaft degrees. Distributors with this system are equipped with vacuum advance. When replacing modules on these three systems, be certain to obtain the correct part: the modules are not interchangeable.

MAJOR REPAIR OPERATIONS (DISTRIBUTOR IN ENGINE)

Internal Ignition Coil Replacement

1. Disconnect the feed and module wire terminal connectors from the distributor cap.
2. Remove the ignition wire set retainer.
3. Remove the 4 coil cover-to-distributor cap screws and the coil cover.
4. Remove the 4 coil-to-distributor cap screws.
5. Using a blunt drift, press the coil wire spade terminals up out of distributor cap.
6. Lift the coil up out of the distributor cap.
7. Remove and clean the coil spring, rubber seal washer and coil cavity of the distributor cap.
8. Reverse the above procedures to install.

External Ignition Coil Replacement

1. Remove the ignition switch-to-coil lead from the coil.
2. Unfasten the distributor leads from the coil.
3. Remove the screws which secure the coil to the engine and lift it off.
Installation is the reverse of removal.

Distributor Cap Replacement, All Engines

1. Remove the feed and module wire terminal connectors from the distributor cap.
2. Remove the retainer and spark plug wires from the cap.
3. Depress and release the 4 distributor cap-to-housing retainers and lift off the cap assembly.
4. If the cap has an internal coil, remove the coil from the old cap and install into the new cap.
5. Using a new distributor cap, reverse the above procedures to assemble.

Rotor Replacement, All Engines

1. Disconnect the feed and module wire connectors from the distributor.
2. Depress and release the 4 distributor

cap to housing retainers and lift off the cap assembly.

3. Remove the two rotor attaching screws and rotor.

4. Reverse the above procedure to install.

Vacuum Advance Unit Replacement, All Engines So Equipped

1. Remove the distributor cap and rotor as previously described.

2. Disconnect the vacuum hose from the vacuum advance unit. Remove the module.

3. Remove the two vacuum advance retaining screws, pull the advance unit outward, rotate and disengaged the operating rod from its tang.

4. Reverse the above procedure to install.

Module Replacement, All Engines

1. Remove the distributor cap and rotor as previously described.

2. Disconnect the harness connector and pick-up coil spade connectors from the module (note their positions):

3. Remove the two screws and module from the distributor housing.

4. Coat the bottom of the new module with silicone lubricant.

NOTE: *The lubricant is required for proper module cooling.*

Reverse the above procedure to install. Be sure that the leads are installed correctly.

NOTE: *If a five terminal or seven terminal module is replaced, the ignition timing must be checked and reset as necessary.*

SERVICE PROCEDURES (DISTRIBUTOR REMOVED)

Driven Gear Replacement, All Engines

1. Mark the distributor shaft and gear so they can be reassembled in the same position. With the distributor removed, use a ⅛ in. pin punch and tap out the driven gear roll pin.

2. Hold the rotor end of shaft and rotate the driven gear to shear any burrs in the roll pin hole.

3. Remove the driven gear from the shaft.

4. Reverse the above procedure to install.

Mainshaft Replacement, All Engines

1. With the driven gear and rotor removed, gently pull the mainshaft out of the housing.

2. Remove the advance springs, weights and slide the weight base plate off the mainshaft.

3. Reverse the above procedure to install.

Pole Piece, Magnet or Pick-Up Coil Replacement, All Engines

The pole piece, magnet, and pickup coil are serviced as an assembly.

1. With the mainshaft out of its housing, remove the three screws and the magnetic shield (1981–82), remove the thin "C" washer on top of the pickup coil assembly, remove the pickup coil leads from the module, and remove the pickup coil as an assembly. Do not remove the three screws and attempt to servide the parts individually on models through 1980. They are aligned at the factory.

2. Reverse the removal procedure to install. Note the alignment marks when the drive gear is reinstalled.

TROUBLESHOOTING THE HEI SYSTEM

An accurate diagnosis is the first step to problem solution and repair. For several of the following steps, a modified spark plug (side electrode removed) is needed. GM makes a modified plug (tool ST 125) which also has a spring clip to attach it to ground. Use of this tool is recommended, as there is less chance of being shocked. If a tachometer is connected to the TACH terminal on the distributor, disconnect it before proceeding with this test.

Engine Cranks But Will Not Run

1. Check for spark at the spark plugs by attaching the modified spark plug to one of the plug wires, grounding the modified plug shell on the engine and cranking the starter. Wear heavy gloves, use insulated pliers and make sure the ground is good. If no spark on one wire, check a second. If spark is present, HEI system is good. Check fuel system, plug wires, and spark plugs. If no spark (except EST), proceed to next step. If no spark on EST distributor, disconnect the 4 terminal EST connector and recheck for spark. If spark is present, EST system service check should be performed by qualified service department. If no spark, proceed to Step 2.

2. Check voltage at the BAT terminal of the distributor while cranking the engine. If under 7V, repair the primary circuit to the ignition switch. If over 7V, proceed to Step 3.

3. With the ignition switch on, check volt-

age at the TACH terminal of the distributor or coil (external). If under IV, coil connection or coil are faulty. If over 10V, proceed to Step 4. If 1 to 10V, replace module and check for spark from coil. See Step 4.

4. On external coil models, disconnect coil wire from distributor and connect to grounded modified spark plug. On integral coils, remove distributor cap from distributor without removing its electrical connectors, remove the rotor, then modify a plug boot so that the modified plug can be connected directly to the center terminal of the distributor cap. Ground the shell of the modified plug to the engine block with a jumper wire. Make sure no wires, clothing, etc., are in the way of moving parts and crank the engine. On external coils, if no spark, check secondary coil wire continuity and repair. On both external and integral coils, if spark is present, inspect distributor cap for moisture, cracks, etc. If cap is OK, install new rotor. If no spark, proceed to Step 5.

5. Remove the pick-up coil leads from the module and check TACH terminal voltage with the ignition on. Watch the voltmeter and momentarily (not more than 5 seconds) connect a test light from the positive battery terminal to the appropriate module terminal: 4 terminal module, terminal "G" (small terminal); 5 terminal module (ESS or ESC), terminal "D"; 5 terminal module (EMR) terminal "H"; 7 terminal module, terminal "P". If no drop in voltage, check module ground, and check for open in wires from cap to distributor. If OK, replace module. If voltage drops, proceed to next step.

6. Reconnect modified plug to ignition coil as instructed in step 4, and check for spark as the test light is removed from the appropriate module terminal (see step 5 for appropriate terminal). Do not connect test light for more than 5 seconds. If spark is present, problem is with pick-up coil or connections. Pick-up coil resistance should be 500–1500 ohms and not grounded. If no spark, proceed to next step.

7. On integral coil distributors, check the coil ground by attaching a test light from the BAT terminal of the cap to the coil ground wire. If the light lights when the ignition is on, replace the ignition coil and repeat Step 6. If the light does not light, repair the ground. On external coil models, replace the ignition coil and repeat Step 6. On both the integral and external coil distributors, if no spark is present, replace the module and

reinstall the original coil. Repeat Step 6 again. If no spark is present, replace the original ignition coil with a good one.

Alternator

A variety of alternators were used:
- 1975: Motorola and Delco
- 1976: 6 cyl.–Delco
  8 cyl.–Motorcraft'
- 1977–78: 4 & 6 cyl.–Delco
  8 cyl.–Motorcraft
- 1979: 4 & 6 cyl.–Delco
  8 cyl.–Bosch
- 1980: All Delco, exc. Eagle
  with heated rear
  window (Bosch)
- 1981–82: All Delco

The alternator needs no lubrication or adjustments except for drive belt tension.

ALTERNATOR PRECAUTIONS

Certain safety precautions should be observed concerning the alternator:

1. Do not polarize the unit.
2. Do not short across or ground any of the terminals.
3. Never operate the unit with the output terminal disconnected.
4. Make sure that the battery is installed with the correct polarity.
5. When connecting a booster battery or a charger, always connect positive terminal to positive terminal and negative terminal to negative terminal.
6. Disconnect the battery ground cable when working on any electrical equipment.
7. If any electric welding is done on the car, disconnect the alternator completely.

REMOVAL AND INSTALLATION

1. Disconnect the battery cables.
   NOTE: *Always disconnect the ground cable first, and connect it last, and then you needn't fear sparks.*
2. Disconnect the alternator wires or wiring plug.
3. Remove the adjusting bolt.
4. Take off the drive belt.
5. Remove the mounting bolts and the alternator.
6. Reverse the procedure for installation.
7. Adjust the drive belt.

BELT TENSION ADJUSTMENT

The alternator drive belt, or any engine V-belt, is correctly tensioned when the long-

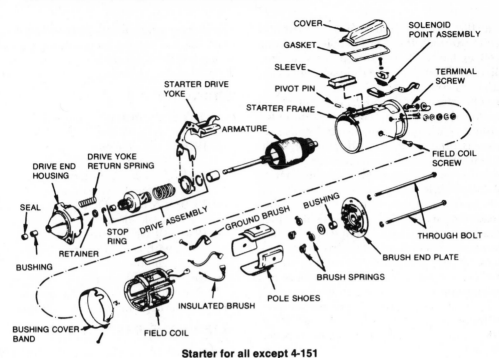

COVER
SOLENOID POINT ASSEMBLY
GASKET
SLEEVE
TERMINAL SCREW
STARTER DRIVE YOKE
PIVOT PIN
STARTER FRAME
ARMATURE
DRIVE YOKE RETURN SPRING
FIELD COIL SCREW
DRIVE END HOUSING
SEAL
BUSHING
STOP RING
DRIVE ASSEMBLY
GROUND BRUSH
BUSHING
THROUGH BOLT
RETAINER
BRUSH END PLATE
BUSHING
BRUSH SPRINGS
INSULATED BRUSH
POLE SHOES
BUSHING COVER BAND
FIELD COIL

Starter for all except 4-151

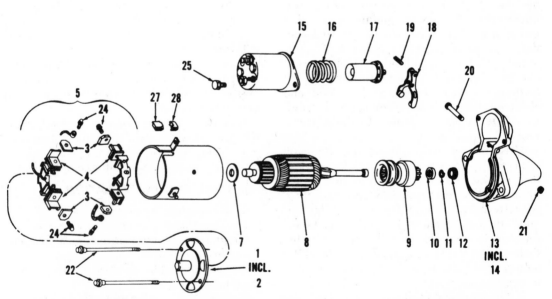

15 16 17 19 18
25
20
5
27 28
24
3
4
3
24
7
8
9 10 11 12 13
INCL. 14
22
1
INCL. 2
21

1. Frame—commutator end
2. Brush and holder pkg.
3. Brush
4. Brush holder
5. Housing—drive end
6. Frame and field asm.
7. Solenoid switch
8. Armature
9. Drive asm.
10. Plunger
11. Shift lever
12. Plunger return springer
13. Shift lever shaft
14. Lock washer
15. Screw—Brush attaching
16. Screw—field lead to switch
17. Screw—Switch attaching
18. Washer—brake
19. Thru bolt
20. Bushing—commutator end
21. Bushing—drive end
22. Pinion stop collar
23. Thrust collar
24. Grommet
25. Grommet
26. Plunger pin
27. Pinion stop retainer ring
28. Lever shaft retaining ring

4-151 starter

est span of belt between pulleys can be depressed about ½ in. in the middle by moderate thumb pressure. To adjust, loosen the slotted adjusting bracket bolt. If the alternator hinge bolt(s) is very tight, it may be necessary to loosen it slightly to move the alternator. V8 engines have a hole in the alternator bracket, so that you can insert a big screwdriver and pry out on the alternator. Some V8s have a square hole into which you can insert a ½ in. square socket drive. The best way is to pull the alternator out by hand to avoid overtightening.

CAUTION: *Be careful not to overtighten the belt, as this will damage the alternator bearings.*

Regulator

The regulator is sealed at the factory and thus cannot be adjusted. It is mounted to the fender well inside the engine compartment. To remove it, simply unplug it and remove the sheet metal screws holding it in place.

Starter

REMOVAL AND INSTALLATION

1. Disconnect the battery ground cable.
2. Disconnect the leads from the starter.
3. Unbolt and remove the starter.
4. Reverse the procedure on installation.

STARTER DRIVE REPLACEMENT

1. Remove the starter from the car.
2. Remove the brush cover band and protective tape, drive yoke cover, and gasket.
3. Remove the brushes from the holders.
4. Remove the through-bolts, drive end housing, and drive yoke return spring.
5. Remove the pivot pin and starter drive yoke.
6. Remove the armature and drive assembly.
7. Remove the brush end plate.
8. To remove the drive assembly, pry the stop ring off. Remove the drive from the armature shaft. The replacement assembly is prelubricated. Apply a few drops of 10W-30 oil to the armature shaft and end bushings. Apply a thin coat of silicone lubricant to the armature shaft splines.
9. When installing the drive assembly, make sure that the snap-ring fits tightly on the shaft. Slide the drive assembly over the

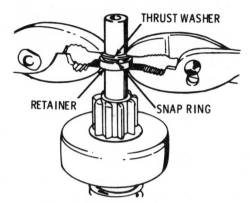

Installing starter drive snap ring

shaft and install the stop ring and the original retainer.

10. The remainder of the assembly procedure is the reverse of disassembly.

SOLENOID REPLACEMENT

The solenoid is usually fastened to the wheel-well inside the engine compartment. To replace the solenoid, first disconnect the battery ground cable. Disconnect and tag all the solenoid wires, then unscrew the solenoid from the sheet metal.

Battery

Refer to Chapter 1 for details on the battery.

REMOVAL AND INSTALLATION

1. Disconnect the negative (ground) cable terminal and then the positive cable terminal. Special pullers are available to remove battery terminals.

NOTE: *Always disconnect the battery ground cable first, and connect it last.*

2. Remove the hold-down clamp.
3. Remove the battery, being careful not to spill the acid.

NOTE: *Spilled acid can be neutralized with a baking soda/water solution. If you somehow get acid into your eyes, flush with lots of water and visit a doctor.*

4. Clean the cable terminals of any corrosion, using a wire brush or an old jackknife inside and out.
5. Install the battery. Replace the hold-down clamp.
6. Connect the positive and then the negative cable terminal. Do not hammer them in place. The terminals should be coated lightly (externally) with petroleum jelly or grease to prevent corrosion.

CAUTION: *Make absolutely sure that the battery is connected properly before you start the engine. Reversed polarity can destroy your alternator and regulator in a matter of seconds.*

ENGINE MECHANICAL

Design

FOUR-CYLINDER

During the 1977 model year, a four cylinder 2 litre (121 CID) engine, manufactured by Volkswagen, was introduced for the Gremlin. The engine is of overhead camshaft design, belt driven from the crankshaft. The cylinder head is cast aluminum alloy and has removable camshaft bearing caps. Valve lash is controlled by manual adjustment of a tapered adjusting screw, located at the base of the tappet, under the camshaft. The intake and exhaust manifolds are on the opposite sides of the cylinder head. The block is of cast iron and the crankshaft is set into five main bearings. Three grooved aluminum alloy pistons are used with full floating piston pins.

The oil pump is located at the front of the block and is driven by the crankshaft.

Beginning in 1980, the 151 cubic inch engine, manufactured by Pontiac, replaced the 121. The 151 is an inline four cylinder engine with a cast iron cylinder head and block. The pistons are made of light weight cast aluminum. The cylinder head is of a crossflow design for more efficient combustion. The camshaft, gear driven by the crankshaft, operates the overhead valves through hydraulic lifters and pushrods.

SIX-CYLINDER

The 232 and 258 sixes are virtually identical in construction. The design was originally adopted in 1966 and has remained unchanged. The engines are overhead valve with a seven main bearing crankshaft.

V8

All the AMC V8s are similar in design, having five main bearing crankshafts and overhead valves with hydraulic lifters.

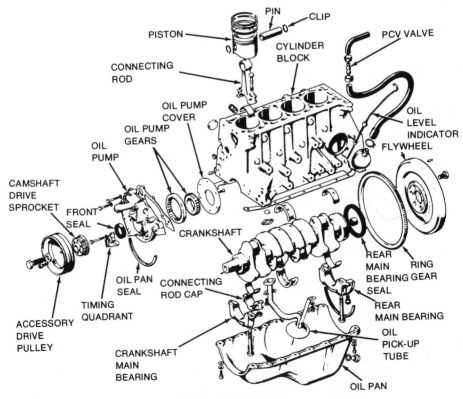

4-121 cylinder block

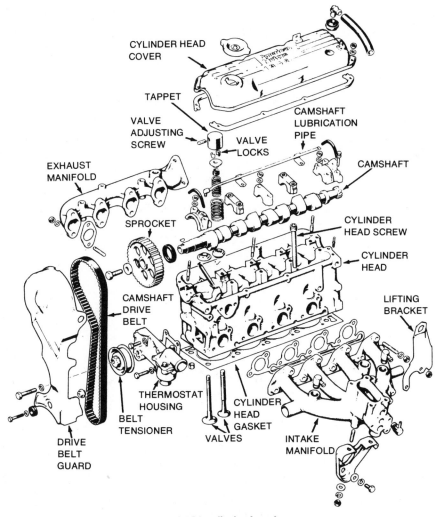

CYLINDER HEAD
COVER

TAPPET

VALVE
ADJUSTING
SCREW

VALVE
LOCKS

CAMSHAFT
LUBRICATION
PIPE

CAMSHAFT

EXHAUST
MANIFOLD

SPROCKET

CYLINDER
HEAD SCREW

CYLINDER
HEAD

CAMSHAFT
DRIVE
BELT

LIFTING
BRACKET

THERMOSTAT
HOUSING

BELT
TENSIONER

CYLINDER
HEAD
GASKET

VALVES

INTAKE
MANIFOLD

DRIVE
BELT
GUARD

4-121 cylinder head

Engine Removal and Installation

4-121

NOTE: *It is recommended by the manufacturer that the engine be removed from the car separately, and the transmission remain in the car.*

1. Mark the hinge locations and remove the hood.

2. Drain the coolant and remove the air cleaner and TAC hose.

3. Detach the negative cable at the alternator bracket and battery.

4. Remove the fuel and vacuum lines from the engine. Plug the fuel line.

5. Disconnect the necessary wiring, the throttle cable, and automatic transmission throttle valve linkage.

6. If your car has air conditioning, the system must be bled, the hoses disconnected, and the condenser moved.

CAUTION: *Do not attempt to bleed the system unless you are familiar with air conditioning systems. Have it done by a qualified mechanic. Compressed refrigerant will freeze any surface it contacts, including your eyes. It also forms a poisonous gas in the presence of flame.*

With air conditioning, bleed off the compressor charge, remove the service valves, cap the compressor ports and service valves, and disconnect the clutch wire.

7. Raise the car, disconnect and remove the starter motor and exhaust pipe support bracket. Unbolt the exhaust pipe from the manifold.

8. Remove the torque convertor nuts and

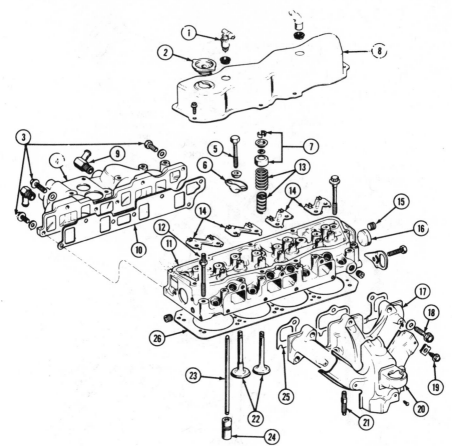

1. PCV valve
2. Oil filler cap
3. Intake manifold attaching bolts
4. Intake manifold
5. Rocker arm capscrew
6. Rocker arm
7. Valve spring retainer assembly
8. Cylinder head cover (rocker cover)
9. Coolant hose fitting
10. Intake manifold gasket
11. Cylinder head
12. Cylinder head stud bolt
13. Valve spring
14. Push rod guide
15. Cylinder head plug
16. Cylinder head core plug
17. Exhaust manifold
18. Exhaust manifold bolt
19. Oil level indicator tube
    attaching screw
20. Exhaust manifold heat shroud
    (heat shield)
21. Exhaust manifold to exhaust
    pipe stud
22. Valves
23. Push rod
24. Tappet
25. Exhaust manifold gasket
26. Cylinder head gasket

4-151 cylinder head

fluid cooler lines, if the car has automatic transmission.

9. Disconnect the wiring at the backup lamp switch and from the alternator.

10. Remove the lower radiator hose and heater hose from the radiator.

11. Remove all the bell housing bolts, except the top center bolt.

12. Lower the car and remove the top radiator hose and the cold air induction manifold at the radiator.

13. Remove the radiator screws, move the radiator one inch to the left, rotate, and lift the radiator and shroud assembly out of the car. With air conditioning, first remove the condenser attaching bolts and move the condenser away from the radiator.

14. Remove any other heater hoses and wiring that are still attached to the car.

15. With power steering, disconnect the hoses from the steering gear. Remove the transmission filler tube support screws with automatic transmission.

16. Remove the engine support cushion nuts on both sides of the engine and attach a lifting device.

17. With the engine partially raised, support the transmission and remove the center bolt from the transmission bell housing. Carefully remove the engine from the car.

18. The installation procedure is in the reverse order of removal.

NOTE: *When mating the engine to the transmission bell housing, install three bolts*

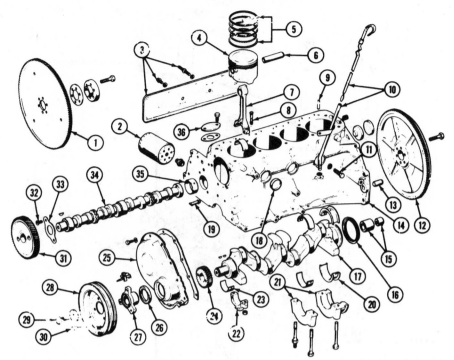

1. Drive plate and ring gear
   (automatic trans)
2. Oil filter
3. Push rod cover and bolts
4. Piston
5. Piston ring
6. Piston pin
7. Connecting rod
8. Connecting rod bolt
9. Dowel
10. Oil level indicator and tube
11. Block drain
12. Flywheel and ring gear (manual
    trans)

13. Dowel
14. Cylinder block
15. Pilot and/or converter bushing
16. Rear oil seal
17. Crankshaft
18. Block core plug
19. Timing gear oil nozzle
20. Main bearings
21. Main bearing caps
22. Connecting rod bearing cap
23. Connecting rod bearing
24. Crankshaft gear
25. Timing gear cover (front)

26. Timing gear cover oil seal
27. Crankshaft pulley
28. Crankshaft pulley hub
29. Crankshaft pulley hub bolt
30. Crankshaft pulley bolt
31. Crankshaft timing gear
32. Camshaft thrust plate screw
33. Camshaft thrust plate
34. Camshaft
35. Camshaft bearing
36. Oil pump driveshaft retainer
    plate, gasket and bolt

4-151 cylinder block

for a more secure mounting until the engine is bolted into place.

4-151

The engine and transmission are removed as an assembly.

1. Disconnect the engative battery cable. Mark the hood hinge locations and remove the hood.

2. Drain the cooling system. Disconnect the hoses. If equipped with automatic transmission, disconnect and plug the coolant lines from the radiator. Remove the fan and shroud; remove the radiator. Disconnect the heater hose from the intake manifold.

3. If equipped with power steering, remove the pump and set it aside, without disconnecting any hoses. If equipped with air conditioning, unbolt the compressor and move it aside without disconnecting any hoses. Remove the evaporator-to-dryer line from the sill clips, but do not disconnect the line. Unbolt the condenser and move it aside, without disconnecting any hoses.

4. Disconnect and label the alternator harness, starter wires, vacuum hoses and electrical connections to the carburetor, carburetor linkage, and vacuum and electrical connections to the distributor. Disconnect the coolant and oil pressure sending unit wires.

5. Disconnect the oil dipstick tube from the exhaust manifold, and pull the tube from the block.

6. Raise and support the car. Remove the engine mount nuts from the crossmember. Remove the ground cable at the left mount bracket.

7. Loosen the crossmember and lower it

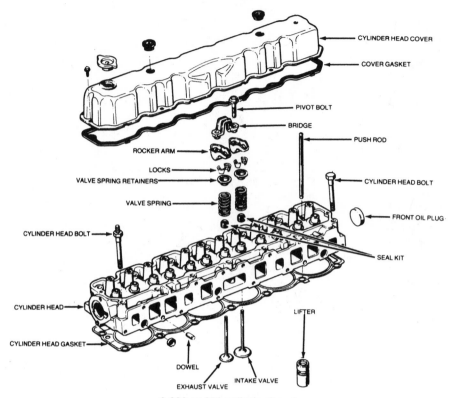

6-232 or 258 cylinder head

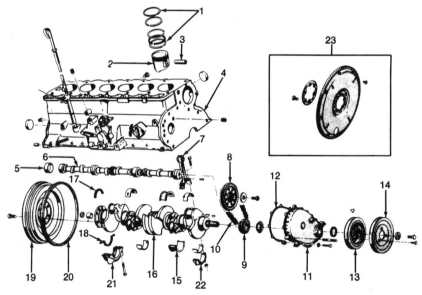

1. Piston rings
2. Piston
3. Piston pin
4. Block
5. Camshaft bearing
6. Camshaft
7. Connecting rod
8. Camshaft sprocket

9. Crankshaft sprocket
10. Timing chain
11. Timing case cover
12. Cover gasket
13. Vibration damper
14. Pulley
15. Main bearing
16. Crankshaft

17. Upper seal
18. Lower seal
19. Flywheel
20. Ring gear
21. Main bearing cap
22. Connecting rod bearing cap
23. Converter drive plate and spacer
    (with auto. trans.)

6-232 or 258 cylinder block

General Engine Specifications

Year	Engine No. Cyl. Displacement Cu. In.	Carburetor Type	Horsepower @ rpm■	Torque @ rpm (ft. lbs.)■	Bore and Stroke (in.)	Compression Ratio	Oil Pressure @ 2000 rpm
'75	6-232	1 bbl	100 @ 3600	185 @ 1800	3.750 x 3.500	8.0:1	46
	6-258	1 bbl	110 @ 3500	195 @ 2000	3.750 x 3.900	8.0:1	46
	8-304	2 bbl	150 @ 4200	245 @ 2500	3.750 x 3.440	8.4:1	46
	8-360	2 bbl	175 @ 4000	285 @ 2400	4.080 x 3.440	8.25:1	46
	8-360	4 bbl	195 @ 4400	295 @ 2900	4.080 x 3.440	8.25:1	46
	8-360 ①	4 bbl	220 @ 4400	315 @ 3100	4.080 x 3.440	8.25:1	46
	8-401 ②	4 bbl	255 @ 4600	345 @ 3300	4.165 x 3.680	8.25:1	46
'76	6-232	1 bbl	90 @ 3050	170 @ 2000	3.750 x 3.500	8.0:1	46
	6-258	1 bbl	95 @ 3050	180 @ 2100	3.750 x 3.900	8.0:1	46
	6-258	2 bbl	120 @ 3400	200 @ 2000	3.750 x 3.900	8.0:1	46
	8-304	2 bbl	120 @ 3200	220 @ 2200	3.750 x 3.440	8.4:1	46
	8-360	2 bbl	140 @ 3200	260 @ 1600	4.080 x 3.440	8.25:1	46
	8-360	4 bbl	180 @ 3600	280 @ 2800	4.080 x 3.440	8.25:1	46
	8-401 ②	4 bbl	215 @ 4200	320 @ 2800	4.165 x 3.680	8.25:1	46
'77	4-121	2 bbl	80 @ 5000	105 @ 2800	3.410 x 3.320	8.1:1	28.5 ③
	6-232	1 bbl	88 @ 3400	164 @ 1600	3.750 x 3.500	8.0:1	46
	6-258	1 bbl	98 @ 3200	193 @ 1600	3.750 x 3.900	8.0:1	46
	6-258	2 bbl	114 @ 3600	192 @ 2000	3.750 x 3.900	8.0:1	46
	8-304	2 bbl	121 @ 3450	219 @ 2000	3.750 x 3.440	8.4:1	46
	8-360	2 bbl	129 @ 3700	245 @ 1600	4.080 x 3.440	8.25:1	46
'78	4-121	2 bbl	80 @ 5000	105 @ 2800	3.410 x 3.320	8.1:1	28.5 ③
	6-232	1 bbl	90 @ 3400	168 @ 1600	3.750 x 3.500	8.0:1	46
	6-258	1 bbl	100 @ 3400	200 @ 1600	3.750 x 3.900	8.0:1	46
	6-258	2 bbl	120 @ 3600	201 @ 1800	3.750 x 3.900	8.0:1	46

General Engine Specifications (cont.)

Year	Engine No. Cyl. Displacement Cu. In.	Carburetor Type	Horsepower @ rpm ▪	Torque @ rpm (ft. lbs.) ▪	Bore and Stroke (in.)	Compression Ratio	Oil Pressure @ 2000 rpm
'78	8-304	2 bbl	130 @ 3200	238 @ 2000	3.750 x 3.440	8.4:1	46
	8-360	2 bbl	140 @ 3350	278 @ 2000	4.080 x 3.440	8.25:1	46
'79	4-121	2 bbl	80 @ 5000	105 @ 2800	3.410 x 3.320	8.1:1	28.5 ③
	6-232	1 bbl	90 @ 3400	168 @ 1600	3.750 x 3.500	8.0:1	46
	6-258	1 bbl	100 @ 3400	200 @ 1600	3.750 x 3.900	8.0:1	46
	6-258	2 bbl	110 @ 3200	210 @ 1800	3.750 x 3.900	8.3:1	46
	8-304	2 bbl	125 @ 3200	220 @ 2400	3.750 x 3.440	8.4:1	46
'80–'82	4-151	2 bbl	99 @ 4000	134 @ 2400	4.000 x 3.000	8.2:1 ④	36–41
	6-258	2 bbl	110 @ 3200	210 @ 1800	3.750 x 3.900	8.3:1	46

▪ Horsepower and torque, since 1972, are SAE net figures. They are measured at the rear of the transmission with all accessories installed and operating. Since the figures vary when a given engine is installed in different models, some are representative rather than exact.

① Dual exhaust ③ At sending unit
② Police only ④ 1981–82 8.3:1

Torque Specifications
All specifications in ft. lb.

Year	Engine	Cylinder Head Bolts	Connecting Rod Bearing Bolts	Main Bearing Bolts	Crank Pulley Bolt	Flywheel Bolts	Manifold Intake	Manifold Exhaust
1977–79	4-121	65 cold 80 hot	41	58 47 rear	181	65	18	18
1975–76	6-232, 258	95–115	26–30	75–85	48–64	95–120	18–28	18–28
1977–80	6-232, 258	95–115	30–35	75–85	70–90 ①	95–120	18–28	18–28
1981–82	6-258	80–90	30–35	75–85	70–90	95–115	18–28	18–28
1975	8-304, 360	100–120	26–30	90–105	70–90	95–120	37–47	20–30
1976–79	8-304, 360	100–120	30–35	90–105	80–100 ②	95–120	37–47	20–30 ③
1975–76	8-401	100–120	35–40	90–105	70–90	95–120	37–47	20–30
1980–82	4-151	80–103	27–33	62–68	157–163	65–71	34–40	36–42

① 1977: 48–64   ③ ⅜ inch bolts: 25
② 1976–77: 70–90   5/16 inch bolts: 15

Camshaft Specifications
(All measurements in inches)

Engine	Journal Diameter					Bearing Clearance	Lobe Lift		Camshaft End Play
	1	2	3	4	5		Intake	Exhaust	
4-121	1.2579–1.2569	1.0220–1.0212	1.0220–1.0212	1.0220–1.0212	1.0220–1.0212	#1 .004–.002 2–5 .003–.002	.396 .396	.366	.0019–.0061
4-151	1.8690	1.8690	1.8690	—	—	.0007–.0027	.398	.398	.0015–.0050
6-232, 258	2.0290–2.0300	2.0190–2.0200	2.0090–2.0100	1.9990–2.0000	—	.001–.003	.254 ②	.254 ②	0
8-304, 360, 401	2.1195–2.1205	2.0895–2.0905	2.0595–2.0605	2.0295–2.0305	1.9995–2.0005	.001–.003	.266 ①	.266 ①	0

① 401: .286
② 258 2-bbl: .248

Valve Specifications

Year	Engine No. Cyl. Displacement (cu. in.)	Seat Angle (deg) ■	Face Angle (deg) ●	Outer Spring Test Pressure (lbs. @ in.)	Spring Installed Height (in.)	Stem to Guide Clearance (in.)		Stem Diameter (in.)	
						Intake	Exhaust	Intake	Exhaust
'75	6-232	44.5	44	195 @ 1.44	$1^{13}/_{16}$	.0010–.0030	.0010–.0027	.3720	.3720
	6-258	44.5	44	195 @ 1.44	$1^{13}/_{16}$	.0010–.0030	.0010–.0027	.3720	.3720
	8-304	44.5	44	213 @ 1.38	$1^{13}/_{16}$	.0010–.0030	.0010–.0030	.3720	.3720
	8-360	44.5	44	213 @ 1.38 ②	$1^{13}/_{16}$	.0010–.0030	.0010–.0030	.3720	.3720
	8-401	44.5	44	223 @ 1.35 ②	$1^{13}/_{16}$	.0010–.0030	.0010–.0030	.3720	.3720
'76	6-232, 258	44.5	44	195 @ 1.44	$1^{13}/_{16}$	.0010–.0030	.0010–.0027	.3720	.3720
	8-304, 360	44.5	44	213 @ 1.38 ②	$1^{13}/_{16}$	.0010–.0030	.0010–.0030	.3720	.3720
	8-401	44.5	44	223 @ 1.35 ②	$1^{13}/_{16}$	.0010–.0030	.0010–.0030	.3720	.3720
'77	4-121	45.75	45.33	160 @ 1.319	1.7	.0012–.0026	.0015–.0030	.3529	.3525
	6-232, 258	44.5	44	195 @ 1.411 ④	$1^{13}/_{16}$	.0010–.0030	.0010–.0027	.3720	.3722

	8-304, 360	44.5	44	213 @ 1.382	1 13/16	.0010–.0030	.0010–.0027	.3720	.3722
'78	4-121	45.75	45.33	160 @ 1.319 ⑧	1.7 ⑨	.0012–.0026	.0015–.0030	.3529	.3525
	6-232, 258	44.5	44	195 @ 1.411 ④	1 13/16	.0010–.0030	.0010–.0027	.3720	.3722
	8-304, 360	44.5	44	213 @ 1.356	1 13/16	.0010–.0030	.0010–.0027	.3720	.3722
'79	4-121	44.75	45.33	160 @ 1.319 ⑧	1.7 ⑨	.0012–.0026	.0015–.0030	.3529	.3525
	6-232, 258, 8-304	44.5	44	195 @ 1.411 ④	1 13/16	.0010–.0030	.0010–.0027	.3720	.3722
'80–'82	4-151	46	45	176 @ 1.254	①	.0010–.0027	.0010–.0027	.3423	.3423
	6-258	44.5	44	195 @ 1.411	1 13/16	.0010–.0030	.0010–.0030	.3720	.3720

● Exhaust valve face angles are shown. All intake valve face angles are 29°, except 121 and 151 cu. in. engines

■ Exhaust valve seat angles are shown. All intake valve seat angles are 30°, except 121 and 151 cu. in. engines

① Intake: 2.057 in.; exhaust: 1.730 in.
② 1975 Police 360, 401: intake—270 @ 1.38; exhaust—270 @ 1.19, exhaust installed height—1⅝ in.
③ Not used
④ 204 @ 1.39 in. for two barrel 258
⑤ Not used
⑥ Not used
⑦ Not used
⑧ Intake—166 @ 1.299
⑨ Inner spring—1.49 in.

Crankshaft and Connecting Rod Specifications

Year	Engine	Crankshaft				Connecting Rod		
		Main Brg. Journal Dia.	Main Brg. Oil Clearance	Shaft End Play	Thrust on No.	Journal Diameter	Oil Clearance	Side Clearance
1977–79	4-121	2.5177–2.5185	.001–.003	.004–.008	3	1.8880–1.8890	.001–.002	.002–.012
1975–76	All 6	2.4986–2.5001	.001–.003	.002–.007	3	2.0934–2.0955	.001–.002	.005–.014
1977–79	All 6	2.4986–2.5001	.0003–.0024	.002–.007	3	2.0934–2.0955	.001–.002	.005–.014
1975–76	All 8	2.7474–2.7489 ①	.001–.002 ②	.003–.008	3	③	.001–.003	.006–.018
1977–79	All 8	2.7474–2.7489 ①	.0003–.0020 ②	.003–.008	3	③	.001–.003	.006–.018
1980–82	4-151	2.2988	.0005–.0022	.0035–.0085	5	2.0000	.0005–.0026	.017
	6-258	2.4986–2.5001	.001–.003	.0015–.0065	3	2.0934–2.0955	.001–.003	.005–.014

①No. 5: 2.7464–2.7479
②Rear main 1975–76: .002–.003
    1977–79: .001–.003
③304, 360: 2.0934–2.0955
   401: 2.2464–2.2485

Piston Clearance

Year	Engine	Piston-to-Bore Clearance (in.)
1975–82	6-232, 258	.0009–.0017
	8-304, 401	.0010–.0018 ②
	8-360	.0012–.0020 ①
1977	4-121	.0009–.0015
1978–79	4-121	.0007–.0017
1980–82	4-151	.0025–.0033

① police 8-360: .0016–.0024
② police 8-401: .0014–.0022

Ring Side Clearance
All measurements in inches

Year	Engine	Top Compression	Bottom Compression	Oil Control
1975–80	6-232, 258	.0015–.0030	.0015–.0030	.001–.008
1981–82	6-258	.0017–.0032	.0017–.0032	.001–.008
1975–79	8-304	.0015–.0035	.0015–.0030	.001–.008
1975–78	8-360, 401	.0015–.0030	.0015–.0035	0–.007
1977–79	4-121	.0012–.0024	.0012–.0024	.0012–.0024
1980–82	4-151	.0030	.0030	0

Ring Gap
All measurements in inches

Year	Engine	Top Compression	Bottom Compression	Oil Control
1975–82	6-232, 258, 8-304	.010–.020	.010–.020	.010–.025
1975–79	8-360	.010–.020	.010–.020	.015–.045
1975–76	8-401	.010–.020	.010–.020	.015–.055
1977–79	4-121	.010–.020	.010–.020	.010–.016
1980–82	4-151	.010–.022	.010–.028	.015–.055

conditioner or alternator bracket and raise and remove the engine/transmission assembly.

Installation is the reverse.

6 CYLINDER AND V8

The engine is removed without the transmission on all models except the Pacer.

1. Mark the hood hinge locations, disconnect the underhood light, if equipped, and remove the hood.

2. Drain the coolant and engine oil. Remove the filter on the Pacer.

3. Disconnect and remove the battery and air cleaner. On Pacers, first run the wipers to the center of the windshield.

4. Disconnect and tag the alternator, ignition coil, distributor, temperature and oil sender wiring. On Pacers, also disconnect the brake warning switch wiring.

5. If equipped with TCS, remove the switch bracket and vacuum solenoid wire harness.

6. Disconnect and plug the hose from the fuel pump. On Pacers, also disconnect the automatic transmission fluid cooler line.

7. Disconnect the engine ground strap at the block and the starter cable at the starter. Remove the right front engine support cushion-to-bracket bolt.

8. If your car has air conditioning, the system must be bled, the hoses disconnected, and the system removed.

CAUTION: *Do not perform this operation if you are unfamiliar with A/C systems. Have the system bled by a qualified mechanic. Compressed refrigerant will freeze any surface it contacts, including your eyes.*

slightly. Remove the speedometer cable from the transmission. Remove the cooler tubes if equipped with automatic transmission. Remove the transmission linkage and backup light switch wiring. Remove the rear transmission mount.

8. Matchmark the driveshaft and remove.

9. Remove the crossmember.

10. Disconnect the exhaust pipe from the manifold.

11. Disconnect the fuel line.

12. Check that all hoses and wires have been disconnected. Lower the car. Attach a chain to the engine rear bracket and the air

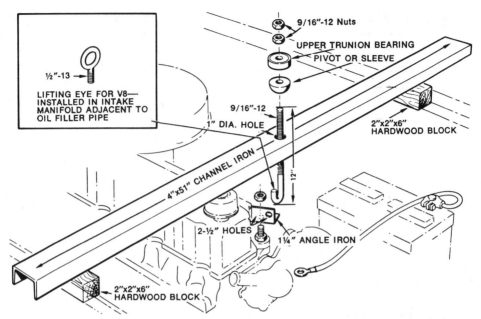

A lifting fixture can be fabricated as illustrated to facilitate oil pan and/or engine mount removal

It also forms a poisonous gas in the presence of flame.

Bleed the refrigerant from the system. Remove the service valves, cap the compressor ports and the service valves, and disconnect the clutch wire. On Pacers, also disconnect the receiver outlet at the coupling, and remove the receiver and condenser assembly.

9. Disconnect the return hose from the fuel filter. TAC hose from the manifold, carburetor vent hose, heater or A/C vacuum hose and/or power brake hose at intake manifold, and power brake vacuum check valve from booster, if equipped.

10. Disconnect the throttle cable and throttle valve rod, if equipped.

11. Disconnect the radiator and heater hoses from the engine, automatic transmission cooler lines from the radiator, radiator shroud, fan, and spacer, and remove the radiator.

12. Install a $5/16 \times 1/2$ in. bolt through the fan pulley into the water pump flange to maintain alignment (all but Pacer).

13. With power steering, disconnect the hoses, drain the reservoir, and cap the fittings. With power brakes, remove the vacuum check valve from the booster.

14. On Pacers only, remove the carburetor and plug the fitting, remove the valve cover(s) and remove the vibration damper.

15. With automatic transmission, remove the filler tube.

16. Jack and support the front of the car. Remove the starter.

17. With automatic transmission on all except the Pacer, remove the converter cover, converter bolts (rotate the crankshaft for access), and the exhaust pipe/transmission linkage support.

With manual transmission on all but the Pacer, remove the clutch cover, bellcrank inner support bolts and springs, the bellcrank, outer bellcrank-to-strut retainer, and disconnect the back-up lamp wire harness at the firewall for access later.

On Pacers, disconnect the transmission and clutch linkage, speedometer cable at the transmission, remove the driveshaft (plug the transmission), and support the transmission with a jack. Remove the rear crossmember.

18. Attach the lifting device and support the engine. Remove the engine mount bolts.

19. Disconnect the exhaust pipe from the manifold.

20. On all but the Pacer, remove the upper converter or clutch housing bolts and loosen the lower bolts. Raise the car and move the jackstands to the jack pad area. Remove the A/C idler pulley and bracket, if equipped. Lift the engine off the front supports, support the transmission, remove the lower transmission cover attaching bolts, and lift the engine out of the car.

On Pacers, lift the engine slightly and remove the front support cushions. Remove the transmission support, raise the front of the car so that the bottom of the bumper is three feet from the floor, and partially remove the engine/transmission assembly until the rear of the cylinder head clears the cowl. Lower the car and remove the engine.

21. On installation with manual transmission, insert the transmission shaft into the clutch spline and align the clutch housing to the engine. Install and tighten the lower housing bolts. With automatic transmission, align the converter housing to the engine and loosely install the bottom housing bolts. Then install the next higher bolts and tighten all four bolts. With both transmissions, next remove the transmission support, lower the engine onto the mounts, and install the mounting bolts. The remainder of the installation is the reverse of removal.

On Pacers, raise the car with a jack as in Step 20. Lower the engine/transmission assembly into the compartment. Raise the transmission into position with a jack and install the rear crossmember. Install the front engine support cushions. The remainder of installation is the reverse of removal.

Intake Manifold

REMOVAL AND INSTALLATION

4-121

1. Drain the cooling system.
2. Remove the EGR tube at the exhaust manifold and remove the air cleaner assembly.
3. Disconnect the fuel and vacuum lines and plug the main fuel line to avoid gasoline leakage.
4. Remove the accelerator cable and the air hose from the diverter valve.
5. Remove the fuel pump and the power brake cylinder vacuum hose. Loosen the air conditioner compressor mounting bracket, if so equipped. Do not discharge the system.
6. Remove the water inlet and outlet hoses from the manifold and the PCV hose at the block.
7. Remove the wires from the carburetor, accessories, and from the ignition coil.
8. Remove the manifold bracket lower screw, loosen and remove the manifold nuts, and remove the manifold and lift bracket from the engine.
9. Remove the gasket and clean the mating surfaces on the manifold and the cylinder head.
10. The installation of the intake manifold

is in the reverse of the disassembly. When installing the manifold, don't tighten the manifold retaining nuts until the EGR tube is connected to the exhaust manifold. Then tighten the retaining nuts to 18 ft. lbs. torque and the bracket lower screw to 30 ft. lbs. When the installation is completed, operate the engine for 3 to 5 minutes and check for leaks.

4-151

1. Remove the air cleaner. Drain the cooling system. Disconnect the heater hose from the intake manifold.
2. Disconnect and label the fuel line, all vacuum lines and electrical connectors from the carburetor, insulator and the intake manifold.
3. Disconnect the throttle linkage.
4. Remove the carburetor and insulator.
5. Remove the alternator rear support bracket from the manifold.
6. Remove the A/C compressor, if so equipped.
7. Remove the intake manifold bolts and remove the manifold.
8. To install, place a new gasket against the cylinder head, then install the manifold in place by starting all bolts finger tight.
9. Torque the intake manifold bolts to 25 ft. lbs. in two stages, using the torque sequence shown. The rest of installation is the reverse of removal.

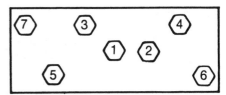

4-151 intake manifold bolt torque sequence

6 Cylinder

The intake manifold is mounted on the left-hand side of the engine and bolted to the cylinder head. A gasket is used between the intake manifold and the head; none is required for the exhaust manifold.

1. Remove the air cleaner. Disconnect the fuel line, vent hose, and solenoid wire, if equipped.
2. Disconnect the accelerator cable from the accelerator bellcrank.
3. Disconnect the PCV vacuum hose from the intake manifold and the TCS solenoid and bracket, if so equipped.

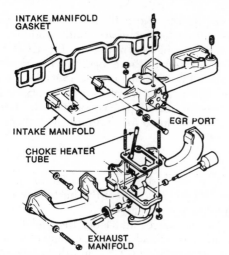

INTAKE MANIFOLD
GASKET

INTAKE MANIFOLD

EGR PORT

CHOKE HEATER
TUBE

EXHAUST
MANIFOLD

6 cylinder intake and exhaust manifold through 1980

4. Remove the spark CTO switch, if so equipped, and EGR valve (or exhause back-pressure sensor) vacuum lines from each of these components.

5. Disconnect the hoses from the air pump and the injection manifold check valve. Disconnect the vacuum line from the diverter valve and remove the diverter valve with hoses, if so equipped.

6. Remove the air pump and power steering bracket (if so equipped) and remove the air pump. Move the power steering pump aside, out of the way, without disconnecting the hoses.

7. Remove the air conditioning drive belt idler assembly from the cylinder head, if so equipped. On some models it is necessary to remove the A/C compressor. Do not discharge the A/C system; just lay the compressor aside.

8. Disconnect the throttle valve linkage if equipped with automatic transmission.

9. Disconnect the exhaust pipe from the manifold.

10. On some 1981 and later models, an oxygen sensor is screwed in the exhaust mani-

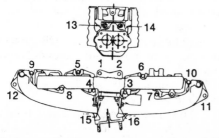

6 cylinder manifold torque sequences through 1980

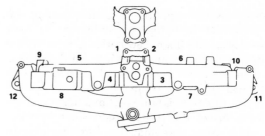

1981–82 6 cylinder manifold torque sequences

fold just above the exhaust pipe connection. Disconnect the wire and remove the sensor, if so equipped.

11. Remove the manifold attaching bolts, nuts, and clamps and remove the intake and exhaust manifolds as an assembly. Discard the gasket. The two manifolds are separated at the heat riser. Discard the asbestos gasket if they are separated. The asbestos gasket is not used on 1980 and later models.

To install the intake and exhaust manifolds:

1. Clean all of the mating surfaces on the cylinder head and the manifolds.

2. Assemble the two manifolds together with a new gasket (through 1979) and tighten the heat riser retaining nuts to 5 ft. lbs.

3. Position the manifold to the engine to-

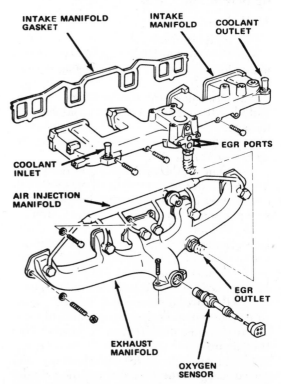

INTAKE MANIFOLD
GASKET

INTAKE
MANIFOLD

COOLANT
OUTLET

EGR PORTS

COOLANT
INLET

AIR INJECTION
MANIFOLD

EGR
OUTLET

EXHAUST
MANIFOLD

OXYGEN
SENSOR

1981–82 6 cylinder intake and exhaust manifold assemblies

gether with a new intake manifold gasket and tighten the manifold attaching bolts and nuts in the proper sequence to the specified torque.

4. Install the remaining components in the reverse order of removal. Adjust the automatic transmission throttle linkage, if so equipped. Adjust the drive belt(s) tension.

V8

The cast iron manifold completely encloses and seals the tappet valley between the cylinder heads. The manifold contains water passages, a crankcase vent passage, exhaust crossover, induction, and in some cases EGR passages. A one-piece metal gasket seals the intake manifold to cylinder head joint and also serves as an oil splash baffle. The left-hand carburetor bores supply cylinders No. 1, 7, 4 and 6; the right-hand bores cylinders No. 3, 5, 2 and 8.

1. Drain the cooling system.

2. Remove the air cleaner assembly from the carburetor.

3. Mark and remove the spark plug wires.

4. Remove the spark plug wire guides from the rocker cover, ignition coil and by-pass valve brackets.

5. Disconnect the radiator upper hose and the by-pass hoses from their fittings on the intake manifold. Disconnect the temperature gauge sending unit electrical lead.

6. Remove the ignition coil and bracket. Set the coil/bracket assembly out of the way.

7. Remove the TCS solenoid if so equipped, from the right-hand valve cover. Remove the A/C compressor bracket, if equipped. Do not discharge the system, just move the compressor aside with lines attached.

8. Disconnect any of the emission control wiring or hoses as necessary. Disconnect the heater hose from the rear of the intake manifold.

9. Disconnect the throttle linkage and fuel and vacuum lines from the carburetor.

10. On the cars equipped with air injection, remove the by-pass (diverter) valve bracket. Set the valve assembly (with hoses) out of the way, forward of the engine.

11. If the car is equipped with "Cruise Command" (automatic speed control), remove the vacuum speed control), remove the vacuum servo mounting bracket and set the servo assembly aside.

12. Remove the carburetor assembly from the manifold.

13. Remove the intake manifold assembly complete with gasket and end seals.

Always use a new gasket when installing the intake manifold. Use a good commercial sealer on both sides of the metal gasket and on the rubber end seals. Align the gasket at the rear first, then at the front.

The rest of the installation procedure is the reverse of removal. Torque the manifold bolts evenly to the specified torque, working from the center out.

Exhaust Manifold

REMOVAL AND INSTALLATION

4-121

1. Remove the TAC cold air induction manifold assembly and components.

2. Disconnect the EGR tube from the manifold.

3. Remove the exhaust pipe from the manifold.

4. Remove the manifold retaining nuts and washers.

5. Remove the manifold and gasket from the engine.

6. Clean the mating surfaces of the manifold and the head.

7. The installation of the manifold is the reverse of disassembly. Do not tighten the exhaust manifold nuts until the EGR tube is attached to the exhaust manifold, then torque the manifold nuts to 18 ft. lbs.

4-151

1. Remove the air cleaner and the hot air tube.

2. Remove the Pulsair system from the exhaust manifold.

3. Disconnect the exhaust pipe from the manifold at the flange. Spray the bolts first with penetrating sealer, if necessary.

4. Remove the engine oil dipstick bracket bolt.

5. Remove the exhaust manifold bolts and remove the manifold from the head.

6. To install, place a new gasket against the cylinder head, then install the exhaust mani-

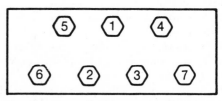

4-151 exhaust manifold torque sequence

fold over it. Start all the bolts into the head finger tight.

7. Torque the exhaust manifold bolts to 37 ft. lbs. in two stages, using the torque sequence illustrated.

8. The remainder of installation is the reverse of removal.

6 Cylinder

The exhaust manifold is removed along-with the intake manifold; previous instructions.

V8—Except Gremlin and Hornet w/Air Pump Through 1976

NOTE: *The mating surfaces of both the exhaust manifold and the cylinder head are machined smooth, thus eliminating any need for a gasket between them.*

1. Disconnect the wires from the spark plugs after marking them for firing order.

2. On models equipped with air injection, disconnect the air delivery hoses from the injection manifold. Remove the injection manifold and nozzles from the exhaust manifold.

3. Disconnect the exhaust pipe from the exhaust manifold flange.

4. Remove the bolts and washers used to retain the manifold.

5. Remove the shields from the spark plugs. On 1977 and later Hornets and Concords only, before removing the right side manifold, remove the transmission filler tube bolt and tube. Use a new O-ring when installing the tube.

6. Remove the exhaust manifold from the cylinder head.

7. Clean the machined surfaces of the manifold and head. Installation is the reverse of removal.

Gremlin and Hornet V8 With Air Pump Through 1976

The exhaust manifold on the left side may be removed in the same manner as detailed for other V8 engines; however, the right-side manifold on Gremlins and Hornets equipped with air pumps must be removed in the following order:

1. Raise the car and securely support it with jackstands.

2. Disconnect the exhaust pipe from the manifold flange.

3. Support the engine at the vibration damper, by placing a jack with a block of wood on its lifting pad underneath it.

4. Remove the bolts which secure the engine mounting bracket on the right side.

5. Remove the air cleaner assembly, including the tube which runs to the manifold heat stove.

6. Disconnect the battery cables. Remove the spark plug leads after marking them for installation.

7. Disconnect the air supply hose from the air injection manifold.

8. Remove the air injection tubes from the exhaust manifold.

9. On cars with automatic transmissions, remove the dipstick and the screw which secures the transmission dipstick tube.

10. Working from the rear, unscrew the exhaust manifold mounting bolts.

11. Raise the engine. Remove the exhaust manifold and the air injection manifold as an assembly.

Prior to installation, clean the joining surfaces of the manifold and cylinder head. Be careful not to nick or scratch either surface.

The rest of installation is the reverse of removal. Torque the manifold securing bolts to specification, starting from the rear and working forward.

Valve System

4-121

The valves are operated by an overhead cam, driven by a toothed rubber belt, connected to the crankshaft. The cam lobes contact "bucket" type tappets, which are set over the valve and valve springs, and force the valve and springs to move downward, moving the valve from its seat on the cylinder head. Both intake and exhaust valves are manually ad-

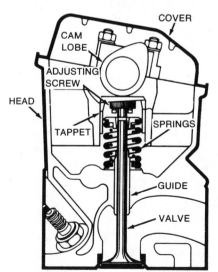

4-121 valve train

justed by a wedge type screw angled into the tappet, perpendicular to the valve stem. A flat area is milled onto the screw, which contacts the valve stem end. The threaded area locks to a threaded area within the tappet. Each turn changes the clearance .002 in. When tappet adjustment is done, the flat side of the adjusting screw must be toward the valve stem end at the completion of the adjustment. Refer to the Tune-Up Specifications Chart for hot valve clearances. Cold assembly clearances are 0.004–0.007, intake; and 0.014–0.017, exhaust.

4 Cylinder-121 Valve Adjustment

NOTE: *Valve adjustment must be made with the engine at normal operating temperature*

1. Remove the TAC hose, the cylinder head cover, the spark plug wires and distributor cap.
2. Rotate the crankshaft to bring the number one cylinder to TDC (the beginning of its firing stroke). The position of the distributor rotor will assist in determining this position.

NOTE: *There is a mark on the edge of the distributor housing at number one terminal position. Do not attempt to rotate the engine by turning the camshaft. Turn the crankshaft in the direction of normal rotation to avoid damage to the timing belt.*

3. With number one cylinder on TDC of its firing stroke, the clearance of the exhaust valves on cylinders number one and three, and of the intake valves on cylinders number one and two, can be checked.

NOTE: *The front valve in each pair per cylinder is the intake valve. If the clearance requires adjustment, a special tool is required to move the adjusting screw.*

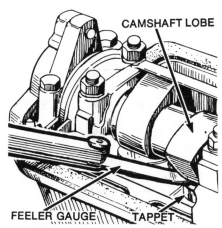

CAMSHAFT LOBE

FEELER GAUGE   TAPPET

4-121 valve clearance measurement

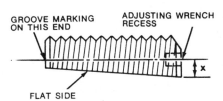

GROOVE MARKING ON THIS END   ADJUSTING WRENCH RECESS

FLAT SIDE

4-121 valve adjusting screw

4. Adjust the screw by turning one complete turn until it clicks, and continue until the proper clearance is obtained.
5. After adjusting the clearance, use the special AMC gauge J-26860 to check the position of the screw in the tappet. If the gauge indicates the adjusting screw is turned too far into the tappet, the screw must be replaced. Five sizes of screws are available, identified by grooves on the end of the screws.

NOTE: *If the adjusting screws must be replaced, the tappets must be removed from the head. Note which tappets must be removed, then continue the adjustment procedure. When all eight adjustments are made, remove those tappets requiring screw replacement. Refer to camshaft removal and installation.*

6. Rotate the crankshaft 360 degrees. The distributor rotor should be 180 degrees opposite the mark on the distributor housing.
7. The clearance can now be checked on the exhaust valves for cylinders two and four, and the intake valve on cylinders three and four.
8. Reinstall the head cover, using a new gasket.
9. Reinstall the distributor cap and spark plug wiring. Reinstall the TAC flexible hose.

4-151

The 151 uses hydraulic lifters, eliminating periodic valve adjustments. The cylinder head has integral valve guides. Oversized valves are available in 0.003 and 0.005 in. sizes. To fit these, the valve guide bores must be enlarged with a reamer. If a large oversize clearance is given in the Valve Specifications table at the beginning of this section.

As an alternate procedure, some automotive machine shops fit replacement valve guides which accept the standard size valves.

Rocker Assembly
REMOVAL AND INSTALLATION
4-151

1. Remove the valve cover.
2. Remove the rocker arm nut and rocker arm ball.

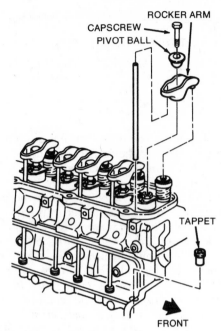

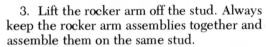

4-151 rocker arm assembly

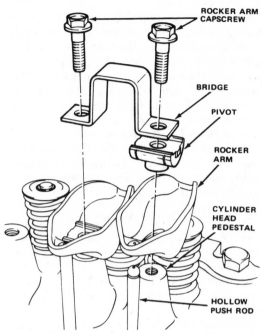

6 cylinder rocker arm assembly; V8 is almost identical

3. Lift the rocker arm off the stud. Always keep the rocker arm assemblies together and assemble them on the same stud.

4. Remove the pushrod from its bore. Make sure the rods are returned to their original bores, with the same end in the block.

5. Reverse the removal procedure to install. Lubricate all parts before installation. Tighten the rocker arm ball retaining nut to 20 ft. lbs.

6 Cylinder and V8

American Motors six and V8 engines use hydraulic tappets; thus, no mechanical valve adjustment is necessary. Special tappets to permit higher sustained rpm are used in police engines. The valve guides are integral with the head on all engines.

The valve stem oil deflectors should be replaced whenever valve service is performed.

American Motors engines do not have replaceable valve guides. If stem to guide clearance is excessive, guides must be reamed to the proper oversize. Three oversize valves are available with stems 0.003, 0.015 and 0.030 in. larger than standard diameter.

The intake and exhaust rocker arms for each cylinder pivot on a bridged pivot assembly bolted to the cylinder head. The pushrods are hollow to supply lubrication to the rocker arms. The pushrods act as guides to keep the rocker arms in alignment, so it is not abnor-

mal for them to rub slightly on the cylinder head.

NOTE: *Be careful when ordering new valve train components, not to get parts for the wrong year.*

1. Remove any accessories which are in the way and remove the valve cover, complete with gasket.

2. Unscrew the rocker arm capscrews evenly to avoid breaking the bridge.

3. Remove the pivot assemblies, rocker arms, and pushrods.

NOTE: *Be sure to keep all parts in the same order in which they were removed.*

4. Clean all parts in solvent. Blow all oil passages in the rocker arms and pushrods dry with compressed air.

Replace any deeply pitted rocker arms and scuffed or worn pushrods. If the pushrod is worn from lack of oil, replace it, its valve lifter and rocker arm, as well.

Installation is performed in the following order:

1. Insert the pushrods in their bores. Be sure to center the bottom of each rod in the plunger cap of the hydraulic valve lifter.

2. Install the rocker arms, pivot assemblies and capscrews. Tighten the capscrews evenly to 21 ft. lbs. on six cylinders through 1975, and 19 ft. lbs. on all other engines.

NOTE: *Be sure that the pushrods, pivot*

assemblies, and capscrews are returned to exactly the same places from which they were removed.

3. Wipe the gasket surface clean.

a. If a silicone sealer is being used, wipe the surface with an oily rag and apply a ⅛ in. bead of silicone along the sealing surface. Before the silcone begins to harden, install the cover, being careful not to touch the silcone to the rocker arms. Apply a small amount of sealer to each screw hole and tighten the screws to specifications.

b. When using a gasket, cement the gasket in several places with a quick drying adhesive. Correctly position the cover and gasket on the engine and install the attaching screws.

4. Install anything which was removed to gain access to the valve covers.

Cylinder Head

REMOVAL AND INSTALLATION

CAUTION: *Don't loosen the head bolts until the engine is thoroughly cool, to prevent warping. Do not remove block drain plugs or loosen radiator draincock with the system hot and under pressure, as serious burns from coolant can occur.*

If the head sticks, operate the starter to loosen it by compression or rap it upward with a soft hammer. Do not force anything between the head and the block.

NOTE: *Resurfacing (milling or grinding) the cylinder head will increase the compression ratio, and can affect the emission output, as well as the fuel octane requirement. For this reason the factory recommends replacing rather than resurfacing cylinder heads.*

Cylinder head bolts should be retorqued after the first 500 miles or so unless a special AMC gasket is used. The special gasket doesn't require retorquing.

CAUTION: *Make sure to blow any coolant out of the cylinder head bolt holes before reassembly to prevent inaccurate torque readings.*

4-121

1. Drain the coolant from the system and disconnect the negative cable from the battery.

2. Remove the air cleaner assembly, vacuum hoses and flexible hoses from the cylinder head area.

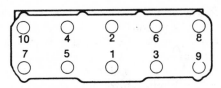

4-121 head bolt torque sequence

3. Remove the radiator hoses, radiator bypass hose and the heater hoses.

4. Remove the accessory drive belts, camshaft drive belt cover, and the camshaft drive belt. Loosen the compressor mounting bracket if equipped with A/C.

5. Remove the fan belt, fan blades, spacer and pulley. Remove the air pump and also the alternator pivot bolt. Do not disconnect the wire harness from the alternator.

6. Remove the air pump front bracket, and the exhaust pipe from the manifold. Remove the air hose from the diverter valve and remove the EGR tube to bell housing screw.

7. Disconnect the remaining wires to the electrical units of the cylinder head, marking the wires for connection during assembly.

8. Remove the fuel line at the bottom of the intake manifold, and remove the screw from the bottom of the manifold bracket.

9. Disconnect the power brake vacuum hose. Remove the remaining fuel vapor control hoses, PCV hoses, and the remaining vacuum lines.

10. Disconnect the accelerator cable.

11. Remove the coolant inlet and outlet hoses from the intake manifold.

12. Remove the cylinder head cover. Loosen and remove the head bolts. Loosen the bolts in the reverse order of the tightening sequence, in two passes. Remove the cylinder head, manifolds and carburetor as a unit.

13. Clean the machined surfaces of the cylinder head and the engine block. With a straight edge and feeler gauge, check the flatness of the mating surfaces. There should not be a distortion of over 0.002 in. on both surfaces.

14. After the necessary services have been done to the cylinder head and/or the block assembly, prepare the mating surfaces by cleaning thoroughly. Install a new head gasket, and place the head on the block with the aid of locating dowels. Torque the cylinder head bolts to 65 ft. lbs. following the cylinder head torque sequence illustration, and in three stages.

15. Complete cylinder head replacement

by following the reverse procedure of disassembly. Temporarily install the head cover. Start the engine and allow it to warm up for five minutes.

16. When the engine has warmed up to operating temperature, stop the engine and remove the top engine cover.

17. Following the head torque sequence, loosen the first head bolt ⅛ of a turn and retorque the bolt to 80 ft. lbs. Proceed to the second bolt and repeat the procedure for each head bolt until all the bolts have been retorqued to the new specification.

18. Replace the head cover and complete the assembly of the lines, tubes, wires, and air cleaner assembly.

19. Check the engine for leakage.

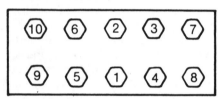

4-151 head bolt torque sequence

4-151

1. Disconnect the negative battery cable. Drain the cooling system.

2. Disconnect the accelerator cable at the bellcrank, and the manifold vacuum and fuel lines at the carburetor.

3. Remove the intake and exhaust manifolds.

4. Remove the alternator and power steering power. Unbolt the A/C compressor (if equipped) and move it aside, without disconnecting any lines.

5. Disconnect all electrical connectors at the head.

6. Disconnect the radiator and heater hoses, and the battery ground strap.

7. Remove the spark plugs.

8. Remove the rocker arm cover, rocker arms, and push rods. Keep all parts in order.

9. Unbolt and remove the cylinder head.

10. Clean the gasket surfaces thoroughly.

11. Install a new gasket over the dowels, and position the cylinder head.

12. Coat the head bolt threads with sealer and install finger tight.

13. Tighten the bolts in sequence, in three equal steps to the specified torque.

14. Install all parts in the reverse of removal.

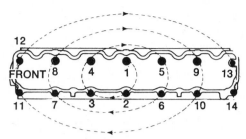

6 cylinder head bolt torque sequence

6 Cylinder

NOTE: *On Pacers, run the wipers to the center of the windshield to ease valve cover removal.*

1. Drain the cooling system. Disconnect throttle linkage, fuel lines, water hoses, spark plug wires and vacuum line. Remove the air cleaner, PCV hose, and the temperature sender.

2. Remove the valve cover and its gasket. Remove the rocker arm assembly and the pushrods. With bridged pivots, loosen each bolt alternately, one turn at a time, to avoid damage. Keep the pushrods in order. If equipped with power steering, remove the power steering pump bracket and Air Guard pump and set them aside. Don't disconnect the hoses.

3. Remove the intake and exhaust manifold assembly from the head.

4. Disconnect the spark plug wires and remove the plugs.

5. Disconnect the battery ground cable, the coil, and the coil bracket from the head. Disconnect the temperature sending unit wire.

6. If the vehicle is equipped with air conditioning, remove the drive belt idler pulley bracket from the cylinder head. Loosen the alternator drive belt and remove the bolts from the compressor mounting bracket. Set the compressor aside, all hoses attached.

7. Remove the bolts and remove the cylinder head from the block.

8. Clean the gasket surfaces of both the head and the block. Remove the carbon deposits from the top of each piston and from the combustion chambers.

9. Check the head for straightness. If the head (or the block) is 0.008 in. out of true over its entire length, 0.001 in. in 1 in., or 0.002 in. in 6 in., the head requires resurfacing.

Installation of the cylinder head is performed in the following order:

1. Use a new head gasket and coat both of its sides with sealer. The word "top," on the gasket, faces upward.

2. Tighten the head bolts in three stages and proper sequence to the proper torque specification.

3. The rest of installation is the reverse of the removal. Refill the cooling system when completed.

V8

Maximum out of true is 0.006 in. for the entire length of head, 0.001 in every 1 in., or 0.002 in. in 6 in.

1. Drain the cooling system.

2. Remove the cylinder head cover and gasket.

3. Remove the rocker arm assemblies. Alternately loosen the capscrews on the bridged pivots to avoid damage to the bridge.

4. Remove the pushrods.

NOTE: *Keep the rocker arms and push rods in order so they can be replaced in the same order as removed.*

5. Remove the ignition wires and spark plugs.

6. Remove the intake and exhaust manifolds.

7. Loosen all drive belts.

8. Remove the A/C compressor mounting bracket if so equipped. Remove the alternator support brace.

9. Remove the air pump and power steering mounting bracket, if so equipped.

10. Remove the cylinder head retaining bolts in the reverse order of the installation sequence, and in two stages.

11. Remove the cylinder head and gasket. To install:

12. Apply a coat of sealer to both sides of the new head gasket. Position the gasket on the block with the word Top facing up.

13. Install the cylinder head and gasket.

14. Tighten the cylinder bolts to 80 ft. lbs. following the torquing sequence chart. Following the sequence chart again, torque the bolts to 110 ft. lbs.

The remainder of the installation procedure is in the reverse of removal.

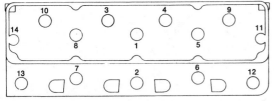

V8 head bolt torque sequence

Timing Cover, Chain, and Camshaft

VIBRATION DAMPER REMOVAL

4-151, 6 Cylinder and V8

Remove the radiator core, all drive belts, and the fan. Remove the nut from the center of the pulley. The best way to do this is to affix a heavy wrench and rap it with a substantial hammer. It may be necessary to lock up the engine at the flywheel to prevent crankshaft rotation. The nut must be unscrewed in the opposite direction of normal engine rotation. Using a puller, remove the pulley from the front of the crankshaft.

Timing Case Cover

REMOVAL AND INSTALLATION

4-151

1. Remove the crankshaft hub.

2. Remove the oil pan-to-front cover screws.

3. Remove the front cover-to-block screws.

4. Pull the cover slightly forward, just enough to allow cutting of the oil pan front seal flush with the block on both sides.

5. Remove the front cover and attached portion of the pan seal.

6. Clean the gasket surfaces thoroughly.

7. Cut the tabs from the new oil pan front seal.

8. Install the seal on the front cover, pressing the tips into the holes provided.

9. Coat the new gasket with sealer and position it on the front cover.

10. Apply a ⅛ in. bead of silicone sealer to the joint formed at the oil pan and block.

11. Align the front cover seal with a centering tool and install the front cover. Tighten the screws to 7.5 ft. lbs. Install the hub.

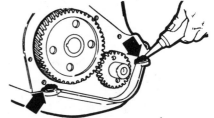

Applying sealer to the 4-151 front cover prior to installation

6 Cylinder

1. Remove all V-belts, fan and pulley.

2. Remove the vibration damper.

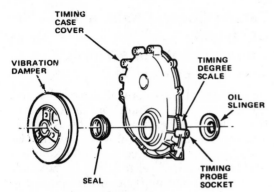

6 cylinder timing case cover

3. Remove oil pan to cover bolts and cover to block bolts.

4. Raise cover and pull oil pan front seal up far enough to extract the tabs from the holes in cover.

CAUTION: *If this isn't done, the oil pan will have to be removed to get the seals into place.*

5. Remove cover gasket from block; cut off seal tab flush with front face of block.

6. Clean all mating surfaces and remove oil seal.

7. Install a new front oil seal.

8. Install new neoprene front oil pan seal, cutting off protruding tabs to match original. Use sealer on the end tabs and the gasket surfaces.

9. Position cover on block and install bolts. Align the front cover with a centering tool. Tighten cover bolts to 4–6 ft. lbs.; four lower bolts to 10–12 ft. lbs. Remove the centering tool.

10. Install vibration damper, tightening the bolt to the specified torque.

NOTE: *Front oil seal can be installed with*

cover in place only if proper tool or duplicate is available.

V8

The die-cast timing cover incorporates an oil seal at the vibration damper hub. This seal must be installed from the rear through 1976; therefore the cover must be removed from engine in every case to replace front seal. 1977–79 oil seals are installed from the front, and can be replaced without removing the cover using a special AMC tool.

1. Drain coolant and remove hoses from water pump.

2. Remove distributor, fuel pump, alternator drive belt, accessory drive belts, fan and hub assembly, alternator and bracket, and back idler pulley.

3. Remove the vibration damper bolts, then pull off the damper.

4. Remove air conditioner compressor and power steering pump, if so equipped, and swing them out of the way *without* disconnecting hoses.

5. Remove the two front oil pan bolts from beneath the car, then remove the cover bolts.

NOTE: *The timing case cover attaching bolts are of different lengths and must be replaced in their original locations.*

6. Remove cover from block, then clean all parts and mating surfaces and remove oil seal.

7. Coat new seal lips with Petroleum jelly and seal surface with sealer, then drive the seal into the cover bore until it seats against the outer cover face. Use a proper size arbor for this job. Install from the back through 1976; 1977 and later seals go on the front.

8. Remove lower dowel pin from cylin-

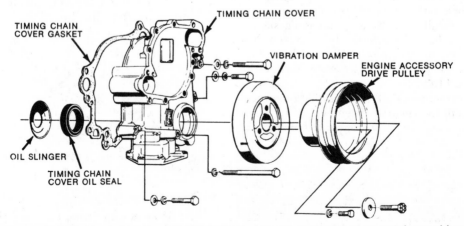

V8 timing case cover assembly, through 1976. 1977 and later are identical except for seal location

der block; this must be replaced when cover is in position but before bolts are installed.

9. Cut the oil pan gasket flush with the block on both sides of the oil pan.

10. Cut corresponding pieces of gasket from another oil pan gasket and cement them to cover. Install neoprene oil pan front seal into cover and align gasket tabs with pan seal.

11. Apply sealant to gaskets, then position cover. Install oil pan bolts and tighten evenly until cover lines up with upper dowel pin.

12. Install lower dowel pin, then cover to block bolts; tighten to 20–30 ft. lbs.

13. Install all removed pieces and adjust ignition timing.

Timing Chain, Belt or Gear and Sprocket or Pulley

REMOVAL AND INSTALLATION

4-121

This engine uses a toothed rubber belt to drive the camshaft. Belt tension is controlled by an adjustable idler pulley. The distributor is at the rear of the cylinder head and is driven by a gear pressed on the rear of the camshaft.

CAUTION: *Do not turn the engine backwards. Damage to the drive belt teeth could result. Turn the engine by the crankshaft bolt, not the camshaft.*

BELT REMOVAL AND INSTALLATION

1. Rotate the crankshaft in the normal direction of rotation, until the timing mark on the pulley is pointing to the zero position on the degree scale on the block. The timing mark on the rear of the camshaft pulley should be aligned with the pointer on the cylinder head cover.

2. Loosen the accessory pulley attaching bolts. Remove the V belts and the cam drive belt shield.

3. Loosen the adjuster retaining screw to allow the belt to slacken and remove the belt.

4. To replace the belt, install the belt on the crankshaft pulley, and position it on the tensioner pulley. Slip the belt over the camshaft pulley using hand pressure only, while maintaining the pulleys at their respective timing marks.

NOTE: *Do not pry the belt with metal tools. The belt drive surface can be damaged and premature belt failure can result.*

5. Turn the offset adjusting nut on the tensioning pulley counterclockwise to increase the belt tension. The belt is properly ten-

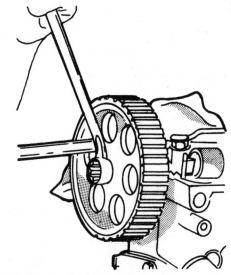
Removing the 4-121 camshaft pulley

sioned when the drive side of the belt can be twisted 90 degrees with finger pressure.

NOTE: *When checking belt tension, apply tension on the crankshaft with a wrench, in a cosnterclockwise direction, to get all the slack on one side of the belt.*

6. With pressure on the tensioning pulley nut, tighten the retaining nut to 29 ft. lbs. torque. Recheck the belt tension.

7. Install the drive belt shield. Install the alternator belts and adjust their tension. Tighten the accessory pulley bolts to 15 ft. lbs.

8. Start the engine and adjust the ignition timing.

CAMSHAFT PULLEY REMOVAL AND INSTALLATION

1. Remove the drive belt.

2. Insert a bar or other suitable tool through the camshaft pulley to prevent it from turning.

3. Remove the pulley retaining bolt. Remove the pulley, woodruff key, and washer from the camshaft.

4. To replace the pulley reverse the disassembly procedure. Hold the camshaft pulley and torque the retaining bolt to 58 ft. lbs.

5. Refer to Belt Removal and Installation for installation and tensioning.

CRANKSHAFT PULLEY REMOVAL AND INSTALLATION

1. Raise and support the front of the car with stands.

2. Remove the camshaft drive belt.

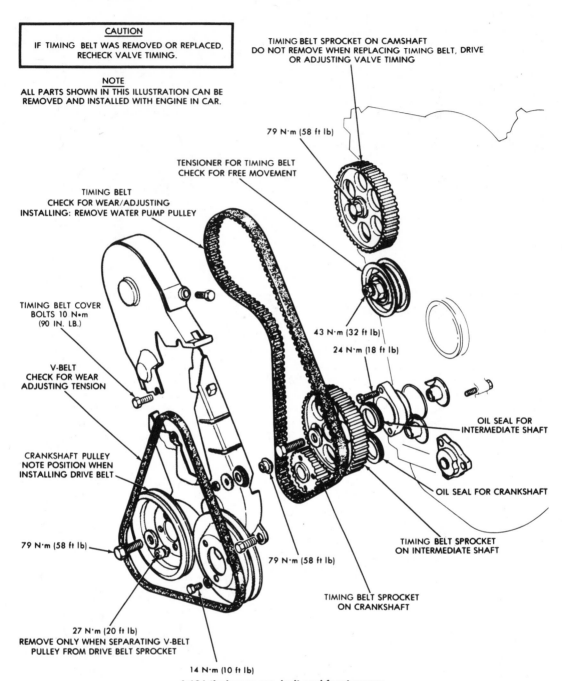

CAUTION
IF TIMING BELT WAS REMOVED OR REPLACED, RECHECK VALVE TIMING.

NOTE
ALL PARTS SHOWN IN THIS ILLUSTRATION CAN BE REMOVED AND INSTALLED WITH ENGINE IN CAR.

TIMING BELT SPROCKET ON CAMSHAFT
DO NOT REMOVE WHEN REPLACING TIMING BELT, DRIVE OR ADJUSTING VALVE TIMING

79 N·m (58 ft lb)

TENSIONER FOR TIMING BELT
CHECK FOR FREE MOVEMENT

TIMING BELT
CHECK FOR WEAR/ADJUSTING
INSTALLING: REMOVE WATER PUMP PULLEY

TIMING BELT COVER
BOLTS 10 N•m
(90 IN. LB.)

V-BELT
CHECK FOR WEAR
ADJUSTING TENSION

43 N·m (32 ft lb)

24 N·m (18 ft lb)

OIL SEAL FOR INTERMEDIATE SHAFT

CRANKSHAFT PULLEY
NOTE POSITION WHEN
INSTALLING DRIVE BELT

OIL SEAL FOR CRANKSHAFT

TIMING BELT SPROCKET
ON INTERMEDIATE SHAFT

79 N·m (58 ft lb)

79 N·m (58 ft lb)

TIMING BELT SPROCKET
ON CRANKSHAFT

27 N·m (20 ft lb)
REMOVE ONLY WHEN SEPARATING V-BELT
PULLEY FROM DRIVE BELT SPROCKET

14 N·m (10 ft lb)

4-121 timing gears, belt and front cover

3. Remove the accessory drive pulley from the crankshaft pulley using a no. 40 Torx head bit to remove the pulley screws.

4. the sprocket retaining bolt can be loosened and removed from the crankshaft. Hold the pulley from turning while the bolt is loosened.

5. Remove the pulley from the crankshaft.

6. Install in the pulley so that the index-ing hole in the pulley engages with the pin on the crankshaft.

7. Hold the pulley from turning. Install the retaining bolt and torque to 181 ft. lbs.

8. Install the drive belt. See Belt Removal and Installation for tensioning.

9. Replace the belt guard. Replace the accessory drive pulley and torque the attaching bolts to 15 ft. lbs.

10. Complete the assembly in the reverse

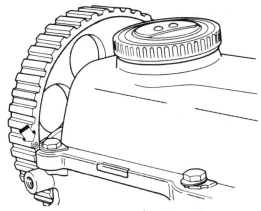

Aligning the camshaft timing dot with the edge of the cylinder head on the 4-121

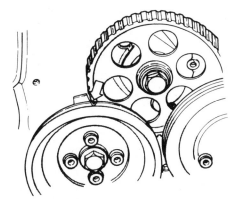

Aligning the timing marks on the crankshaft and intermediate shaft on the 4-121

order of disassembly. Start the engine and reset the ginition timing.

4-151

The 151 uses timing gears instead of a chain and sprockets or a belt. The cam timing gear is pressed onto the camshaft. The camshaft must be removed to remove the gear, which must be pressed off the camshaft. See the camshaft removal procedure for details. The replacement cam gear must be pressed onto the camshaft. To replace the gear, first place the gear spacer ring and thrust plate over the

end of the camshaft, then install the woodruff key. Press the camshaft gear onto the cam until it bottoms against the gear spacer ring. End clearance of the thrust plate must be 0.0015–0.0050 in. If less than 0.0015 in., the spacer ring must be replaced. If more than 0.0050 in., the thrust plate must be replaced.

6 Cylinder

1. Remove the drive belt(s).
2. Remove the engine fan and hub assembly.

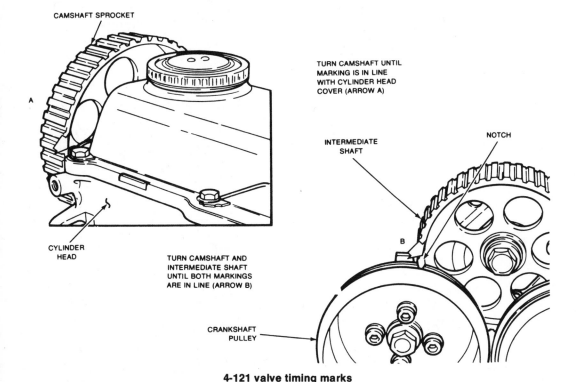

CAMSHAFT SPROCKET

A

CYLINDER HEAD

TURN CAMSHAFT AND INTERMEDIATE SHAFT UNTIL BOTH MARKINGS ARE IN LINE (ARROW B)

TURN CAMSHAFT UNTIL MARKING IS IN LINE WITH CYLINDER HEAD COVER (ARROW A)

INTERMEDIATE SHAFT

NOTCH

B

CRANKSHAFT PULLEY

4-121 valve timing marks

Timing Belt Wear

DESCRIPTION	FLAW CONDITIONS

1. Hardened back surface rubber — Back surface glossy. Non-elastic and so hard that even if a finger nail is forced into it, no mark is produced.

2. Cracked back surface rubber

3. Cracked or exfoliated' canvas

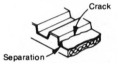

Crack   Crack

Separation   Separation

4. Badly worn teeth (initial stage) — Canvas on load side tooth flank worn (Fluffy canvas fibers, rubber gone and color changed to white, and unclear canvas texture)

Flank worn (On load side)

5. Badly worn teeth (last stage) — Canvas on load side tooth flank worn down and rubber exposed (tooth width reduced)

Rubber exposed

6. Cracked tooth bottom

Crack

7. Missing tooth

Tooth missing and canvas fiber exposed

8. Side of belt badly worn

Rounded belt side

Abnormal wear (Fluffy canvas fiber)

NOTE: *Normal belt should have clear-cut sides as if cut by a sharp knife.*

9. Side of belt cracked

4-121 timing belt wear diagnosis

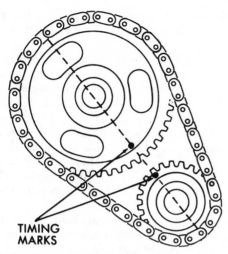

TIMING
MARKS

Aligning the 6 cylinder timing marks

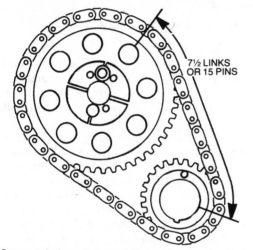

7½ LINKS
OR 15 PINS

Correct timing chain installation for the 6 cylinder

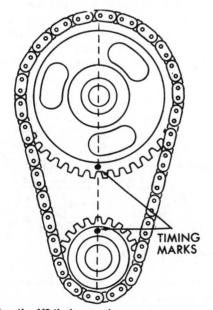

TIMING
MARKS

Aligning the V8 timing marks

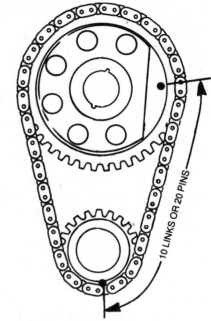

10 LINKS OR 20 PINS

Correct timing chain installation on the V8

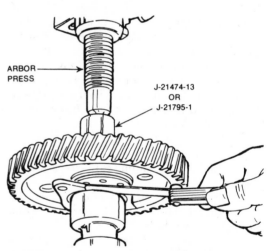

ARBOR
PRESS

J-21474-13
OR
J-21795-1

Installing the 4-151 camshaft timing gear and measuring the thrust plate end clearance

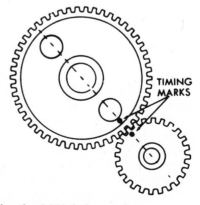

TIMING
MARKS

Aligning the 4-151 timing marks

3. Remove the vibration damper pulley and remove the vibration damper.

4. Remove the timing case cover. Remove the seal from the timing case cover, because the seal should be replaced every time the cover is removed from the engine.

5. Remove the camshaft sprocket retaining bolt and washer.

6. Turn the crankshaft until the 0 timing mark on the crankshaft sprocket is closest to and on a centerline with the timing pointer of the camshaft sprocket.

7. Remove the crankshaft sprocket, camshaft sprocket and timing chain as an assembly. Disassemble the chain and sprockets.

To install:

8. Assemble the timing chain, crankshaft sprocket, and camshaft sprocket with the timing marks aligned.

9. Install the assembly to the crankshaft and camshaft.

10. Install the camshaft sprocket retaining bolt and washer and tighten the bolt to 50 ft. lbs.

11. To ensure the correct installation of the timing chain, locate the timing mark of the camshaft sprocket at about the 1 o'clock position. This should place the timing mark on the crankshaft sprocket where the sprocket teeth mesh with the chain. There must be 15 timing chain pins between the timing marks of both sprockets.

V8

1. Remove the timing case cover and gasket.

2. Remove the crankshaft oil slinger

3. Remove the camshaft sprocket retaining bolt and washer.

4. Remove the distributor drive gear and the fuel pump eccentric.

5. Turn the crankshaft until the 0 timing mark on the crankshaft sprocket is closest to and on a center line with the 0 timing mark on the camshaft sprocket.

6. Remove the crankshaft sprocket, camshaft sprocket and the timing chain as an assembly.

To install:

7. Assemble the timing chain, and the two sprockets with the timing marks aligned vertically and install the assembly to the crankshaft and camshaft.

8. Install the fuel pump eccentric and the distributor drive gear. The fuel pump eccentric is installed with the word "REAR" toward the camshaft sprocket.

9. Install the camshaft sprocket, washer, and retaining bolt, tightening the bolt to 30 ft. lbs.

10. To ensure the timing chain is installed correctly, turn the crankshaft until the timing mark on the camshaft sprocket is placed horizontally at the 3 o'clock position. Starting with the timing chain pin directly opposite the camshaft sprocket timing mark, count the number of pins down to the timing mark on the crankshaft sprocket. There should be 20 pins between the two timing marks. The crankshaft timing mark must be between the 20th and 21st pin.

11. Install the crankshaft oil slinger.

12. Install the timing case cover together with a new gasket and seal.

Camshaft
REMOVAL AND INSTALLATION
4-121

1. Remove the air cleaner assembly, and the distributor cap with the wires attached.

2. Remove the accessory belts, and the belt guard. Loosen and remove the camshaft drive belt.

3. Remove the distributor and housing assembly from the rear of the cylinder head.

4. Remove the cylinder head cover, and the camshaft pulley from the camshaft.

NOTE: *Use a tool to prevent the sprocket from turning while removing the retaining bolt, and protect the head surface by wrapping a cloth around the end of the tool.*

5. Remove the bolts from number 5 camshaft bearing cap (rear cap), and then remove the retaining nuts from caps 1, 3, and 5. Next remove the nuts on bearing caps number 2 and 4, backing off each nut ¼ turn at a time to relieve tension on the camshaft. Remove

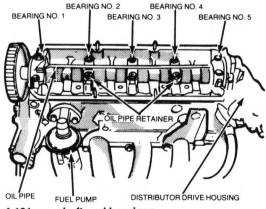

BEARING NO. 2   BEARING NO. 4
BEARING NO. 1   BEARING NO. 3   BEARING NO. 5

OIL PIPE RETAINER

OIL PIPE   FUEL PUMP   DISTRIBUTOR DRIVE HOUSING

4-121 camshaft and bearings

the oil pipe retainers from the bolts on bearing caps number 2 and 4.

6. Remove all the camshaft bearing caps from the cylinder head. Keep them in order.

7. Remove the camshaft from the cylinder head.

NOTE: *The distributor drive gear should be removed from the camshaft with a puller. It can be replaced by driving the gear on the camshaft with the use of a block of wood and a hammer. Note the gear location before removal.*

8. The tappets may be removed for service by lifting them out of their bores in the cylinder head.

9. On installation, lubricate the camshaft lobes and bearing surfaces and install the shaft into the cylinder head. Install the camshaft bearing caps on their respective seats, and install the retaining nuts on cap numbers 2 and 4, tightening to 13 ft. lbs.

10. Torque numbers 3 and 5 retaining nuts to 13 ft. lbs. Install the bolts in bearing cap number 5 and torque to 7 ft. lbs.

11. Install a replacement seal on the camshaft and tighten the number 1 bearing cap to 13 ft. lbs. torque. Install the oil pipe and tighten the nuts to 13 ft. lbs.

12. Install the camshaft sprocket and torque the retaining bolt to 58 ft. lbs., while holding the sprocket to prevent its turning.

13. Temporarily install the cylinder head cover and position the camshaft pulley timing mark in line with the indicator on the cylinder head cover.

14. Install the distributor and housing on the rear of the cylinder head, setting the rotor to the number one cylinder position.

15. Install the distributor cap and wiring, attach the vacuum line, and connect the primary wire.

16. Rotate the crankshaft to the TDC mark. Install the camshaft drive belt and adjust. Refer to Belt Removal and Installation.

17. Reassemble the drive belt guard, replace the accessory belts and adjust.

18. Remove the cylinder head cover and adjust the tappet to camshaft clearance.

19. Install the cylinder head cover and complete the assembly. Start the engine and adjust the ignition timing.

4-151

1. Drain the cooling system.
2. Remove the radiator.
3. Remove the fan and water pump pulley.

4. Remove the grille and bumper if necessary for clearance.

5. Remove the rocker cover, rocker arms, and pushrods.

6. Remove the distributor, spark plugs, and fuel pump.

7. Remove the pushrod cover and gasket. Remove the lifters.

8. Remove the crankshaft hub and timing gear cover.

9. Remove the two camshaft thrust plate screws by working through the holes in the gear.

10. Remove the camshaft and gear assembly by pulling it through the front of the block. Take care not to damage the bearings.

11. Install in the reverse order. Torque the thrust plate screws to 75 in. lbs.

6 Cylinder

1. Drain the cooling system and remove the radiator. Remove the hood (Pacers only).

2. If the car is equipped with air conditioning, remove the condenser and the receiver unit as a *charged assembly*, only.

NOTE: *Do not discharge the A/C system.*

3. Remove the valve cover and gasket.

4. Remove the rocker arm assembly and the cylinder head. Remove the pushrods and tappets.

NOTE: *Pushrods and tappets should be kept in the proper order. They must be returned to their original places during assembly.*

5. Remove the drivebelt(s), fan assembly, accessory pulley(s), vibration damper, and the timing chain cover.

6. Remove the fuel pump. Remove the distributor assembly, including spark plug wires.

7. Turn the crankshaft until the "0" timing mark on the crankshaft sprocket is nearest to, on a centerline with, and aligns with the timing pointer on the camshaft sprocket.

8. Remove the sprockets and the timing chain as an assembly.

9. Remove the front bumper and/or grille as necessary. Withdraw the camshaft through the opening. On the Pacer, unbolt the front engine mounts from the crossmember and raise the engine.

10. Inspect the bearing journals, distributor drive, cam lobes, and tappets for wear or damage. Replace parts, as required.

Camshaft installation is performed in the following order:

1. Use a generous amount of an engine

oil supplement on the camshaft. Install it in the block, using care not to damage any surfaces. On the Pacer, lower the engine and connect the engine mounts.

2. Install the timing chain and sprocket assembly.

3. Install the timing chain cover and a new oil seal.

4. Install the vibration damper and the accessory drive pulley(s).

5. Install the engine fan assembly and the drive belt(s). Tighten the belts to the proper tension.

6. Install the fuel pump.

7. With the number one piston at TDC of its compression stroke, fit the distributor so that the rotor is aligned with the no. one terminal on the cap (distributor fully seated on the block). Install the cap and the spark plug wires.

8. Install the tappets, cylinder head, its gasket, valve train (pushrods in the same order, as removed), valve cover and its gasket.

NOTE: *All valve train components must be lubricated with engine oil supplement. The supplement must remain in the engine for at least the first 1,000 miles. It does not require draining until the next regular oil change.*

9. Install the air conditioner receiver and condenser, without discharging any coolant (if so equipped).

10. Install the radiator and top up the cooling system.

11. Install the front bumper and/or grille. Bolt down the Pacer engine mounts and install the hood.

12. Check ignition timing and reset as required.

V8

1. Disconnect the battery cable.

2. Drain the radiator and both banks of the cylinder block. Remove the radiator, the hoses, and the thermostat housing. Remove the air conditioning condenser and receiver assembly as a charged unit, if so equipped.

3. Remove the distributor, complete with spark plug wires and the coil from the intake manifold.

4. Remove the intake manifold as a complete assembly.

5. Take off the valve cover and take out the valve train, including the hydraulic tappets.

NOTE: *Keep the valve train components in*

proper order. They must be returned to their original place during assembly.

6. Remove the power steering pump from its bracket, without disconnecting the hoses. Set it out of the way.

7. Remove the fan assembly and then the fuel pump. Disconnect heater hose at the water pump.

8. Unbolt the alternator bracket and set it out of the way, complete with the alternator. Do not disconnect the alternator wiring.

9. Remove the crankshaft pulley and the vibration damper.

10. Remove the timing case cover. With the timing marks in vertical alignment, remove the front cover, distributor/olil pump drive gear, fuel pump eccentric, sprockets, and the timing chain.

11. Remove the hood latch upper support bracket attachment screws. Move the bracket, as necessary, to permit removal of the camshaft. Remove the bumper and grille if necessary.

12. Use care during camshaft removal, so that the journal bearings are not damaged.

13. Inspect all parts for wear and damage. Replace them as required.

Installation of the cam is the reverse of removal. Install the timing chain and cover. Adjust the belt tension and fill up the cooling system.

NOTE: *Lubricate the camshaft tappets, and the valve train with an engine oil supplement. Add the remaining supplement to the crankcase, and leave it in the engine for at least the first 1000 miles. It does not require draining until the next regular oil change.*

Piston and Rod Assembly

The piston and rod assemblies are installed from the top, and the dimple, notch, or dot, marked on the top of the piston, goes toward the front. On the 121 four cylinder, the rod and piston assemblies must be marked on disassembly; the projections on the connecting rods must face towards the front of the engine. On the 151 four cylinder, the raised notch side of the rod (near the bearing end) must be 180° opposite the notch in the piston. On the six cylinder, the connecting rod numbers must go toward the camshaft; on the V8, the numbers must go toward the outside of the engine.

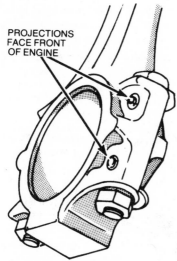

4-121 connecting rod installation

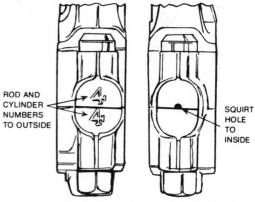

4-151 connecting rod numbering and oil squirt hole

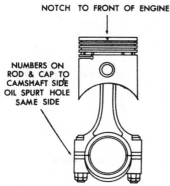

6 cylinder piston and connecting rod

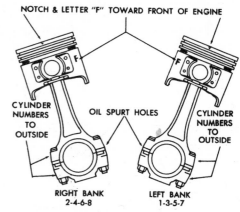

V8 piston and rod assemblies

ENGINE LUBRICATION

Oil Pan

REMOVAL AND INSTALLATION

NOTE: *It is much easier to remove the engine in most cases.*

4-121

1. Raise the car and support it with stands. Drain the oil.

2. Install an engine lifting device and support the weight of the engine, while removing the engine bracket to mount cushion nuts. Loosen the strut and bracket screws.

3. Raise the engine approximately two inches and remove the crossmember to sill attaching parts.

4. Remove the steering gear idler bracket from the frame rail.

5. Pry the crossmember down and insert wooden blocks between the crossmember and the side sill on both sides.

6. Remove the oil pan and clean the gasket from the mating surfaces of the block and oil pan.

7. The installation of the oil pan is the reverse of removal. Cement the gasket to the engine block; use sealer between side gaskets and end seals; tighten the side pan bolts to 80 in. lbs. and the end bolts to 90 in. lbs.

4-151

1. Follow Steps 1 through 6 of the 121 4 cylinder procedure.

2. To install the pan, thoroughly clean all the gasket mating surfaces.

3. Install a new rear oil pan gasket in the rear main bearing cap. Apply a small quantity of RTV silicone sealer into the depressions where the rear pan gasket engages the block.

4. Install a new front oil pan gasket onto the timing gear cover. Press the tips into the holes in the cover.

5. Install the side gaskets onto the block,

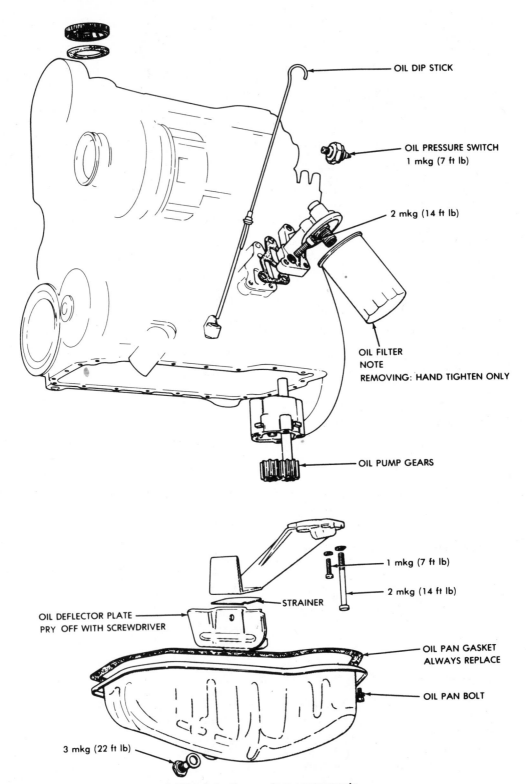

OIL DIP STICK

OIL PRESSURE SWITCH
1 mkg (7 ft lb)

2 mkg (14 ft lb)

OIL FILTER
NOTE
REMOVING: HAND TIGHTEN ONLY

OIL PUMP GEARS

1 mkg (7 ft lb)

2 mkg (14 ft lb)

STRAINER

OIL DEFLECTOR PLATE
PRY OFF WITH SCREWDRIVER

OIL PAN GASKET
ALWAYS REPLACE

OIL PAN BOLT

3 mkg (22 ft lb)

4-121 lubrication system components

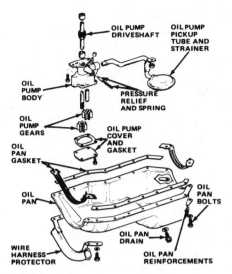

OIL PUMP DRIVESHAFT

OIL PUMP PICKUP TUBE AND STRAINER

OIL PUMP BODY

PRESSURE RELIEF AND SPRING

OIL PUMP GEARS

OIL PUMP COVER AND GASKET

OIL PAN GASKET

OIL PAN

OIL PAN BOLTS

OIL PAN DRAIN

WIRE HARNESS PROTECTOR

OIL PAN REINFORCEMENTS

4-151 lubrication system components

not the oil pan. Retain them with a thin film of grease. Apply a ¼ in. long bead of RTV silicone sealer to the split lines of the front and side gaskets; the bead should be ⅛ in. wide.

6. Install the oil pan onto the engine. The timing cover bolts should be installed last. They are installed at an angle; the holes will line up after the rest of the pan bolts have been snugged down. The bolts should be tightened to 6 ft. lbs. all around. The rest of installation is the reverse of removal.

6 Cylinder and V8 (Except Pacer)

1. Turn the steering wheel to full left lock. Support the engine with a hoist. Raise and support the car at the side sills. Disconnect the engine ground cable.

2. Unbolt the steering idler arm at the side sill, and the engine cushions at the brackets.

3. Remove the sway bar, if equipped. Remove the front crossmember-to-side sill bolts and pull the crossmember down. Remove the right engine bracket. Loosen but do not remove the strut rods at the lower control arm.

4. Drain the engine oil.

5. Remove the starter.

6. Remove the oil pan bolts and pan. Remove the front and rear seats, and clean the gasket surfaces.

7. Install the new pan front seal to the timing cover, and apply sealer to end tabs. Cement new pan side gaskets to the block, and apply sealer to the ends of the gasket.

8. Coat the inside surface of the new rear seal with soap, and apply sealer to end tabs. Install the seal in the rear main cap.

9. Coat front and rear seal contact surfaces with engine oil, and install the pan. The remainder of the installation is the reverse of removal.

Pacer

1. Drain the engine oil.

2. Install an engine lifting device and support the weight of the engine.

3. Disconnect the steering shaft flexible joint and hold it aside with a length of wire.

4. Raise and support the car.

5. Remove the front engine support through bolts.

6. Disconnect the front brake lines at the wheel cylinders.

7. Disconnect the upper ball joints from the spindles. Make sure the shock absorbers are attached securely.

8. Remove the upper control arm and move it aside.

9. Support the front crossmember with a jack.

10. Remove the nuts from the front crossmember rear mounts and swing the crossmember down and forward.

11. Follow Steps 5–9 of the preceding six cylinder and V8 procedure.

12. Install and assemble the remaining components in the reverse order of removal, tightening the ¼ in. oil pan screws to 7 ft. lbs., the ⁵/₁₆ in. oil pan screws to 11 ft. lbs., the crossmember attaching nuts to 50 ft. lbs., the upper control arm cross shaft bolt and nut to 60 ft. lbs., and the engine mount and

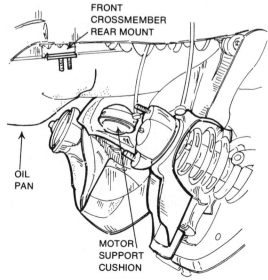

FRONT CROSSMEMBER REAR MOUNT

OIL PAN

MOTOR SUPPORT CUSHION

Pacer oil pan removal

steering shaft nuts to 25 ft. lbs. Fill the crankcase with oil and bleed the brakes.

Oil Pump

REMOVAL AND INSTALLATION

CAUTION: *Anytime the oil pump cover is removed or the pump disassembled, the pump must be primed by filling the spaces around the gears with petroleum jelly. Do not use grease.*

4-121

The oil pump is on the lower front of the engine block. It consists of two gears with meshing teeth, one with internal teeth and the other with external teeth. Oil pressure is controlled by a pressure relief valve and spring assembly. The inner gear is driven by the crankshaft at twice the speed of distributor driven oil pumps. To service the oil pump assembly, removal is necessary. Proceed as follows.

1. Remove the fan shroud.
2. Raise the car and support it on stands.
3. Loosen the crankshaft pulley screws but don't remove them.
4. Loosen and remove the power steering pump belt, air conditioner belt and alternator belt.
5. Remove the crankshaft pulley. Attach a crankshaft sprocket wrench using all of the pulley screws and remove the crankshaft screw.
6. Remove the camshaft drive sprocket from the cranksahft.
7. Remove the oil pump screws and the front oil pan screws and remove the oil pump by prying in the slots with a large screwdriver.

8. Replace the gasket and the crankshaft seal. Trim the edges of the gasket.
9. Rotate the crankshaft so the oil pump lugs are either vertical or horizontal.
10. Cut off the oil pan gasket flush with the front of the block.
11. Align the gears of the oil pump with the crankshaft lugs and carefully tap the pump on as far as possible.
12. Apply silicone sealant to the edges of the pump and the oil pan and to the pump sealing surfaces. Tighten the screws to 87 in. lbs.
13. Install the crankshaft seal with a seal installing tool.
14. Install the camshaft drive sprocket and the crankshaft accessory drive pulley, making sure the pins align with the holes. Install the crankshaft screw.
15. Install the camshaft drive belt, belt guard, accessory drive belts and the fan shroud. Start the engine and check for leaks or low oil pressure, and adjust the timing.

CAUTION: *An oil filter with a built-in by-pass valve must be used on the 121–4 cylinder engine.*

4-151

1. Remove engine oil pan. (See previous procedure.)
2. Remove the two bolts and one nut, and carefully lower the pump.
3. Reinstall in reverse order. To ensure immediate oil pressure on start-up, the oil pump gear cavity can be packed with petroleum jelly.

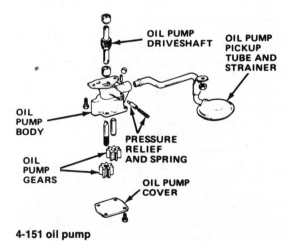

4-151 oil pump

6 Cylinder

The oil pump is driven by the distributor drive shaft. Oil pump replacement does not,

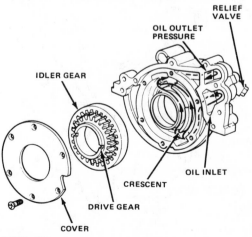

4-121 oil pump

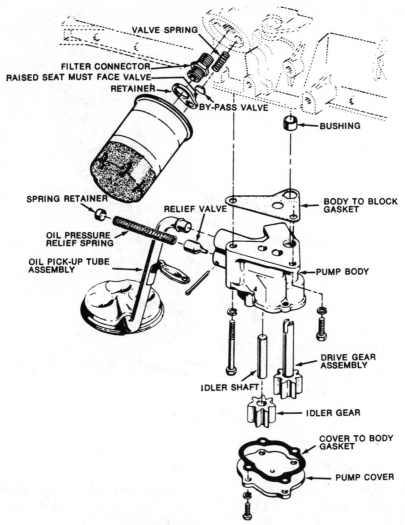

VALVE SPRING

FILTER CONNECTOR
RAISED SEAT MUST FACE VALVE

RETAINER

BY-PASS VALVE

BUSHING

SPRING RETAINER

RELIEF VALVE

BODY TO BLOCK
GASKET

OIL PRESSURE
RELIEF SPRING

OIL PICK-UP TUBE
ASSEMBLY

PUMP BODY

DRIVE GEAR
ASSEMBLY

IDLER SHAFT

IDLER GEAR

COVER TO BODY
GASKET

PUMP COVER

6 cylinder oil pump and filter

however, affect distributor timing because the drive gear remains in mesh with the camshaft gear.

1. Drain the oil and remove the oil pan.
2. Remove the oil pump attaching screws. Remove the pump and gasket from the engine block.

Installation is the reverse of removal. Prime the pump before installation; use a new cover gasket.

Chilton Time Saver

The original equipment-type oil filters for AMC engines have an anti-drainback diaphragm. This prevents the filter from emptying or partially emptying while the engine is stopped overnight. If a replacement filter without this feature is used, the result will be low or no oil pressure on startup. If this continues for any length of time, bearing damage will occur.

V8

The oil pump is located in, and is part of, the timing cover. The pump is driven by the distributor drive shaft. Oil pump replacement does not, however, affect distributor timing.

1. Remove the retaining bolts and separate the oil pump cover, complete with filter and gasket, from the timing cover.
2. The drive gear and shaft and the idler gear will slide out of the timing cover after removal of the pump cover.
3. Prime the pump before installation, and use a new gasket.

Rear Main Bearing Oil Seal
REPLACEMENT
4-121

The rear main bearing oil seal consists of a single piece of formed neoprene with a single

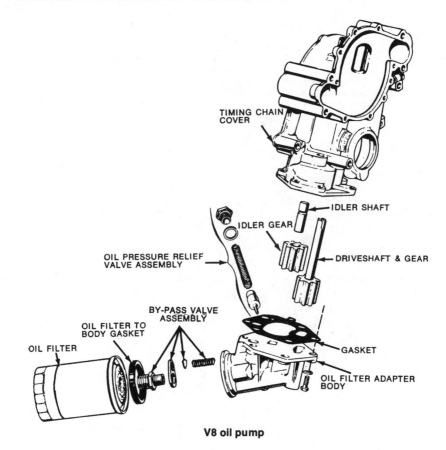

TIMING CHAIN COVER

IDLER SHAFT

IDLER GEAR

OIL PRESSURE RELIEF VALVE ASSEMBLY

DRIVESHAFT & GEAR

BY-PASS VALVE ASSEMBLY

OIL FILTER TO BODY GASKET

OIL FILTER

GASKET

OIL FILTER ADAPTER BODY

V8 oil pump

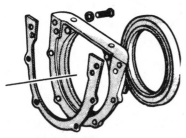

4-121 rear main oil seal

lip. To replace the seal, proceed as follows.

1. Remove the transmission assembly. If manual transmission, remove the pressure plate and flywheel.

2. Remove the crankshaft seal from its seat in the block, while exercising care not to scratch the seal contacting area of the crankshaft.

3. Install the seal, after lubricating the lip with engine oil, into the recess of the block, until the seal bottoms. The seal should be about $1/32$ inch below the surface of the block.

4. Reinstall the flywheel and components. Reinstall the transmission assembly, adjust as necessary, start the engine and check for oil leakage.

4-151

The rear main oil seal is a one piece unit, and is removed or installed without removal of the oil pan or crankshaft.

1. Remove the transmission, flywheel or torque converter bellhousing, and the flywheel or flex plate.

4-151 upper rear main oil seal removal

2. Remove the rear main oil seal with a screwdriver. Be extremely careful not to scratch the crankshaft.

3. Oil the lips of the new seal with clean engine oil. Install the new seal by hand onto the rear crankshaft flange. The helical lip side of the seal should face the engine. Make sure the seal is firmly and evenly installed.

4. Replace the flywheel or flexplate, bell-housing and transmission.

6 Cylinder and V8

1. Remove oil pan, as previously described.

2. Scrape clean all gasket surfaces, then remove rear main cap.

3. Discard lower portion of seal. Clean the main bearing cap thoroughly and loosen all remaining bearing capscrews.

4. Using a brass drift and a hammer, tap the upper seal out until it can be grasped by pliers and pull it out.

5. Coat the lip of the new upper seal with SAE 40 engine oil.

6. Install upper seal portion with the lip facing the front.

7. Coat both sides of the lower seal end tabs with sealant.

NOTE: *Do not apply sealer to the cylinder block mating surfaces of the cap.*

8. Coat the back surface of new lower seal with soap, the lip with SAE 40 engine oil. Install lower seal firmly into main cap.

9. Coat both chamfered edges of rear main cap with sealant, install bearing inserts (if removed) and tighten all cap bolts to 100 ft. lbs. on V-8s, 80 ft. lbs. on six cylinders.

10. Install the pan.

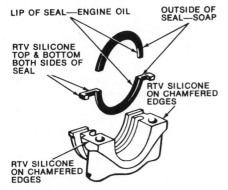

LIP OF SEAL—ENGINE OIL   OUTSIDE OF SEAL—SOAP

RTV SILICONE TOP & BOTTOM BOTH SIDES OF SEAL

RTV SILICONE ON CHAMFERED EDGES

RTV SILICONE ON CHAMFERED EDGES

6 and V8 rear main oil seal

COOLING SYSTEM

American Motors cars are equipped with a conventional cooling system which utilizes a vertical flow radiator (except Pacer), a water pump, and a thermostat. The Pacer has a crossflow radiator. An internal by-pass port is used on four and six-cylinder engines, which allows water to flow through the engine when the thermostat is closed. The V8 engine uses an external hose to perform the same function.

Information on the water temperature gauge can be found in the Unit Repair Section.

Radiator

REMOVAL AND INSTALLATION

1. Raise the hood and remove the radiator cap. Be sure the engine is cold.

2. Drain the radiator. If the coolant appears to be clean, drain it into a clean container and save it for re-use.

3. Remove the upper and lower radiator hoses. Disconnect the coolant recovery hose, if so equipped.

4. On four cylinder models, remove the ambient air intake from the radiator support.

5. On four cylinder air-conditioned models, remove the charcoal canister and the bracket.

6. Remove the fan shroud, if so equipped.

7. On automatic transmission models, disconnect and plug the fluid cooler lines. Remove battery on Pacers for access.

8. Remove the radiator attaching screws and bolts and lift out the radiator.

9. Installation is the reverse of removal.

Water Pump

REMOVAL AND INSTALLATION

The water pump is a centrifugal unit having a non-adjustable packless seal. It is non-serviceable and must be replaced if defective—no maintenance is required

4-121

1. Drain the cooling system. Disconnect the negative (−) cable from the battery. Remove the fan shroud.

2. Rotate the crankshaft until the camshaft and crankshaft are at TDC for number one cylinder.

3. If equipped with power steering, loosen the pump and remove the belt. Loosen the air conditioner idler pulley and remove the belt, if so equipped.

4. Loosen the alternator and air pump.

5. Remove the fan, spacer, and pulley.

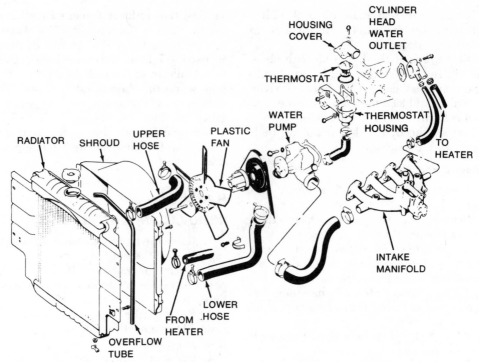

4-121 cooling system components

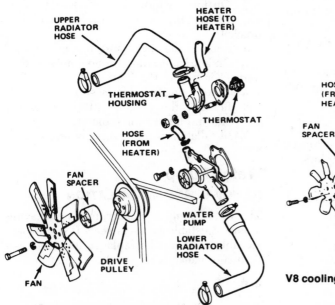

6 cylinder cooling system components

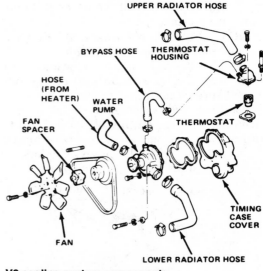

V8 cooling system components

6. Remove the belt guard and air pump bracket.

7. Remove the camshaft and drive belt idler pulley.

8. Disconnect all the hoses from the pump except the hose from the thermostat.

9. Remove the water pump attaching bolts and pull the pump out of the hose from the thermostat.

10. Clean the gasket from the block, install a new gasket on the pump or block.

11. Insert the pump into the thermostat hose, install the pump attaching bolts and torque the small bolts to 7 ft. lbs. and the large bolts to 16 ft. lbs.

12. Reassemble in the reverse order, align the timing belt, apply tension to alternator,

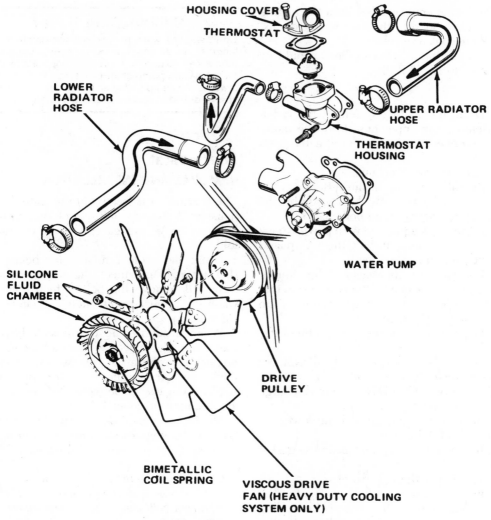

HOUSING COVER

THERMOSTAT

LOWER
RADIATOR
HOSE

UPPER RADIATOR
HOSE

THERMOSTAT
HOUSING

WATER PUMP

SILICONE
FLUID
CHAMBER

DRIVE
PULLEY

BIMETALLIC
COIL SPRING

VISCOUS DRIVE
FAN (HEAVY DUTY COOLING
SYSTEM ONLY)

4-151 cooling system components

air pump, power steering (if equipped), belts.

13. Install coolant, operate engine for 3 to 5 minutes with the heater on to check for leaks and correct fluid level.

4-151

1. Drain the cooling system.
2. Remove all drive belts.
3. Remove the fan and pump pulley.
4. Unbolt and remove the pump from the engine.
5. Clean the gasket surfaces, coat the new gasket with non-hardening type sealer and position the gasket on the block.
6. Coat the threaded areas of the bolts with waterproof sealer and install the pump. Torque the bolts to 25 ft. lbs.
7. Install the pulley and fan.
8. Install the drive belts. The belts should be adjusted so that a ½″ deflection is present when they are depressed mid-point along their longest straight run.

6 Cylinder

1. Drain the cooling system. Disconnect the negative (−) cable from the battery.
2. Unfasten the radiator and the heater hoses at the pump.
3. Loosen the adjustment bolts from the alternator and the power steering pump (if so equipped). Remove the V-belts.
4. Unfasten the fan ring securing belts. Remove the fan and pump pulley assembly. Withdraw the fan ring (or shroud).
5. Remove the securing bolts from the water pump. Withdraw the pump along with its gasket.

Installation is the reverse order of removal. Always use a new pump gasket. Bleed the radiator by running the engine and opening the heater control valve. Run the engine long enough so that the thermostat opens. Check the coolant level.

The water pump securing bolts should be tightened to 10–15 ft. lbs.

V8

1. Drain the cooling system at the radiator. Remove the upper hose from the radiator. Disconnect the negative (−) cable from the battery.

2. Remove the air cleaner.

3. Remove the fan shroud. Remove the drive belts, the fan, and hub assembly by withdrawing the attaching bolts.

4. If the car is equipped with power steering or an air pump, unbolt the pump and move it aside (hoses attached).

5. Loosen the bolts attaching the alternator bracket. Leave one bolt in position, so that the alternator may be swung to one side. Do not disconnect the wires.

6. Disconnect the heater hose at the water pump.

7. On cars equipped with A/C, disconnect the compressor bracket and set it and the compressor out of the way. Do not discharge the air conditioning system.

8. Remove the by-pass and the lower radiator hoses from the pump.

9. Remove the pump and clean the gasket areas.

Installation is the reverse of removal. Always install a new pump gasket. Tighten the pump bolts to 18 ft. lbs. Bleed the cooling system by starting the engine and opening the heater valve. Leave it open until the thermostat opens. Check the coolant level.

Chilton Time Saver

On V8 engines, water pumps have two different shaft lengths depending on application. Long-shaft pumps can be used in short-shaft applications if the flange on the pump shaft is pressed further down towards the pump (using an axle press) and the fan spacer drilled to receive the longer shaft.

Thermostat

REMOVAL AND INSTALLATION

The thermostat is located in the water outlet housing at the top or front of the cylinder head, or on V8 models in front of the manifold.

Drain the coolant to a point below the thermostat. Disconnect the upper radiator hose and remove the bolts which hold the water outlet neck to the engine. Remove the thermostat.

When installing the thermostat, be sure that the pellet or coil spring are facing the engine. Thermostats are marked on the outer flange with the proper installing direction. Replace the gasket between the thermostat and the housing cover.

The bleed hole on the thermostats used on six-cylinder engines must be installed up (at 12 o'clock), to prevent "burping" caused by trapped air.

CAUTION: *Tightening the housing bolts unevenly, or with the thermostat cocked in its recess, will cause the housing to crack.*

Refill the cooling system and run the engine for a while with the heater on to bleed the system of air. Recheck the coolant level.

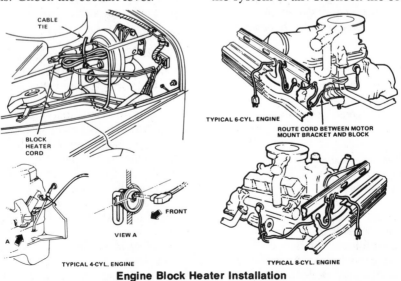

Engine Block Heater Installation

ENGINE REBUILDING

Most procedures involved in rebuilding an engine are fairly standard, regardless of the type of engine involved. This section is a guide to accepted rebuilding procedures. Examples of standard rebuilding practices are illustrated and should be used along with specific details concerning your particular engine, found earlier in this chapter.

The procedures given here are those used by any competent rebuilder. Obviously some of the procedures cannot be performed by the do-it-yourself mechanic, but are provided so that you will be familiar with the services that should be offered by rebuilding or machine shops. As an example, in most instances, it is more profitable for the home mechanic to remove the cylinder heads, buy the necessary parts (new valves, seals, keepers, keys, etc.) and deliver these to a machine shop for the necessary work. In this way you will save the money to remove and install the cylinder head and the mark-up on parts.

On the other hand, most of the work involved in rebuilding the lower end is well within the scope of the do-it-yourself mechanic. Only work such as hot-tanking, actually boring the block or Magnafluxing (invisible crack detection) need be sent to a machine shop.

Tools

The tools required for basic engine rebuilding should, with a few exceptions, be those included in a mechanic's tool kit. An accurate torque wrench, and a dial indicator (reading in thousandths) mounted on a universal base should be available. Special tools, where required, are available from the major tool suppliers. The services of a competent automotive machine shop must also be readily available.

Precautions

Aluminum has become increasingly popular for use in engines, due to its low weight and excellent heat transfer characteristics. The following precautions must be observed when handling aluminum (or any other) engine parts:

—Never hot-tank aluminum parts.

—Remove all aluminum parts (identification tags, etc.) from engine parts before hot-tanking (otherwise they will be removed during the process).

—Always coat threads lightly with engine oil or anti-seize compounds before installation, to prevent seizure.

—Never over-torque bolts or spark plugs in aluminum threads. Should stripping occur, threads can be restored using any of a number of thread repair kits available (see next section).

Inspection Techniques

Magnaflux and Zyglo are inspection techniques used to locate material flaws, such as stress cracks. Magnaflux is a magnetic process, applicable only to ferrous materials. The Zyglo process coats the matrial with a fluorescent dye penetrant, and any material may be tested using Zyglo. Specific checks of suspected surface cracks may be made at lower cost and more readily using spot check dye. The dye is sprayed onto the suspected area, wiped off, and the area is then sprayed with a developer. Cracks then will show up brightly.

Overhaul

The section is divided into two parts. The first, Cylinder Head Reconditioning, assumes that the cylinder head is removed from the engine, all manifolds are removed, and the cylinder head is on a workbench. The camshaft should be removed from overhead cam cylinder heads. The second section, Cylinder Block Reconditioning, covers the block, pistons, connecting rods and crankshaft. It is assumed that the engine is mounted on a work stand, and the cylinder head and all accessories are removed.

Procedures are identified as follows:

Unmarked—Basic procedures that must be performed in order to successfully complete the rebuilding process.

Starred (*)—Procedures that should be performed to ensure maximum performance and engine life.

Double starred (**)—Procedures that may be performed to increase engine performance and reliability.

When assembling the engine, any parts that will be in frictional contact must be prelubricated, to provide protection on initial start-up. Any product specifically formulated for this purpose may be used. NOTE: *Do not use engine oil. Where semi-permanent* (locked but removable) installation of bolts or nuts is desired, threads should be cleaned and located with Loctite ® or a similar product (non-hardening).

Repairing Damaged Threads

Several methods of repairing damaged threads are available. Heli-Coil® (shown here), Keenserts® and Microdot® are among the most widely used. All involve basically the same principle—drilling out stripped threads, tapping the hole and installing a pre-wound insert—making welding, plugging and oversize fasteners unnecessary.

Two types of thread repair inserts are usually supplied—a standard type for most Inch Coarse, Inch Fine, Metric Coarse and Metric Fine thread sizes and a spark plug type to fit most spark plug port sizes. Consult the individual manufacturer's catalog to determine exact applications. Typical thread repair kits will contain a selection of pre-wound threaded inserts, a tap (corresponding to the outside diameter threads of the insert) and an installation tool. Spark plug inserts usually differ because they require a tap equipped with pilot threads and a combined reamer/tap section. Most manufacturers also supply blister-packed thread repair inserts separately in addition to a master kit containing a variety of taps and inserts plus installation tools.

Before effecting a repair to a threaded hole, remove any snapped, broken or damaged bolts or studs. Penetrating oil can be used to free frozen threads; the offending item can be removed with locking pliers or with a screw or stud extractor. After the hole is clear, the thread can be repaired, as follows:

Drill out the damaged threads with specified drill. Drill completely through the hole or to the bottom of a blind hole

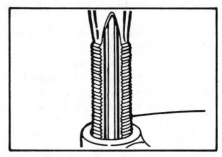

With the tap supplied, tap the hole to receive the thread insert. Keep the tap well oiled and back it out frequently to avoid clogging the threads

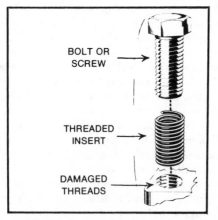

BOLT OR SCREW

THREADED INSERT

DAMAGED THREADS

Damaged bolt holes can be repaired with thread repair inserts

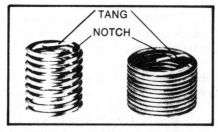

TANG

NOTCH

Standard thread repair insert (left) and spark plug thread insert (right)

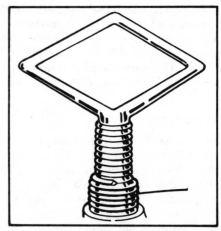

Screw the threaded insert onto the installation tool until the tang engages the slot. Screw the insert into the tapped hole until it is ¼–½ turn below the top surface. After installation break off the tang with a hammer and punch

Standard Torque Specifications and Fastener Markings

The Newton-metre has been designated the world standard for measuring torque and will gradually replace the foot-pound and kilogram-meter. In the absence of specific torques, the following chart can be used as a guide to the maximum safe torque of a particular size/grade of fastener.

- There is no torque difference for fine or coarse threads.
- Torque values are based on clean, dry threads. Reduce the value by 10% if threads are oiled prior to assembly.
- The torque required for aluminum components or fasteners is considerably less.

U. S. BOLTS

SAE Grade Number	1 or 2			5			6 or 7		
Bolt Markings Manufacturer's marks may vary—number of lines always 2 less than the grade number.									
Usage	Frequent			Frequent			Infrequent		
Bolt Size (inches)—(Thread)	Maximum Torque			Maximum Torque			Maximum Torque		
	Ft-Lb	kgm	Nm	Ft-Lb	kgm	Nm	Ft-Lb	kgm	Nm
¼—20	5	0.7	6.8	8	1.1	10.8	10	1.4	13.5
—28	6	0.8	8.1	10	1.4	13.6			
⁵⁄₁₆—18	11	1.5	14.9	17	2.3	23.0	19	2.6	25.8
—24	13	1.8	17.6	19	2.6	25.7			
⅜—16	18	2.5	24.4	31	4.3	42.0	34	4.7	46.0
—24	20	2.75	27.1	35	4.8	47.5			
⁷⁄₁₆—14	28	3.8	37.0	49	6.8	66.4	55	7.6	74.5
—20	30	4.2	40.7	55	7.6	74.5			
½—13	39	5.4	52.8	75	10.4	101.7	85	11.75	115.2
—20	41	5.7	55.6	85	11.7	115.2			
⁹⁄₁₆—12	51	7.0	69.2	110	15.2	149.1	120	16.6	162.7
—18	55	7.6	74.5	120	16.6	162.7			
⅝—11	83	11.5	112.5	150	20.7	203.3	167	23.0	226.5
—18	95	13.1	128.8	170	23.5	230.5			
¾—10	105	14.5	142.3	270	37.3	366.0	280	38.7	379.6
—16	115	15.9	155.9	295	40.8	400.0			
⅞— 9	160	22.1	216.9	395	54.6	535.5	440	60.9	596.5
—14	175	24.2	237.2	435	60.1	589.7			
1— 8	236	32.5	318.6	590	81.6	799.9	660	91.3	894.8
—14	250	34.6	338.9	660	91.3	849.8			

METRIC BOLTS

NOTE: *Metric bolts are marked with a number indicating the relative strength of the bolt. These numbers have nothing to do with size.*

Description	Torque ft-lbs (Nm)			
Thread size x pitch (mm)	Head mark—4		Head mark—7	
6 x 1.0	2.2–2.9	(3.0–3.9)	3.6–5.8	(4.9–7.8)
8 x 1.25	5.8–8.7	(7.9–12)	9.4–14	(13–19)
10 x 1.25	12–17	(16–23)	20–29	(27–39)
12 x 1.25	21–32	(29–43)	35–53	(47–72)
14 x 1.5	35–52	(48–70)	57–85	(77–110)
16 x 1.5	51–77	(67–100)	90–120	(130–160)
18 x 1.5	74–110	(100–150)	130–170	(180–230)
20 x 1.5	110–140	(150–190)	190–240	(160–320)
22 x 1.5	150–190	(200–260)	250–320	(340–430)
24 x 1.5	190–240	(260–320)	310–410	(420–550)

NOTE: *This engine rebuilding section is a guide to accepted rebuilding procedures. Typical examples of standard rebuilding procedures are illustrated. Use these procedures along with the detailed instructions earlier in this chapter, concerning your particular engine.*

Cylinder Head Reconditioning

Procedure	Method
Remove the cylinder head:	See the engine service procedures earlier in this chapter for details concerning specific engines.
Identify the valves:	Invert the cylinder head, and number the valve faces front to rear, using a permanent felt-tip marker.
Remove the rocker arms (OHV engines only):	Remove the rocker arms with shaft(s) or balls and nuts. Wire the sets of rockers, balls and nuts together, and identify according to the corresponding valve.
Remove the camshaft (OHC engines only):	See the engine service procedures earlier in this chapter for details concerning specific engines.
Remove the valves and springs:	Using an appropriate valve spring compressor (depending on the configuration of the cylinder head), compress the valve springs. Lift out the keepers with needlenose pliers, release the compressor, and remove the valve, spring, and spring retainer. See the engine service procedures earlier in this chapter for details concerning specific engines.

Cylinder Head Reconditioning

Procedure	Method
Check the valve stem-to-guide clearance: 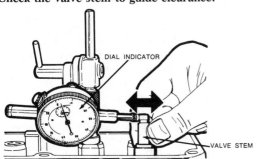 **Check the valve stem-to-guide clearance**	Clean the valve stem with lacquer thinner or a similar solvent to remove all gum and varnish. Clean the valve guides using solvent and an expanding wire-type valve guide cleaner. Mount a dial indicator so that the stem is at 90° to the valve stem, as close to the valve guide as possible. Move the valve off its seat, and measure the valve guide-to-stem clearance by rocking the stem back and forth to actuate the dial indicator. Measure the valve stems using a micrometer, and compare to specifications, to determine whether stem or guide wear is responsible for excessive clearance. NOTE: *Consult the Specifications tables earlier in this chapter.*
De-carbon the cylinder head and valves: 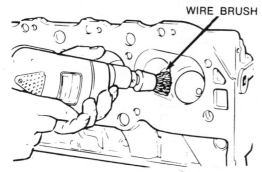 **Remove the carbon from the cylinder head with a wire brush and electric drill**	Chip carbon away from the valve heads, combustion chambers, and ports, using a chisel made of hardwood. Remove the remaining deposits with a stiff wire brush. NOTE: *Be sure that the deposits are actually removed, rather than burnished.*
Hot-tank the cylinder head (cast iron heads only): CAUTION: *Do not hot-tank aluminum parts.*	Have the cylinder head hot-tanked to remove grease, corrosion, and scale from the water passages. NOTE: *In the case of overhead cam cylinder heads, consult the operator to determine whether the camshaft bearings will be damaged by the caustic solution.*
Degrease the remaining cylinder head parts:	Clean the remaining cylinder head parts in an engine cleaning solvent. Do not remove the protective coating from the springs.
Check the cylinder head for warpage: 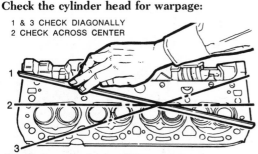 **Check the cylinder head for warpage**	Place a straight-edge across the gasket surface of the cylinder head. Using feeler gauges, determine the clearance at the center of the straight-edge. If warpage exceeds .003″ in a 6″ span, or .006″ over the total length, the cylinder head must be resurfaced. NOTE: *If warpage exceeds the manufacturer's maximum tolerance for material removal, the cylinder head must be replaced.* When milling the cylinder heads of V-type engines, the intake manifold mounting position is altered, and must be corrected by milling the manifold flange a proportionate amount.

Cylinder Head Reconditioning

Procedure	Method

Knurl the valve guides:

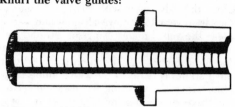

Cut-away view of a knurled valve guide

*Valve guides which are not excessively worn or distorted may, in some cases, be knurled rather than replaced. Knurling is a process in which metal is displaced and raised, thereby reducing clearance. Knurling also provides excellent oil control. The possibility of knurling rather than replacing valve guides should be discussed with a machinist.

Replace the valve guides:
NOTE: *Valve guides should only be replaced if damaged or if an oversize valve stem is not available.*

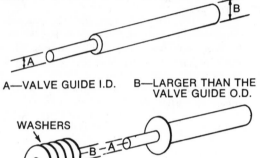

A—VALVE GUIDE I.D.   B—LARGER THAN THE VALVE GUIDE O.D.

WASHERS

A—VALVE GUIDE I.D.   B—LARGER THAN THE VALVE GUIDE O.D.

Valve guide installation tool using washers for installation

See the engine service procedures earlier in this chapter for details concerning specific engines. Depending on the type of cylinder head, valve guides may be pressed, hammered, or shrunk in. In cases where the guides are shrunk into the head, replacement should be left to an equipped machine shop. In other cases, the guides are replaced using a stepped drift (see illustration). Determine the height above the boss that the guide must extend, and obtain a stack of washers, their I.D. similar to the guide's O.D., of that height. Place the stack of washers on the guide, and insert the guide into the boss.
NOTE: *Valve guides are often tapered or beveled for installation.* Using the stepped installation tool (see illustration), press or tap the guides into position. Ream the guides according to the size of the valve stem.

Replace valve seat inserts:

Replacement of valve seat inserts which are worn beyond resurfacing or broken, if feasible, must be done by a machine shop.

Resurface (grind) the valve face:

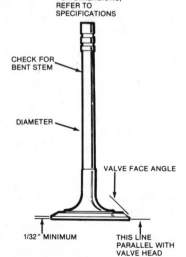

FOR DIMENSIONS, REFER TO SPECIFICATIONS

CHECK FOR BENT STEM

DIAMETER

VALVE FACE ANGLE

1/32" MINIMUM   THIS LINE PARALLEL WITH VALVE HEAD

Critical valve dimensions

Using a valve grinder, resurface the valves according to specifications given earlier in this chapter.
CAUTION: *Valve face angle is not always identical to valve seat angle.* A minimum margin of

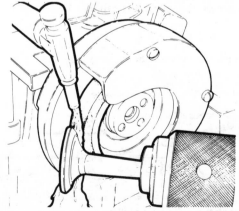

Valve grinding by machine

Cylinder Head Reconditioning

Procedure	Method
	$1/32''$ should remain after grinding the valve. The valve stem top should also be squared and resurfaced, by placing the stem in the V-block of the grinder, and turning it while pressing lightly against the grinding wheel. **NOTE:** *Do not grind sodium filled exhaust valves on a machine. These should be hand lapped.*
Resurface the valve seats using reamers or grinder: 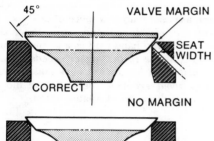 **Valve seat width and centering**  **Reaming the valve seat with a hand reamer**	Select a reamer of the correct seat angle, slightly larger than the diameter of the valve seat, and assemble it with a pilot of the correct size. Install the pilot into the valve guide, and using steady pressure, turn the reamer clockwise. **CAUTION:** *Do not turn the reamer counterclockwise.* Remove only as much material as necessary to clean the seat. Check the concentricity of the seat (following). If the dye method is not used, coat the valve face with Prussian blue dye, install and rotate it on the valve seat. Using the dye marked area as a centering guide, center and narrow the valve seat to specifications with correction cutters. **NOTE:** *When no specifications are available, minimum seat width for exhaust valves should be $5/64''$, intake valves $1/16''$.* After making correction cuts, check the position of the valve seat on the valve face using Prussian blue dye.
	To resurface the seat with a power grinder, select a pilot of the correct size and coarse stone of the proper angle. Lubricate the pilot and move the stone on and off the valve seat at 2 cycles per second, until all flaws are gone. Finish the seat with a fine stone. If necessary the seat can be corrected or narrowed using correction stones.
Check the valve seat concentricity: 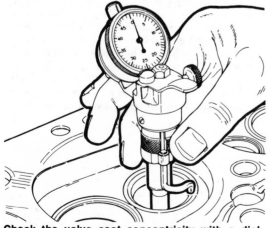 **Check the valve seat concentricity with a dial gauge**	Coat the valve face with Prussian blue dye, install the valve, and rotate it on the valve seat. If the entire seat becomes coated, and the valve is known to be concentric, the seat is concentric. *Install the dial gauge pilot into the guide, and rest of the arm on the valve seat. Zero the gauge, and rotate the arm around the seat. Run-out should not exceed $.002''$.

Cylinder Head Reconditioning

Procedure	Method

*Lap the valves:
NOTE: *Valve lapping is done to ensure efficient sealing of resurfaced valves and seats.*

Lapping the valves by hand

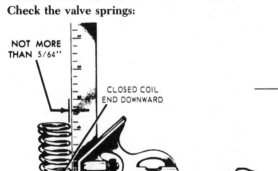

HAND DRILL

ROD

SUCTION CUP

Home-made valve lapping tool

*Invert the cylinder head, lightly lubricate the valve stems, and install the valves in the head as numbered. Coat valve seats with fine grinding compound, and attach the lapping tool suction cup to a valve head.
NOTE: *Moisten the suction cup.* Rotate the tool between the palms, changing position and lifting the tool often to prevent grooving. Lap the valve until a smooth, polished seat is evident. Remove the valve and tool, and rinse away all traces of grinding compound.

** Fasten a suction cup to a piece of drill rod, and mount the rod in a hand drill. Proceed as above, using the hand drill as a lapping tool.
CAUTION: *Due to the higher speeds involved when using the hand drill, care must be exercised to avoid grooving the seat.* Lift the tool and change direction of rotation often.

Check the valve springs:

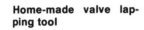

NOT MORE THAN 5/64"

CLOSED COIL END DOWNWARD

Check the valve spring free length and squareness

Check the valve spring test pressure

Place the spring on a flat surface next to a square. Measure the height of the spring, and rotate it against the edge of the square to measure distortion. If spring height varies (by comparison) by more than $1/16"$ or if distortion exceeds $1/16"$, replace the spring.

** In addition to evaluating the spring as above, test the spring pressure at the installed and compressed (installed height minus valve lift) height using a valve spring tester. Springs used on small displacement engines (up to 3 liters) should be ∓ 1 lb of all other springs in either position. A tolerance of ∓ 5 lbs is permissible on larger engines.

Cylinder Head Reconditioning

Procedure	Method

***Install valve stem seals:**

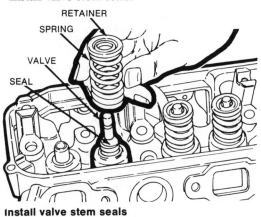

RETAINER
SPRING
VALVE
SEAL

Install valve stem seals

* Due to the pressure differential that exists at the ends of the intake valve guides (atmospheric pressure above, manifold vacuum below), oil is drawn through the valve guides into the intake port. This has been alleviated somewhat since the addition of positive crankcase ventilation, which lowers the pressure above the guides. Several types of valve stem seals are available to rocker arms and balls, and install them on the the stem and guide boss, while others require that the boss be machined. Recently, Teflon guide seals have become popular. Consult a parts supplier or machinist concerning availability and suggested usages.
NOTE: *When installing seals, ensure that a small amount of oil is able to pass the seal to lubricate the valve guides; otherwise, excessive wear may result.*

Install the valves:

See the engine service procedures earlier in this chapter for details concerning specific engines.

Lubricate the valve stems, and install the valves in the cylinder head as numbered. Lubricate and position the seals (if used) and the valve springs. Install the spring retainers, compress the springs, and insert the keys using needle-nose pliers or a tool designed for this purpose.
NOTE: *Retain the keys with wheel bearing grease during installation.*

Check valve spring installed height:

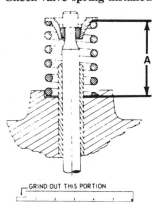

A

GRIND OUT THIS PORTION

Measure the valve spring installed height (A) with a modified steel rule

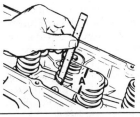

Valve spring installed height (A)

Measure the distance between the spring pad and the lower edge of the spring retainer, and compare to specifications. If the installed height is incorrect, add shim washers between the spring pad and the spring.
CAUTION: *Use only washers designed for this purpose.*

Install the camshaft (OHC engines only) and check end-play:

See the engine service procedures earlier in this chapter for details concerning specific engines.

Cylinder Head Reconditioning

Procedure	Method
Inspect the rocker arms, balls, studs, and nuts (OHV engines only): 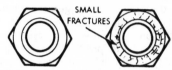 **Stress cracks in the rocker nuts**	Visually inspect the rocker arms, balls, studs, and nuts for cracks, galling, burning, scoring, or wear. If all parts are intact, liberally lubricate the rocker arms and balls, and install them on the cylinder head. If wear is noted on a rocker arm at the point of valve contact, grind it smooth and square, removing as little material as possible. Replace the rocker arm if excessively worn. If a rocker stud shows signs of wear, it must be replaced (see below). If a rocker nut shows stress cracks, replace it. If an exhaust ball is galled or burned, substitute the intake ball from the same cylinder (if it is intact), and install a new intake ball. NOTE: *Avoid using new rocker balls on exhaust valves.*
Replacing rocker studs (OHV engines only): 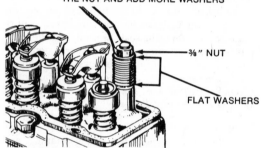 **Extracting a pressed-in rocker stud** 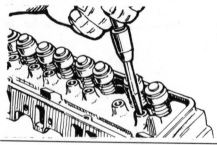 **Ream the stud bore for oversize rocker studs**	In order to remove a threaded stud, lock two nuts on the stud, and unscrew the stud using the lower nut. Coat the lower threads of the new stud with Loctite, and install. Two alternative methods are available for replacing pressed in studs. Remove the damaged stud using a stack of washers and a nut (see illustration). In the first, the boss is reamed .005–.006″ oversize, and an oversize stud pressed in. Control the stud extension over the boss using washers, in the same manner as valve guides. Before installing the stud, coat it with white lead and grease. To retain the stud more positively drill a hole through the stud and boss, and install a roll pin. In the second method, the boss is tapped, and a threaded stud installed.
Inspect the rocker shaft(s) and rocker arms (OHV engines only) 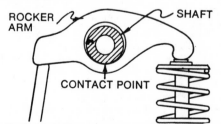 **Check the rocker arm-to-rocker shaft contact area**	Remove rocker arms, springs and washers from rocker shaft. NOTE: *Lay out parts in the order as they are removed.* Inspect rocker arms for pitting or wear on the valve contact point, or excessive bushing wear. Bushings need only be replaced if wear is excessive, because the rocker arm normally contacts the shaft at one point only. Grind the valve contact point of rocker arm smooth if necessary, removing as little material as possible. If excessive material must be removed to smooth and square the arm, it should be replaced. Clean out all oil holes and passages in rocker shaft. If shaft is grooved or worn, replace it. Lubricate and assemble the rocker shaft.

Cylinder Head Reconditioning

Procedure	Method
Inspect the pushrods (OHV engines only):	Remove the pushrods, and, if hollow, clean out the oil passages using fine wire. Roll each pushrod over a piece of clean glass. If a distinct clicking sound is heard as the pushrod rolls, the rod is bent, and must be replaced.
	*The length of all pushrods must be equal. Measure the length of the pushrods, compare to specifications, and replace as necessary.
Inspect the valve lifters (OHV engines only): 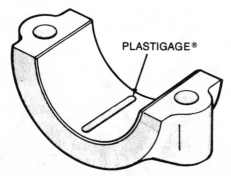 CHECK FOR CONCAVE WEAR ON FACE OF TAPPET USING TAPPET FOR STRAIGHT EDGE **Check the lifter face for squareness**	Remove lifters from their bores, and remove gum and varnish, using solvent. Clean walls of lifter bores. Check lifters for concave wear as illustrated. If face is worn concave, replace lifter, and carefully inspect the camshaft. Lightly lubricate lifter and insert it into its bore. If play is excessive, an oversize lifter must be installed (where possible). Consult a machinist concerning feasibility. If play is satisfactory, remove, lubricate, and reinstall the lifter.
*Testing hydraulic lifter leak down (OHV engines only):	Submerge lifter in a container of kerosene. Chuck a used pushrod or its equivalent into a drill press. Position container of kerosene so pushrod acts on the lifter plunger. Pump lifter with the drill press, until resistance increases. Pump several more times to bleed any air out of lifter. Apply very firm, constant pressure to the lifter, and observe rate at which fluid bleeds out of lifter. If the fluid bleeds very quickly (less than 15 seconds), lifter is defective. If the time exceeds 60 seconds, lifter is sticking. In either case, recondition or replace lifter. If lifter is operating properly (leak down time 15–60 seconds), lubricate and install it.

Cylinder Block Reconditioning

Procedure	Method

Checking the main bearing clearance:
 	
PLASTIGAGE®
 	
Plastigage® installed on the lower bearing shell
	Invert engine, and remove cap from the bearing to be checked. Using a clean, dry rag, thoroughly clean all oil from crankshaft journal and bearing insert.
	NOTE: *Plastigage® is soluble in oil; therefore, oil on the journal or bearing could result in erroneous readings.*
	    Place a piece of Plastigage along the full length of journal, reinstall cap, and torque to specifications.
	NOTE: *Specifications are given in the engine specifications earlier in this chapter.*
	    Remove bearing cap, and determine bearing clearance by comparing width of Plastigage to the scale on Plastigage envelope. Journal taper is determined by comparing width of the Plastigage strip near its ends. Rotate crankshaft 90° and retest, to determine journal eccentricity.
	NOTE: *Do not rotate crankshaft with Plastigage*

Cylinder Block Reconditioning

Procedure	Method

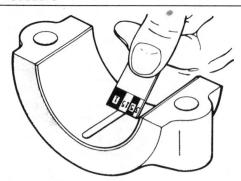

Measure Plastigage® to determine main bearing clearance

installed. If bearing insert and journal appear intact, and are within tolerances, no further main bearing service is required. If bearing or journal appear defective, cause of failure should be determined before replacement.

* Remove crankshaft from block (see below). Measure the main bearing journals at each end tiwce (90° apart) using a micrometer, to determine diameter, journal taper and eccentricity. If journals are within tolerances, reinstall bearing caps at their specified torque. Using a telescope gauge and micrometer, measure bearing I.D. parallel to piston axis and at 30° on each side of piston axis. Subtract journal O.D. from bearing I.D. to determine oil clearance. If crankshaft journals appear defective, or do not meet tolerances, there is no need to measure bearings; for the crankshaft will require grinding and/or undersize bearings will be required. If bearing appears defective, cause for failure should be determined prior to replacement.

Check the connecting rod bearing clearance:

Connecting rod bearing clearance is checked in the same manner as main bearing clearance, using Plastigage. Before removing the crankshaft, connecting rod side clearance also should be measured and recorded.

* Checking connecting rod bearing clearance, using a micrometer, is identical to checking main bearing clearance. If no other service is required, the piston and rod assemblies need not be removed.

Remove the crankshaft:

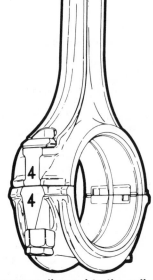

Using a punch, mark the corresponding main bearing caps and saddles according to position (i.e., one punch on the front main cap and saddle, two on the second, three on the third, etc.). Using number stamps, identify the corresponding connecting rods and caps, according to cylinder (if no numbers are present). Remove the main and connecting rod caps, and place sleeves of plastic tubing or vacuum hose over the connecting rod bolts, to protect the journals as the crankshaft is removed. Lift the crankshaft out of the block.

Match the connecting rod to the cylinder with a number stamp

Match the connecting rod and cap with scribe marks

Cylinder Block Reconditioning

Procedure	Method
Remove the ridge from the top of the cylinder: 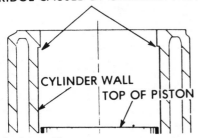 RIDGE CAUSED BY CYLINDER WEAR CYLINDER WALL TOP OF PISTON **Cylinder bore ridge**	In order to facilitate removal of the piston and connecting rod, the ridge at the top of the cylinder (unworn area; see illustration) must be removed. Place the piston at the bottom of the bore, and cover it with a rag. Cut the ridge away using a ridge reamer, exercising extreme care to avoid cutting too deeply. Remove the rag, and remove cuttings that remain on the piston. **CAUTION:** *If the ridge is not removed, and new rings are installed, damage to rings will result.*
Remove the piston and connecting rod: 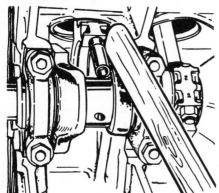 **Push the piston out with a hammer handle**	Invert the engine, and push the pistons and connecting rods out of the cylinders. If necessary, tap the connecting rod boss with a wooden hammer handle, to force the piston out. **CAUTION:** *Do not attempt to force the piston past the cylinder ridge* (see above).
Service the crankshaft:	Ensure that all oil holes and passages in the crankshaft are open and free of sludge. If necessary, have the crankshaft ground to the largest possible undersize.
	**Have the crankshaft Magnafluxed, to locate stress cracks. Consult a machinist concerning additional service procedures, such as surface hardening (e.g., nitriding, Tuftriding) to improve wear characteristics, cross drilling and chamfering the oil holes to improve lubrication, and balancing.
Removing freeze plugs:	Drill a small hole in the middle of the freeze plugs. Thread a large sheet metal screw into the hole and remove the plug with a slide hammer.
Remove the oil gallery plugs:	Threaded plugs should be removed using an appropriate (usually square) wrench. To remove soft, pressed in plugs, drill a hole in the plug, and thread in a sheet metal screw. Pull the plug out by the screw using pliers.
Hot-tank the block: **NOTE:** *Do not hot-tank aluminum parts.*	Have the block hot-tanked to remove grease, corrosion, and scale from the water jackets. **NOTE:** *Consult the operator to determine whether the camshaft bearings will be damaged during the hot-tank process.*

Cylinder Block Reconditioning

Procedure	Method

Check the block for cracks:	Visually inspect the block for cracks or chips. The most common locations are as follows:
	    Adjacent to freeze plugs.
	    Between the cylinders and water jackets.
	    Adjacent to the main bearing saddles.
	    At the extreme bottom of the cylinders.
	Check only suspected cracks using spot check dye (see introduction). If a crack is located, consult a machinist concerning possible repairs.

	** Magnaflux the block to locate hidden cracks. If cracks are located, consult a machinist about feasibility of repair.
Install the oil gallery plugs and freeze plugs:	Coat freeze plugs with sealer and tap into position using a piece of pipe, slightly smaller than the plug, as a driver. To ensure retention, stake the edges of the plugs. Coat threaded oil gallery plugs with sealer and install. Drive replacement soft plugs into block using a large drift as driver.
	* Rather than reinstalling lead plugs, drill and tap the holes, and install threaded plugs.
Check the bore diameter and surface: 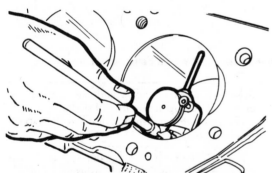 Measure the cylinder bore with a dial gauge	Visually inspect the cylinder bores for roughness, scoring, or scuffing. If evident, the cylinder bore must be bored or honed oversize to eliminate imperfections, and the smallest possible oversize piston used. The new pistons should be given to the machinist with the block, so that the cylinders can be bored or honed exactly to the piston size (plus clearance). If no flaws are evident, measure the bore diameter using a telescope gauge and micrometer, or dial gauge, parallel and perpendicular to the engine centerline, at the top (below the ridge) and bottom of the bore. Subtract the bottom measurements from the top to determine taper, and the parallel to the centerline measurements from the perpendicular measurements to determine eccentricity. If the measurements are not within specifications, the cylinder must be bored or honed, and an oversize piston installed. If the measurements are within specifications the cylinder may be used as is, with only finish honing (see below).

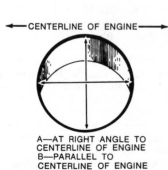

CENTERLINE OF ENGINE

A—AT RIGHT ANGLE TO CENTERLINE OF ENGINE
B—PARALLEL TO CENTERLINE OF ENGINE

Cylinder bore measuring points

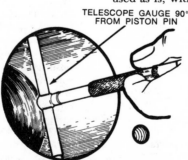

TELESCOPE GAUGE 90° FROM PISTON PIN

Measure the cylinder bore with a telescope gauge

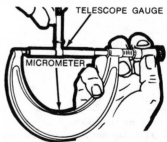

TELESCOPE GAUGE

MICROMETER

Measure the telescope gauge with a micrometer to determine the cylinder bore

Cylinder Block Reconditioning

Procedure	Method
	NOTE: *Prior to submitting the block for boring, perform the following operation(s).*
Check the cylinder block bearing alignment: **Check the main bearing saddle alignment**	Remove the upper bearing inserts. Place a straightedge in the bearing saddles along the centerline of the crankshaft. If clearance exists between the straightedge and the center saddle, the block must be alignbored.
*Check the deck height:	The deck height is the distance from the crankshaft centerline to the block deck. To measure, invert the engine, and install the crankshaft, retaining it with the center main cap. Measure the distance from the crankshaft journal to the block deck, parallel to the cylinder centerline. Measure the diameter of the end (front and rear) main journals, parallel to the centerline of the cylinders, divide the diameter in half, and subtract it from the previous measurement. The results of the front and rear measurements should be identical. If the difference exceeds .005″, the deck height should be corrected. NOTE: *Block deck height and warpage should be corrected at the same time.*
Check the block deck for warpage:	Using a straightedge and feeler gauges, check the block deck for warpage in the same manner that the cylinder head is checked (see Cylinder Head Reconditioning). If warpage exceeds specifications, have the deck resurfaced. NOTE: *In certain cases a specification for total material removal (Cylinder head and block deck) is provided. This specification must not be exceeded.*
Clean and inspect the pistons and connecting rods: RING EXPANDER **Remove the piston rings**	Using a ring expander, remove the rings from the piston. Remove the retaining rings (if so equipped) and remove piston pin. NOTE: *If the piston pin must be pressed out, determine the proper method and use the proper tools; otherwise the piston will distort.* Clean the ring grooves using an appropriate tool, exercising care to avoid cutting too deeply. Thoroughly clean all carbon and varnish from the piston with solvent. CAUTION: *Do not use a wire brush or caustic solvent on pistons.* Inspect the pistons for scuffing, scoring, cracks, pitting, or excessive ring groove wear. If wear is evident, the piston must be replaced. Check the connecting rod length by measuring the rod from the inside of the large end to the

Cylinder Block Reconditioning

Procedure	Method

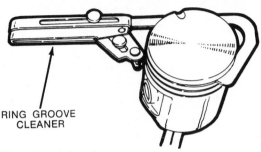

RING GROOVE
CLEANER

Clean the piston ring grooves

inside of the small end using calipers (see illustration). All connecting rods should be equal length. Replace any rod that differs from the others in the engine.

* Have the connecting rod alignment checked in an alignment fixture by a machinist. Replace any twisted or bent rods.

* Magnaflux the connecting rods to locate stress cracks. If cracks are found, replace the connecting rod.

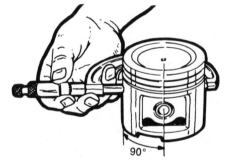

Check the connecting rod length (arrow)

Fit the pistons to the cylinders:

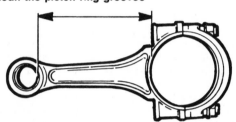

90°

Measure the piston prior to fitting

Using a telescope gauge and micrometer, or a dial gauge, measure the cylinder bore diameter perpendicular to the piston pin, 2½″ below the deck. Measure the piston perpendicular to its pin on the skirt. The difference between the two measurements is the piston clearance. If the clearance is within specifications or slightly below (after boring or honing), finish honing is all that is required. If the clearance is excessive, try to obtain a slightly larger piston to bring clearance within specifications. Where this is not possible, obtain the first oversize piston, and hone (or if necessary, bore) the cylinder to size.

Assemble the pistons and connecting rods:

Install the piston pin lock-rings (if used)

Inspect piston pin, connecting rod small end bushing, and piston bore for galling, scoring, or excessive wear. If evident, replace defective part(s). Measure the I.D. of the piston boss and connecting rod small end, and the O.D. of the piston pin. If within specifications, assemble piston pin and rod.
CAUTION: *If piston pin must be pressed in, determine the proper method and use the proper tools; otherwise the piston will distort.*
    Install the lock rings; ensure that they seat properly. If the parts are not within specifications, determine the service method for the type of engine. In some cases, piston and pin are serviced as an assembly when either is defective. Others specify reaming the piston and connecting rods for an oversize pin. If the connecting rod bushing is worn, it may in many cases be replaced. Reaming the piston and replacing the rod bushing are machine shop operations.

Cylinder Block Reconditioning

Procedure	Method
Clean and inspect the camshaft:	Degrease the camshaft, using solvent, and clean out all oil holes. Visually inspect cam lobes and bearing journals for excessive wear. If a lobe is questionable, check all lobes as indicated below. If a journal or lobe is worn, the camshaft must be reground or replaced. NOTE: *If a journal is worn, there is a good chance that the bushings are worn.* If lobes and journals appear intact, place the front and rear journals in V-blocks, and rest a dial indicator on the center journal. Rotate the camshaft to check straightness. If deviation exceeds .001″, replace the camshaft.

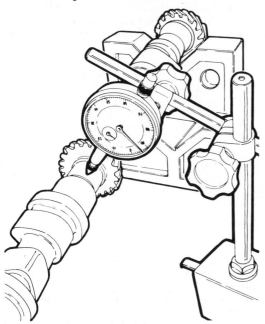

Check the camshaft for straightness

* Check the camshaft lobes with a micrometer, by measuring the lobes from the nose to base and again at 90° (see illustration). The lift is determined by subtracting the second measurement from the first. If all exhaust lobes and all intake lobes are not identical, the camshaft must be reground or replaced.

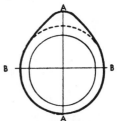

Camshaft lobe measurement

Replace the camshaft bearings (OHV engines only):	If excessive wear is indicated, or if the engine is being completely rebuilt, camshaft bearings should be replaced as follows: Drive the camshaft rear plug from the block. Assemble the removal puller with its shoulder on the bearing to be removed. Gradually tighten the puller nut until bearing is removed. Remove remaining bearings, leaving the front and rear for last. To remove front and rear bearings, reverse position of the tool, so as to pull the bearings in toward the center of the block. Leave the tool in this position, pilot the new front and rear bearings on the installer, and pull them into position: Return the tool to its original position and pull remaining bearings into position. NOTE: *Ensure that oil holes align when installing bearings.* Replace camshaft rear plug, and stake it into position to aid retention.

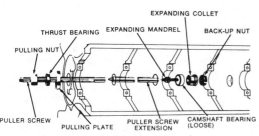

Camshaft bearing removal and installation tool (OHV engines only)

Finish hone the cylinders:	Chuck a flexible drive hone into a power drill, and insert it into the cylinder. Start the hone, and move it up and down in the cylinder at a rate which will produce approximately a 60° cross-hatch pattern. NOTE: *Do not extend the hone below the cylin-*

Cylinder Block Reconditioning

Procedure	*Method*

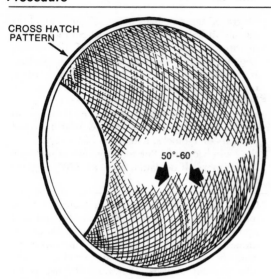

CROSS HATCH PATTERN

50°-60°

Cylinder bore after honing

der bore. After developing the pattern, remove the hone and recheck piston fit. Wash the cylinders with a detergent and water solution to remove abrasive dust, dry, and wipe several times with a rag soaked in engine oil.

Check piston ring end-gap:

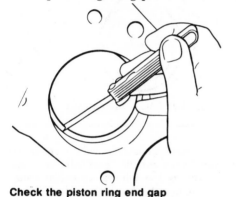

Check the piston ring end gap

Compress the piston rings to be used in a cylinder, one at a time, into that cylinder, and press them approximately 1″ below the deck with an inverted piston. Using feeler gauges, measure the ring end-gap, and compare to specifications. Pull the ring out of the cylinder and file the ends with a fine file to obtain proper clearance.
CAUTION: *If inadequate ring end-gap is utilized, ring breakage will result.*

Install the piston rings:

PISTON RING

FEELER GAUGE

RING GROOVE

Check the piston ring side clearance

Inspect the ring grooves in the piston for excessive wear or taper. If necessary, recut the grooves(s) for use with an overwidth ring or a standard ring and spacer. If the groove is worn uniformly, overwidth rings, or standard rings and spacers may be installed without recutting. Roll the outside of the ring around the groove to check for burrs or deposits. If any are found, remove with a fine file. Hold the ring in the groove, and measure side clearance. If necessary, correct as indicated above.
NOTE: *Always install any additional spacers above the piston ring.*
 The ring groove must be deep enough to allow the ring to seat below the lands (see illustration). In many cases, a "go-no-go" depth gauge will be provided with the piston rings. Shallow grooves may be corrected by recutting, while deep grooves require some type of filler or expander behind the piston. Consult the piston ring sup-

Cylinder Block Reconditioning

Procedure	Method
	plier concerning the suggested method. Install the rings on the piston, lowest ring first, using a ring expander. NOTE: *Position the ring as specified by the manufacturer.* Consult the engine service procedures earlier in this chapter for details concerning specific engines.
Install the camshaft (OHV engines only):	Liberally lubricate the camshaft lobes and journals, and install the camshaft. CAUTION: *Exercise extreme care to avoid damaging the bearings when inserting the camshaft.* Install and tighten the camshaft thrust plate retaining bolts. See the engine service procedures earlier in this chapter for details concerning specific engines.
Check camshaft end-play (OHV engines only): 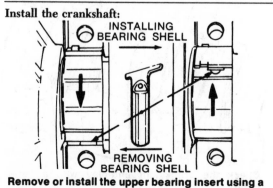 Check the camshaft end-play with a feeler gauge DIAL INDICATOR CAMSHAFT Check the camshaft end-play with a dial indicator	Using feeler gauges, determine whether the clearance between the camshaft boss (or gear) and backing plate is within specifications. Install shims behind the thrust plate, or reposition the camshaft gear and retest endplay. In some cases, adjustment is by replacing the thrust plate. See the engine service procedures earlier in this chapter for details concerning specific engines.
	* Mount a dial indicator stand so that the stem of the dial indicator rests on the nose of the camshaft, parallel to the camshaft axis. Push the camshaft as far in as possible and zero the gauge. Move the camshaft outward to determine the amount of camshaft endplay. If the endplay is not within tolerance, install shims behind the thrust plate, or reposition the camshaft gear and retest. See the engine service procedures earlier in this chapter for details concerning specific engines.
Install the rear main seal:	See the engine service procedures earlier in this chapter for details concerning specific engines.
Install the crankshaft: INSTALLING BEARING SHELL REMOVING BEARING SHELL **Remove or install the upper bearing insert using a roll-out pin**	Thoroughly clean the main bearing saddles and caps. Place the upper halves of the bearing inserts on the saddles and press into position. NOTE: *Ensure that the oil holes align.* Press the corresponding bearing inserts into the main bearing caps. Lubricate the upper main bearings, and lay the crankshaft in position. Place a strip of Plastigage on each of the crankshaft journals, install the main caps, and torque to specifications. Remove the main caps, and compare the Plastigage to the scale on the Plastigage envelope. If clearances are within tolerances, remove the Plastigage, turn the crankshaft 90°, wipe off all oil and retest. If all clearances are correct, re-

Cylinder Block Reconditioning

Procedure	Method

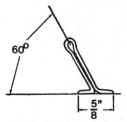

Home-made bearing roll-out pin

move all Plastigage, thoroughly lubricate the main caps and bearing journals, and install the main caps. If clearances are not within tolerance, the upper bearing inserts may be removed, without removing the crankshaft, using a bearing roll out pin (see illustration). Roll in a bearing that will provide proper clearance, and retest. Torque all main caps, excluding the thrust bearing cap, to specifications. Tighten the thrust bearing cap finger tight. To properly align the thrust bearing, pry the crankshaft the extent of its axial travel several times, the last movement held toward the front of the engine, and torque the thrust bearing cap to specifications. Determine the crankshaft end-play (see below), and bring within tolerance with thrust washers.

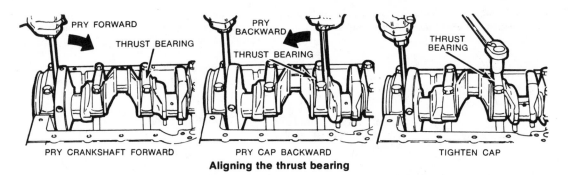

Aligning the thrust bearing

Measure crankshaft end-play:

Mount a dial indicator stand on the front of the block, with the dial indicator stem resting on the nose of the crankshaft, parallel to the crankshaft axis. Pry the crankshaft the extent of its travel rearward, and zero the indicator. Pry the crankshaft forward and record crankshaft end-play.

NOTE: *Crankshaft end-play also may be measured at the thrust bearing, using feeler gauges (see illustration).*

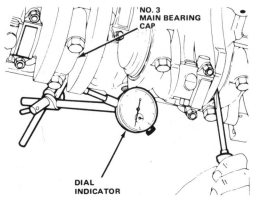

Check the crankshaft end-play with a dial indicator

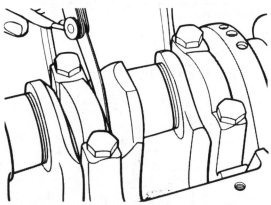

Check the crankshaft end-play with a feeler gauge

Cylinder Block Reconditioning

Procedure	*Method*

Install the pistons:

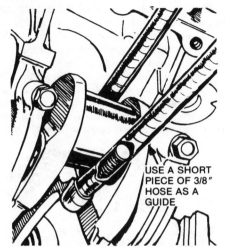

USE A SHORT PIECE OF 3/8" HOSE AS A GUIDE

Use lengths of vacuum hose or rubber tubing to protect the crankshaft journals and cylinder walls during piston installation

RING COMPRESSOR

Install the piston using a ring compressor

Press the upper connecting rod bearing halves into the connecting rods, and the lower halves into the connecting rod caps. Position the piston ring gaps according to specifications (see car section), and lubricate the pistons. Install a ring compresser on a piston, and press two long (8") pieces of plastic tubing over the rod bolts. Using the tubes as a guide, press the pistons into the bores and onto the crankshaft with a wooden hammer handle. After seating the rod on the crankshaft journal, remove the tubes and install the cap finger tight. Install the remaining pistons in the same manner. Invert the engine and check the bearing clearance at two points (90° apart) on each journal with Plastigage.
NOTE: *Do not turn the crankshaft with Plastigage installed.* If clearance is within tolerances, remove *all* Plastigage, thoroughly lubricate the journals, and torque the rod caps to specifications. If clearance is not within specifications, install different thickness bearing inserts and recheck.
CAUTION: *Never shim or file the connecting rods or caps.* Always install plastic tube sleeves over the rod bolts when the caps are not installed, to protect the crankshaft journals.

Check connecting rod side clearance:

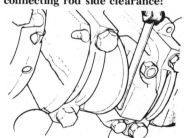

Check the connecting rod side clearance with a feeler gauge

Determine the clearance between the sides of the connecting rods and the crankshaft, using feeler gauges. If clearance is below the minimum tolerance, the rod may be machined to provide adequate clearance. If clearance is excessive, substitute an unworn rod, and recheck. If clearance is still outside specifications, the crankshaft must be welded and reground, or replaced.

Inspect the timing chain (or belt):

Visually inspect the timing chain for broken or loose links, and replace the chain if any are found. If the chain will flex sideways, it must be replaced. Install the timing chain as specified. Be sure the timing belt is not stretched, frayed or broken.
NOTE: *If the original timing chain is to be reused, install it in its original position.*

Cylinder Block Reconditioning

Procedure	Method
Check timing gear backlash and runout (OHV engines):	Mount a dial indicator with its stem resting on a tooth of the camshaft gear (as illustrated). Rotate the gear until all slack is removed, and zero the indicator. Rotate the gear in the opposite direction until slack is removed, and record gear backlash. Mount the indicator with its stem resting on the edge of the camshaft gear, parallel to the axis of the camshaft. Zero the indicator, and turn the camshaft gear one full turn, recording the runout. If either backlash or runout exceed specifications, replace the worn gear(s).

Check the camshaft gear backlash

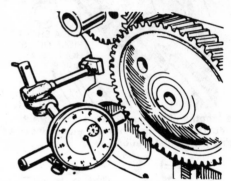

Check the camshaft gear run-out

Completing the Rebuilding Process

Following the above procedures, complete the rebuilding process as follows:

Fill the oil pump with oil, to prevent cavitating (sucking air) on initial engine start up. Install the oil pump and the pickup tube on the engine. Coat the oil pan gasket as necessary, and install the gasket and the oil pan. Mount the flywheel and the crankshaft vibration damper or pulley on the crankshaft. NOTE: *Always use new bolts when installing the flywheel.* Inspect the clutch shaft pilot bushing in the crankshaft. If the bushing is excessively worn, remove it with an expanding puller and a slide hammer, and tap a new bushing into place.

Position the engine, cylinder head side up. Lubricate the lifters, and install them into their bores. Install the cylinder head, and torque it as specified. Insert the pushrods (where applicable), and install the rocker shaft(s) (if so equipped) or position the rocker arms on the pushrods. Adjust the valves.

Install the intake and exhaust manifolds, the carburetor(s), the distributor and spark plugs. Adjust the point gap and the static ignition timing. Mount all accessories and install the engine in the car. Fill the radiator with coolant, and the crankcase with high quality engine oil.

Break-in Procedure

Start the engine, and allow it to run at low speed for a few minutes, while checking for leaks. Stop the engine, check the oil level, and fill as necessary. Restart the engine, and fill the cooling system to capacity. Check the point dwell angle and adjust the ignition timing and the valves. Run the engine at low to medium speed (800–2500 rpm) for approximately ½ hour, and retorque the cylinder head bolts. Road test the car, and check again for leaks.

Follow the manufacturer's recommended engine break-in procedure and maintenance schedule for new engines.

Emission Controls and Fuel System

EMISSION CONTROLS

Description

1975

All American Motors cars built for sale in California are equipped with the following emission control equipment:

• Air guard air injection system
• Catalytic converter (all V8s have two converters)
• Exhaust gas recirculation (EGR)
• Fuel tank vapor control system (FTVC)
• Fuel vapor return system
• Positive crankcase ventilation system (PCV)

• Thermostatically controlled air cleaner (TAC)
• Transmission controlled spark (TCS)
• Exhaust back-pressure sensor (BPS)
• EGR coolant temperature override switch
• Vacuum advance (distributor) coolant temperature override switch

American Motors cars built for sale in the remaining 49 states are equipped with all of the emission control devices California cars have with the following exceptions:

• All six cylinder vehicles except manual transmission Matadors, do not have catalytic converters. All V8s and the 258 Matador six with manual transmission have one catalytic

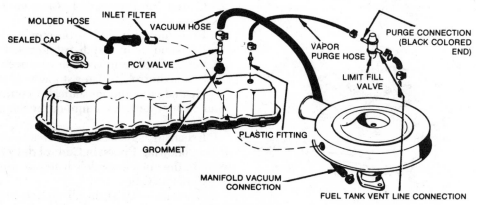

Typical PCV system

converter; the 360 4 bbl V8 has two converters.

• All Gremlin sixes and automatic transmission Hornet sixes and Pacers do not have the Air Guard air injection system.

• All six cylinder vehicles except the Matador and Pacer automatic do not have the Fuel Vapor Return System.

See the Emission Controls Unit Repair Section for more information.

1976

No new emission control devices were introduced for 1976, but applications were changed as follows:

• Air pump
  49 States:
    Used on all V8 engines
    Pacer and Hornet 6 cylinder
      Manual Transmission only
    Matador, all 6 cylinder
  California:
    All models
• Closed positive crankcase ventilation
• Emission calibrated carburetor
• Emission calibrated distributor
• Single diaphragm vacuum advance
• Exhaust gas recirculation
• Vapor control, canister storage
• Heated air cleaner
• Transmission controlled spark
  49 States:
    Not used
  California:
    All models
• Catalytic converter, single
  49 States:
    Matador 258 1 bbl. Manual
      Transmission only.
    All 2 bbl. V8

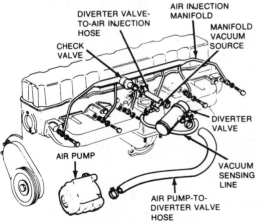

DIVERTER VALVE-TO-AIR INJECTION HOSE
AIR INJECTION MANIFOLD
MANIFOLD VACUUM SOURCE
CHECK VALVE
DIVERTER VALVE
AIR PUMP
VACUUM SENSING LINE
AIR PUMP-TO-DIVERTER VALVE HOSE

Typical air pump system, except V8

California:
  All 6 cylinder
• Catalytic converter, dual
  49 States:
    All 4 bbl. V8
  California:
    All V8
• Electric choke
  49 States:
    Hornet 6 cylinder manual
      transmission only
    Pacer 1 bbl. 6 cylinder manual
      transmission only
    Matador 6 cylinder manual
      transmission only
    All 4 bbl. V8
  California:
    Hornet 6 cylinder automatic
      transmission only
    Gremlin 6 cylinder automatic
      transmission only
    Pacer 1 bbl. 6 cylinder automatic
      transmission only
    Pacer 1 bbl. 6 cylinder automatic
      transmission only.
    All 4 bbl. V8

1977–82

Vehicles manufactured for sale at altitudes higher than 4,000 feet must now be equipped with special emission control components. The emission control devices have been changed on some models and remain the same on others. All models have as standard equipment the following emission control components:

NOTE: *Refer to the Emission Control Systems section in the Unit Repair Section for further details on the emission control coponents.*

• Air Guard system (air pump and components) or Pulsair system on 4-151
• Closed positive crankcase ventilation system
• Emission calibrated carburetor
• Emission calibrated distributor
• Single diaphragm vacuum advance unit
• Vapor control, canister storage
• Heated and thermostatically controlled air cleaner (either vacuum or mechanically operated)
• Exhaust gas recirculation valve

The following Emission Control devices are used on the vehicle models listed by area.

• Catalytic Converter:
    49 States—Used on all models that do not have transmission controlled spark,

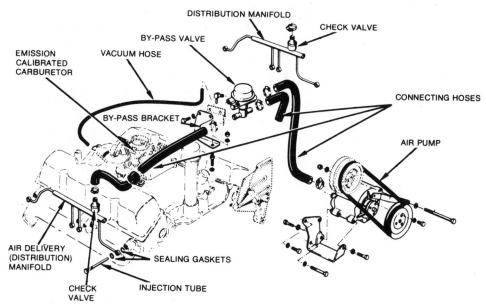

Typical V8 air pump system

except Matador 6 cylinder automatic through 1977; used on all 1978–82 models
Altitude—Used on all models
California—4 cylinder uses one pellet converter
6 cylinder uses one warm up converter and one pellet converter
8 cylinder through 1978
uses two warm up converters and two pellet converters
• Transmission Controlled Spark:
49 States—Used on all models without catalytic converters, except Matador 6 cylinder automatic and 4 cylinder Gremlin models through 1977
Altitude—Used on all automatic transmission models 1977 only
California—Used on all models except 4 cylinder 121 through 1978, the four cylinder 151, and on the 258 engine, 1979–82
• Spark Coolant Temperature Override:
49 States—Used with 232 6 cylinder automatic and all other models except catalytic converter equipped manual transmission, and Matador 6 cylinder through 1977; used on some models in 1978 and on 1979–82 four and six cylinder engines
Altitude—Used on all models
California—Used on all models
• Carburetor Vent To Canister:
49 States—Used on all 4 and 6 cylinder models in 1977, and all 1978–82 models

Altitude—Used on all models except 360 V8 Matador in 1977, and all 1978–82 models
California—Used on all 4 and 6 cylinder in 1977, and all 1978–82 models
• Electric Choke:
49 States—Used on 4-121 and all 1980–82 models
Altitude—Used on 4 cylinder and Matador 360 V8. '78–'79 304 V8 and all 1980–82 models
California—Used on all 4 cylinder and V8 and all 1980–82 models
• Throttle Solenoid:
49 States—Used on 4 cylinder, 258 6 cylinder 2 bbl automatic and all V8
Altitude—Used on 4 cylinder and Matador 360 V8 and '78–'79 304 V8
California—Used on all models
• Computer Controlled Carburetor:
49 States—All six cylinder models except Eagle use Computerized Emission Control (CEC), 1980–82
California—All four cylinder models use C-4 system. All six cylinder except 1980 Eagle use CEC, 1980–82
Altitude—Same as California

Component Removal and Installation

AIR PUMP

CAUTION: *Never place the pump in a vise or attempt to dismantle it. The pump has no internal parts that are replaceable and*

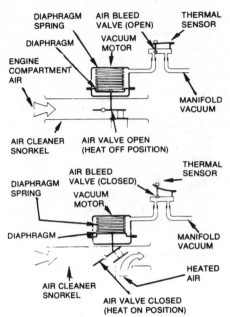

Vacuum controlled thermostatic air cleaner

it is serviced as a unit. Never pry or hammer on the pump housing.

1. Loosen the bolts on the pump pulley.

2. Loosen the air pump attachment bracket. On V8 models with air conditioning, loosen the power steering pump to aid in drive belt removal.

3. Detach the air supply hoses at the pump.

4. Remove the drivebelt and pulley from the hub.

5. Unfasten the bolts on the bracket and remove the pump.

Installation is as follows:

1. Place the pump on its mounting bracket and install, but do not tighten, the attachment bolts.

2. With the rotor shaft used as a center, fit the pulley into the hub and install the drive belt over the pulley.

3. Tighten the pulley attachment bolts, using care not to snap them off.

4. Adjust the pump until the belt is secure. Tighten the mounting bolts and the adjusting screw to 18–22 ft. lbs.; do not overtighten.

5. Attach the hoses and clamps.

AIR PUMP RELIEF VALVE

1. Use a gear puller and a steel bridge to remove the relief valve from the pump.

2. Remove the pressure plug from the new relief valve assembly.

3. Insert the relief valve into its housing mounting hole.

4. Place a block of wood over the valve. Use a hammer to tap the valve until it lightly registers against the housing. Use care not to distort the housing.

5. Press the pressure plug into the center of the relief valve.

CENTRIFUGAL FILTER FAN

NOTE: *Never attempt to clean the filter fan. It is impossible to remove the fan without destroying it.*

1. Remove the air pump from the car, as detailed above.

2. Gently pry the outer disc off and pull off the remaining portion. Be careful that no fragments from the fan enter the pump air intake.

3. Install a new filter fan pulling it into place with the pump pulley and attaching bolts.

4. Alternately tighten the bolts so that the fan is drawn down *evenly*. Be sure that the outer edge of the fan fits into the pump housing.

CAUTION(*Never hammer or press the fan into place; damage to it and the pump will result.*

5. Install the pump on the car.

NOTE: *For the first 20–30 miles of operation, the fan may squeal until its lip has worn in. This is normal and does not indicate a damaged pump.*

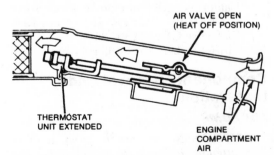

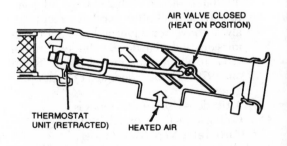

Non-vacuum controlled thermostatic air cleaner

EXHAUST TUBE

1. Remove the exhaust tube by grasping *it* (never the pump body) in a vise or a pair of pliers. Pull the tube out with a gentle twisting motion.

2. Install the new exhaust tube by tapping it into the hole with a hammer and a wooden block. Be careful not to damage its end.

3. Tap it until ⅞ in. of the tube remains above the pump cover.

NOTE: *Do not clamp the pump in a vise while installing the exhaust tube.*

BY-PASS (DIVERTER) VALVE

1. Disconnect the hoses from the valve.

2. Remove the screws that attach the valve bracket to the engine. Remove the valve and bracket assembly.

3. Installation is the reverse of removal.

AIR INJECTION MANIFOLD AND CHECK VALVE ASSEMBLY

Six-Cylinder

1. Remove the intake/exhaust manifold assembly, after disconnecting the hoses from the air injection manifold.

2. Place the assembly in a vise and unfasten the retaining nuts on the air injection manifold at each cylinder exhaust port.

3. Lightly tap the injection tubes, then pull the injection manifold away from the exhaust manifold.

4. If the tubes have become fused to the injection manifold, remove them by applying heat while rotating them with pliers.

Installation of the injection manifold and tubes is performed as follows:

1. Insert new air injection tubes into the exhaust manifold.

NOTE: *The shorter tubes go into the Nos. 3 and 4 cylinders.*

2. Using a new gasket, assemble the exhaust/intake manifold to the engine.

3. Using new gaskets, install the air injection manifold on to the exhaust manifold in the reverse order of removal.

V8

1. Detach the air delivery hose at the check valve.

2. Unfasten the air injection manifold attachment nuts from the cylinder head. Carefully, ease the air injection manifold away from the head.

NOTE: *On some models it may be necessary to lower the bottom steering shaft clamp to gain access to the left rear mounting bolt; or to disconnect the right engine support and raise the engine to remove the right air injection manifold assembly.*

3. On newer cars, the air injection tubes and the manifold are removed as an assembly.

4. On older models, or if the tubes are hard to remove, use an "easy-out" to twist the tube out gradually.

NOTE: *Some interference may be encountered because of the normal carbon buildup on the tubes. Injection tubes which are removed with an "easy-out" must be replaced with new ones.*

Installation is the reverse of removal.

PCV VALVE

This job is covered in Chapter 1.

EGR VALVE

1. Remove the air cleaner assembly from the carburetor.

2. Unfasten the vacuum line from the top of the EGR valve.

3. Loosen and remove the two screws which secure the valve to the manifold.

4. Remove the EGR valve, complete with its gasket.

Installation of the EGR valve is the reverse of its removal. Always use a new gasket. Tighten the valve securing bolts to 13 ft. lbs.

Valve and Passage Cleaning

1. Remove the EGR valve.

2. Use a wire brush to clean all of the deposits from the stainless steel pintle.

3. Press down on the pintle to open the EGR valve and then release it to close the valve. Replace the valve assembly if it will not close fully.

4. Inspect the manifold passages. If necessary, clean them with a spiral wire brush.

NOTE: *On six-cylinder engines, deposits will build up most rapidly in the upper passage. If the deposits cannot be removed with the wire brush, use a ⁹/₁₆ in. drill bit. Rotate the drill by hand, after coating it with heavy grease.*

5. Install the EGR valve with a new gasket.

Emission Control Troubleshooting

POSITIVE CRANKCASE VENTILATION (PCV) SYSTEM

Valve Test

1. See if there are any deposits in the carburetor passages, the oil filler cap, or the hoses. Clean these as required.

2. Connect a tachometer to the engine.

3. With the engine idling, do one of the following:

    a. Remove the PCV valve hose from the crankcase or the oil filler connection.

    b. On cars with the PCV valve located in a grommet on the valve cover, remove both the valve and the grommet.

NOTE: *If the valve and the hoses are not clogged-up, there should be a hissing sound.*

4. Check the tachometer reading. Place a finger over the valve or hose opening (a suction should be felt).

5. Check the tachometer again. The engine speed should have dropped at least 50 rpm. It should return to normal when the finger is removed from the opening.

6. If the engine does not change speed or if the change is less than 50 rpm, the hose is clogged or the valve is defective. Check the hose first. If the hose is not clogged, replace, do not attempt to repair the PCV valve.

7. Test the new valve in the above manner, to make sure that it is operating properly.

NOTE: *There are several commercial PCV valve testers available. Be sure that the one used is suitable for the valve to be tested, as the testers are not universal.*

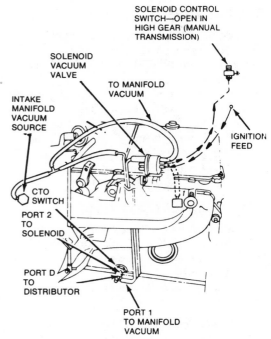

6 cylinder TCS system

AIR INJECTION SYSTEM

CAUTION: *Do not hammer on, pry, or bend the pump housing while tightening the drive belt or testing the pump.*

Belt Tension and Air Leaks

1. Check the pump drive belt tension. There should be about ½ in. play in the longest span of belt between pulleys.

2. Turn the pump by hand. If it has seized, the belt will slip, producing noise. Disregard any chirping, squealing, or rolling sounds from inside the pump; these are normal when it is turned by hand.

3. Check the hoses and connections for leaks. Hissing or a blast of air is indicative of a leak. Soapy water, applied lightly around the area in question, is a good method for detecting leaks.

Air Output Tests

1. Disconnect the air supply hose at the antibackfire valve.

2. Connect a vacuum pressure gauge to the air supply hose.

NOTE: *If there are two hoses plug the second one.*

3. With the engine at normal operating temperature, increase the idle speed and watch the gauge.

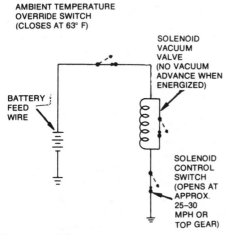

TCS electrical diagram

4. The airflow from the pump should be steady and between 2–6 psi. If it is unsteady or falls below this, the pump is defective and must be replaced.

Pump Noise Diagnosis

The air pump is normally noisy; as engine speed increases, the noise of the pump will rise in pitch. The rolling sound the pump bearings make is normal; however, if this sound becomes objectionable at certain speeds, the pump is defective and will have to be replaced.

A continual hissing sound from the air pump pressure relief valve at idle, indicates a defective valve. Replace the relief valve.

If the pump rear bearing fails, a continual knocking sound will be heard. Since the rear bearing is not separately replaceable, the pump will have to be replaced as an assembly.

Antibackfire Valve Tests

There are two different types of antibackfire valves used with air injection systems. A by-pass (diverter) valve is used on most current engines, while most older engines use a gulp type antibackfire valve. Test procedures for both types are given below.

GULP VALVE

1. Detach the air supply hose which runs between the pump and the gulp valve.
2. Connect a tachometer and run the engine between 1,500–2,000 rpm.
3. Allow the throttle to snap closed. This should produce a loud sucking sound from the gulp valve.
4. Repeat this operation several times. If there is no sound, the valve is not working or the vacuum connections are loose.
5. Check the vacuum connections. If they are secure, replace the gulp valve.

BY-PASS (DIVERTER) VALVE

1. Detach the hose, which runs from the by-pass valve to the check valve, at the by-pass valve hose connection.
2. Connect a tachometer to the engine. With the engine running at normal idle speed, check to see that air is flowing from the by-pass valve hose connection.
3. Speed the engine up, so that it is running at 1,500–2,000 rpm. Allow the throttle to snap shut. The flow of air from the by-pass valve at the check valve hose connection should stop momentarily and air should then

flow from the exhaust port on the valve body or the silencer assembly.
4. Repeat Step 3 several times. If the flow of air is not diverted into the atmosphere from the valve exhaust port or if it fails to stop flowing from the hose connection, check the vacuum lines and connections. If these are tight, the valve is defective and requires replacement.
5. A leaking diaphragm will cause the air to flow out both the hose connection and the exhaust port at the same time. If this happens, replace the valve.

Check Valve Test

1. Before starting the test, check all of the hoses and connections for leaks.
2. Detach the air supply hose(s) from the check valve(s).
3. Insert a suitable probe into the check valve and depress the plate. Release it; the plate should return to its original position against the valve seat. If binding is evident, replace the valve.
4. Repeat Step 3 if two valves are used.
5. With the engine running at normal operating temperature, gradually increase its speed to 1,500 rpm. Check for exhaust gas leakage. If any is present, replace the valve assembly.

NOTE: *Vibration and flutter of the check valve at idle speed is a normal condition and does not mean that the valve should be replaced.*

THERMOSTATICALLY CONTROLLED AIR CLEANER
Non-Vacuum-Operated Air Door Test

1. Unfasten the temperature sensing valve and snorkle assembly from the air cleaner. Place it in a container of cold water. Make sure that the thermostat is completely covered with water.
2. Place a thermometer, of known accuracy, in the water. Heat the water slowly and watch the temperature.
3. At 105°F, or less, the door should be closed (manifold heat position).
4. Continue heating the water until it reaches 130°F. The door should be fully open to the outside air position.
5. If the door does not open at or near this temperature, check it for binding or a detached spring. If the door doesn't open or close properly, the sensor is defective and must be replaced.

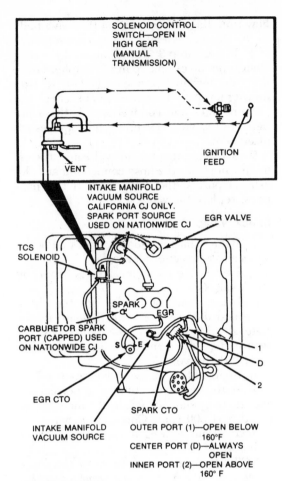

8 cylinder TCS system

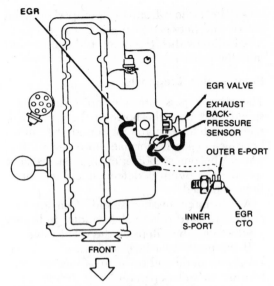

1975–79 6 cylinder EGR system

NOTE: *This usually requires that the entire snorkle assembly must be replaced.*

Vacuum-Operated Air Door Test

1. Either start with a cold engine or remove the air cleaner from the engine for at least half an hour. While cooling the air cleaner, leave the hood open.

2. Tape a thermometer, of known accuracy, to the inside of the air cleaner so that it is near the temperature sensor unit. Install the air cleaner on the engine but do not fasten its securing nut.

3. Start the engine. With the engine cold and the outside temperature less than 90°F., the door should be in the "heat on" position (closed to outside air).

NOTE: *Due to the position of the air cleaner on some cars, a mirror may be necessary when observing the position of the air door.*

4. Operate the throttle rapidly to ½–¾ of its opening and release it. The air door should

open to allow outside air to enter and then close again.

5. Allow the engine to warm up to normal temperature. Watch the door. When it opens to the outside air, remove the cover from the air cleaner. The temperature should be over 90°F and no more than 130°F; 115°F is about normal. If the door does not work within these temperature ranges, or fails to work at all, check for linkage or door binding.

If there is no binding and the air door is not working, proceed with the vacuum test below. If these indicate no faults in the vacuum motor and the door is not working, the temperature sensor is defective and must be replaced.

Vacuum Motor Test

NOTE: *Be sure that the vacuum hose that runs between the temperature switch and the vacuum motor is not pinched by the retaining clip under the air cleaner. This could prevent the air door from closing.*

1. Check all of the vacuum lines and fittings for leaks. Correct any leaks. If none are found, proceed with the test.

2. Remove the hose which runs from the sensor to the vacuum motor. Run a hose directly from the manifold vacuum source to the vacuum motor.

3. If the motor closes the air door, it is functioning properly and the temperature sensor is defective.

4. If the motor does *not* close the door and no binding is present in its operation, the

vacuum motor is defective and must be replaced.

NOTE: *If an alternate vacuum source is applied to the motor, insert a vacuum gauge in the line by using a T-fitting. Apply at least 9 in. Hg of vacuum in order to operate the motor.*

DISTRIBUTOR CONTROLS

Dual Diaphragm Distributor Test

1. Connect a timing light to the engine. Check the ignition timing.

NOTE: *First disconnect any spark control devices, distributor vacuum valves, etc. If these are left connected, inaccurate results may be obtained.*

2. Remove the retard hose from the distributor and plug it. Increase the engine speed. The timing should advance. If it fails to do so, then the vacuum unit is faulty and must be replaced.

3. Check the timing with the engine at normal idle speed. Unplug the retard hose and connect it to the vacuum unit. The timing should instantly be retarded from 4–10°. If this does not occur, the retard diaphragm has a leak and the vacuum unit must be replaced.

Deceleration Valve Test

NOTE: *Timing, idle speed and air/fuel mixture should be correct before beginning this test.*

1. Connect a vacuum gauge to the distributor vacuum advance line.

2. If the carburetor has a dashpot, tape its plunger down so that it cannot touch the throttle lever at idle.

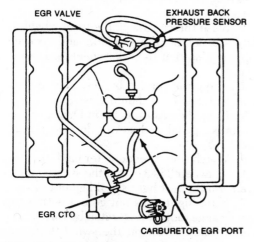

1975–79 8 cylinder EGR system

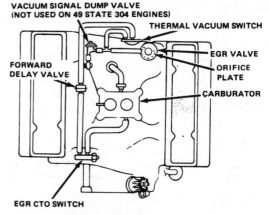

1980 8 cylinder EGR system

3. Speed the engine up to about 2,000 rpm and retain this speed for about ten seconds.

4. Release the throttle, allowing the engine to return to normal idle.

5. The vacuum reading should rise to about 20 in. Hg and stay there for one second. It should take about three seconds for the vacuum to return to its normal 4 in. Hg reading.

6. If the valve does not hold its high reading for about one second or if it takes over three seconds for the reading to return to normal, the valve should be adjusted.

To check for a leaking valve diaphragm:

1. Remove the vacuum gauge and connect it to the manifold vacuum line with a T-connection.

2. Clamp shut the valve-to-distributor vacuum line and, with the engine at normal idle speed, check the vacuum reading.

3. Clamp the line shut between the deceleration valve and the T-connection. Check the vacuum gauge reading again.

4. If the second reading is higher than the first, the valve diaphragm is leaking and the valve should be replaced.

Deceleration Valve Adjustment

If the deceleration valve test indicated a need for adjustment, proceed as follows:

1. Remove the cover to gain access to the adjusting screw.

2. If an *increase* in valve opening time is desired, turn the adjusting screw counterclockwise.

3. If a *decrease* in time is desired, turn the adjusting screw clockwise.

NOTE: *Each complete turn of the adjusting screw equals ½ in. Hg.*

4. After finishing the adjustments, retest the valve. If the valve cannot be adjusted, it is defective and must be replaced.

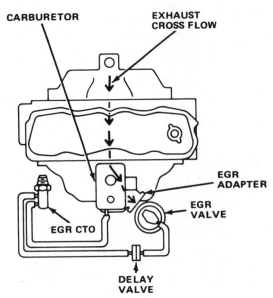

CARBURETOR

EXHAUST
CROSS FLOW

EGR
ADAPTER

EGR
VALVE

EGR CTO

DELAY
VALVE

4-151 EGR system

Transmission Controlled Spark System Test

MANUAL TRANSMISSION SYSTEM TEST

1. Connect a vacuum gauge between the distributor and the solenoid vacuum valve, using a T-connector.

NOTE: *This won't work unless the temperature switch on the front crossmember is above 63°F.*

2. Start the engine. With the transmission in Neutral, the vacuum gauge should read zero.

3. Increase engine speed to between 1000–1500 rpm with the clutch pedal depressed. The vacuum reading should remain at zero.

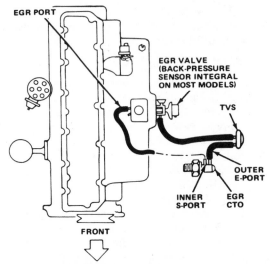

EGR PORT

EGR VALVE
(BACK-PRESSURE
SENSOR INTEGRAL
ON MOST MODELS)

TVS

OUTER
E-PORT

INNER
S-PORT

EGR
CTO

FRONT

1980–82 6 cylinder EGR system

4. With the clutch still depressed, place the transmission in High gear. Increase engine speed, as before. The vacuum gauge should now read at least 6 in. Hg. If it does not, proceed further with testing.

5. Unfasten the transmission switch lead from the solenoid vacuum valve terminal. Connect the lead in series with a low amperage test lamp and the positive side of the battery.

6. Move the shift lever through all of the gears. The test lamp should remain on until high gear is entered.

7. If the lamp stays on when the transmission is in High, either the switch is defective or the circuit is grounded. If it fails to come on at all, the switch is defective or the circuit has a loose wire.

8. If the transmission switch is functioning properly but the system check indicates that something is still wrong, check the temperature switch.

AUTOMATIC TRANSMISSION SYSTEM TEST

NOTE: *The spark control system used on AMC cars with automatic transmission made after 15 March 1973, is controlled by a switch which operates on transmission governor oil pressure.*

1. Disconnect the electrical lead from the terminal of the governor pressure switch.

NOTE: *The switch may easily be reached with the hood opened. On sixes, the switch is located on the right rear of the cylinder block; on V8s, it is attached to a bracket at the rear of the right-hand rocker cover.*

2. Connect a 12V test light in series, between the lead and the terminal on the switch.

CAUTION: *Use a low amperage test light, so that the switch contacts will not be damaged.*

3. Raise the car, block the front wheels (if they are not off the ground), and securely support it so that the rear wheels are free to turn.

4. Apply the service brakes. Start the engine. The test light should glow.

5. Place the gear selector in Drive, release the brake pedal and slowly depress the gas pedal.

6. Watch the speedometer and the test light; between 33–37 mph the switch should open and the test light should go out.

7. If the light does not go out within this speed range, adjust the switch by turning the $1/16$ in. allen screw on the switch terminal. Turn the screw clockwise to increase or coun-

terclockwise to decrease the switch cut-out speed. The switch should be adjusted to open at 35 mph.

8. If the switch cannot be adjusted, replace it.

9. If the switch is working properly, but the TCS system is not working, the solenoid vacuum valve is probably defective.

TRANSMISSION SWITCH TEST

1. Leave the rear wheels of the car off the ground as in the system test above.

2. Disconnect the transmission switch leads. Connect a low-amperage test lamp in series with the switch and the positive side of the battery.

3. Accelerate to the speed specified in Step 3 of the system test and watch the test lamp. It should remain on until the specified speed is reached. If the lamp fails to go out or if it does not light at all, the switch is defective and must be replaced.

4. If the switch is working properly, reconnect it and go on with the next test.

VACUUM ADVANCE SOLENOID TEST

1. Disconnect the vacuum advance solenoid leads. Connect a vacuum gauge to the solenoid hose as in the system test.

2. Place the transmission in Neutral and start the engine. Increase engine speed. The gauge should indicate the presence of a vacuum.

3. Connect the hot lead to a 12 V power source. Ground the other lead. Increase the engine speed again. The solenoid should energize, resulting in a vacuum reading of zero.

4. Replace the vacuum advance solenoid if it is faulty. If it is not, reconnect the wiring and go on with the next appropriate test.

AMBIENT TEMPERATURE OVERRIDE SWITCH TEST

1. Disconnect the ambient temperature switch leads.

2. Replace the switch in the circuit with a jumper wire.

3. Repeat the system test. If the vacuum gauge now reads zero or below the specified speed, i.e., the solenoid energizes, the temperature switch is defective.

4. If the switch proves not to be defective when tested in Step 3, reconnect it after removing the jumper lead.

5. Cool the switch, using either ice, cold water, or an aerosol spray, to below 63°F. Repeat the system test. If there is no vacuum

below the specified speed, the switch is stuck closed and must be replaced.

CARBURETOR CONTROLS

Antidieseling Solenoid Test

NOTE: *Antidieseling solenoids are also referred to as, "throttle stop" or "idle stop" solenoids.*

1. Turn the ignition key on and open the throttle. The solenoid plunger should extend (solenoid energized).

2. Turn the ignition off. The plunger should retract, allowing the throttle to close.

NOTE: *With the antidieseling solenoid de-energized, the carburetor idle speed adjusting screw must make contact with the throttle shaft to prevent the throttle plates from jamming in the throttle bore when the engine is turned off.*

3. If the solenoid is functioning properly and the engine is still dieseling, check for one of the following:

   a. High idle or engine shut off speed;

   b. Engine timing not set to specifications;

   c. Binding throttle linkage;

   d. Too low an octane fuel being used.

Correct any of these problems, as necessary.

4. If the solenoid fails to function as outlined in steps 1–2, disconnect the solenoid leads; the solenoid should de-energize. If it does not, it is jammed and must be replaced.

5. Connect the solenoid to a 12 V power source and to ground. Open the throttle so that the plunger can extend. If it does not, the solenoid is defective.

6. If the solenoid is functioning correctly and no other source of trouble can be found, the fault probably lies in the wiring between the solenoid and the ignition switch or in the ignition switch itself.

Electrically Assisted Choke Test

1. Detach the electrical lead from the choke cap.

2. Use a jumper lead to connect the terminal on the choke cap and the wire terminal, so that the electrical circuit is still completed.

3. Start the engine.

4. Hook up a test light between the connector on the choke lead and ground.

5. The test light should glow. If it does not, current is not being supplied to the electrically assisted choke.

6. Connect the test light between the terminal on the alternator and the terminal on the choke cap. If the light now glows, replace the lead, since it is not passing current to the choke assist.

CAUTION: *Do not ground the terminal on the alternator while performing Step 6.*

7. If the light still does not glow, the fault lies somewhere in the electrical system.

If the electrically assisted choke receives power, but still does not appear to be functioning properly, reconnect the choke lead and proceed with the rest of the test.

8. Tape the bulb end of a thermometer to the metallic portion of the choke housing.

9. If the electrically assisted choke operates below 55°F, it is defective and must be replaced.

10. Allow the engine to warm up to between 80 and 110°F; at these temperatures the choke should operate for about 1½ minutes.

11. If it does not operate for this length of time, check the bi-metallic spring to see if it is connected to the tang on the choke lever.

12. If the spring is connected and the choke is not operating properly, replace the cap assembly.

EVAPORATIVE EMISSION CONTROL SYSTEM

There are several things to check for if a malfunction of the evaporative emission control system is suspected.

1. Leaks may be traced by using an infrared hydrocarbon tester. Run the test probe along the lines and connections. The meter will indicate the presence of a leak by a high hydrocarbon (HC) reading. This method is much more accurate than a visual inspection which would indicate only the presence of a leak large enough to pass liquid.

2. Leaks may be caused by any of the following, so always check these areas when looking for them:

    a. Defective or worn lines;
    b. Disconnected or pinched lines;
    c. Improperly routed lines;
    d. A defective filler cap.

NOTE: *If it becomes necessary to replace any of the lines used in the evaporative emission control system, use only hoses which are fuel resistant or are marked "EVAP."*

3. If the fuel tank has collapsed, it may be the fault of clogged or pinched vent lines, a defective vapor separator, or a plugged or incorrect fuel filler cap.

4. To test the filler cap, clean it and place it against the mouth. Blow into the relief valve housing. If the cap passes pressure with light blowing or if it fails to release with hard blowing, it is defective and must be replaced.

NOTE: *Replace the cap with one marked "pressure/vacuum" only. An incorrect cap will render the system inoperative or damage its components.*

General Motors Computer Controlled Catalytic Converter (C-4) System, and Computer Command Control (CCC) System

INTRODUCTION

The GM designed Computer Controlled Catalytic Converter System (C-4 System), was introduced in 1979 and used on 4-151 engines through 1980. The C-4 System primarily maintains the ideal air/fuel ratio at which the catalytic converter is most effective. Some versions of the system also control ignition timing of the distributor.

The Computer Command Control System (CCC System), introduced on some 1980 California models and used on all 1981 and later carbureted car lines, is an expansion of the C-4 System. The CCC System monitors up to fifteen engine/vehicle operating conditions which it uses to control up to nine engine and emission control systems. In addition to maintaining the ideal air/fuel ratio for the catalytic converter and adjusting ignition timing, the CCC System also controls the Air Management System so that the Catalytic converter can operate at the highest efficiency possible. The system also controls the lockup on the transmission torque converter clutch (certain automatic transmission models only), adjusts idle speed over a wide range of conditions, purges the evaporative emissions charcoal canister, controls the EGR valve operation and operates the early fuel evaporative (EFE) system. Not all engines use all of the above sub-systems.

There are two operation modes for both the C-4 System and the CCC System: closed loop and open loop fuel control. Closed loop fuel control means the oxygen sensor is controlling the carburetor's air/fuel mixture ratio. Under open loop fuel control operating conditions (wide open throttle, engine and/or ox-

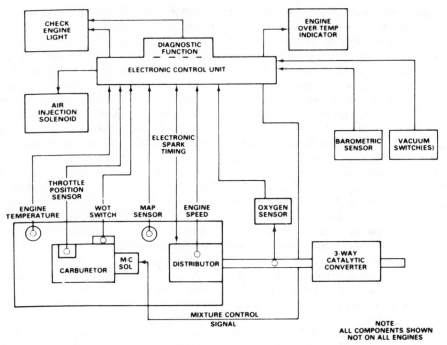

GM Computer Controlled Catalytic Converter (C-4) system

ygen sensor cold), the oxygen sensor has no effect on the air/fuel mixture.

NOTE: *On some engines, the oxygen sensor will cool off while the engine is idling, putting the system into open loop operation. To restore closed loop operation, run the engine at part throttle and accelerate from idle to part throttle a few times.*

COMPUTER CONTROLLED CATALYTIC CONVERTER (C-4) SYSTEM OPERATION

Major components of the system include an Electronic Control Module (ECM), an oxygen sensor, and electronically controlled variable-mixture carburetor, and a three-way oxidation-reduction catalytic converter.

The oxygen sensor generates a voltage which varies with exhaust gas oxygen content. Lean mixtures (more oxygen) reduce voltage; rich mixtures (less oxygen) increase voltage. Voltage output is sent to the ECM.

An engine temperature sensor installed in the engine coolant outlet monitors coolant temperatures. Vacuum control switches and throttle position sensors also monitor engine conditions and supply signals to the ECM.

The Electronic Control Module (ECM) monitors the voltage input of the oxygen sensor along with information from other input signals. It processes these signals and generates a control signal sent to the carburetor.

The control signal cycles between ON (lean command) and OFF (rich command). The amount of ON and OFF time is a function of the input voltage sent to the ECM by the oxygen sensor. The ECM has a calibration unit called a PROM (Programable Read Only Memory) which contains the specific instructions for a given engine application. In other words, the PROM unit is specifically programed or "tailor made" for the system in which it is installed. The PROM assembly is a replacable component which plugs into a socket on the ECM and requires a special tool for removal and installation.

NOTE: *Electronic Spark Timing (EST) allows continuous spark timing adjustments to be made by the ECM. Engines with EST can easily be identified by the absence of vacuum and mechanical spark advance mechanisms on the distributor. Engines with EMR systems may be recognized by the presence of five connectors, instead of the HEI module's usual four.*

To maintain good idle and driveability under all conditions, other input signals are used to modify the ECM output signal. Besides the sensors and switches already mentioned, these input signals include the manifold absolute pressure (MAP) or vacuum sensors and the barometric pressure (BARO) sensor. The MAP or vacuum sensors sense changes in manifold vacuum, while the BARO sensor senses changes in barometric pressure. One important function of the BARO sensor is the maintenance of good engine performance at various altitudes. These sensors act as throttle position sensors on some engines. See the following paragraph for description.

A Rochester Dualjet carburetor is used with the C-4 System. It may be an E2SE, E2ME, E4MC or E4ME model, depending on engine application. An electronically operated mixture control solenoid is installed in the carburetor float bowl. The solenoid controls the air/fuel mixture metered to the idle and main metering systems. Air metering to the idle system is controlled by an idle air bleed valve. It follows the movement of the mixture solenoid to control the amount of air bled into the idle system, enrichening or leaning out the mixture as appropriate. Air/fuel mixture enrichment occurs when the fuel valve is open and the air bleed is closed. All cycling of this system, which occurs ten times per second, is controlled by the ECM. A throttle position switch informs the ECM of open or closed throttle operation. A number of different switches are used, varying with application. The four cylinder engine (151 cu. in.) uses two vacuum switches to sense open throttle and closed throttle operation.

COMPUTER COMMAND CONTROL (CCC) SYSTEM OPERATION

The CCC has many components in common with the C-4 system (although they should probably not be interchanged between systems). These include the Electronic Control Module (ECM), which is capable of monitoring and adjusting more sensors and components than the ECM used on the C-4 System, an oxygen sensor, an electronically controlled variable-mixture carburetor, a three way catalytic converter, throttle position and coolant sensors, a barometric pressure (BARO) sensor, a manifold absolute pressure (MAP) sensor, a "check engine" light on the instrument cluster, and an Electronic Spark Timing (EST) distributor, which on some engines (turbcharged) is equipped with an Electronic Spark Control (ESC) which retards ignition spark under some conditions (detonation, etc.).

Components used almost exclusively by the CCC System include the Air Injection Reaction (AIR) Management System, charcoal canister purge solenoid, EGR valve control, vehicle speed sensor (located in the instrument cluster), transmission torque converter clutch solenoid (automatic transmission models only), idle speed control, and early fuel evaporative (EFE) system.

See the operation descriptions under C-4 System for those components (except the ECM) the CCC System shares with the C-4 System.

The CCC System ECM, in addition to monitoring sensors and sending a control signal to the carburetor, also control the following components or sub-systems: charcoal

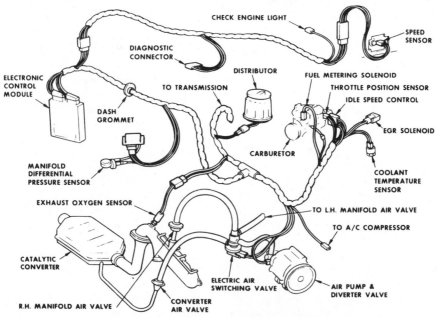

GM Computer Command Control (CCC) system

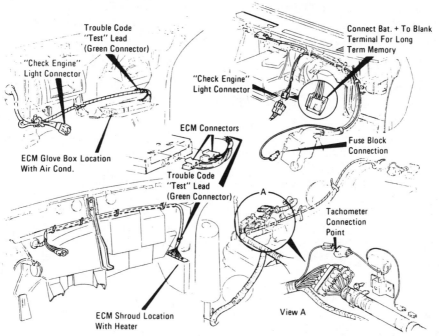

Typical C-4 system harness layout. Ground the trouble code test lead for a readout

canister purge, AIR Management System, idle speed control, automatic transmission converter lockup, distributor ignition timing, EGR valve control, EFE control, and the air conditioner compressor clutch operation. The CCC ECM is equipped with a PROM assembly similar to the one used in the C-4 ECM. See above for description.

The AIR Management System is an emission control which provides additional oxygen either to the catalyst or the cylinder head ports (in some cases exhaust manifold). An AIR Management System, composed of an air switching valve and/or an air control valve, controls the air pump flow and is itself controlled by the ECM. A complete description of the AIR system is given elsewhere in this unit repair section. The major difference between the CCC AIR System and the systems used on other cars is that the flow of air from the air pump is controlled electrically by the ECM, rather than by vacuum signal.

The charcoal canister purge control is an electrically operated solenoid valve controlled by the ECM. When energized, the purge control solenoid blocks vacuum from reaching the canister purge valve. When the ECM de-energizes the purge control solenoid, vacuum is allowed to reach the canister and operate the purge valve. This releases the fuel vapors collected in the canister into the induction system.

The EGR valve control solenoid is activated by the ECM in similar fashion to the canister purge solenoid. When the engine is cold, the ECM energizes the solenoid, which blocks the vacuum signal to the EGR valve. When the engine is warm, the ECM de-energizes the solenoid and the vacuum signal is allowed to reach and activate the EGR valve.

The Transmission Converter Clutch (TCC) lock is controlled by the ECM through an electrical solenoid in the automatic transmission. When the vehicle speed sensor in the instrument panel signals the ECM that the vehicle has reached the correct speed, the ECM energizes the solenoid which allows the torque converter to mechanically couple the engine to the transmission. When the brake pedal is pushed or during deceleration, passing, etc., the ECM returns the transmission to fluid drive.

The idle speed control adjusts the idle speed to load conditions, and will lower the idle speed under no-load or low-load conditions to conserve gasoline.

The Early Fuel Evaporative (EFE) system is used on some engines to provide rapid heat to the engine induction system to promote smooth start-up and operation. There are two types of system: vacuum servo and electrically heated. They use different means to achieve the same end, which is to pre-heat the incoming air/fuel mixture. They are controlled by the ECM.

BASIC TROUBLESHOOTING

NOTE: *The following explains how to activate the Trouble Code signal light in the instrument cluster and gives an explanation of what each code means. This is not a full C-4 or CCC System troubleshooting and isolation procedure.*

Before suspecting the C-4 or CCC System or any of its components as faulty, check the ignition system including distributor, timing, spark plugs and wires. Check the engine compression, air cleaner, and emission control components not controlled by the ECM. Also check the intake manifold, vacuum hoses and hose connectors for leaks and the carburetor bolts for tightness.

The following systems could indicate a possible problem with the C-4 or CCC System.

1. Detonation;
2. Stalls or rough idle—cold;
3. Stalls or rough idle—hot;
4. Missing;
5. Hesitation;
6. Surges;
7. Poor gasoline mileage;
8. Sluggish or spongy performance;
9. Hard starting—cold;
10. Hard starting—hot;
11. Objectionable exhaust odors;
12. Cuts out.

As a bulb and system check, the "Check Engine" light will come on when the ignition switch is turned to the ON position but the engine is not started.

The "Check Engine" light will also produce the trouble code or codes by a series of flashes which translate as follows. When the diagnostic test lead (C-4) or terminal (CCC) under the dash is grounded, with the ignition in the ON position and the engine not running, the "Check Engine" light will flash once, pause, then flash twice in rapid succession. This is a code 12, which indicates that the diagnostic system is working. After a longer pause, the code 12 will repeat itself two more times. The cycle will then repeat itself until the engine is started or the ignition is turned off.

When the engine is started, the "Check Engine" light will remain on for a few seconds, then turn off. If the "Check Engine" light remains on, the self-diagnostic system has detected a problem. If the test lead (C-4) or test terminal (CCC) is then grounded, the

trouble code will flash three times. If mor than one problem is found, each trouble code will flash three times. Trouble codes will flash in numerical order (lowest code number to highest). The trouble codes series will repeat as long as the test lead or terminal is grounded.

A trouble code indicates a problem with a given circuit. For example, trouble code 14 indicates a problem in the cooling sensor circuit. This includes the coolant sensor, its electrical harness, and the Electronic Control Module (ECM).

Since the self-diagnostic system cannot diagnose every possible fault in the system, the absence of a trouble code does not mean the system is trouble-free. To determine problems within the system which do not activate a trouble code, a system performance check must be made. This job should be left to a qualified technician.

In the case of an intermittant fault in the system, the "Check Engine" light will go out when the fault goes away, but the trouble code will remain in the memory of the ECM. Therefore, if a trouble code can be obtained even though the "Check Engine" light is not on, the trouble code must be evaluated. It must be determined if the fault is intermittant or if the engine must be at certain operating conditions (under load, etc.) before the "Check Engine" light will come on. Some trouble codes will not be recorded in the ECM until the engine has been operated at part throttle for about 5 to 18 minutes.

On the C-4 System, the ECM erases all trouble codes every time the ignition is turned off. In the case of intermittent faults, a long term memory is desirable. This can be produced by connecting the orange connector/lead from terminal "S" of the ECM directly to the battery (or to a "hot" fuse panel terminal). This terminal must be disconnected after diagnosis is complete or it will drain the battery.

On the CCC System, a trouble code will be stored until terminal "R" of the ECM has been disconnected from the battery for 10 seconds.

An easy way to erase the computer memory on the CCC System is to disconnect the battery terminals from the battery. If this method is used, don't forget to reset clocks and electronic preprogramable radios. Another method is to remove the fuse marked ECM in the fuse panel. Not all models have such a fuse.

ACTIVATING THE TROUBLE CODE

On the C-4 System, activate the trouble code by grounding the trouble code test lead. Use the illustrations to locate the test lead under the instrument panel (usually a white and black wire or a wire with a green connector). Run a jumper wire from the lead to ground.

On the CCC System, locate the test terminal under the instrument panel. Ground the test lead. On many systems, the test lead is situated side by side with a ground terminal. In addition, on some models, the partition between the test terminal and the ground terminal has a cut out section so that a spade terminal can be used to connect the two terminals.

NOTE: *Ground the test lead or terminal according to the instructions given in "Basic Troubleshooting", above.*

Explanation of Trouble Codes
GM C-4 and CCC Systems
Ground test lead or terminal AFTER engine is running.

Trouble Code	Applicable System	Notes	Possible Problem Area
12	C-4, CCC		No tachometer or reference signal to computer (ECM). This code will only be present while a fault exists, and will not be stored if the problem is intermittent.
13	C-4, CCC		Oxygen sensor circuit. The engine must run for about five minutes at part throttle (and under road load—CCC equipped cars) before this code will show.
13 & 14 (at same time)	C-4		See code 43.
14	C-4, CCC		Shorted coolant sensor circuit. The engine has to run 2 minutes before this code will show.
15	C-4, CCC		Open coolant sensor circuit. The engine has to operate for about five minutes at part throttle (some models) before this code will show.
21	C-4		Shorted wide open throttle switch and/or open closed-throttle switch circuit (when used).
	C-4, CCC		Throttle position sensor circuit. The engine must be run up to 10 seconds (25 seconds—CCC System) below 800 rpm before this code will show.
21 & 22 (at same time)	C-4		Grounded wide open throttle switch circuit.
22	C-4		Grounded closed throttle or wide open throttle switch circuit.
23	C-4, CCC		Open or grounded carburetor mixture control (M/C) solenoid circuit.

Explanation of Trouble Codes (cont.)
GM C-4 and CCC Systems

Ground test lead or terminal AFTER engine is running.

Trouble Code	Applicable System	Notes	Possible Problem Area
24	CCC		Vehicle speed sensor (VSS) circuit. The car must operate up to five minutes at road speed before this code will show.
32	C-4, CCC		Barometric pressure sensor (BARO) circuit output low.
32 & 55 (at same time)	C-4		Grounded +8V terminal or V(REF) terminal for barometric pressure sensor (BARO), or faulty ECM computer.
34	C-4		Manifold absolute pressure (MAP) sensor output high (after ten seconds and below 800 rpm).
	CCC		Manifold absolute pressure (MAP) sensor circuit or vacuum sensor circuit. The engine must run up to five minutes below 800 RPM before this code will set.
35	CCC		Idle speed control (ISC) switch circuit shorted (over ½ throttle for over two seconds).
41	CCC		No distributor reference pulses to the ECM at specified engine vacuum. This code will store in memory.
42	CCC		Electronic spark timing (EST) bypass circuit grounded.
43	C-4		Throttle position sensor adjustment (on some models, engine must run at part throttle up to ten seconds before this code will set).
44	C-4, CCC		Lean oxygen sensor indication. The engine must run up to five minutes in closed loop (oxygen sensor adjusting carburetor mixture), at part throttle and under road load (drive car) before this code will set.
44 & 55 (at same time)	C-4, CCC		Faulty oxygen sensor circuit.
45	C-4, CCC	Restricted air cleaner can cause code 45.	Rich oxygen sensor system indication. The engine must run up to five minutes in closed loop (oxygen sensor adjusting carburetor mixture), at part throttle under road load before this code will set.
51	C-4, CCC		Faulty calibration unit (PROM) or improper PROM installation in electronic control module (ECM). It takes up to thirty seconds for this code to set.

Explanation of Trouble Codes (cont.)
GM C-4 and CCC Systems
Ground test lead or terminal AFTER engine is running.

Trouble Code	Applicable System	Notes	Possible Problem Area
52 & 53	C-4		"Check Engine" light off: Intermittent ECM computer problem. "Check Engine" light on: Faulty ECM computer (replace).
52	C-4, CCC		Faulty ECM computer.
53	CCC		Faulty ECM computer.
54	C-4, CCC		Faulty mixture control solenoid circuit and/or faulty ECM computer.
55	C-4		Faulty throttle position sensor or ECM computer. Faulty ECM computer.
55	CCC		Grounded +8 volt supply (terminal 19 of ECM computer connector), grounded 5 volt reference (terminal 21 of ECM computer connector), faulty oxygen sensor circuit or faulty ECM computer.

American Motors Feedback System

American Motors introduced feedback systems on all cars (except Eagle) in 1980. Two different, but similar, systems are used. The four cylinder engine uses the G.M. C-4 feedback system, which is covered earlier in this section. Component usage is identical to that of the G.M. 151 cu. in four cylinder engine, including an oxygen sensor, a vacuum switch (which is closed at idle and partial throttle positions), a wide open throttle switch, a coolant temperature sensor (set to open at 150°F), an Electronic Control Module (ECM) equipped with modular Programmable Read Only Memory (PROM), and a mixture control solenoid installed in the air horn on the E2SE carburetor. A "Check Engine" light is included on the instrument panel as a service and diagnostic indicator.

The six cylinder engine is equipped with a Computerized Emission Control (CEC) System.

1980 CEC components include an oxygen sensor; two vacuum switches (one ported and one manifold) to detect three operating conditions: idle, partial throttle, and wide open throttle; a coolant temperature switch; a Micro Computer Unit (MCU), the control unit

for the system which monitors all data and sends an output signal to the carburetor; and a stepper motor installed in the main body of the BBD carburetor, which varies the position of the two metering pins controlling the size of the air bleed orifices in the carburetor. The MCU also interprets signals from the distributor (rpm voltage) to monitor engine rpm.

On 1981 and later models with CEC, the number of sensors has been increased. Three vacuum operated electric switches, two mechanically operated electric switches, one engine coolant switch and an air temperature operated switch are used to detect and send engine operating data to the MCU concerning the following engine operating conditions: cold engine start-up and operation; wide open throttle; idle (closed throttle); and partial and deep throttle.

Both AMC systems are conventional in operation. As in other feedback systems, two modes of operation are possible: open loop and closed loop. Open loop operation occurs during engine starting, cold engine operation, cold oxygen sensor operation, engine idling, wide open throttle operation, and low battery voltage operation. In open loop, a fixed air/fuel mixture signal is provided by the ECM or MCU to the carburetor, and oxygen sensor data is ignored. Closed loop operation occurs at all other times, and in this mode all signals are used by the control unit to determine the optimum air/fuel mixture.

OXYGEN SENSOR REPLACEMENT

1. Disconnect the two wire plug.
2. Remove the sensor from the exhaust manifold on the four cylinder, or the exhaust pipe on the six.
3. Clean the threads in the manifold or pipe.
4. Coat the threads of the replacement sensor with an electrically-conductive antiseize compound. Do not use a conventional antiseize compound, which may electrically insulate the sensor.
5. Install the sensor. Installation torque is 25 ft. lbs. for the four cylinder, 31 ft. lbs. for the six cylinder.
6. Connect the sensor lead. Do not push the rubber boot into the sensor body more than ½ inch above the base.
7. If the sensor's pigtail is broken, replace the sensor. The wires cannot be spliced or soldered.

VACUUM SWITCH REPLACEMENT

The vacuum switches are mounted in a bracket bolted to the left inner fender panel in the engine compartment. They are not replaceable individually; the complete unit must be replaced.
1. Tag all the vacuum hoses, then disconnect them from the switches. Disconnect the electrical plugs. The four cylinder has two plugs and the six has one.
2. Remove the switch and bracket assembly from the fender panel.
3. Installation is the reverse.

CONTROL UNIT REPLACEMENT

The control unit, whether ECM or MCU, is mounted in the passenger compartment, beneath the right side of the instrument panel.
1. The ECM is installed in a mounting bracket; remove it from the bracket. The MCU is attached with bolts; remove the bolts and remove the unit.
2. Disconnect the electrical plugs.
3. Installation is the reverse. The four cylinder ECM is electrically insulated from the chassis; *do not ground the ECM bracket!*

MIXTURE CONTROL SOLENOID REPLACEMENT

The E2SE mixture control solenoid is installed in the air horn.

1. Remove the air cleaner case.
2. Disconnect the solenoid electrical plug.
3. Remove the solenoid retaining screws.
4. Remove the solenoid from the air horn.
5. Before installation, coat the rubber seal on the end of the stem with silicone grease or light engine oil. Install the solenoid, accurately aligning the stem with the recess at the bottom of the bowl. Use a new gasket. Connect the electrical plug and install the air cleaner.

STEPPER MOTOR REPLACEMENT

The BBD stepper motor is installed in the side of the main body of the carburetor.
1. Remove the air cleaner case.
2. Disconnect the electrical plug.
3. Remove the retaining screw and remove the motor from the side of the carburetor. Be careful not to drop the metering pins or the spring when removing the motor.
4. Installation is the reverse.

FUEL SYSTEM

Fuel Pump

REMOVAL AND INSTALLATION

1. Detach both fuel lines from the pump.
2. Remove the two bolts holding the pump to the engine.
3. Remove the pump. If it is defective, it should be replaced.
4. Bolt the new pump in place and replace the lines.
5. Start the engine and check for leaks.

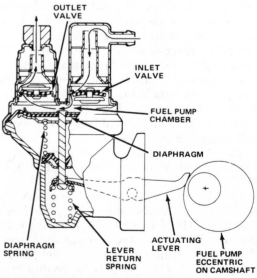

OUTLET VALVE

INLET VALVE

FUEL PUMP CHAMBER

DIAPHRAGM

DIAPHRAGM SPRING

LEVER RETURN SPRING

LEVER

ACTUATING LEVER

FUEL PUMP ECCENTRIC ON CAMSHAFT

Typical fuel pump

NOTE: *When installing the 4-121 pump, be sure that the push-rod is positioned properly against the actuating lever or the pump may damaged when the screws are tightened.*

TESTING

Fuel pump output can be tested by rigging the pump to discharge into a container. It should pump one quart of fuel in a minute or less, with the engine running at 500 rpm.

CAUTION: *Use a big container so that it doesn't overflow. Have an assistant ready to stop the engine. Be extremely careful not to spill fuel on hot engine parts.*

Carburetors

REMOVAL AND INSTALLATION

1. Remove the air cleaner.
2. Disconnect the fuel and vacuum lines. It might be a good idea to tag them to avoid confusion when the time comes to put them back.
3. Disconnect the choke rod.
4. Disconnect the accelerator linkage.
5. Disconnect the automatic transmission linkage.
6. Unbolt and remove the carburetor.
7. Remove the base gasket.
8. Before installation, make sure that the carburetor and manifold sealing surfaces are clean.
9. Install a new carburetor base gasket.
10. Install the carburetor and start the fuel and vacuum lines.
11. Bolt down the carburetor evenly.
12. Tighten the fuel and vacuum lines.
13. Connect the accelerator and automatic transmission linkage. If the transmission linkage was disturbed, it will have to be adjusted. The procedure is in Chapter 6.
14. Connect the choke rod.
15. Install the air cleaner. Adjust the idle speed and mixture as described in Chapter 2. Depending on the vintage, it may not be necessary (or possible) to adjust the idle mixture.

OVERHAUL

Whenever wear or dirt causes a carburetor to perform poorly, there are two possible solutions to the problem. The simplest is to trade in the old unit for a rebuilt one. The other, cheaper alternative is to buy an overhaul kit and rebuild the original unit. Some of the better overhaul kits contain complete step-by-step instructions along with exploded views and gauges. Other kits, intended for the professional, have only a few general overhaul hints. The second type can be moderately confusing to the novice, especially since a kit may have extra parts so that one kit can cover several variations of the same carburetor. In any event, it is not a good idea to dismantle any carburetor without at least replacing all the gaskets. The carburetor adjustments should all be checked during or after overhaul.

NOTE: *Before you tear off to the parts store for a rebuilding kit, make sure that you know what make and model your carburetor is.*

Efficient carburetion depends greatly on careful cleaning and inspection during overhaul, since dirt, gum, water, or varnish in or on the carburetor parts are often responsible for poor performance.

Overhaul your carburetor in a clean, dust-free area. Carefully disassemble the carburetor, referring often to the exploded views. Keep all similar and lookalike parts segregated during disassembly and cleaning to avoid accidental interchange during assembly. Make a note of all jet sizes.

When the carburetor is disassembled, wash all parts (except diaphragms, electric choke units, pump plunger, and any other plastic, leather, fiber, or rubber parts) in clean carburetor solvent. Do not leave parts in the solvent any longer than is necessary to sufficiently loosen the deposits. Excessive cleaning may remove the special finish from the float bowl and choke valve bodies, leaving these parts unfit for service. Rinse all parts in clean solvent and blow them dry with compressed air or allow them to air dry. Wipe clean all cork, plastic, leather, and fiber parts with a clean, lint-free cloth.

Blow out all passages and jets with compressed air and be sure that there are no restrictions or blockages. Never use wire or similar tools to clean jets, fuel passages, or air bleeds. Clean all jets and valves separately to avoid accidental interchange.

Check all parts for wear or damage. If wear or damage is found, replace the defective parts. Especially check the following:

1. Check the float needle and seat for wear. If wear is found, replace the complete assembly.
2. Check the float hinge pin for wear and the float(s) for dents or distortion. Replace the float if fuel has leaked into it.
3. Check the throttle and choke shaft bores for wear or an out-of-round condition. Damage or wear to the throttle arm, shaft, or shaft

bore will often require replacement of the throttle body. These parts require a close tolerance of fit; wear may allow air leakage, which could affect starting and idling.

NOTE: *Throttle shafts and bushings are not included in overhaul kits. They can be purchased separately.*

4. Inspect the idle mixture adjusting needles for burrs or grooves. Any such condition requires replacement of the needle, since you will not be able to obtain a satisfactory idle.

5. Test the accelerator pump check valves. They should pass air one way but not the other. Test for proper seating by blowing and sucking on the valve. Replace the valve as necessary. If the valve is satisfactory, wash the valve again to remove breath moisture.

6. Check the bowl cover for warped surfaces with a straightedge.

7. Closely inspect the valves and seats for wear and damage, replacing as necessary.

8. After the carburetor is assembled, check the choke valve for freedom of operation.

Carburetor overhaul kits are recommended for each overhaul. These kits contain all gaskets and new parts to replace those that deteriorate most rapidly. Failure to replace all parts supplied with the kit (especially gaskets) can result in poor performance later.

Some carburetor manufacturers supply overhaul kits of three basic types: minor repair; major repair; and gasket kits. Basically, they contain the following:

Minor Repair Kits:
- All gaskets
- Float needle valve
- Volume control screw
- All diaphragms
- Spring for the pump diaphragm

Major Repair kits:
- All jets and gaskets
- All diaphragms
- Float needle valve
- Volume control screw
- Pump ball valve
- Float
- Complete intermediate rod
- Intermediate pump lever
- Complete injector tube
- Some cover hold-down screws and washers

Gasket Kits:
- All gaskets

After cleaning and checking all components, reassemble the carburetor, using new parts and referring to the exploded view.

When reassembling, make sure that all screws and jets are tight in their seats, but do not overtighten as the tips will be distorted. Tighten all screws gradually, in rotation. Do not tighten needle valves into their seats; uneven jetting will result. Always use new gaskets. Be sure to adjust the float level when reassembling.

THROTTLE LINKAGE ADJUSTMENT

Throttle linkage adjustments are rarely required; sometimes there is no provision for adjustment. However, it is a good idea to check that the throttle valve(s) open all the way when the accelerator pedal is held all the way down. This is occasionally the source of poor performance on new cars.

Carburetor Adjustments

CARTER YF

The YF carburetor is a single-barrel downdraft carburetor with a diaphragm type accelerator pump and diaphragm operated metering rods.

Float Adjustment

1. Invert the air horn assembly and check the clearance from the top of the float to the surface of the air horn with a T-scale. The air horn should be held at eye level when gauging and the float arm should be resting on the needle pin.

2. Do not exert pressure on the needle valve when measuring or adjusting the float. Bend the float arm as necessary to adjust the float level.

Float Drop Adjustment

1. Hold the air horn up with the float hanging free.

2. Measure the distance between the top of the float at the extreme outer end and the air horn under surface.

3. Adjust by bending the tab at the rear of the float lever.

Metering Rod Adjustment

1. Back out the idle speed adjusting screw until the throttle plate is seated fully in its bore.

2. Press down on the upper end of the diaphragm shaft until the diaphragm bottoms in the vacuum chamber.

3. The metering rod should contact the bottom of the metering rod well and lifter link at the outer end nearest the springs and at

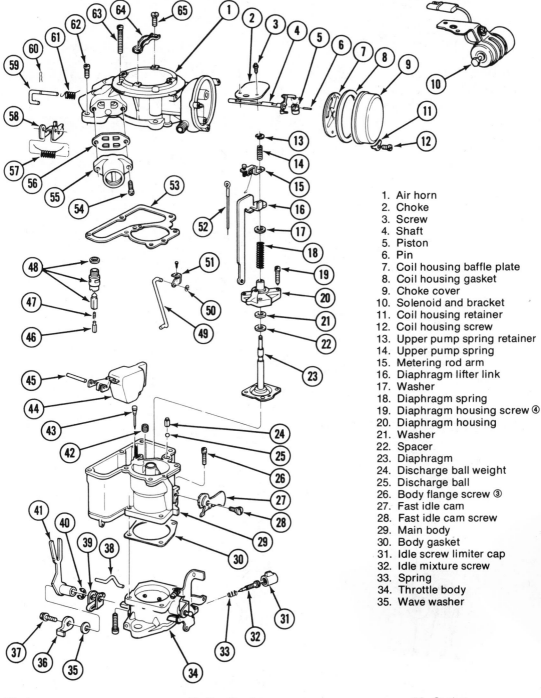

1. Air horn
2. Choke
3. Screw
4. Shaft
5. Piston
6. Pin
7. Coil housing baffle plate
8. Coil housing gasket
9. Choke cover
10. Solenoid and bracket
11. Coil housing retainer
12. Coil housing screw
13. Upper pump spring retainer
14. Upper pump spring
15. Metering rod arm
16. Diaphragm lifter link
17. Washer
18. Diaphragm spring
19. Diaphragm housing screw ④
20. Diaphragm housing
21. Washer
22. Spacer
23. Diaphragm
24. Discharge ball weight
25. Discharge ball
26. Body flange screw ③
27. Fast idle cam
28. Fast idle cam screw
29. Main body
30. Body gasket
31. Idle screw limiter cap
32. Idle mixture screw
33. Spring
34. Throttle body
35. Wave washer

36. Arm	46. Needle pin	56. Gasket
37. Screw	47. Needle spring	57. Spring
38. Pump connector link	48. Needle, needle seat, gasket	58. Lifter
39. Throttle shaft arm	49. Choke connector rod	59. Bellcrank
40. Retainer	50. Choke connector rod retainer	60. Retainer
41. Lever	51. Lever	61. Spring
42. Metering rod jet	52. Metering rod	62. Air horn screw (short)
43. Low speed jet	53. Air horn gasket	63. Air horn screw (long)
44. Float	54. Screw ②	64. Stud support
45. Float pin	55. Chamber	65. Screw

Carter YF with altitude compensator

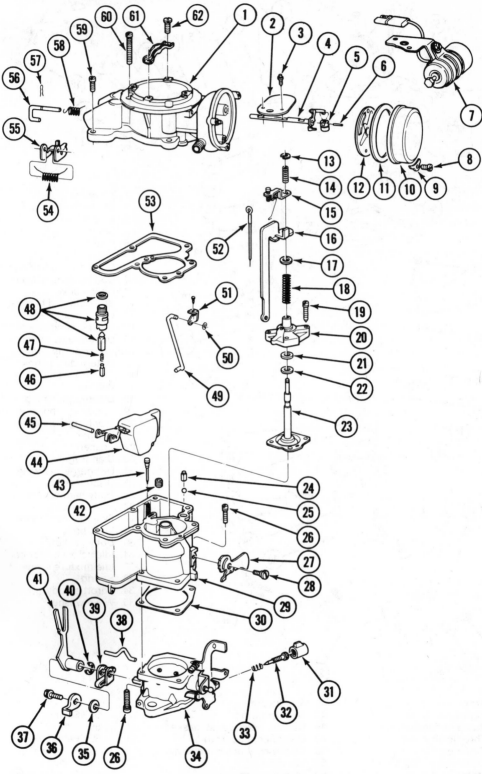

Carter YF without altitude compensator

the supporting link. The eyelet of the rod should slide freely on the pin of the metering rod arm.

4. On models not equipped with an adjusting screw, adjust by bending the metering rod pin tab.

5. On models with an adjusting screw, turn the screw until the metering rod just bottoms in the body casting. For final adjustment, turn the screw one additional turn clockwise.

Fast Idle Cam Adjustment

1. Open the throttle wide enough to allow full closing of the choke valve. Be sure that the fast idle screw is not contacting the fast idle cam.

2. Close the throttle valve and the fast idle cam should revolve to the fast idle position.

3. If adjustment is necessary, bend the choke rod at its upper angle.

4. Position the fast idle screw on the second step of the fast idle cam and against the shoulder of the high step. Measure the specified clearance between the lower edge of the choke plate and the air horn wall. Bend the choke rod to adjust.

5. Fast idle speed may be checked with the engine warmed up. Speed adjustment is made by bending the choke rod at the lower angle. The speed is given with the adjusting screw on the second step and against the highest step. Adjustment is made with the adjusting screw.

NOTE: *EGR hoses must be blocked off and TCS solenoid vacuum valve wires must be disconnected to do this.*

Choke Unloader Adjustment

1. With the throttle valve held wide open and the choke valve held in the closed position, bend the unloader lug on the choke trip lever to obtain the specified clearance between the lower edge of the choke valve and the air horn wall.

Automatic Choke Adjustment

1. Loosen the choke cover retaining screws.

2. Turn the choke over so that the index mark on the cover lines up with the specified mark on the choke housing. Never set it more than two graduations in either direction of the specified setting.

Electrically-Assisted Choke

Starting with the 1976 models, some single-barrel Carter YF carburetors use an electrically-assisted choke to reduce hydrocarbon and carbon monoxide exhaust emissions during warm-up.

Once underhood temperatures reach 95°F (±15°F), a bimetallic switch located in the choke cap closes, allowing a ceramic heating element to draw power from a special tap on the alternator.

This causes the choke valve to open faster than normal, thus reducing CO emission during engine warm-up.

After the engine is shut off, the bimetallic switch remains closed until underhood temperature drops below 65°F. Thus, if the engine is turned off for only a short time or if the ambient temperature is above 65°F, the

1. Air horn	22. Spacer	43. Low speed jet
2. Choke	23. Diaphragm	44. Float
3. Screw	24. Discharge ball weight	45. Float pin
4. Shaft	25. Discharge ball	46. Needle pin
5. Piston	26. Body flange screw ③	47. Needle spring
6. Pin	27. Fast idle cam	48. Needle, needle seat, gasket
7. Solenoid and bracket	28. Fast idle cam screw	49. Choke connector rod
8. Coil housing screw	29. Main body	50. Choke connector rod retainer
9. Coil housing retainer	30. Body gasket	51. Lever
10. Choke cover	31. Idle screw limiter cap	52. Metering rod
11. Coil housing gasket	32. Idle mixture screw	53. Air horn gasket
12. Coil housing baffle plate	33. Spring	54. Spring
13. Upper pump spring retainer	34. Throttle body	55. Lifter
14. Upper pump spring	35. Wave washer	56. Bellcrank
15. Metering rod arm	36. Arm	57. Retainer
16. Diaphragm lifter link	37. Screw	58. Spring
17. Washer	38. Pump connector link	59. Air horn screw (short)
18. Diaphragm spring	39. Throttle shaft arm	60. Air horn screw (long)
19. Diaphragm housing screw ④	40. Retainer	61. Stud support
20. Diaphragm housing	41. Lever	62. Screw
21. Washer	42. Metering rod jet	

choke will function for only a limited period of time.

TESTING

1. Detach the electrical lead from the choke cap.

2. Use a jumper lead to connect the terminal on the choke cap and the wire terminal, so that the electrical circuit is still completed.

3. Start the engine.

4. Hook up a test light between the connector on the choke lead and ground.

5. The test light should glow. If it does not, current is not being supplied to the electrically-assisted choke.

6. Connect the test light between the terminal on the alternator and the terminal on the choke cap. If the light now glows, replace the lead, since it is not passing current to the choke assist.

CAUTION: *Do not ground the terminal on the alternator while performing Step 6.*

7. If the light still does not glow, the fault lies somewhere in the electrical system. Check the system out.

If the electrically-assisted choke receives power, but still does not appear to be functioning properly, reconnect the choke lead and proceed with the rest of the test.

8. Tape the bulb end of a thermometer to the metallic portion of the choke housing.

9. If the electrically-assisted choke operates below 55°F, it is defective and must be replaced.

10. Allow the engine to warm-up to between 80 and 110°F; at these temperatures the choke should operate for about 1½ minutes.

11. If it does not operate for this length of time, check the bimetallic spring to see if it is connected to the tang on the choke lever.

12. If the spring is connected and the choke is not operating properly, replace the cap assembly.

REMOVAL AND INSTALLATION

1. Unfasten the electrical lead from the choke cover.

2. Remove the choke cover retaining screws and clamp.

3. Remove the choke cover and gasket from the carburetor.

Installation is performed in the reverse order of removal. Adjust the choke cover.

CARTER BBD 2-BBL

Float Adjustment

1. Remove the carburetor air horn.

2. Gently hold the lip of the float against its needle to raise the float.

3. Measure float level by placing a straightedge across the float bowl. Float level should be maintained at 0.250 in., plus or minus 0.032 in. Release the floats.

4. If necessary, adjust by bending the float lip as required.

NOTE: *Do not bend float lip while it is resting against the needle as this may deform the synthetic needle tip and cause a false setting.*

5. Install the air horn.

Fast Idle Adjustment

NOTE: *Perform this adjustment with the carburetor installed on the engine. If the car is equipped with a transmission con-*

1. Diaphragm connector link	22. Idle fuel pick-up tube	42. Screw
2. Screw	23. Gasket	43. Throttle body
3. Choke vacuum diaphragm	24. Venturi cluster	44. Choke housing
4. Hose	25. Gasket	45. Baffle
5. Valve	26. Check ball (small)	46. Gasket
6. Metering rod	27. Float	47. Retainer
7. S-link	28. Fulcrum pin	48. Choke coil
8. Pump arm	29. Baffle	49. Lever
9. Gasket	30. Clip	50. Choke rod
10. Rollover check valve	31. Choke link	51. Clip
11. Screw	32. Screw	52. Needle and seat assembly
12. Lock	33. Fast idle cam	53. Main body
13. Rod lifter	34. Gasket	54. Main metering jet
14. Bracket	35. Thermostatic choke shaft	55. Check ball (large)
15. Nut	36. Spring	56. Accelerator pump plunger
16. Solenoid	37. Screw	57. Fulcrum pin retainer
17. Screw	38. Pump link	58. Gasket
18. Air horn retaining screw (short)	39. Clip	59. Spring
19. Air horn retaining screw (long)	40. Gasket	60. Air horn
20. Pump lever	41. Limiter cap	61. Lever
21. Venturi cluster screw		

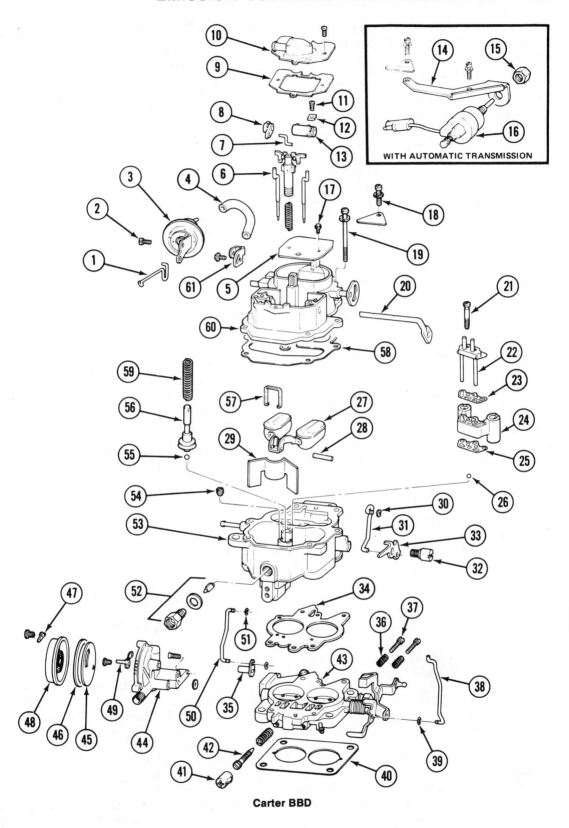

WITH AUTOMATIC TRANSMISSION

Carter BBD

trolled spark (TCS) system and/or an exhaust gas recirculation (EGR) system, be sure that both are disconnected before attempting to set fast idle speed.

1. Start the engine and allow it to reach normal operating temperature.

2. Connect a tachometer to the engine.

3. Set the fast idle adjusting screw so that it contacts the second step of the fast idle cam and rests against the shoulder of the high step.

4. Rotate the fast idle adjusting screw until a fast idle speed of 1,700 rpm is obtained.

5. Remove the tach and return the engine to normal idle speed after the adjustment is completed.

Automatic Choke Adjustment

NOTE: *This adjustment may be made with the carburetor either on or off the engine.*

1. Loosen the choke cover retaining screws.

2. Rotate the choke cover in the direction of its arrow to the setting specified in the chart below.

3. Tighten the retaining screws.

4. If the car stumbles or stalls at the specified choke setting during engine warm-up, adjust the setting to (richer or leaner) until the car runs properly.

NOTE: *Never set the choke more than two notches in either direction of the recommended setting.*

Choke Unloader Adjustment

1. Hold the throttle in the wide open position and apply pressure on the choke plate toward the closed position.

2. Measure the distance between the lower edge of the choke plate and the air horn wall (see the "Carburetor Specifications" chart).

3. If necessary, adjust by bending the unloader tang where it contacts the fast idle cam. Bend toward the cam to increase clearance, and away from the cam to decrease clearance.

NOTE: *Do not bend the unloader tang down from the horizontal plane. After adjusting, make sure that the unloader tang maintains at least a 0.070 in. clearance from the flange of the main body at wide open throttle position.*

4. Operate the throttle and make sure that the unloader does not bind against the carburetor or linkage. Also make sure that wide open throttle can be reached by fully depressing the gas pedal. If not, remove excess padding from beneath the floormat or reposition the throttle cable bracket.

Initial Choke Valve Adjustment

1. Remove the choke cover.

2. Using a vacuum source which holds a minimum of 19 in. Hg, pull the diaphragm in against its stop.

3. Open the throttle valve slightly so that the fast idle screw locates on the high step of the cam.

4. Hold the choke bimetallic coil tang in the closed position and measure the clearance between the choke plate and the air horn wall. The distance should be 0.128 in., plus or minus 0.010 in.

5. Adjust as necessary by bending the "S"-shaped section of the diaphragm connector link.

Vacuum Step-Up Piston Gap Adjustment

1. Remove the step-up piston cover plate and gasket from the carburetor air horn.

2. Adjust the gap in the step-up piston to 0.040 in., plus or minus 0.015 in. using the allen head screw on top of the piston. Turning the screw clockwise richens the fuel mixture and turning counterclockwise leans it out.

3. Back off the curb idle adjustment until the throttle valves are fully closed, then rotate the idle screw inward one complete turn. Make a note of the number of turns so that the idle screw can be returned to its original position.

4. While keeping moderate pressure on the rod lifter tab, fully depress the step-up piston and tighten the rod lifter lockscrew.

5. Release the piston and rod lifter, and return the curb idle screw to its original position.

6. Install the step-up piston cover plate and gasket.

Accelerator Pump Adjustment

1. Back off the curb idle screw until the throttle valves (plates) are completely closed. Then, open the choke valve (plate) so that the fast idle cam permits the throttle valves to seat in their bores. Make sure that the accelerator pump "S" link is located in the outer hole of the pump arm.

2. Turn the curb idle screw clockwise until it just contacts its stop, and then continue to rotate two complete turns.

3. Measure the distance between the surface of the air horn and the top of the accel-

erator pump shaft. This distance should be 0.500 in.

4. Adjust the pump travel as necessary, by loosening the pump arm adjusting lockscrew and rotating the sleeve until the proper measurement is obtained. Then, tighten the lockscrew.

AUTOLITE/MOTORCRAFT 2100 AND 2150

The Model 2100 2150 two-barrel carburetors have an air horn assembly that covers the main body and houses the choke plate and the internal fuel bowl vents. The throttle plate, accelerator pump assembly, power valve assembly, and fuel bowl are contained in the main body. The automatic choke is also attached to the main body. Each bore contains a main and booster venturi, a main fuel discharge, an accelerating pump discharge, an idle fuel discharge, and a throttle plate. They are used on V8 engines.

Float Level (Dry)

The dry float level measurement is a preliminary check and must be followed by a wet float level measurement with the carburetor mounted on the engine.

1. With the air horn removed and the fuel inlet needle seated lightly, gently raise the float and measure the distance between the main body gasket surface (gasket removed) and the top of the float.

2. If necessary, bend the float tab to obtain the correct level.

Float Level (Wet)

1. Remove the screws that hold the air horn to the main body and break the seal between the air horn and main body. Leave the air horn and gasket loosely in place on top of the main body.

2. Start the engine and allow it to idle for at least 3 minutes.

3. After the engine has idled long enough to stabilize the fuel level, remove the air horn assembly.

4. With the engine idling, use a T-scale to measure the distance from the top of the fuel bowl machined surface to the surface of the fuel. The scale must be held at least ¼ in. away from any vertical surface to ensure proper measurement.

5. If any adjustment is required, stop the engine to avoid a fire from fuel spraying on the engine.

6. Bend the float tab upward to raise the level and downward to lower the level.

CAUTION: *Be sure to hold the fuel inlet needle off its seat when bending the float tab so as not to damage the Viton® tip.*

7. Each time the float level is changed, the air horn must be temporarily positioned and the engine started to stabilize the fuel level before again checking it.

Initial Choke Valve Clearance Adjustment

1. Loosen the choke cover screws. Rotate the cover ¼ turn counterclockwise.

2. Disconnect the choke heat inlet tube. Align the fast idle speed adjusting screw with the indexed (second) step of the fast idle cam.

3. Start the engine without moving the accelerator linkage.

4. Turn the fast idle cam lever adjusting screw out 3 full turns. Measure the clearance between the lower edge of the choke valve and the air horn wall.

5. Adjust by grasping the modulator arm with a pair of pliers and twisting with a second pair of pliers. Twist to the front to increase the clearance and toward the rear to decrease the clearance.

CAUTION: *Be very careful not to damage the nylon piston rod of the modulator assembly.*

6. Stop the engine and connect the heat tube. Turn the fast idle cam lever in 3 full turns.

7. Don't reset the choke cover until the fast idle cam linkage adjustment is done.

Fast Idle Cam

1. Push down on the fast idle cam lever until the fast idle screw is in contact with the second step of the fast idle cam and against the shoulder of the high step.

2. The specified clearance should be present between the lower edge of the choke valve and the air horn wall.

3. The adjustment is made by turning the fast idle cam lever screw.

4. The choke cover may now be adjusted.

Choke Unloader (Dechoke)

1. With the throttle held completely open, move the choke valve to the closed position.

2. Measure the distance between the lower edge of the choke valve and the air horn wall.

3. Adjust by bending the gang on the fast idle speed lever which is located on the throttle shaft.

NOTE: *Final unloader adjustment must be*

performed on the car and the throttle should be opened by using the accelerator pedal of the car. This is to be sure that full throttle operation is achieved.

Accelerator Pump

The accelerator pump operating rod must be positioned in the proper holes of the accelerator pump lever and the throttle over-travel lever to assure correct pump travel. If adjusting is required, additional holes are provided in the throttle over-travel lever.

Fast Idle

Adjust the fast idle setting with the engine at operating temperature. The fast idle screw should be resting against the second step of the fast idle cam. Adjust by turning the fast idle screw.

AUTOLITE/MOTORCRAFT 4300 AND 4350 4-BBL

The model 4300/4350 4-barrel carburetor is composed of three main assemblies: the air

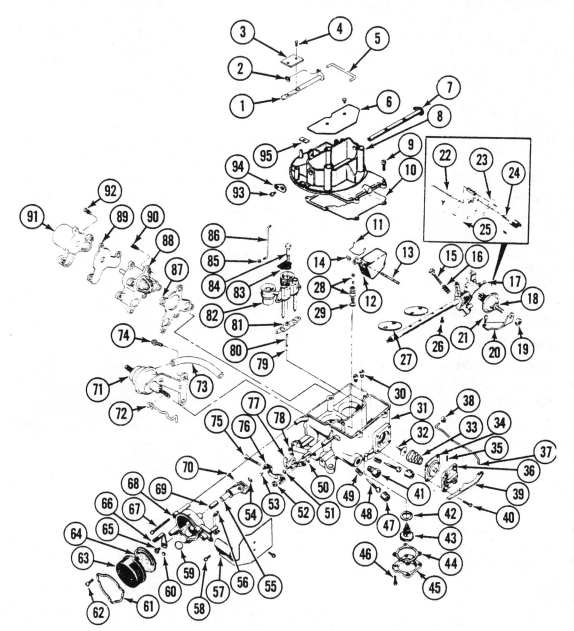

Motorcraft 2150

horn, the main body, and the throttle body. The air horn assembly serves as the fuel bowl cover as well as the housing for the choke valve and shaft. It contains the accelerator pump linkage, fuel inlet seat, float and lever, booster venturi, and internal fuel bowl vents.

The main body houses the fuel metering passages, accelerator pump mechanism, and the power valve.

The throttle body contains the primary and secondary throttle valves and shafts, the curb idle adjusting screw, the fast idle adjusting screw, the idle mixture adjusting screws, and

the automatic choke assembly. It is used on V8 engines.

Float Adjustment, 4300

1. Adjustments to the fuel level are best made with the carburetor removed from the engine and the carburetor cleaned upon disassembly.

2. Invert the air horn assembly and remove the gasket from the surface.

3. Use a T-scale to measure the distance from the floats to the air horn casting. Position the scale horizontally over the flat sur-

1. Compensator choke shaft
2. Retainer
3. Compensator choke valve
4. Choke valve screw
5. Compensator choke rod
6. Choke valve
7. Choke shaft
8. Air horn
9. Air horn retaining screw ④
10. Air horn gasket
11. Float shaft retainer
12. Float and lever assembly
13. Float shaft
14. Needle retaining clip
15. Curb idle adjusting screw
16. Curb idle adjusting screw spring
17. Throttle shaft and lever assembly
18. Dashpot
19. Dashpot locknut
20. Dashpot bracket
21. Dashpot bracket
    retaining screw
22. Adjusting screw
23. Carriage
24. Electric solenoid
25. Mounting bracket
26. Throttle valve
    retaining screw ④
27. Throttle valve ②
28. Needle and seat assembly
29. Needle seat gasket
30. Main jet ②
31. Main body
32. Elastomer valve
33. Pump return spring
34. Pump diaphragm
35. Pump lever pin
36. Pump cover
37. Pump rod
38. Pump rod retainer
39. Pump lever
40. Pump cover retaining screw ④
41. Fuel inlet fitting
42. Power valve gasket
43. Power valve
44. Power valve cover gasket
45. Power valve cover
46. Power valve cover
    retaining screw ④
47. Idle limiter cap ②
48. Idle mixture
    screw ②

49. Idle mixture
    screw spring ②
50. Retainer
51. Retainer
52. Fast idle lever
    retaining nut
53. Fast idle lever pin
54. Retainer
55. Thermostatic
    choke shaft
56. Fast idle cam rod
57. Choke shield
58. Choke shield retaining screw ②
59. Piston passage plug
60. Heat passage plut
61. Choke cover retaining clamp
62. Choke cover retaining screw ③
63. Choke cover
64. Choke cover gasket
65. Thermostat lever retaining screw
66. Thermostat lever
67. Choke housing retaining screw ③
68. Choke housing
69. Choke shaft bushing
70. Fast idle cam lever adjusting screw
71. Choke diaphragm
72. Hose
73. Link
74. Screw
75. Fast idle speed adjusting screw
76. Fast idle lever
77. Fast idle cam
78. Choke housing gasket
79. Pump discharge check ball
80. Pump discharge weight
81. Booster venturi gasket
82. Booster venturi assembly
83. Air distribution plate
84. Pump discharge screw
85. Retainer
86. Choke rod
87. Gasket
88. Compensation chamber
89. Gasket
90. Screw
91. Aneroid
92. Screw
93. Choke lever retaining screw
94. Choke plate lever
95. Choke rod seal

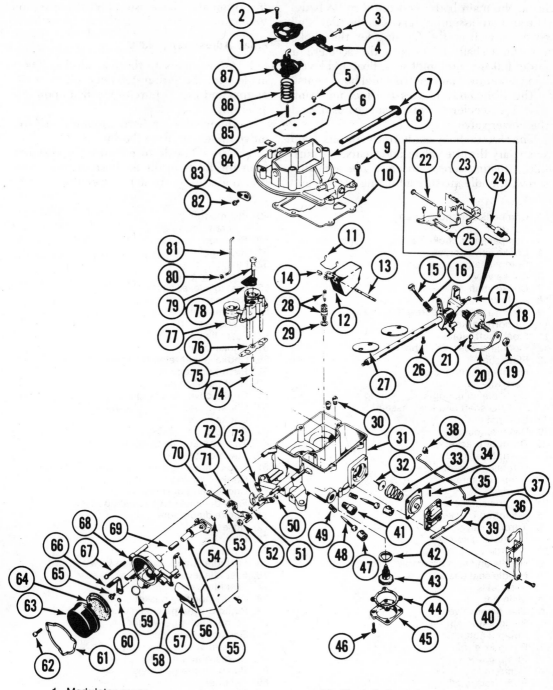

1. Modulator cover
2. Modulator retaining screw ③
3. Pivot pin
4. Modulator arm
5. Choke valve retaining screw ②
6. Choke valve
7. Choke shaft
8. Air horn
9. Air horn retaining screw ④
10. Air horn gasket
11. Float and lever assembly

12. Float shaft retainer
13. Float shaft
14. Needle retaining clip
15. Curb idle adjusting screw
16. Curb idle adjusting screw spring
17. Throttle shaft and lever assembly
18. Dashpot
19. Dashpot locknut
20. Dashpot bracket
21. Dashpot bracket retaining screw
22. Adjusting screw

Motorcraft 2100

face of both floats at the free ends and parallel to the air horn casting. Hold the lower end of the vertical scale in full contact with the smooth surface of the air horn.

CAUTION: *The end of the vertical scale must not come into contact with any gasket sealing ridges while measuring the float level.*

4. The free end of each float should just touch the horizontal scale, if one float is lower than the other; twist the float and lever assembly slightly to correct.

5. Adjust the float level by bending the tab which contacts the needle and seat assembly.

Float Adjustment, 4350

1. Invert the air horn assembly and remove the gasket.

2. Measure the distance from the floats to the air horn rim using a T-scale. Position the horizontal scale over the flat surface of both floats at the free ends, parallel to the air horn casting. Hold the lower end of the vertical scale in full contact with the smooth area of the casting, midway between the main discharge nozzles.

CAUTION: *Do not allow the end of the vertical scale to contact any gasket sealing ridge while measuring the float setting.*

3. The free end of the floats should just touch the horizontal scale. Float-to-air horn casting distance should be $29/64$ inch. Bend the vertical tab on the float arm to adjust the distance.

Initial Choke Valve Clearance Adjustment

1. Remove the choke thermostatic spring housing.

2. Bend a wire gauge (0.035 in. diameter) at a 90 degree angle about 1/8 in. from one end.

3. Block the throttle open so that the fast idle screw does not contact the fast idle cam.

4. Insert the bend end of the wire gauge between the lower edge of the piston slot and the upper edge of the righthand slot in the choke housing.

5. Pull the choke piston lever counterclockwise until the gauge is snug in the piston slot. Hold the wire in place by exerting light pressure in a rearward direction on the choke piston lever. Check the distance from the lower edge of the choke valve to the air horn wall.

6. Adjustment is done by loosening the hex head screw (left-hand thread) on the choke valve shaft and rotating the choke shaft.

23. Carriage
24. Electric solenoid
25. Mounting bracket
26. Throttle valve retaining screw ④
27. Throttle valve ②
28. Needle and seat assembly
29. Needle seat gasket
30. Main jet ②
31. Main body
32. Elastomer valve
33. Pump return spring
34. Pump diaphragm
35. Pump lever pin
36. Pump cover
37. Pump rod
38. Pump rod retainer
39. Pump lever
40. Bowl vent bellcrank
41. Fuel inlet fitting
42. Power valve gasket
43. Power valve
44. Power valve cover gasket
45. Power valve cover
46. Power valve cover retaining screw ④
47. Idle limiter cap ②
48. Idle mixture screw ②
49. Idle mixture screw spring ②
50. Retainer
51. Retainer
52. Fast idle lever retaining nut
53. Fast idle lever pin
54. Retainer

55. Lever and shaft
56. Fast idle cam rod
57. Choke shield
58. Choke shield retaining screw ②
59. Piston passage plug
60. Heat passage plug
61. Choke cover retaining clamp
62. Choke cover retaining screw ③
63. Choke cover
64. Choke cover gasket
65. Thermostat lever retaining screw
66. Thermostat lever
67. Choke housing retaining screw ③
68. Choke housing
69. Choke shaft bushing
70. Fast idle speed adjusting screw
71. Fast idle lever
72. Fast idle cam
73. Choke housing gasket
74. Pump discharge check ball
75. Pump discharge weight
76. Booster venturi gasket
77. Booster venturi assembly
78. Air distribution plate
79. Pump discharge screw
80. Retainer
81. Choke rod
82. Choke lever retaining screw
83. Choke plate lever
84. Choke rod seal
85. Stop screw
86. Modulator return spring
87. Modulator diaphragm assembly

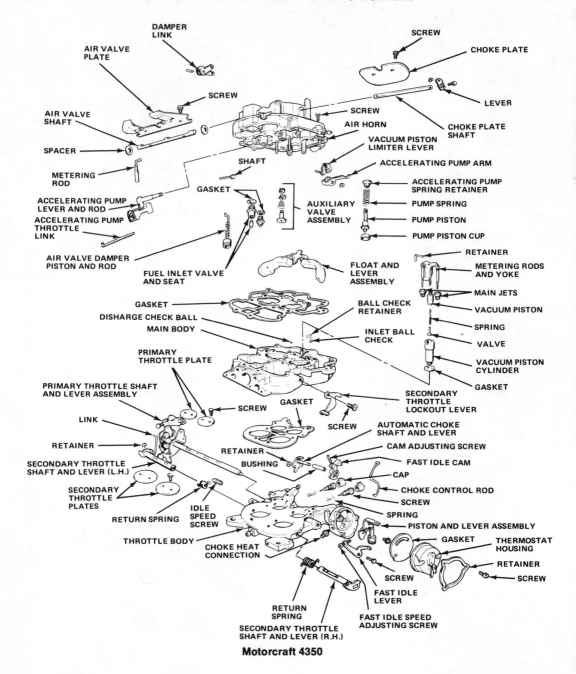

DAMPER LINK
AIR VALVE PLATE
SCREW
CHOKE PLATE
SCREW
LEVER
AIR VALVE SHAFT
AIR HORN
CHOKE PLATE SHAFT
SPACER
VACUUM PISTON LIMITER LEVER
METERING ROD
SHAFT
ACCELERATING PUMP ARM
GASKET
ACCELERATING PUMP SPRING RETAINER
ACCELERATING PUMP LEVER AND ROD
AUXILIARY VALVE ASSEMBLY
PUMP SPRING
ACCELERATING PUMP THROTTLE LINK
PUMP PISTON
PUMP PISTON CUP
AIR VALVE DAMPER PISTON AND ROD
RETAINER
FUEL INLET VALVE AND SEAT
FLOAT AND LEVER ASSEMBLY
METERING RODS AND YOKE
GASKET
MAIN JETS
DISHARGE CHECK BALL
BALL CHECK RETAINER
VACUUM PISTON
MAIN BODY
SPRING
INLET BALL CHECK
VALVE
PRIMARY THROTTLE PLATE
VACUUM PISTON CYLINDER
PRIMARY THROTTLE SHAFT AND LEVER ASSEMBLY
GASKET
SECONDARY THROTTLE LOCKOUT LEVER
LINK
SCREW
GASKET
SCREW
AUTOMATIC CHOKE SHAFT AND LEVER
RETAINER
RETAINER
CAM ADJUSTING SCREW
SECONDARY THROTTLE SHAFT AND LEVER (L.H.)
BUSHING
FAST IDLE CAM
CAP
SECONDARY THROTTLE PLATES
CHOKE CONTROL ROD
IDLE SPEED SCREW
SCREW
RETURN SPRING
SPRING
PISTON AND LEVER ASSEMBLY
THROTTLE BODY
GASKET
THERMOSTAT HOUSING
CHOKE HEAT CONNECTION
RETAINER
SCREW
SCREW
RETURN SPRING
FAST IDLE LEVER
FAST IDLE SPEED ADJUSTING SCREW
SECONDARY THROTTLE SHAFT AND LEVER (R.H.)

Motorcraft 4350

Fast Idle Cam Adjustment, 4300

1. Loosen the screws on the choke thermostatic spring cover and rotate the housing ¼ turn counterclockwise. Tighten the screws.

2. Open the throttle and allow the choke valve to close completely.

3. Push down on the fast idle cam counterweight until the fast idle screw is in contact with the second step of the cam and against the high step.

4. Measure the clearance between the lower edge of the choke valve and the air horn wall.

5. Adjust by turning the fast idle cam adjusting screw.

6. Return the housing to its original position.

Fast Idle Cam Adjustment, 4350

1. Run the engine to normal operating temperature. Connect an accurate tachometer to the engine.

CHILTON'S
FUEL ECONOMY
& TUNE-UP TIPS

55 WAYS TO IMPROVE FUEL ECONOMY

Tune-up • Spark Plug Diagnosis • Emission Controls

Fuel System • Cooling System • Tires and Wheels

General Maintenance

CHILTON'S FUEL ECONOMY & TUNE-UP TIPS

Fuel economy is important to everyone, no matter what kind of vehicle you drive. The maintenance-minded motorist can save both money and fuel using these tips and the periodic maintenance and tune-up procedures in this Repair and Tune-Up Guide.

There are more than 130,000,000 cars and trucks registered for private use in the United States. Each travels an average of 10-12,000 miles per year, and, and in total they consume close to 70 billion gallons of fuel each year. This represents nearly ⅔ of the oil imported by the United States each year. The Federal government's goal is to reduce consumption 10% by 1985. A variety of methods are either already in use or under serious consideration, and they all affect you driving and the cars you will drive. In addition to "down-sizing", the auto industry is using or investigating the use of electronic fuel delivery, electronic engine controls and alternative engines for use in smaller and lighter vehicles, among other alternatives to meet the federally mandated Corporate Average Fuel Economy (CAFE) of 27.5 mpg by 1985. The government, for its part, is considering rationing, mandatory driving curtailments and tax increases on motor vehicle fuel in an effort to reduce consumption. The government's goal of a 10% reduction could be realized — and further government regulation avoided — if every private vehicle could use just 1 less gallon of fuel per week.

How Much Can You Save?

Tests have proven that almost anyone can make at least a 10% reduction in fuel consumption through regular maintenance and tune-ups. When a major manufacturer of spark plugs sur-

TUNE-UP

1. Check the cylinder compression to be sure the engine will really benefit from a tune-up and that it is capable of producing good fuel economy. A tune-up will be wasted on an engine in poor mechanical condition.

2. Replace spark plugs regularly. New spark plugs alone can increase fuel economy 3%.

3. Be sure the spark plugs are the correct type (heat range) for your vehicle. See the Tune-Up Specifications.

Heat range refers to the spark plug's ability to conduct heat away from the firing end. It must conduct the heat away in an even pattern to avoid becoming a source of pre-ignition, yet it must also operate hot enough to burn off conductive deposits that could cause misfiring.

The heat range is usually indicated by a number on the spark plug, part of the manufacturer's designation for each individual spark plug. The numbers in bold-face indicate the heat range in each manufacturer's identification system.

Manufacturer	Typical Designation
AC	R **45** TS
Bosch (old)	WA **145** T30
Bosch (new)	HR **8** Y
Champion	RBL **15** Y
Fram/Autolite	**415**
Mopar	P-**62** PR
Motorcraft	BRF-**42**
NGK	BP **5** ES-15
Nippondenso	W **16** EP
Prestolite	14GR **5** 2A

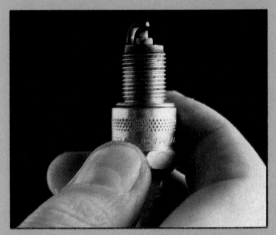

Periodically, check the spark plugs to be sure they are firing efficiently. They are excellent indicators of the internal condition of your engine.

On AC, Bosch (new), Champion, Fram/Autolite, Mopar, Motorcraft and Prestolite, a higher number indicates a hotter plug. On Bosch (old), NGK and Nippondenso, a higher number indicates a colder plug.

4. Make sure the spark plugs are properly gapped. See the Tune-Up Specifications in this book.

5. Be sure the spark plugs are firing efficiently. The illustrations on the next 2 pages show you how to "read" the firing end of the spark plug.

6. Check the ignition timing and set it to specifications. Tests show that almost all cars have incorrect ignition timing by more than 2°.

veyed over 6,000 cars nationwide, they found that a tune-up, on cars that needed one, increased fuel economy over 11%. Replacing worn plugs alone, accounted for a 3% increase. The same test also revealed that 8 out of every 10 vehicles will have some maintenance deficiency that will directly affect fuel economy, emissions or performance. Most of this mileage-robbing neglect could be prevented with regular maintenance.

Modern engines require that all of the functioning systems operate properly for maximum efficiency. A malfunction anywhere wastes fuel. You can keep your vehicle running as efficiently and economically as possible, by being aware of your vehicle's operating and performance characteristics. If your vehicle suddenly develops performance or fuel economy problems it could be due to one or more of the following:

PROBLEM	POSSIBLE CAUSE
Engine Idles Rough	Ignition timing, idle mixture, vacuum leak or something amiss in the emission control system.
Hesitates on Acceleration	Dirty carburetor or fuel filter, improper accelerator pump setting, ignition timing or fouled spark plugs.
Starts Hard or Fails to Start	Worn spark plugs, improperly set automatic choke, ice (or water) in fuel system.
Stalls Frequently	Automatic choke improperly adjusted and possible dirty air filter or fuel filter.
Performs Sluggishly	Worn spark plugs, dirty fuel or air filter, ignition timing or automatic choke out of adjustment.

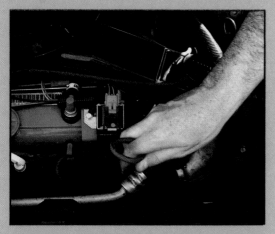

Check spark plug wires on conventional point type ignition for cracks by bending them in a loop around your finger.

Be sure that spark plug wires leading to adjacent cylinders do not run too close together. (Photo courtesy Champion Spark Plug Co.)

7. If your vehicle does not have electronic ignition, check the points, rotor and cap as specified.

8. Check the spark plug wires (used with conventional point-type ignitions) for cracks and burned or broken insulation by bending them in a loop around your finger. Cracked wires decrease fuel efficiency by failing to deliver full voltage to the spark plugs. One misfiring spark plug can cost you as much as 2 mpg.

9. Check the routing of the plug wires. Misfiring can be the result of spark plug leads to adjacent cylinders running parallel to each other and too close together. One wire tends to pick up voltage from the other causing it to fire "out of time".

10. Check all electrical and ignition circuits for voltage drop and resistance.

11. Check the distributor mechanical and/or vacuum advance mechanisms for proper functioning. The vacuum advance can be checked by twisting the distributor plate in the opposite direction of rotation. It should spring back when released.

12. Check and adjust the valve clearance on engines with mechanical lifters. The clearance should be slightly loose rather than too tight.

SPARK PLUG DIAGNOSIS

Normal

APPEARANCE: This plug is typical of one operating normally. The insulator nose varies from a light tan to grayish color with slight electrode wear. The presence of slight deposits is normal on used plugs and will have no adverse effect on engine performance. The spark plug heat range is correct for the engine and the engine is running normally.

CAUSE: Properly running engine.

RECOMMENDATION: Before reinstalling this plug, the electrodes should be cleaned and filed square. Set the gap to specifications. If the plug has been in service for more than 10-12,000 miles, the entire set should probably be replaced with a fresh set of the same heat range.

Oil Deposits

APPEARANCE: The firing end of the plug is covered with a wet, oily coating.

CAUSE: The problem is poor oil control. On high mileage engines, oil is leaking past the rings or valve guides into the combustion chamber. A common cause is also a plugged PCV valve, and a ruptured fuel pump diaphragm can also cause this condition. Oil fouled plugs such as these are often found in new or recently overhauled engines, before normal oil control is achieved, and can be cleaned and reinstalled.

RECOMMENDATION: A hotter spark plug may temporarily relieve the problem, but the engine is probably in need of work.

Incorrect Heat Range

APPEARANCE: The effects of high temperature on a spark plug are indicated by clean white, often blistered insulator. This can also be accompanied by excessive wear of the electrode, and the absence of deposits.

CAUSE: Check for the correct spark plug heat range. A plug which is too hot for the engine can result in overheating. A car operated mostly at high speeds can require a colder plug. Also check ignition timing, cooling system level, fuel mixture and leaking intake manifold.

RECOMMENDATION: If all ignition and engine adjustments are known to be correct, and no other malfunction exists, install spark plugs one heat range colder.

Photos Courtesy Fram Corporation

Carbon Deposits

APPEARANCE: Carbon fouling is easily identified by the presence of dry, soft, black, sooty deposits.

CAUSE: Changing the heat range can often lead to carbon fouling, as can prolonged slow, stop-and-start driving. If the heat range is correct, carbon fouling can be attributed to a rich fuel mixture, sticking choke, clogged air cleaner, worn breaker points, retarded timing or low compression. If only one or two plugs are carbon fouled, check for corroded or cracked wires on the affected plugs. Also look for cracks in the distributor cap between the towers of affected cylinders.

RECOMMENDATION: After the problem is corrected, these plugs can be cleaned and reinstalled if not worn severely.

MMT Fouled

APPEARANCE: Spark plugs fouled by MMT (Methycyclopentadienyl Maganese Tricarbonyl) have reddish, rusty appearance on the insulator and side electrode.

CAUSE: MMT is an anti-knock additive in gasoline used to replace lead. During the combustion process, the MMT leaves a reddish deposit on the insulator and side electrode.

RECOMMENDATION: No engine malfunction is indicated and the deposits will not affect plug performance any more than lead deposits (see Ash Deposits). MMT fouled plugs can be cleaned, regapped and reinstalled.

High Speed Glazing

APPEARANCE: Glazing appears as shiny coating on the plug, either yellow or tan in color.

CAUSE: During hard, fast acceleration, plug temperatures rise suddenly. Deposits from normal combustion have no chance to fluff-off; instead, they melt on the insulator forming an electrically conductive coating which causes misfiring.

RECOMMENDATION: Glazed plugs are not easily cleaned. They should be replaced with a fresh set of plugs of the correct heat range. If the condition recurs, using plugs with a heat range one step colder may cure the problem.

Ash (Lead) Deposits

APPEARANCE: Ash deposits are characterized by light brown or white colored deposits crusted on the side or center electrodes. In some cases it may give the plug a rusty appearance.

CAUSE: Ash deposits are normally derived from oil or fuel additives burned during normal combustion. Normally they are harmless, though excessive amounts can cause misfiring. If deposits are excessive in short mileage, the valve guides may be worn.

RECOMMENDATION: Ash-fouled plugs can be cleaned, gapped and reinstalled.

Detonation

APPEARANCE: Detonation is usually characterized by a broken plug insulator.

CAUSE: A portion of the fuel charge will begin to burn spontaneously, from the increased heat following ignition. The explosion that results applies extreme pressure to engine components, frequently damaging spark plugs and pistons.

Detonation can result by over-advanced ignition timing, inferior gasoline (low octane) lean air/fuel mixture, poor carburetion, engine lugging or an increase in compression ratio due to combustion chamber deposits or engine modification.

RECOMMENDATION: Replace the plugs after correcting the problem.

Photos Courtesy Champion Spark Plug Co.

EMISSION CONTROLS

13. Be aware of the general condition of the emission control system. It contributes to reduced pollution and should be serviced regularly to maintain efficient engine operation.

14. Check all vacuum lines for dried, cracked or brittle conditions. Something as simple as a leaking vacuum hose can cause poor performance and loss of economy.

15. Avoid tampering with the emission control system. Attempting to improve fuel econ-

FUEL SYSTEM

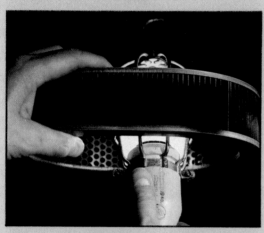

Check the air filter with a light behind it. If you can see light through the filter it can be reused.

Extremely clogged filters should be discarded and replaced with a new one.

18. Replace the air filter regularly. A dirty air filter richens the air/fuel mixture and can increase fuel consumption as much as 10%. Tests show that ⅓ of all vehicles have air filters in need of replacement.

19. Replace the fuel filter at least as often as recommended.

20. Set the idle speed and carburetor mixture to specifications.

21. Check the automatic choke. A sticking or malfunctioning choke wastes gas.

22. During the summer months, adjust the automatic choke for a leaner mixture which will produce faster engine warm-ups.

COOLING SYSTEM

29. Be sure all accessory drive belts are in good condition. Check for cracks or wear.

30. Adjust all accessory drive belts to proper tension.

31. Check all hoses for swollen areas, worn spots, or loose clamps.

32. Check coolant level in the radiator or expansion tank.

33. Be sure the thermostat is operating properly. A stuck thermostat delays engine warm-up and a cold engine uses nearly twice as much fuel as a warm engine.

34. Drain and replace the engine coolant at least as often as recommended. Rust and scale

TIRES & WHEELS

38. Check the tire pressure often with a pencil type gauge. Tests by a major tire manufacturer show that 90% of all vehicles have at least 1 tire improperly inflated. Better mileage can be achieved by over-inflating tires, but never exceed the maximum inflation pressure on the side of the tire.

39. If possible, install radial tires. Radial tires deliver as much as ½ mpg more than bias belted tires.

40. Avoid installing super-wide tires. They only create extra rolling resistance and decrease fuel mileage. Stick to the manufacturer's recommendations.

41. Have the wheels properly balanced.

omy by tampering with emission controls is more likely to worsen fuel economy than improve it. Emission control changes on modern engines are not readily reversible.

16. Clean (or replace) the EGR valve and lines as recommended.

17. Be sure that all vacuum lines and hoses are reconnected properly after working under the hood. An unconnected or misrouted vacuum line can wreak havoc with engine performance.

23. Check for fuel leaks at the carburetor, fuel pump, fuel lines and fuel tank. Be sure all lines and connections are tight.

24. Periodically check the tightness of the carburetor and intake manifold attaching nuts and bolts. These are a common place for vacuum leaks to occur.

25. Clean the carburetor periodically and lubricate the linkage.

26. The condition of the tailpipe can be an excellent indicator of proper engine combustion. After a long drive at highway speeds, the inside of the tailpipe should be a light grey in color. Black or soot on the insides indicates an overly rich mixture.

27. Check the fuel pump pressure. The fuel pump may be supplying more fuel than the engine needs.

28. Use the proper grade of gasoline for your engine. Don't try to compensate for knocking or "pinging" by advancing the ignition timing. This practice will only increase plug temperature and the chances of detonation or pre-ignition with relatively little performance gain.

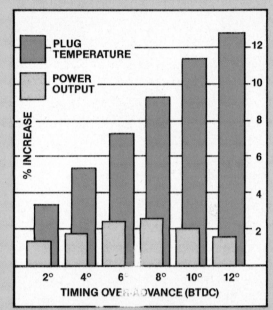

Increasing ignition timing past the specified setting results in a drastic increase in spark plug temperature with increased chance of detonation or preignition. Performance increase is considerably less. (Photo courtesy Champion Spark Plug Co.)

that form in the engine should be flushed out to allow the engine to operate at peak efficiency.

35. Clean the radiator of debris that can decrease cooling efficiency.

36. Install a flex-type or electric cooling fan, if you don't have a clutch type fan. Flex fans use curved plastic blades to push more air at low speeds when more cooling is needed; at high speeds the blades flatten out for less resistance. Electric fans only run when the engine temperature reaches a predetermined level.

37. Check the radiator cap for a worn or cracked gasket. If the cap does not seal properly, the cooling system will not function properly.

42. Be sure the front end is correctly aligned. A misaligned front end actually has wheels going in differed directions. The increased drag can reduce fuel economy by .3 mpg.

43. Correctly adjust the wheel bearings. Wheel bearings that are adjusted too tight increase rolling resistance.

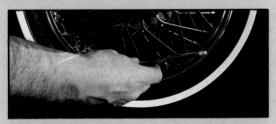

Check tire pressures regularly with a reliable pocket type gauge. Be sure to check the pressure on a cold tire.

GENERAL MAINTENANCE

Check the fluid levels (particularly engine oil) on a regular basis. Be sure to check the oil for grit, water or other contamination.

A vacuum gauge is another excellent indicator of internal engine condition and can also be installed in the dash as a mileage indicator.

44. Periodically check the fluid levels in the engine, power steering pump, master cylinder, automatic transmission and drive axle.

45. Change the oil at the recommended interval and change the filter at every oil change. Dirty oil is thick and causes extra friction between moving parts, cutting efficiency and increasing wear. A worn engine requires more frequent tune-ups and gets progressively worse fuel economy. In general, use the lightest viscosity oil for the driving conditions you will encounter.

46. Use the recommended viscosity fluids in the transmission and axle.

47. Be sure the battery is fully charged for fast starts. A slow starting engine wastes fuel.

48. Be sure battery terminals are clean and tight.

49. Check the battery electrolyte level and add distilled water if necessary.

50. Check the exhaust system for crushed pipes, blockages and leaks.

51. Adjust the brakes. Dragging brakes or brakes that are not releasing create increased drag on the engine.

52. Install a vacuum gauge or miles-per-gallon gauge. These gauges visually indicate engine vacuum in the intake manifold. High vacuum = good mileage and low vacuum = poorer mileage. The gauge can also be an excellent indicator of internal engine conditions.

53. Be sure the clutch is properly adjusted. A slipping clutch wastes fuel.

54. Check and periodically lubricate the heat control valve in the exhaust manifold. A sticking or inoperative valve prevents engine warm-up and wastes gas.

55. Keep accurate records to check fuel economy over a period of time. A sudden drop in fuel economy may signal a need for tune-up or other maintenance.

2. Disconnect and plug the EGR and TCS vacuum lines.

3. Position the fast idle screw against the first step of the fast idle cam. Adjust the fast idle screw to give a reading of 1600 rpm.

4. Return the linkage to its normal position, unplug and reconnect the vacuum lines.

Choke Unloader (Dechoke) Adjustment

1. Open the throttle fully and hold it in this position.

2. Rotate the choke valve toward the closed position.

3. Check the clearance between the lower edge of the choke valve and the air horn wall.

4. Adjust by bending the unloader tang on the fast idle speed lever toward the cam to increase the clearance and away to decrease the clearance.

CAUTION: *Do not bend the unloader tang down from the horizontal. After adjustment, there should be at least 0.070 in. clearance from the choke housing with the throttle fully open.*

Accelerator Pump Stroke Adjustment

The accelerator pump should not need adjustment as its stroke is preset in compliance with exhaust emission control standards. If for any reason the stroke must be altered, it may be done by repositioning the link in the desired holes.

Fast Idle Speed

The fast idle speed is adjusted with the engine at operating temperature and the fast idle screw on the second step of the fast idle cam. Adjust by turning the fast idle screw in or out as required.

NOTE: *To adjust the fast idle speed, you must plug the EGR valve vacuum line and disconnect the TCS solenoid wire.*

Dashpot Adjustment

Some carburetors are equipped with a dashpot to prevent stalling. The dashpot adjustment procedure for these carburetors is as follows:

1. Be sure that the throttle valves are closed tightly and that the diaphragm stem is fully depressed.

2. Measure the clearance between the dashpot stem and the throttle lever with a feeler gauge. For the proper clearance specification, see the chart.

3. If the clearance is not correct, adjust it by loosening the locknut and rotating the dashpot until the proper clearance is obtained. Tighten the locknut.

ROCHESTER E2SE

This carburetor is used on the 4-151 engine.

Float Adjustment

1. Remove the air horn.

2. Hold the float retainer and push down lightly on the float.

3. Using a T-scale, at a point $3/16$ in. from the end of the float, measure the distance from the top surface of the float bowl to the top of the float. The distance should be .208 in. with manual trans., .256 in. with automatic trans., and .208 for all Calif. E2SE models.

4. Bend the float arm as necessary to adjust.

Fast Idle Adjustment

1. Make sure the choke coil adjustment is correct and that the fast idle speed is correct.

2. Obtain a Choke Angle Gauge, tool #J-26701-A. Rotate the degree scale to the zero degree mark opposite the pointer.

3. With the choke valve completely closed, place the magnet on the tool squarely on the choke plate. Rotate the bubble unit until it is centered.

4. Rotate the degree scale until the 25° mark is opposite the pointer. On carburetors with choke cover sticker number 70172, the angle is 18°.

5. Place the fast idle screw on the second step of the cam.

6. Close the choke plate by pushing on the intermediate choke lever.

7. Push the vacuum brake lever toward the open choke position until the lever is against the rear tang on the choke lever.

8. Adjust by bending the fast idle cam rod until the bubble is centered.

Choke Setting Adjustment

NOTE: *Once the rivets and choke cover are removed, a choke cover retainer kit is necessary for assembly.*

1. Remove the rivets, retainers, choke cover and coil following the instructions found in the cover retainer kit.

2. Position the fast idle adjustment screw on the highest step of the fast idle cam.

3. Push on the intermediate choke lever and close the choke plate.

4. Insert the proper plug gauge, .050–.080 in. for manual trans. and .85 in. for automatic trans., in the hole adjacent to the coil lever.

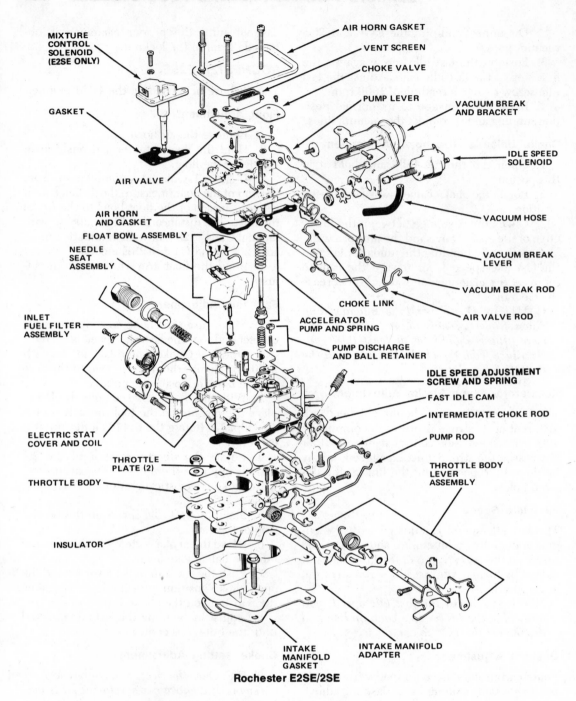

MIXTURE CONTROL SOLENOID (E2SE ONLY)

GASKET

AIR VALVE

AIR HORN AND GASKET

FLOAT BOWL ASSEMBLY

NEEDLE SEAT ASSEMBLY

INLET FUEL FILTER ASSEMBLY

ELECTRIC STAT COVER AND COIL

THROTTLE PLATE (2)

THROTTLE BODY

INSULATOR

AIR HORN GASKET

VENT SCREEN

CHOKE VALVE

PUMP LEVER

VACUUM BREAK AND BRACKET

IDLE SPEED SOLENOID

VACUUM HOSE

VACUUM BREAK LEVER

VACUUM BREAK ROD

AIR VALVE ROD

CHOKE LINK

ACCELERATOR PUMP AND SPRING

PUMP DISCHARGE AND BALL RETAINER

IDLE SPEED ADJUSTMENT SCREW AND SPRING

FAST IDLE CAM

INTERMEDIATE CHOKE ROD

PUMP ROD

THROTTLE BODY LEVER ASSEMBLY

INTAKE MANIFOLD GASKET

INTAKE MANIFOLD ADAPTER

Rochester E2SE/2SE

The edge of the lever should barely contact the plug gauge.

5. Bend the intermediate choke rod to adjust.

Choke Unloader Adjustment

1. Obtain a Carburetor Choke Angle Gauge, tool #J-26701-A. Rotate the scale on the gauge until the 0 mark is opposite the pointer.

2. Close the choke plate completely and set the magnet squarely on top of it.

3. Rotate the bubble until it is centered.

4. Rotate the degree scale until the 32° mark is opposite the pointer. On carburetors with choke cover sticker number 70172 the setting is 19°.

5. Hold the primary throttle valve wide open.

6. Bend the throttle lever tang until the bubble is centered.

HOLLEY 5210-C

This carburetor is used on the 4-121 engine.

Float Level

1. With the carburetor air horn inverted, and the float tang resting lightly on the inlet needle, insert the specified gauge between the air horn and the float.

2. Bend the float tang if an adjustment is needed.

Fast Idle Cam Adjustment

1. Place the fast idle screw on the second step of the fast idle cam and against the shoulder of the high step.

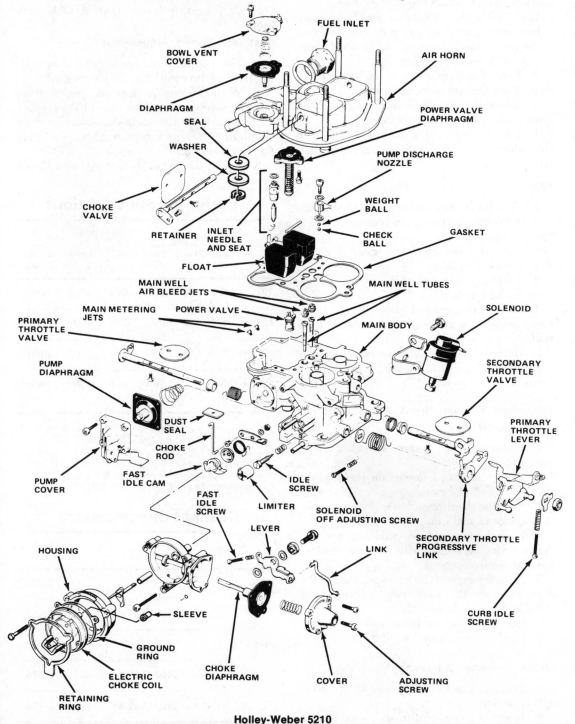

Holley-Weber 5210

2. Place the specified drill or gauge on the down side of the choke plate.

3. To adjust, bend the choke lever tang.

Choke Plate Pulldown (Vacuum Break) Adjustment

THROUGH 1979

1. Remove the three hex headed screws and ring which retain the choke cover.

CAUTION: *Do not remove the choke water housing screw if adjusting on the car. Pull the choke water housing and bimetal cover assembly back out of the way.*

2. Push the diaphragm shaft against the stop. Push the coil lever clockwise.

3. Insert the specified size gauge on the down side of the primary choke plate.

4. Take the slack out of the linkage and turn the adjusting screw with a $5/22$ in. Allen wrench.

1980

1. Attach a hand vacuum pump to the vacuum break diaphragm; apply vacuum and seat the diaphragm.

2. Push the fast idle cam lever down to close the choke plate.

3. Take any slack out of the linkage in the open choke position.

4. Insert the specified gauge between the lower edge of the choke plate and the air horn wall.

5. If the clearance is incorrect, turn the vacuum break adjusting screw, located in the break housing, to adjust.

Secondary Vacuum Break Adjustment

GM THROUGH 1978 ONLY

1. Remove the three screws and the choke coil assembly.

2. Place the cam follower on the highest step of the fast idle cam.

3. Seat the diaphragm by applying an outside source of vacuum.

4. Push the inside choke coil lever counterclockwise for 1977; clockwise for 1978, to close the choke valve.

5. Place a gauge of the size specified in the chart between the lower edge of the choke valve and the air horn wall.

6. Bend the vacuum break rod to adjust.

7. Replace and adjust the choke.

Choke Unloader Adjustment

1. Position the throttle lever at the wide open position.

2. Insert a gauge of the size specified in the chart between the lower edge of the choke valve and the air horn wall.

3. Bend the unloader tang for adjustment.

Secondary Throttle Stop Screw Adjustment

1. Back off the screw until it doesn't touch the throttle lever.

2. Turn the screw in until it touches the secondary throttle lever. Turn it in ¼ turn more.

Fast Idle Speed Adjustment

1. The engine must be at normal operating temperature with the air cleaner off.

2. With the engine running, position the fast idle screw on the high step of the cam for GM cars, or on the second step against the shoulder of the high step for AMC cars. Plug the EGR Port on the carburetor.

3. Adjust the speed by turning the fast idle screw.

Carter YF Specifications

	Float Level (in.)	Float Drop (in.)	Fast Idle Cam (in.)	Choke Un- loader (in.)	Fast Idle Speed (rpm)	Auto- matic Choke Setting
1975	.476	1.38	1.80	.275	1600	1 Rich ①
1976	.476	1.38	1.85	.275	1600	1 Rich ②
1977	.476	1.38	1.95④	.275	1600	1 Rich③
1978– 79	.476	1.38	1.95⑤	.275	1600	1 Rich ⑥

① Carburetor tag numbers 7086 & 7112: 2 Rich
② Carburetor tag numbers 7084 & 7086: 2 Rich
③ Carburetor tag numbers 7111: 2 Rich
④ Carburetor tag numbers 7111 & 7189: .201
⑤ Carburetor tag numbers 7232 & 7333: .201
⑥ Carburetor tag numbers 7232: 2 Rich

Dashpot Specifications

Year	Carburetor	Clearance (in.)
1975	YF (1-V) All	0.075
	2100 (2-V) All	0.093
1976–77	YF (1-V) All	0.075
	2100 (2-V) All	0.075
	BBD (2-V) All	0.104

Carter BBD Specifications

Year	Model ①	Float Level (in.)	Accelerator Pump Travel (in.)	Choke Unloader (in.)	Choke Vacuum Kick	Fast Idle Cam Position	Fast Idle Speed (rpm)	Automatic Choke Adjustment
1976	8067	¼	0.500	0.250	0.128	0.095	1700	2 Rich
	8073	¼	0.500	0.250	0.128	0.095	1700	1 Rich
1977	8103	¼	0.496	0.280	0.150	0.120	1600	1 Rich
	8104	¼	0.520	0.280	0.128	0.095	1500	1 Rich
	8117	¼	0.480	0.280	0.152	0.112	1600	1 Rich
1978	8128	¼	0.496	0.280	0.150	0.110	1600	Index
	8129	¼	0.520	0.280	0.128	0.095	1500	1 Rich
1979	8185	¼	0.470	0.280	0.140	0.110	1600	1 Rich
	8186	¼	0.520	0.280	0.150	0.110	1500	1 Rich
	8187	¼	0.470	0.280	0.140	0.110	1600	1 Rich
	8221	¼	0.530	0.280	0.150	0.110	1600	1 Rich
1980	8216	¼	0.520	0.280	0.140	0.090	1850	2 Rich
	8246	¼	0.520	0.280	0.140	0.095	1850	2 Rich
	8247	¼	0.520	0.280	0.150	0.095	1700	1 Rich
	8248	¼	0.520	0.280	0.150	0.095	1700	1 Rich
	8253	¼	0.470	0.280	0.128	0.095	1850	2 Rich
	8256	¼	0.470	0.280	0.128	0.093	1850	2 Rich
	8278	¼	0.542	0.280	0.140	0.093	1850	Index
1981	8310	¼	0.525	0.280	0.140	0.095	1850	Index
	8302	¼	0.500	0.280	0.128	0.095	1850	1 Rich
	8303	¼	0.500	0.280	0.128	0.090	1700	1 Rich
	8306	¼	0.500	0.280	0.128	0.090	1700	1 Rich
	8307	¼	0.500	0.280	0.128	0.095	1850	1 Rich
	8308	¼	0.500	0.280	0.128	0.095	1850	2 Rich
	8309	¼	0.520	0.280	0.128	0.093	1700	2 Rich
1982	8338	¼	0.520	0.280	0.140	0.095	1850	1 Rich
	8339	¼	0.520	0.280	0.140	0.095	1850	1 Rich

① Model numbers located on the tag or casting

Ford, Autolite, Motorcraft Models 2100, 2150 Specifications

Year	(9510)* Carburetor Identification	Dry Float Level (in.)	Wet Float Level (in.)	Pump Setting Hole #①	Choke Plate Pulldown (in.)	Fast Idle Cam Linkage Clearance (in.)	Fast Idle (rpm)	Dechoke (in.)	Choke Setting	Dashpot (in.)
1975	5DA2	13/32	3/4	3	0.140	0.130	1600	0.250	1 Rich	—
	5DMS	13/32	3/4	3	0.130	0.130	1600	0.250	2 Rich	3/32
	5RAS	13/32	3/4	3	0.140	0.130	1600	0.250	1 Rich	—
1976	6DA2	13/32	3/4	3	0.140	0.130	1600	0.250	1 Rich	—
	6DM2	35/64	15/16	3	0.130	0.120	1600	0.250	2 Rich	—
	6RA2	13/32	3/4	3	0.140	0.130	1600	0.250	1 Rich	—

Year	Code									
1977	7RA2	5/16	0.780	3	0.136	0.126	1600	0.250	1 Rich	—
	7RA2C	5/16	0.780	3	0.130	0.120	1800 ⑥	0.250	1 Rich	—
	7DA2	5/16	0.780	3	0.136	0.126	1600	0.250	Index	—
	7RA2A	5/16	0.780	3	0.104	0.089	1800	0.250	1 Rich	—
1978	8DA2	0.555	0.780	3	0.136	0.126	1600	0.250	Index	—
	8RA2	0.555	0.780	3	0.136	0.126	1600	0.250	1 Rich	—
	8RA2C	0.555	0.780	3	0.136	0.120	1800	0.250	1 Rich	—
	8RA2A	0.555	0.780	3	0.089	0.078	1800	0.170	2 Rich	—
	8DA2A	0.555	0.930	3	0.089	0.078	1600	0.170	2 Rich	—
1979	9DA2	0.313	0.780	3	0.125	0.113	1600 ⑦	0.300	1 Rich	—

Rochester 2SE, E2SE Carburetor Adjustments

Year	Carburetor Identification	Float Level (in.)	Pump Rod (in.)	Fast Idle (rpm)	Choke Coil Lever (in.)	Fast Idle Cam (deg./in.)	Air Valve Rod (in.)	Primary Vacuum Break (deg./in.)	Choke Setting (notches)	Choke Unloader (deg./in.)	Secondary Lockout (in.)
1980	17080681	3/16	17/32	2400	.142	18/0.096	.018	20/.110	Fixed	32/.1950	N.A.
	17080683	3/16	1/2	2400	.142	18/0.096	.018	20/.110	Fixed	32/.195	N.A.
	17080686	3/16	1/2	2600	.142	18/0.096	.018	20/.110	Fixed	32/.195	N.A.
	17080688	3/16	1/2	2600	.142	18/0.096	0.18	20/.110	Fixed	32/.195	N.A.
1981	17081790	0.256	0.128	2600	0.085	25/0.142	.011	19/.103	Fixed	32/.195	0.065
	17081791	0.256	0.128	2400	0.085	25/0.142	.011	19/.103	Fixed	32/.195	0.065
	17081792	0.256	0.128	2400	0.085	25/0.142	.011	19/.103	Fixed	32/1.95	0.065
	17081794	0.256	0.128	2600	0.085	25/0.142	.011	19/.103	Fixed	32/.195	0.065

17081795	0.256	0.128	2600	0.085	25/0.142	.011	19/.103	Fixed	32/.195	0.065
17081796	0.208	0.128	2400	0.065	25/0.142	.011	19/.103	Fixed	32/.1950	.065
17081797	0.208	0.128	2600	0.085	25/0.142	.011	19/.103	Fixed	32/.195	0.085
17081793	0.256	0.128	2400	0.085	25/0.142	.011	19/.103	Fixed	32/.195	0.065
1982										
17082385	0.256	0.128	2400	0.085	18/0.096	.011	21/117	Fixed	34/.204	0.065
17082383	0.256	0.128	2400	0.085	18/0.096	0.011	21/117	Fixed	34/.204	0.065
17082380	0.125	0.128	2400	0.085	18/0.096	0.011	21/117	Fixed	34/.204	0.065
17082386	0.125	0.128	2400	0.065	18/0.096	0.011	19/.103	Fixed	34/.204	0.065
17082387	0.125	0.128	2600	0.085	18/0.096	0.011	19/.103	Fixed	34/.204	0.065
17082388 17082389	0.125	0.128	2500	0.085	18/0.096	0.011	19/.103	Fixed	34/.204	0.065

N.A.: Not Available

1975–76 Ford, Autolite, Motorcraft Models 4300, 4350 Specifications

Year	(9510)* Carburetor Identification ①	Dry Float Level (in.)	Pump Hole Setting	Choke Plate Pulldown (in.)	Fast Idle Cam Linkage	Fast Idle (rpm)	Dechoke (in.)	Choke Setting
1975	5TA4	0.90	Lower	0.140	0.160	1600	0.325	2 Rich
1976	6TA4	0.090	Lower	0.130	0.135	1600	0.325	2 Rich

Holley Model 5210-C

Year	Carb. Part No.	Float Level (Dry) (in.)	Fast Idle Cam (in.)	Choke Plate Pulldown (in.)	Fast Idle Setting (rpm)	Choke Unloader (in.)	Choke Setting
1977	7711	0.420	0.140	0.246	1600	0.300	1 Rich
	7712	0.420	0.140	0.246	1600	0.300	1 Rich
	7799	0.420	0.135	0.215	1600	0.300	Index
	7846	0.420	0.101	0.204	1600	0.300	1 Rich
1978	8163	0.420	0.193	0.191	1800	0.300	1 NR
	8164	0.420	0.204	0.202	1800	0.300	1 NR
	8165	0.420	0.177	0.180	1800	0.300	Index
1979	8548	0.420	0.204	0.191	1800	0.300	1 Rich
	8549	0.420	0.191	0.266	1800	0.300	1 Rich
	7846	0.420	0.193	0.191	1800	0.300	1 Rich
	8675	0.420	0.173	0.177	1800	0.300	Index

Chassis Electrical

HEATER

The following procedures for servicing the components of the heater apply to those cars which have air conditioning as well as to those without it.

CAUTION: *When servicing A/C equipped cars, do not discharge the A/C lines or the evaporator. Damage to the A/C system or personal injury could result.*

Matador

BLOWER REMOVAL AND INSTALLATION

The heater blower may have to be removed in case of excessive motor noise or electrical failure.

1. Disconnect the motor wires, inside the engine compartment.
2. Remove the attaching screws from the motor mounting plate.
3. Remove the motor and fan assembly.

CORE REMOVAL AND INSTALLATION

The heater core may have to be removed for repair in case of clogging or coolant leakage. Repair service can usually be had at radiator repair shops.

1. Disconnect the negative battery cable.

2. Drain about 2 quarts of coolant from the cooling system.
3. Disconnect the heater hoses from the heater core in the engine compartment and plug the core tubes.
4. On air conditioned cars, disconnect the blend-air damper cable at the heater core housing and remove the fuse panel. On non-A/C cars, disconnect the blend-air damper door and fresh air door cables.
5. Remove the lower instrument finish panel and remove the glove box door and liner.
6. Remove the right windshield pillar and corner finish mouldings for access to the upper right heater core housing mounting screws.
7. On air conditioned cars, remove the vacuum motor hoses.
8. Remove the remaining heater core housing attaching screws.
9. On air conditioned cars, remove the capscrew retaining the instrument panel to the right body pillar. Pull the right side of the instrument panel slightly rearward.
10. Remove the heater core housing and heater core. Remove the heater core from the housing.
11. Install the heater core and housing in the reverse order of removal.

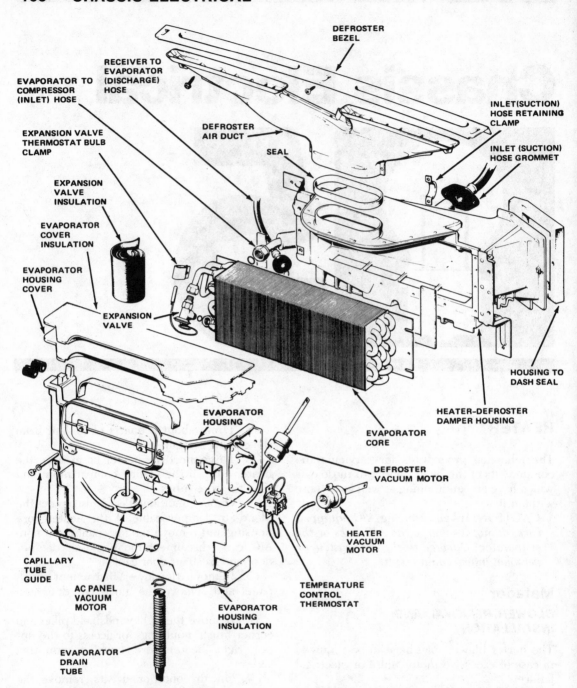

DEFROSTER
BEZEL

RECEIVER TO
EVAPORATOR
(DISCHARGE)
HOSE

EVAPORATOR TO
COMPRESSOR
(INLET) HOSE

INLET(SUCTION)
HOSE RETAINING
CLAMP

DEFROSTER
AIR DUCT

SEAL

INLET (SUCTION)
HOSE GROMMET

EXPANSION VALVE
THERMOSTAT BULB
CLAMP

EXPANSION
VALVE
INSULATION

EVAPORATOR
COVER
INSULATION

EVAPORATOR
HOUSING
COVER

EXPANSION
VALVE

HOUSING TO
DASH SEAL

EVAPORATOR
HOUSING

HEATER-DEFROSTER
DAMPER HOUSING

EVAPORATOR
CORE

DEFROSTER
VACUUM MOTOR

HEATER
VACUUM
MOTOR

CAPILLARY
TUBE
GUIDE

AC PANEL
VACUUM
MOTOR

EVAPORATOR
HOUSING
INSULATION

TEMPERATURE
CONTROL
THERMOSTAT

EVAPORATOR
DRAIN
TUBE

Matador evaporator housing, heater core and defroster/damper on models with air conditioning

Gremlin, Hornet, Concord, Spirit, and Eagle

HEATER CORE REMOVAL AND INSTALLATION

1. Disconnect the negative battery cable and drain 2 qts. of coolant.

2. Disconnect heater hoses and plug hoses and core fittings.

3. Disconnct blower wires and remove motor and fan assembly.

4. Remove the housing attaching nut from the stud in the engine compartment.

5. Remove package shelf, if so equipped.

6. Disconnect wire at resistor, located below glove box.

7. Remove instrument panel center bezel, air outlet and duct, on A/C models.

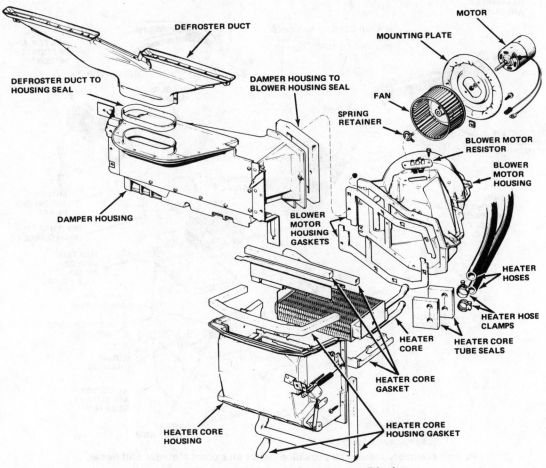

Matador heater assembly without air conditioning

8. Disconnect air and defroster cables from damper levers.

9. Remove right-side windshield pillar molding, the instrument panel upper sheet metal screws and the capscrew at the right door post.

10. Remove the right cowl trim panel and door sill plate.

11. Remove right kick panel and heater housing attaching screws.

12. Pull right side of instrument panel outward slightly and remove housing.

13. Remove core, defroster and blower housing.

14. Remove core from housing.
Installation is the reverse of removal.

BLOWER MOTOR REMOVAL AND INSTALLATION

1. Drain about two quarts of coolant from the radiator.

2. Disconnect the heater hoses from the heater core tubes and plug the core tubes.

3. Disconnect blower wires.

4. Remove cover retaining nut and remove motor and fan assembly.

5. To install, reverse removal procedure.

Pacer

CAUTION: *Unless trained in air conditioning refrigerant evacuation procedures, it is recommended that you do not disconnect any of the refrigerant lines or vessels on cars equipped with air conditioning. Improper evacuation of the lines could result in serious personal injury.*

HEATER CORE REMOVAL AND INSTALLATION

1. Drain about two quarts of coolant from the radiator.

2. Disconnect the heater hoses from the heater core tubes and install plugs in the heater hoses.

3. Remove the vacuum hoses from the

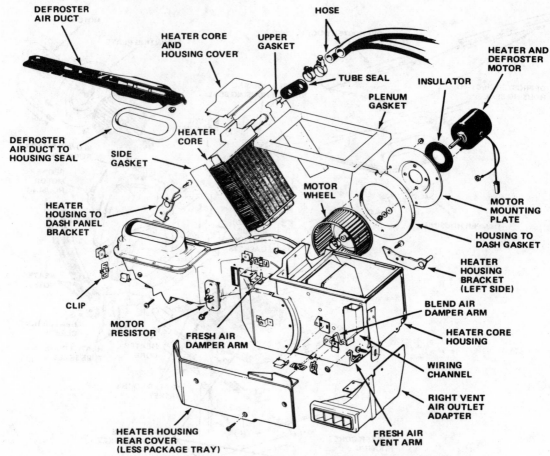

DEFROSTER AIR DUCT

HOSE

HEATER CORE AND HOUSING COVER

UPPER GASKET

TUBE SEAL

HEATER AND DEFROSTER MOTOR

INSULATOR

PLENUM GASKET

DEFROSTER AIR DUCT TO HOUSING SEAL

HEATER CORE

SIDE GASKET

MOTOR WHEEL

HEATER HOUSING TO DASH PANEL BRACKET

MOTOR MOUNTING PLATE

HOUSING TO DASH GASKET

HEATER HOUSING BRACKET (LEFT SIDE)

CLIP

MOTOR RESISTOR

FRESH AIR DAMPER ARM

BLEND AIR DAMPER ARM

HEATER CORE HOUSING

WIRING CHANNEL

HEATER HOUSING REAR COVER (LESS PACKAGE TRAY)

FRESH AIR VENT ARM

RIGHT VENT AIR OUTLET ADAPTER

Heater assembly without air conditioning for all except Matador and Pacer

heater core housing cover clip and move the lines aside.

4. Remove the heater core housing cover screws.

5. Disconnect the overcenter spring from the cover and remove the cover.

6. Remove the heater core-to-housing attaching screws and remove the heater core.

7. Install the heater core in the reverse order of removal.

HEATER BLOWER REMOVAL AND INSTALLATION

Cars Not Equipped with Air Conditioning

1. Disconnect the negative battery cable.

2. Remove the right-side windshield finish moulding.

3. Remove the instrument panel crash pad.

4. Remove the right scuff plate and cowl trim panel.

5. Remove the lower instrument panel-to-right A-pillar attaching screws.

6. Pull the instrument panel to the rear

and replace the lower attaching screw in the right A-pillar. Allow the instrument panel to rest on the screw.

7. Remove the heater core housing attaching nuts and screw.

8. Remove the vacuum hoses from the heater core housing clip and set the lines aside.

9. Disconnect the blend-air door cable from the heater core housing.

10. Pull the heater core housing forward and set atop the upper control arm.

11. Remove the blower motor ground wire at the relay.

12. Disconnect the wires at the blower motor resistor.

13. Remove the blower motor housing brace.

14. Loosen the heater housing-to-dash panel attaching nuts.

15. Pull the blower housing to the rear and downward.

16. Disconnect the vacuum hoses from the vacuum motors.

17. Remove the blower housing.

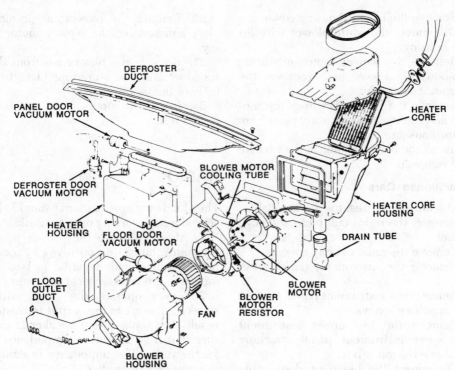

DEFROSTER
DUCT

PANEL DOOR
VACUUM MOTOR

HEATER
CORE

DEFROSTER DOOR
VACUUM MOTOR

BLOWER MOTOR
COOLING TUBE

HEATER CORE
HOUSING

HEATER
HOUSING

FLOOR DOOR
VACUUM MOTOR

DRAIN TUBE

FLOOR
OUTLET
DUCT

FAN

BLOWER
MOTOR
RESISTOR

BLOWER
MOTOR

BLOWER
HOUSING

Pacer heater assembly without air conditioning

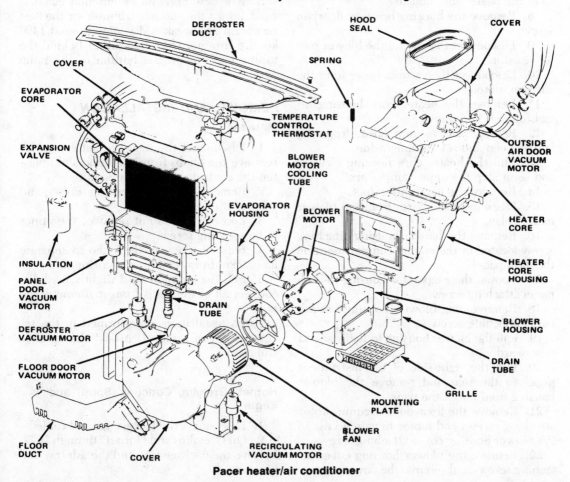

DEFROSTER
DUCT

HOOD
SEAL

COVER

COVER

EVAPORATOR
CORE

TEMPERATURE
CONTROL
THERMOSTAT

SPRING

EXPANSION
VALVE

BLOWER
MOTOR
COOLING
TUBE

OUTSIDE
AIR DOOR
VACUUM
MOTOR

EVAPORATOR
HOUSING

BLOWER
MOTOR

HEATER
CORE

INSULATION

HEATER
CORE
HOUSING

PANEL
DOOR
VACUUM
MOTOR

DRAIN
TUBE

DEFROSTER
VACUUM MOTOR

BLOWER
HOUSING

FLOOR DOOR
VACUUM MOTOR

DRAIN
TUBE

FLOOR
DUCT

COVER

RECIRCULATING
VACUUM MOTOR

BLOWER
FAN

GRILLE

MOUNTING
PLATE

Pacer heater/air conditioner

18. Remove the blower housing cover.

19. Disconnect the white blower wire inside the housing.

20. Remove the blower motor mounting plate-to-housing screws and remove the blower motor assembly.

21. Remove the blower fan from the motor shaft and remove the mounting plate from the motor housing.

22. Install the blower motor in the reverse order of removal.

Air Conditioned Cars

1. Disconnect the negative battery cable.

2. Remove the right scuff plate and cowl trim panel.

3. Remove the radio overlay cover.

4. Remove the instrument panel crash pad.

5. Remove the instrument panel-to-right A-pillar attaching screws.

6. Remove the two upper instrument panel-to-lower instrument panel attaching screws above the glove box.

7. Disconnect the blend-air door cable from the heater core housing.

8. Remove the housing brace-to-floorpan screw.

9. Disconnect the wire at the blower motor resistor.

10. Disconnect the vacuum hoses from the vacuum motors.

11. Remove the heater core housing attaching nuts and screw.

12. Remove the vacuum hoses from the housing clip and set the lines aside.

13. Pull the heater core housing forward and set it atop the upper control arm.

14. Remove the floor outlet duct.

15. Disconnect the wires from the blower motor relay.

16. Remove the blower housing attaching screw located in the engine compartment on the dash panel.

17. Loosen the evaporator housing-to-dash panel attaching screw.

18. Remove the blower housing-to-dash panel attaching screw.

19. Pull the blower housing to the rear and downward.

20. Pull the right-side of the instrument panel to the rear and remove the blower housing from under the panel.

21. Remove the floor door vacuum motor attaching screws and motor to gain access to the blower housing cover attaching screws.

22. Remove the blower housing cover attaching screws and remove the cover.

23. Remove the blower motor mounting plate and remove the blower motor assembly.

24. Remove the blower fan from the motor shaft and the mounting plate from the body of the motor.

25. Install the motor in the reverse order of removal.

RADIO

The following precautions should be observed when working on a car radio:

1. Always observe the proper polarity of the connections; i.e., positive (+) goes to the power source and negative (−) to ground (negative ground electrical system).

2. Never operate the radio without a speaker; damage to the output transistors will result. If a replacement speaker is used, be sure that it is the correct impedance (ohms) for the radio. The impedance is stamped on the case of AMC radios.

3. If a new antenna or antenna cable is used, adjust the antenna trimmer for the best reception of a weak AM station around 1400 kc; the trimmer is located either behind the tuning knob or on the bottom of the radio case.

REMOVAL AND INSTALLATION

Matador

1. Disconnect the negative battery cable. Remove the knobs from the radio and unfasten the control shafts retaining nuts.

2. Remove the bezel securing screws, and remove the bezel.

3. Loosen, but do not remove, the upper radio securing screw.

4. Raise the rear of the radio to separate its bracket from the upper securing screw.

5. Pull the radio forward slightly, and disconnect all of the leads from it. Remove the radio.

Radio installation is performed in the reverse order of removal. Adjust the antenna trimmer.

Hornet, Gremlin, Concord, Spirit, and Eagle

1. Disconnect the battery ground cable.

2. On Gremlins and Hornets through 1977, remove the package tray and the ash tray and bracket.

3. Pull off the radio knobs and remove shaft retaining nuts.

4. Remove the bezel retaining screws and remove the bezel. On 1978 and later models with A/C, remove the center housing of the instrument panel.

5. Disconnect the speaker, antenna, and power leads, and remove the radio.

Installation is the reverse.

Pacer

1. Disconnect the negative battery cable.

2. Remove the radio knobs, attaching nuts, cluster bezel, and overlay cover.

3. Loosen the radio-to-instrument panel attaching screw.

4. Lift the rear of the radio and pull forward slightly. Disconnect the electrical connections and the antenna and remove the radio.

5. Installation is the reverse.

WINDSHIELD WIPERS

Motor

REMOVAL AND INSTALLATION

Gremlin, Hornet, Concord, Eagle, Spirit, and Matador Sedan and Wagon

1. Remove the wiper arms and blades.

2. Remove the screws holding the motor adapter plate to the dash panel.

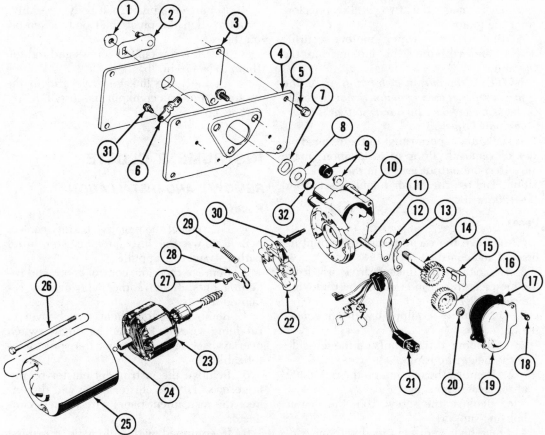

1. Nut	12. Switch washer	23. Armature
2. Drive crank	13. Switch lever	24. Ball
3. Seal	14. Output gear and shaft	25. Motor housing
4. Bracket	15. End play spring	26. Bolt
5. Screw	16. Idler gear and pinion	27. Screw
6. Ground strap	17. Gasket	28. Brush
7. Spring washer	18. Screw	29. Spring
8. Plain washer	19. Cover	30. Parking lever pin
9. Grommet	20. Push nut	31. Screw
10. Gear housing	21. Brushes and harness	32. Seal
11. Shaft	22. End head	

Wiper motor and transmission

3. Separate the wiper wiring harness connector at the motor.

4. Pull the motor and linkage out of the opening to expose the drive link-to-crank stud retaining clip. Raise up the lock tab of the clip with a screwdriver and slide the clip off the stud. Remove the wiper motor assembly.

5. Install the windshield wiper motor in the reverse order of removal.

Matador Coupe

1. Remove the wiper arm/blade assemblies.

2. Open the hood and remove the cowl screen from the cowl opening.

3. Separate the linkage drive arm from the motor arm crankpin, by unfastening the retaining clip.

4. Disconnect the two multiconnectors from the motor.

5. Remove the wiper motor securing screws and withdraw the motor from the opening.

NOTE: *If the output arm hangs up on the firewall panel during motor removal, rotate the arm clockwise by hand, so that it clears the panel opening.*

Installation is performed in the reverse order of removal. Prior to installation, make sure that the output arm is in the "park" position. Tighten the motor retaining screws to 90–120 in. lbs.

Pacer

1. Remove the vacuum canister mounting bracket and canister.

2. Disconnect the linkage drive arm from the motor output arm crankpin by removing the retaining clip.

3. On vehicles equipped with air conditioning:

   a. Remove the two nuts on the left-side of the heater housing;

   b. Remove the one nut on the right-side of the heater housing;

   c. Remove the screw from the heater housing support.

4. On vehicles not equipped with air conditioning:

   a. Remove the two nuts and one screw on the left-side of the heater housing;

   b. Remove the one nut on the right-side of the heater housing;

   c. Remove the screw from the heater housing support. Pull the heater housing forward.

5. Remove the wiper motor mounting plate

attaching screws and remove the wiper motor assembly from the cowl.

6. Disconnect the two wire connectors from the wiper motor.

7. Remove the wiper motor attaching screws and remove the wiper motor.

8. Install the wiper motor in the reverse order of removal.

Wiper Linkage
REMOVAL AND INSTALLATION

1. Remove the wiper arms and blades.

2. Remove the screws retaining the right and left pivot shaft bodies to the cowl.

3. Disconnect the linkage drive arm from the motor output arm crankpin by removing the retaining clip.

4. Remove the pivot shaft body assembly.

5. Position the pivot shaft body assembly on the car.

6. Install the retaining screws and tighten them to 50–70 in. lb.

7. Connect the linkage drive arm to the motor output arm crankpin and install the retaining clip.

INSTRUMENT CLUSTER

REMOVAL AND INSTALLATION
Pacer

1. Disconnect the negative battery cable.

2. Remove the instrument cluster bezel with a straight, firm pull.

3. Remove the radio control knobs and retaining nuts. Remove the radio overlay retaining screws.

4. Remove the headlight switch overlay retaining screws. Pull the headlight switch overlay back and disconnect the speedometer cable.

5. Remove the instrument cluster retaining crews. Tilt the cluster down and disconnect the instrument panel wire harness connectors.

6. If equipped with automatic transmission, disconnect the gear selector dial cable from the steering column.

7. Remove the cluster assembly.

8. Reverse the above procedure to install.

1975–76 Gremlin and Hornet

1. Disconnect battery negative cable.

2. Cover steering column with a cloth to prevent scratching of painted surface.

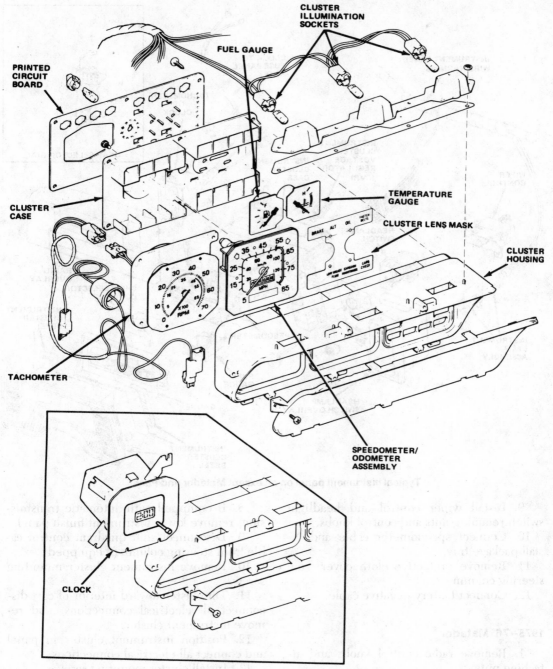

CLUSTER
ILLUMINATION
SOCKETS

FUEL GAUGE

PRINTED
CIRCUIT
BOARD

TEMPERATURE
GAUGE

CLUSTER LENS MASK

BRAKE ALT OIL

FASTEN
BELTS

LOW FUEL CRUISE
FUEL INOPERATIVE

LAMP
CHECK

CLUSTER
CASE

CLUSTER
HOUSING

TACHOMETER

SPEEDOMETER/
ODOMETER
ASSEMBLY

CLOCK

Pacer instrument cluster

3. Remove package tray (if equipped) and disconnect speedometer cable.

4. Remove control knobs and retaining nuts from wiper control and headlight switch.

5. Remove screws attaching instrument cluster housing to instrument panel.

6. Rotate instrument cluster forward, disconnect all electrical connections and lamps, disconnect vacuum line from fuel economy gauge (if equipped), and remove cluster.

7. Position instrument cluster on instrument panel and connect all electrical connections and lamps, connect vacuum line to fuel economy gauge (if equipped).

8. Install cluster housing-to-instrument panel attaching screws.

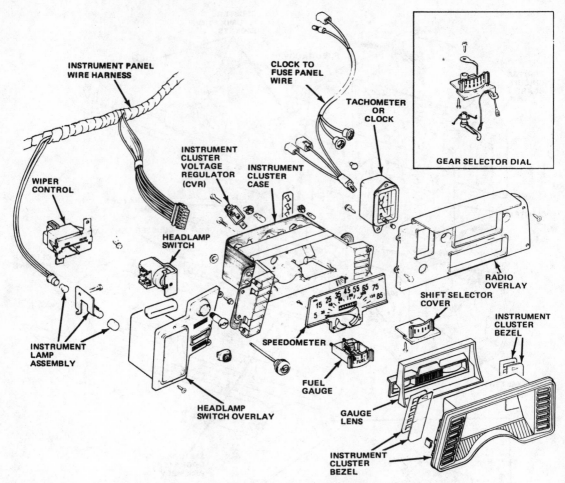

Typical instrument panel on all except Matador and Pacer

9. Install wiper control and headlight switch retaining nuts and control knobs.

10. Connect speedometer cable and install package tray.

11. Remove protective cloth cover from steering column.

12. Connect battery negative cable.

1975–76 Matador

1. Remove radio control knobs and attaching nuts.

2. Remove remote mirror control attaching nut (if equipped).

3. Remove ten bezel attaching screws.

4. Tilt bezel toward interior of car and disconnect all electrical connections.

5. Remove bezel.

6. Remove clock, clock opening cover, or fuel economy gauge.

7. Reach through clock access opening and disconnect speedometer cable from cluster.

8. If equipped with automatic transmission, remove lower instrument finish panel.

9. Disconnect shift quadrant control cable from steering column (if equipped).

10. Remove instrument cluster mounting screws.

11. Tilt cluster toward interior of car, disconnect all electrical connections, and remove instrument cluster.

12. Position instrument cluster in panel and connect all electrical connections.

13. Install cluster mounting screws.

14. Connect shift quadrant control cable (if equipped).

NOTE: *Adjust shift quadrant cable as outlined in Torque-Command Transmission section*

15. Install lower instrument finish panel (if removed).

16. Reach through clock access opening and connect speedometer cable.

17. Install clock, clock opening cover, or fuel economy gauge.

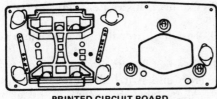

PRINTED CIRCUIT BOARD

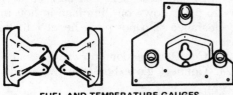

FUEL AND TEMPERATURE GAUGES

INDICATOR BULB LENS

SPEEDOMETER

MASK

GEAR SELECTOR DIAL (AUTO. TRANS)

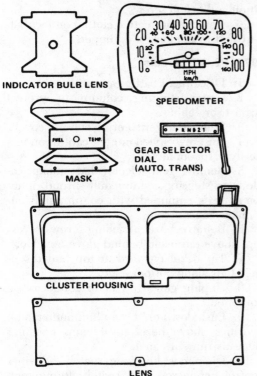

CLUSTER HOUSING

LENS

Matador instrument cluster

18. Position bezel and connect all electrical connections:

19. Install ten bezel attaching screws.

20. Install radio attaching nuts and control knobs.

21. Install remote mirror control attaching nut (if equipped).

NOTE: *Control knob aligning tabs must fit in control shaft slots when installing control knobs.*

1977 Gremlin and Hornet

1. Disconnect battery negative cable.

2. Remove package tray (if equipped) to gain access to speedometer cable.

3. Cover steering column with a cloth to prevent scratches.

4. Disconnect speedometer cable (screw-on type).

5. Remove top and side screws from instrument panel and tilt cluster forward slightly to gain access for disconnecting headlamp switch and wiper control harness connectors.

NOTE: *Lift two locking tabs to disconnect headlamp switch connector.*

6. Disconnect fiber-optic ashtray lamp, if equipped.

7. Disconnect harness connectors and remove instrument cluster assembly.

8. Position instrument cluster on instrument panel and connect all electrical connections and lamps.

NOTE: *Be sure to connect headlamp switch ground wire.*

9. Connect fiber optic ashtray lamp to cluster, if removed.

10. Install cluster housing to instrument panel with attaching screws.

11. Connect speedometer cable and install package tray.

12. Remove protective cloth cover from steering column.

13. Connect battery negative cable.

14. Reset clock, if equipped.

1977–78 Matador

1. Remove radio control knobs and attaching nuts.

2. Remove right remote mirror control attaching nut, if equipped.

3. Remove bezel attaching screws.

4. Tilt bezel toward interior of car and disconnect all electrical connections.

5. Remove bezel. Cover steering column with a cloth to prevent scratching column.

6. Remove clock housing attaching screws, pull assembly away from cluster, and disconnect bulbs and electrical leads. Remove assembly.

7. Using clock access opening, disconnect speedometer cable by depressing locking tab and moving cable away from instrument cluster.

8. Disconnect gear selector dial cable from steering column.

9. Remove cluster mounting screws and disconnect electrical connections.

10. Remove cluster.

11. Position cluster and connect electrical components.

12. Install cluster mounting screws.

13. Connect gear selector dial cable.

14. Connect speedometer cable.

15. Connect clock electrical connector and install bulbs and clock (or cover).

16. Install instrument cluster bezel.

17. Install right mirror remote control, if removed.

18. Install radio attaching nuts and control knobs.

19. Connect battery negative cable.

20. Reset clock, if equipped.

1978 Gremlin, Concord, AMX

1. Disconnect battery negative cable.

2. Cover steering column to protect against scratching.

3. Remove bezel attaching screws across top, above radio and behind glove box door.

4. Tip bezel outward at top and disengage tabs along bottom edge.

5. Unplug glove box lamp connector, if equipped.

6. Depress speedometer cable locking tab and move cable away from cluster.

7. Push down on three illumination lamp housings above bezel until lamp housings are clear from instrument panel.

8. Disconnect headlamp switch and wiper control connectors and switch illumination lamp.

NOTE: *Lift two locking tabs to disconnect headlamp switch connector.*

9. Twist and remove cluster illumination lamp sockets.

10. Disconnect instrument cluster connectors.

11. Remove clock or tachometer screws, if equipped. It is not necessary to remove clock adjusting knob.

12. Disconnect clock or tachometer feed wires from circuit board, if equipped.

13. Remove cluster housing and circuit board-to-bezel screws.

14. Remove cluster housing and circuit board assembly from bezel. If equipped with clock or tachometer, move aside as required.

15. Position instrument cluster to instrument cluster bezel. Move clock or tachometer aside as required.

16. Install cluster housing mounting screws.

NOTE: *Clock ground wire terminal must contact foil on circuit board beneath clock mounting boss.*

17. Connect clock or tachometer feed wires to circuit board, if removed.

18. Install clock or tachometer screws.

19. Connect instrument cluster connectors.

20. Install cluster illumination lamp sockets.

21. Connect headlamp and wiper switch connectors and switch illumination lamp.

22. Align tabs at bottom of bezel with openings and raise bezel. It may be necessary to press down on illumination housings for clearance. Do not push bezel into final position.

23. Connect speedometer cable.

24. Connect glove box lamp wires, if removed.

25. Push bezel forward into installed position and install screws.

26. Remove protective cloth, connect battery and reset clock, if equipped.

1979–82 All Models

1. Disconnect battery negative cable.

2. Cover steering column to protect against scratching.

3. Remove lower steering column cover.

4. Unscrew speedometer cable connector from speedometer.

5. Remove gear selector dial actuator cable from steering column shift shroud, if automobile is equipped with column shift automatic transmission.

6. Remove bezel attaching screws across top, above radio and behind glove box door.

7. Tip bezel outward at top and disengage tabs along bottom edge.

8. Unplug glove box lamp connector, if equipped.

9. Push down on three illumination lamp housings above bezel until lamp housings clear instrument panel.

10. Disconnect headlamp switch and wiper control connectors and switch illumination lamp.

NOTE: *Lift two locking tabs to disconnect headlamp switch connector.*

11. Twist and remove cluster illumination lamp sockets.

12. Disconnect instrument cluster connectors.

13. Remove clock or tachometer screws, if equipped. It is not necessary to remove clock adjusting knob.

14. Disconnect clock or tachometer feed wires from circuit board, if equipped.

15. Remove cluster housing and circuit board-to-bezel screws.

16. Remove cluster housing and circuit board assembly from bezel. If equipped with

clock or tachometer, move aside as required.

17. Position instrument cluster to instrument cluster bezel. Move clock or tachometer aside as required.

18. Install cluster housing mounting screws.

NOTE: *Clock ground and feed wire terminals must contact foil beneath circuit board mounting screws.*

19. Connect clock or tachometer feed wires to circuit board, if removed.

20. Install clock or tachometer screws.

21. Connect instrument cluster connectors.

22. Install cluster illumination lamp sockets.

23. Connect headlamp and wiper switch connectors and switch illumination lamp.

24. If automobile is equipped with column shift automatic transmission, use piece of wire to fish gear selector dial actuator cable through grommet in instrument panel reinforcement and attach to shift column shroud. Adjust cable, if necessary.

25. Align tabs at bottom of bezel with openings and raise bezel. It may be necessary to press down on illumination housings for clearance. Do not push bezel into final position.

26. Connect glove box lamp wires, if removed.

27. Push bezel forward into installed position and install screws.

NOTE: *Make sure gear selector dial actuator cable is adjusted in neutral.*

28. Connect speedometer cable and tighten securely.

29. Install lower steering column cover.

30. Remove protective cloth, connect battery and reset clock, if equipped.

SEAT BELT SYSTEMS

Disabling the Interlock System

Since the legal requirement for seat belt/starter interlock systems was dropped during the 1975 model year, those systems installed on cars built earlier may now be legally disconnected. However, the seat belt warning light is still required to operate.

1. Remove the pink wire and terminal from the two terminal connector at the emergency starter relay, located on the right inner fender panel, under the hood.

2. Cut off the pink wire close to the taped junction of the wire harness.

3. Remove the yellow wire and terminal.

4. Install the yellow wire into the two terminal connector at the location where the pink wire and terminal was removed from the three terminal connector at the starter relay.

5. From under the right side of the dash and along the right side of the glove box area, locate the interlock logic module and remove it from its bracket. Cut off the yellow with black tracer wire close to the taped junction of the wire harness and cut off the remaining end as close to the logic module as possible. Reinstall the logic module on its dash bracket.

6. The warning light should be off when the occupied seat belt is buckled and the car placed in gear with the ignition switch on.

NOTE: *Most models require the seating of both the driver and front seat passenger, prior to buckling of the belts or turning of the ignition system, due to the programming of the logic module for the seat belt warning light to go out. These series can be identified by a buff colored logic module. Other series are equipped with a green colored logic module which allows non-sequential operation and independent use of the seat belts.*

HEADLIGHTS

REMOVAL AND INSTALLATION

1. Remove the headlight cover (surrounding trim panel).

NOTE: *The screws directly above and to one side of the headlight are for adjusting the vertical and horizontal headlight aim. Don't confuse these with the headlight cover retaining screws.*

2. Loosen the screws holding the headlight retainer ring in place.

3. Rotate the retainer ring to disengage the ring from the screws. Remove the ring.

4. Pull the headlight out and pull the wire plug off the back.

There are currently only 3 types of headlights commonly in use on U.S. cars:

    a. Four-lamp system high beam.

    b. Four-lamp system combined high and low beam.

    c. Two-lamp system combined high and low beam.

Knowing this, you can check your required headlight number against the "Light Bulb Specifications" chart and charge off to the discount or auto parts store.

NOTE: *If your two-lamp system takes a*

Light Bulb Specifications

	Bulb Numbers							
	1975	1976	1977	1978	1979	1980	1981	1982
High and low beam headlight	6014	6014	6014	6014 ⑪	4652 ⑫	4652 ⑫	4652	4652
High beam headlight	—	—	—	—	4651	4651	4651	4651
High beam indicator	158	158	158	158	158	158	194	194
Alternator indicator	158	158	158	158	158	158	194	194
Oil pressure indicator	158	158	158	158	158	158	194	194
Brake warning and parking brake indicator	158	158	158	158	158	158	194	194
Low fuel indicator	—	—	—	—	—	—	—	—
Tail and stoplights	1157	1157	1157	1157	1157 ⑭	1157 ⑭	1157	1157
Park and directional lights	1157	1157	1157	1157	1157	1157	1157	1157
Instrument lights	158	158	158	158	158	158	194	194
Headlight and wiper control	1445	1445	1445	1815	1815	1815	1815	1815
Heater and air conditioning controls	1445	1891	1445	1815	1815	1815	1815	1815
Tachometer	1895	—	—	—	—	—	—	—
Clock	1816	1816 ③	1895	1816	1816	1816	—	—
License plate	194	*	*	*	*	*	*	*

Component								
Column shift indicator	1816	④	④	④	④	④	—	—	—
Floor shift indicator	1816	1445	1445	1445	1445	1445	1445	1445 ⑮	1445 ⑮
Radio, tape player	1893	⑤	1892	1893	1893	1893	1893	1893	1893
Ashtray	1445	⑥	1445 ⑨	1891	1445	1445	1445	1815	1815
Front side markers	194	194	194	194	194	194	194	194	194
Rear side markers	194 ①	194 ⑦	194 ⑦	194	194 ⑬	194	194	194	194
Dome	561 ②	561	561	561	561	561	561	561	561
Rallye Pac Gauges	1891	—	—	—	—	—	—	158	158
Cargo	561	561	561 ⑩	561 ⑩	561 ⑩	561 ⑩	212-2	—	561
Courtesy	561	561	561	561	561	561	561	561	561
Glove box	1891	1891	1891	1891	1891	1891	1891	—	1891
Trunk	89	89	89	89	89	89	89	89	89
Turn signal indicators	158	158	158	158	158	158	158	194	194
Back-up	1156	1156 ⑧	1156	1156 ⑧	1156	1156	1156	1156	1156

* Replaced as an assembly
① Hornet: 1895
② Gremlin & Hornet: 562
③ Matador: 1895
④ Tilt wheel: 1445
   w/o tilt wheel: 1816
⑤ Clarion AM: 158
   Motorola AM in Gremlin & Hornet: 1893
      in Matador: 1815
   AM/FM in Gremlin & Hornet: 1893
      in Matador: 1815
⑥ Gremlin & Hornet: 158
   Matador: 1445
⑦ Hornet: 1895
⑧ Matador: 1157
⑨ Gremlin & Hornet: 158
⑩ Pacer: 212-2
⑪ Concord: 6052
⑫ Pacer: 6014
⑬ Spirit & AMX: 1157
⑭ Concord turn: 1156
⑮ Eagle: 1816

6014 headlight, don't buy the 6012 head-light. This is an older headlight that is being phased out. It isn't as bright as a 6014, though it will interchange.

5. Push the plug onto the new headlight. Position the headlight. There are lugs on the headlight to make it impossible to put it in wrong.

6. Replace the retainer ring and tighten the screws.

7. Replace the headlight cover.

NOTE: *When aiming the headlights, each combined high and low beam should be within 6 in. to the right of the vertical centerline of the light and within 2 in. above or below the horizontal centerline, at a distance of 25 ft. The high beams of a four-lamp system should be within 2 in. below the horizontal centerline and within 6 in. right or left from the vertical center line. Some state inspection laws may not allow this much leeway in adjustment.*

PRINTED CIRCUIT BOARD

Current is supplied to the instruments and the instrument panel lights through a printed circuit which is attached to the rear of the instrument cluster. The disconnect plug is part of the panel wiring harness and connects to pins attached to the printed circuit. A keyway located on the printed circuit board insures that the plug is always mounted correctly.

CAUTION: *Never pry under the plug to remove it, or damage to the printed circuit will result.*

An instrument voltage regulator is wired in series with the gauges to supply a constant five volts to them. It is integral with the temperature gauge.

REMOVAL AND INSTALLATION

1. Disconnect the cable from the negative (−) battery terminal.

2. Cover the steering column with a clean cloth, so that it will not be scratched.

3. If equipped with a parcel shelf, unfasten the two screws which secure it at either end, remove the screws which secure it to the center support bracket and withdraw the shelf from underneath the instrument panel.

4. Working from underneath the dash, disconnect the speedometer cable.

5. Remove the knobs from the headlight and wiper switches.

6. Remove the 5 screws that are located around the cluster bezel and partially withdraw the cluster/bezel assembly from the panel.

7. Disconnect all of the wiring and lights from the back of the cluster and remove the cluster/bezel assembly the rest of the way.

Installation is performed in the reverse order of removal.

FUSE LINK

The fuse link is a short length of special, Hypalon (high temperature) insulated wire, integral with the engine compartment wiring harness and should not be confused with standard wire. It is several wire gauges smaller than the circuit which it protects. Under no circumstances should a fuse link replacement repair be made using a length of standard wire cut from bulk stock or from another wiring harness.

To repair any blown fuse link use the following procedure:

1. Determine which circuit is damaged, its location and the cause of the open fuse link. If the damaged fuse link is one of three fed by a common No. 10 or 12 gauge feed wire, determine the specific affected circuit.

2. Disconnect the negative battery cable.

3. Cut the damaged fuse link from the wiring harness and discard it. If the fuse link is one of three circuits fed by a single feed wire, cut it out of the harness at each splice end and discard it.

4. Identify and procure the proper fuse link and butt connectors for attaching the fuse link to the harness.

5. To repair any fuse link in a 3-link group with one feed:

   a. After cutting the open link out of the harness, cut each of the remaining undamaged fuse links close to the feed wire weld.

   b. Strip approximately ½ inch of insulation from the detached ends of the two good fuse links. Then insert two wire ends into one end of a butt connector and carefully push one stripped end of the replacement fuse link into the same end of the butt connector and crimp all three firmly together.

NOTE: *Care must be taken when fitting the three fuse links into the butt connector as the internal diameter is a snug fit for three wires. Make sure to use a proper crimping tool. Pliers, side cutters, etc. will not apply*

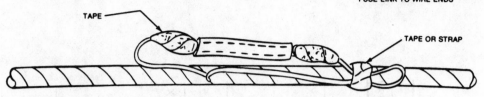

REMOVE EXISTING VINYL TUBE SHIELDING
REINSTALL OVER FUSE LINK BEFORE CRIMPING
FUSE LINK TO WIRE ENDS

TAPE

TAPE OR STRAP

TYPICAL REPAIR USING THE SPECIAL #17 GA. (9.00" LONG-YELLOW) FUSE LINK REQUIRED FOR THE AIR/COND.
CIRCUITS

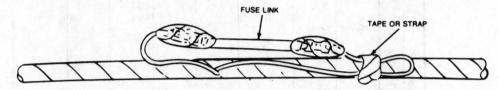

FUSE LINK

TAPE OR STRAP

TYPICAL REPAIR FOR ANY IN-LINE FUSE LINK USING THE SPECIFIED GAUGE FUSE LINK FOR THE SPECIFIC CIRCUIT

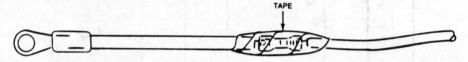

TAPE

TYPICAL REPAIR USING THE EYELET TERMINAL FUSE LINK OF THE SPECIFIED GAUGE FOR ATTACHMENT TO A CIRCUIT WIRE END

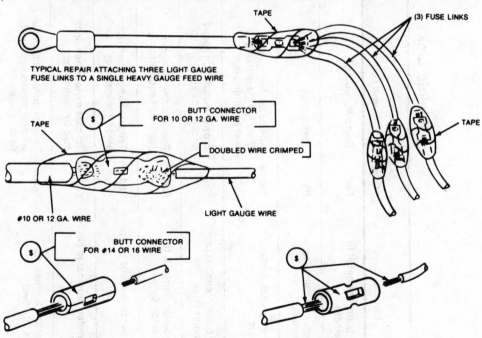

TAPE

(3) FUSE LINKS

TYPICAL REPAIR ATTACHING THREE LIGHT GAUGE
FUSE LINKS TO A SINGLE HEAVY GAUGE FEED WIRE

BUTT CONNECTOR
FOR 10 OR 12 GA. WIRE

TAPE

DOUBLED WIRE CRIMPED

TAPE

#10 OR 12 GA. WIRE

LIGHT GAUGE WIRE

BUTT CONNECTOR
FOR #14 OR 16 WIRE

FUSIBLE LINK REPAIR PROCEDURE

General fuse link repair procedure

the proper crimp to retain the wires and withstand a pull test.

c. After crimping the butt connector to the three fuse links, cut the weld portion from the feed wire and strip approximately ½ inch of insulation from the cut end. In-

sert the stripped end into the open end of the butt connector and crimp very firmly.

d. To attach the remaining end of the replacement fuse link, strip approximately ½ inch of insulation from the wire end of the circuit from which the blown fuse link

Fusible Links

Location	Color	Circuit Protected	1975	1976	1977	1978	1979	1980	1981	1982
Starter relay battery terminal to main wire harness	Red	Complete wiring	X	X	X	X	X	X	X	X
Horn relay battery terminal to main wire harness	Pink	Horn circuit	X	X	X	X	X	X	X	X
Ignition switch ignition terminal to wire harness	Yellow	Alternator, fuel gauge, temp. gauge, parking brake warning light								
Starter relay battery terminal to A/C blower motor relay	Red	Blower motor high speed circuit								
Starter relay battery terminal to rear window defogger switch	Red	Rear window defogger, 1980–82 headlights	X	X	X	X	X	X	X	X
B-3 ignition switch terminal to circuit breaker	Red	Tailgate motor when operated by tailgate key	X	X						
1-3 ignition switch terminal to circuit breaker*	Yellow	Tailgate motor when operated by dash switch	X	X						
1-3 ignition switch terminal (single wire splits into two)*	Yellow	Tailgate motor and/or side window motors and throttle stop solenoid	X	X		X				

Connection	Color	Description	
1-3 ignition switch terminal to throttle stop solenoid*	Yellow	Throttle stop solenoid	X
Ignition switch accessory terminal to wire harness	Brown	Lighter, all fused accessories, electric wipers	X X
Engine compartment harness at AV terminal of dash connector	Yellow	Throttle closing solenoid, feed to interlock relay terminal No. 2	X X
SOL ignition switch terminal to wire harness	Pink or Green	Feed to interlock relay terminal No. 1, feed to logic module pin No. 8 of 9-way connector	X X
Battery terminal of solenoid to lamp	Pink	Engine compartment lamp	X
Battery terminal of solenoid to A/C blower motor relay	Red	A/C blower motor	X
S terminal of ignition switch to wiring harness	Green	Feed to starter solenoid S terminal	X
Battery terminal of starter to harness	Pink	Rally Package Ammeter	X X X
Block terminal to harness	Pink	Rally Package Ammeter	X
Harness to dash conn.	Red	Headlight switch	X X

was removed, and firmly crimp a butt connector or equivalent to the stripped wire. Then, insert the end of the replacement link into the other end of the butt connector and crimp firmly.

e. Using rosin core solder with a consistency of 60 percent tin and 40 percent lead, solder the connectors and the wires at the repairs and insulate with electrical tape.

6. To replace any fuse link on a single circuit in a harness, cut out the damaged portion, strip approximately ½ inch of insulation from the two wire ends and attach the appropriate replacement fuse link to the stripped wire ends with two proper size butt connectors. Solder the connectors and wires and insulate with tape.

7. To repair any fuse link which has an eyelet terminal on one end such as the charging circuit, cut off the open fuse link behind the weld, strip approximately ½ inch of insulation from the cut end and attach the appropriate new eyelet fuse link to the cut stripped wire with an appropriate size butt connector. Solder the connectors and wires at the repair and insulate with tape.

8. Connect the negative battery cable to the battery and test the system for proper operation.

NOTE: *Do not mistake a resistor wire for a fuse link. The resistor wire is generally longer and has print stating, "Resistor-don't cut or splice."*

NOTE: *When attaching a single No. 16, 17, 18 or 20 gauge fuse link to a heavy gauge wire, always double the stripped wire end of the fuse link before inserting and crimping it into the butt connector for positive wire retention.*

FUSE BOX LOCATION

• 1975 and later Pacer: On the left of the glove box
• 1975–78 Gremlin and Hornet: Next to the parking brake mechanism
• 1975–78 Except Pacer, Gremlin and Hornet: In the glove box
• 1979–82 All models: Next to the parking brake mechanism

WIRING DIAGRAMS

Wiring diagrams have been left out of this book. As cars have become more complex, and available with longer and longer option lists, wiring diagrams have grown in size and complexity also. It has become virtually impossible to provide a readable reproduction in a reasonable number of pages. Information on ordering wiring diagrams from the vehicle manufacturer can be obtained from your dealer.

Clutch and Transmission

CLUTCH

NOTE: *Several different clutch assemblies have been used over the years. For correct clutch identification, see the accompanying illustrations.*

REMOVAL AND INSTALLATION

6 and V8

1. Remove the transmission and the starter.

2. Disconnect the clutch linkage at the release lever.

3. Remove the capscrews that hold the bellhousing (clutch housing) to the engine. It may be necessary to move the rear of the engine up or down to gain wrench clearance.

NOTE: *Any shims between the housing and engine must be replaced in exactly the same place to prevent misalignment.*

4. Remove the throwout lever, washer, bearing and sleeve assembly.

5. Matchmark the clutch cover, pressure plate, and flywheel before removal to ensure proper balance.

6. Loosen each clutch cover capscrew a few turns at a time until spring tension is released, then remove the cover, pressure plate, and disc.

7. Check the pilot bushing in the end of the crankshaft for scoring or looseness. If it is

necessary to replace the bushing, use either an expanding-end slidehammer or a suitable tap. Screwing the tap into the bore until it bottoms will force the bushing out. Another way to remove the bushing is to pack it and the crankshaft cavity with grease, then insert the clutch shaft aligning tool (dummy pilot shaft) into the bushing and tap it with a soft hammer. The bushing will be pushed out. It is important to clean out all the grease.

Lubricate the bushing with grease before installing the clutch. Sometimes there is a lu-

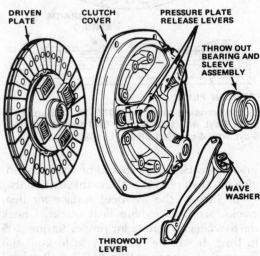

1975–76 9 inch clutch assembly

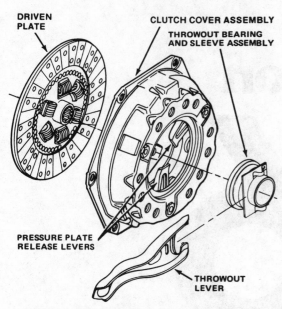

1975–76 10 inch clutch assembly

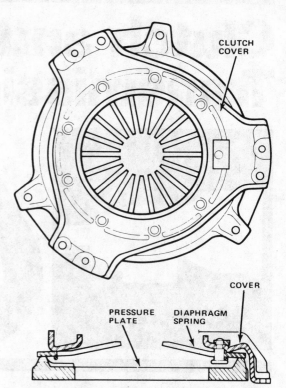

Clutch pressure plate for: 1977 all 4-sp; 1978 all SR4 4-sp; 1979 all Pacer and Concord, and AMX 8-cyl. with SR4 4-sp.; 1980 Pacer, AMX, Concord 6-cyl. with SR4 4-sp; 1982 Spirit and Concord 6-cyl.

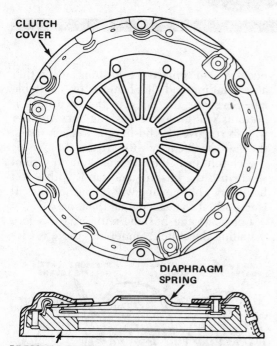

Clutch pressure plate for: 1977–78 all 3-sp; 1979 Spirit 6-cyl. with 150T 3-sp or SR4 4-sp; 1980 Spirit 6-cyl. with 4-sp; 1981 all 6-cyl.; 1982 Eagle 6-cyl.

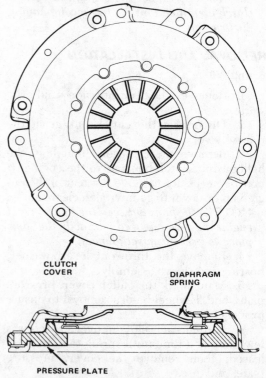

Clutch pressure plate for: 1977–79 4-121 with HR-1 4-sp; 1980–82 all 4-cyl.

bricating wick, which should be soaked in engine oil, then placed in the crankshaft cavity.

8. Inspect the flywheel surface for heat cracks, scoring, or blue heat marks. Check the flywheel capscrews for proper torque (105 ft. lbs.). It will be necessary to lock-up the flywheel ring gear with a block or flywheel

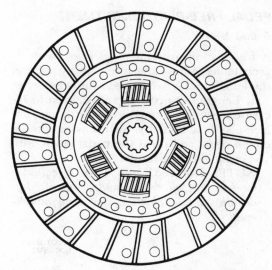

1977–82 clutch driven plate for 6 and 8 cylinder

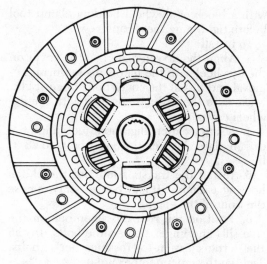

4-151 clutch driven plate

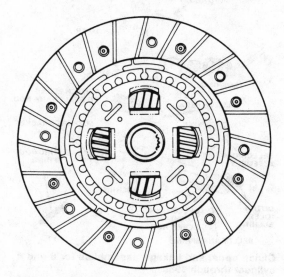

1977–79 4-121 clutch driven plate

holding clamp tool before tightening these capscrews.

The throwout (release) linkage consists of a forked, pivoted lever contacting the bearing at one end and the linkage pushrod on the other. A return spring keeps the lever in contact with the ball pivot.

The throwout bearing itself is prelubricated and cannot be repacked if dry. A bad bearing results in uneven clutch pedal pressure and a grinding, rattling noise when the pedal is depressed. Replace any noisy throwout bearings as soon as is practicable to prevent disintegration and possible transmission or clutch damage.

9. Slide the new clutch disc onto the transmission input shaft to check for binding.

Remove any burrs from either the splines or hub using emery paper, then clean with a safe solvent.

10. Place the clutch disc against the flywheel and secure it by inserting a dummy pilot shaft (such shafts, made of wood, are available from automotive jobbers) or an old transmission input shaft.

11. Place the new pressure plate (it's always a good policy to replace the pressure plate when installing a new disc) in position, after first making sure that the clutch disc is facing the proper direction (the flywheel side is marked), and that the matchmarks are aligned if the old pressure plate is used.

12. Install all the capscrews fingertight. Tighten the screws a little at a time, working around the pressure plate to avoid distorting it, to 40 ft. lbs. Remove the pilot shaft.

NOTE: *Do not depress the clutch pedal until the transmission is installed or the throwout bearing will fall out.*

13. Install the clutch housing, throwout bearing and transmission. Hook up the clutch linkage and check the adjustment.

4-121

1. Remove the transmission.
2. Mark the clutch cover and flywheel for reassembly. Remove the cover and driven plate by loosening the bolts alternately and in several stages to avoid cover distortion.

Inspect the flywheel surface for heat cracks, scoring, or blue heat marks. Check the flywheel capscrews for proper torque. It will be necessary to lock-up the flywheel ring gear with a block or flywheel holding clamp tool before tightening these capscrews.

To install:

3. Align the driven plate and the cover on the flywheel with the marks made during removal and install the cover bolts finger tight. Make sure the cover is engaged with the flywheel dowel pins.

4. Using a clutch alignment tool, align the driven plate. Tighten the cover bolts to 23 ft. lbs.

5. Install the transmission and the clutch housing assembly. It may be necessary to raise the front of the engine.

6. Position the rear crossmember on the side sills and finger tighten the bolts. Install the transmission-to-crossmember bolts. Tighten the crossmember nuts.

The remainder of the installation is the reverse of removal. Be sure, when installing the gearshift lever that the shift rail insert is facing straight down and the offset on the side of the lever fork is facing the right side of the extension housing before installing the lever.

4-151

1. Remove the starter, disconnect the slave cylinder spring at the throwout lever, and remove the transmission.

2. Remove the clutch housing to engine bolts. Remove the housing.

3. Remove the throwout bearing.

4. Matchmark the clutch cover and flywheel for installation. Loosen the clutch cover bolts alternately and evenly, to avoid distortion, and remove the clutch cover and disc.

5. Inspect the parts for signs of overheating (blue color), scoring, or abnormal wear. Overheated parts should be replaced. Deep scoring or wear may require replacement of the disc and cover, and refacing or replacement of the flywheel.

6. Place the disc and cover on the flywheel, aligning the marks made previously if the same cover is being used. Be sure the cover is engaged with the dowel pins. Install the cover bolts finger tight.

7. Align the disc with an alignment tool.

8. Tighten the cover bolts alternately and evenly to 23 ft. lbs. Remove the alignment tool.

9. Install the throwout bearing, clutch housing, and transmission. The housing-to-engine bolts and transmission-to-housing bolts should be tightened to 54 ft. lbs.

PEDAL FREE-PLAY ADJUSTMENT

6 and V8

A free-play measurement of ⅞ to 1⅛ in. is acceptable. Adjust the free-play by varying the length of the bellcrank-to-throwout lever rod. Lengthen to reduce and shorten to increase free-play. The easiest way to measure free-play is to hold a yardstick alongside the clutch pedal and press the pedal down until you can feel spring tension.

NOTE: *The 1981 and later 6 cylinder models and all 4-151 models have a hydraulic clutch which requires no adjustment.*

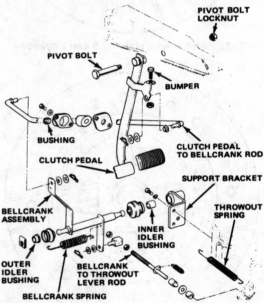

Clutch pedal and linkage assemblies for 6 and 8 cylinder through 1980

4-121

The clutch pedal free play is adjusted by varying the length of the control cable. The preferred free-play is 1⅛ inch.

1. To adjust the cable, loosen the cable locknut at the rear of the cable and pull the cable forward until the free play is eliminated from the throw out lever.

2. Rotate the adjuster nut toward the rear of the cable until the nut tabs contact the clutch housing.

3. Release the cable housing and turn the adjuster nut until the tabs engage the slots on the clutch housing.

4. Tighten the clutch cable locknut. Recheck clutch pedal free play.

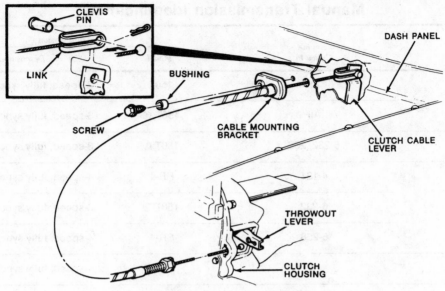

1977–79 4-121 clutch linkage

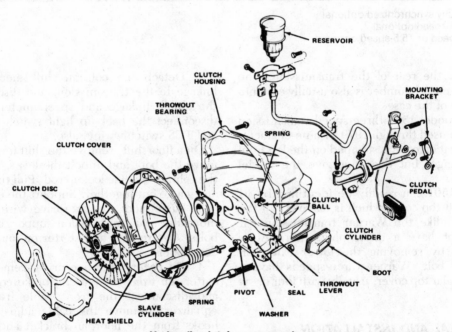

Hydraulic clutch components

MANUAL TRANSMISSION

A lightweight Warner SR4 four-speed was introduced in six cylinder models in late 1976 and is used in all 1980–81 models. The four cylinder uses a Warner HR-1 four-speed transmission through 1979. The SR4 transmission has a cast aluminum case and extension housing, while the HR-1 has a cast iron case and an aluminum extension housing. The SR4 and HR-1 have internal, non-adjustable shift linkage. In 1982 a new Warner (T4) four speed and an optional Warner (T5) five speed transmission were introduced. Both are lightweight and feature an integral mounted shift mechanism.

NOTE: *SR4 and HR-1 transmissions have metric fasteners in most threaded holes.*

An identification tag, containing Warner and American Motors part numbers, is lo-

Manual Transmission Identification

Year	Engine Cyl/cu in.	Transmission	
		Model	Description
1975	All	150T	3-speed, fully synchronized
1976	All	150T ①	3-speed, fully synchronized
1977	6-232, 258	150T ②	3-speed, fully synchronized
1978–79	4-121	HR-1	4-speed, fully synchronized
	6-232	150T ②	3-speed, fully synchronized
	6-258	SR-4	4-speed, fully synchronized
1980–81	All	SR-4	4-speed, fully synchronized
1982	All	SR-4 ③	4-speed, fully synchronized

①T-14, fully synchronized optional
②SR-4, 4-speed optional
③T4 4-speed or T5 5-speed optional

cated at the rear of the transmission. The Warner model number is also usually cast into the side of the case.

The model 150T three-speed transmission was also used through 1979. A nine-character identification code is stamped on the left front case flange, but does not give the model number.

The 150T can readily be identified by its nine-bolt top cover which is narrower in the front. Unlike the Warner transmissions, it does not have a drain plug: lubricant is drained by removing the lower extension housing bolt. Warner three-speeds have a rectangular top cover, usually with four or six bolts.

REMOVAL AND INSTALLATION

All except Eagle

NOTE: *Open the hood to avoid damage when the rear crossmember is removed. If the overdrive and transmission are to be separated, first engage then disengage the overdrive with the clutch pedal depressed and the engine running.*

1. Matchmark the driveshaft and rear axle yoke for correct installation. Split the rear universal joint and slide the driveshaft off the back of the transmission. Support the transmission with a jack.

2. Detach the column shift mechanism linkage to the transmission, and disconnect the clutch linkage and speedometer cable; disconnect the back-up light switch wiring, and TCS switch wiring, also.

On a floorshift, remove the shift lever. Remove the boot and unbolt the lever. Detach the column reverse lockup rod. Pull the lever and gauge out together. Support the engine.

3. Disconnect the overdrive wiring. Remove the rear transmission support cushion bolts. Also remove the starter on four cylinder models.

4. On Pacers with overdrive, remove the cotter pin from the parking brake equalizer and disconnect the front cable from the equalizer. Remove the cable adjuster and hooks from the floorpan bracket and lower equalizer and rear brake cables to provide clearance. Also, remove the ground strap from the floorpan.

NOTE: *On V8 models with dual exhaust or dual catalytic converters, exhaust pipes must be disconnected from manifolds and lowered so to gain working clearance.*

5. On HR1s, remove the throwout lever protective boot and disengage the clutch cable from the lever. Also remove the inspection cover at the front of the clutch housing.

6. Remove the transmission support crossmember except on Pacers; remove the cross-

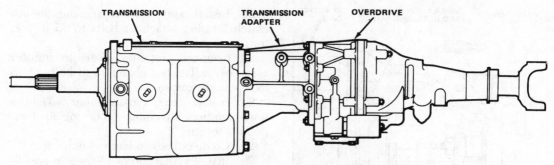

Pacer overdrive unit attached to the transmission

member with the transmission on those models. Remove the two lower studs which hold the transmission to the bell housing and replace these two studs with two long pilot studs on 150Ts and SR4s. On the HR1, remove the catalytic converter support bracket attaching bolts from the transmission rear support.

7. Remove the two top studs and slide the transmission assembly along the pilot studs and out of the car. On HR1s, support the engine and remove the clutch housing to engine bolts and remove the clutch and transmission as an assembly.

Installation is as follows:

1. Fill the slots in the inner groove of the throwout bearing with high temperature grease and soak the crankshaft pilot bushing wick in engine oil. Fit the throwout bearing and the sleeve assembly in the clutch fork. Center the bearing over the clutch lever. Shift 150Ts and SR4s into first gear.

2. Install two pilot studs in the clutch housing, instead of the lower clutch housing cap screws on 150Ts and SR4s.

3. Carefully slide the transmission into place. Be careful not to damage the clutch driven plate splines while mating them with the transmission input shaft. It may be necessary to raise the front of the engine for the HR1.

4. Install the upper screws, which attach the case to the housing. Remove the pilot studs and install the lower cap screws.

5. If the car is equipped with a floor shift, install the shift lever retainer and shift rods, if removed.

6. Attach the speedometer cable, connect the back-up light switch wires and the transmission controlled spark (TCS) wire, if so equipped. On the HR1, connect the clutch cable and adjust as necessary. Also install the inspection cover and the catalytic converter bracket bolts.

7. Raise the transmission. Attach the rear crossmember and support to the transmission. Fasten the crossmember to the side sills and finger tighten the bolts. Install and tighten the crossmember-to-support bolts. Tighten the crossmember stud nuts. Install the parking brake cables and ground strap on Pacer.

8. Attach the exhaust pipes to the exhaust manifolds, on V8 engines, if they were removed.

9. Install the front U-joint yoke on the transmission. Do the same for the rear U-joint at the differential. Be sure the alignment marks made earlier line up.

10. Connect the shift rods on the column shift transmissions and the reverse lockup rod on the floorshift transmission. Check the transmission oil level and add lubricant, as needed.

11. Remove the supports and lower the car.

12. Install the shift lever if the car is a floorshift transmission.

13. Adjust the shift linkage, if it was disturbed.

1980–81 Eagle

1. Shift transmission into neutral.

2. Remove screws attaching gearshift lever bezel and boot to floorpan.

3. Slide bezel and boot upward on gearshift lever to provide access to lever attaching bolts.

4. Remove bolts attaching gearshift lever to lever mounting cover on transmission adapter housing and remove gearshift lever.

5. Remove bolts attaching gearshift lever mounting cover to transmission adapter and remove mounting cover to provide access to transfer case upper mounting stud nut in transmission adapter housing.

6. Remove nut from transfer case upper

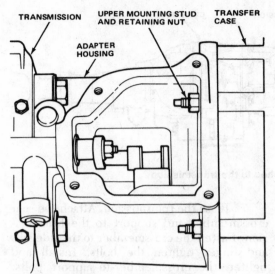

TRANSMISSION   UPPER MOUNTING STUD   TRANSFER
                AND RETAINING NUT   CASE

ADAPTER
HOUSING

Eagle offset lever and retaining nut

mounting stud located inside transmission adapter housing.

7. Raise automobile.

8. Remove skid plate.

9. Remove speedometer adapter retainer bolt and remove retainer, adapter, and cable. Discard adapter O-ring and plug adapter opening in transfer case to prevent excessive oil spillage.

NOTE: *Mark the position of the speedometer adapter for assembly alignment reference before removing it.*

10. Mark propeller shafts and axle yokes for assembly alignment reference and disconnect propeller shafts at transfer case.

11. Disconnect backup lamp switch wire.

12. Place support stand under engine.

13. Support transmission and transfer case using transmission jack.

14. Remove rear crossmember.

15. Remove catalytic converter bracket from transfer case.

16. Remove bolts attaching transmission to clutch housing.

17. Remove transmission and transfer case as assembly.

18. Remove nuts from transfer case mounting studs and remove transmission from transfer case.

19. Install transmission on transfer case. Install and tighten all transfer case mounting stud nuts to 26 foot-pounds torque.

20. Support transmission-transfer case assembly on transmission jack.

21. Align transmission clutch shaft with throwout bearing and clutch disc splines and seat transmission against clutch housing.

22. Install and tighten transmission-to-clutch housing attaching bolts to 55 ft. lbs. torque.

23. Connect propeller shafts to transfer case yokes. Tighten clamp strap bolts to 15 foot-pounds torque.

24. Install rear crossmember. Tighten crossmember attaching bolts to 30 foot-pounds torque.

25. Connect backup lamp switch wire.

26. Install replacement O-ring on speedometer adapter and install adapter and cable, and retainer. Tighten retainer bolt to 100 in. lbs. torque.

CAUTION: *Do not attempt to reuse the original adapter O-ring. The ring is designed to swell in service to improve its sealing qualities and could be cut or torn during installation if reuse is attempted.*

27. Attach catalytic converter bracket to transfer case. Tighten retaining nuts to 26 foot-pounds torque.

28. Check and correct lubricant levels in transmission and transfer case if necessary.

29. Install skid plate. Tighten skid plate attaching bolts to 30 ft. lbs. torque.

30. Remove stand used to support engine and remove transmission jack if not removed previously.

31. Lower automobile.

32. Clean mating surfaces of gearshift lever mounting cover and transmission adapter housing.

33. Apply RTV-type sealant to gearshift lever mounting cover and intall cover on transmission adapter housing. Tighten cover bolts to 13 ft. lbs. torque.

34. Install gearshift lever on mounting cover. Be sure lever is engaged with shift rail before tightening lever attaching bolts. Tighten lever attaching bolts to 18 ft. lbs. torque.

35. Position gearshift lever boot and bezel in floorpan and install bezel attaching screws.

1982 Eagle

1. Shift transmission into neutral.

2. Remove screws attaching gearshift lever bezel and boot to floorpan.

3. Slide bezel and boot upward on gearshift lever to provide access to lever attaching bolts.

4. Remove bolts attaching gearshift lever to lever mounting cover on transmission adapter housing and remove gearshift lever.

5. Remove bolts attaching gearshift lever mounting cover to transmission adapter and

remove mounting cover to provide access to transfer case upper mounting stud nut in transmission adapter housing.

6. Remove nut from transfer case upper mounting stud located inside transmission adapter housing.

7. Raise automobile.

8. Remove skid plate.

9. Remove speedometer adapter retainer bolt and remove retainer, adapter, and cable. Discard adapter O-ring and plug adapter opening in transfer case to prevent excessive oil spillage.

NOTE: *Mark the position of the speedometer adapter for assembly alignment reference before removing it.*

10. Mark propeller shafts and axle yokes for assembly alignment reference and disconnect propeller shafts at transfer case.

11. Disconnect backup lamp switch wire.

12. Place support stand under engine.

13. Support transmission and transfer case using transmission jack.

14. Remove rear crossmember.

15. Remove catalytic converter bracket from transfer case and brace rod from bracket.

16. Remove bolts attaching transmission to clutch housing.

17. Remove transmission and transfer case as assembly.

18. Remove nuts from transfer case mounting studs and remove transmission from transfer case.

19. Install transmission on transfer case. Install and tighten all transfer case mounting stud nuts to 26 ft. lbs. torque.

20. Support transmission-transfer case assembly on transmission jack.

21. Align transmission clutch shaft without throwout bearing and clutch disc splines and seat transmission against clutch housing.

22. Install and tighten transmission-to-clutch housing attaching bolts to 55 ft. lbs. torque.

23. Connect propeller shafts to transfer case yokes. Tighten clamp strap bolts to 15 foot-pounds torque.

24. Install brace rod and rear crossmember. Tighten attaching bolts to 30 foot-pounds torque.

25. Connect backup lamp switch wire.

26. Install replacement O-ring on speedometer adapter and install adapter and cable, and retainer. Tighten retainer bolt to 100 in. lbs. torque.

CAUTION: *Do not attempt to reuse the original adapter O-ring. The ring is de-signed to swell in service to improve its sealing qualities and could be cut or torn during installation if reuse is attempted.*

27. Attach catalytic converter bracket to transfer case. Tighten retaining nuts to 26 ft. lbs. torque.

28. Check and correct lubricant levels in transmission and transfer case, if necessary.

29. Install skid plate. Tighten skid plate attaching bolts to 30 ft. lbs. torque.

30. Remove stand used to support engine and remove transmission jack if not removed previously.

31. Lower automobile.

32. Clean mating surfaces of gearshift lever mounting cover and transmission adapter housing.

33. Apply RTV-type sealant to gearshift lever mounting cover and install cover bolts to 13 foot-pounds torque.

34. Install gearshift lever on mounting cover. Be sure lever is engaged with shift rail before tightening lever attaching bolts. Tighten lever attaching bolts to 18 ft. lbs. torque.

35. Position gearshift lever boot and bezel in floorpan and install bezel attaching screws.

Linkage Adjustment
PACER
Column Shift Linkage Adjustment

1. Detach the shift rods from the shift levers. Insert a $3/16$ in. drill through the column shift lever holes.

2. Shift into Reverse and lock the column with the ignition key. Position the First/Reverse shift lever in Reverse.

3. Adjust the shift rod trunnion to a free pin fit in the outer shift lever. Tighten the trunnion locknuts.

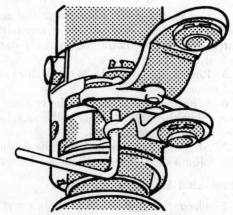

Aligning shift levers on column shift models

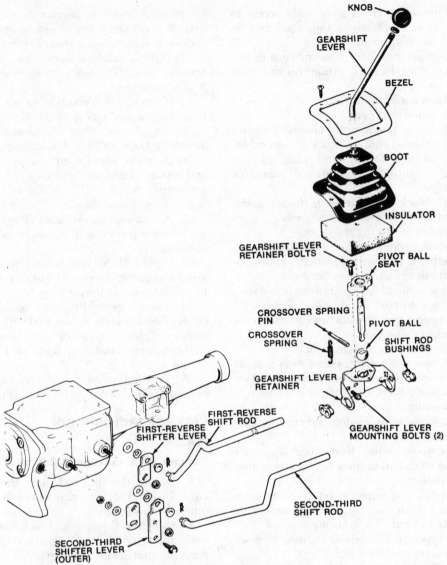

Three speed floor shift linkage

4. Unlock the column and move the gearshift to Neutral. Both of the transmission outer shift levers should be in the Neutral detent.

5. Repeat Step 3 for the Second/Third shift rod trunnion.

6. Withdraw the drill from the column levers. Shift through all gears and check for a free crossover into Neutral.

7. Shift into Reverse and lock the column. The column should lock without any binding.

Floor Shift Linkage Adjustment

1. Place the transmission shift levers in Neutral.

2. Loosen the Second/Third transmission lever attaching nut and adjusting bolt.

3. With the First/Reverse shift rod in the Neutral position, align the Second/Third shift rod so that its notch is exactly aligned with the notch in the First-Reverse shift rod.

4. Tighten the adjustment bolt and attaching nut.

5. Shift through all of the gears being particularly careful to check for binding in the First-to-Second shift.

6. To adjust the back-up light switch, loosen the jam nuts and then slide the switch forward or backward, as necessary. Tighten the jam nuts.

ALL EXCEPT PACER

Column Shift

1. Disconnect the shift rods from the transmission shift levers. Insert a $3/16$ in. drill through the column shift lever holes.

2. Shift into Reverse and lock the column with the ignition key. Position the transmission First/Reverse shift lever in Reverse.

3. Adjust the shift rod trunnion to a free pin fit in the transmission shift lever. Tighten the trunnion locknuts.

4. Unlock the column and move the gearshift to Neutral. Both of the transmission shift levers should be in the Neutral detent.

5. Repeat step three for the Second/Third shift rod trunnion.

6. Remove the drill from the column levers. Shift through all gears and check for a free crossover into Neutral.

7. Shift into Reverse and lock the column. The column should lock without any binding.

Three-Speed Floorshift

1. Place the transmission shift levers in their neutral positions.

2. Loosen the second-third lever adjuster.

3. Keeping the first-reverse shift rod and transmission lever in the neutral position, align the second-third rod so the shift notch is exactly aligned with the first-reverse shift notch. Tighten the adjuster.

4. Operate the linkage and check for full engagement of all gears and a smooth crossover from first to second.

5. If there is a reverse lockup rod to the steering column, loosen both of the locknuts about ½ in. each. Shift into reverse and lock the column. You may have to rotate the lever at the bottom of the column up into the locked position. Tighten the lower locknut until it contacts the trunnion. Tighten the upper locknut while holding the trunnion centered. Unlock the column and shift through the gears. Shift into reverse and lock the binding.

PACER OVERDRIVE

The Laycock de Normanville overdrive unit for the Pacer is an electro-hydraulic-actuated, planetary gear-type, mounted to a special adapter at the rear of the transmission.

When the overdrive is in the direct drive position (overdrive switched off), and the car is driven forward, power from the transmission mainshaft is transmitted through the freewheel rollers and unidirectional clutch to the overdrive output shaft. When the car is backing up or during periods of engine braking, torque is transmitted through the clutch sliding member which is held by spring pressure against the tapered portion of the output shaft. When the overdrive is actuated, the clutch sliding member is pressed by hydraulic pressure against the brake disc (ring), which locks the sun wheel. As a result, the output shaft of the overdrive rotates at a higher speed than the mainshaft thereby accomplishing a 30% reduction in engine speed in relation to vehicle speed.

The overdrive is actuated by a switch located beneath the steering wheel. This switch energizes a solenoid on the overdrive unit, via a switch on the transmission, which is cut in only when Third gear is engaged. The solenoid has two windings: a heavy control winding and a lower current, hold winding. When actuated, the control winding opens the overdrive control valve, whereupon the control winding is cut off and the valve is held in the open position by the hold winding. The control valve regulates the pressurized oil flow from the cam-operated pump to the hydraulic pistons which operate the overdrive clutch sliding member.

REMOVAL AND INSTALLATION

To facilitate removal, the vehicle should first be driven in Third gear with the overdrive engaged, and then coasted for a few seconds with the overdrive disengaged and the clutch pedal depressed.

1. Remove the transmission from the vehicle as previously outlined in the "Transmission Removal and Installation" section.

2. Disconnect the solenoid cables.

3. If the overdrive unit has not already been drained, remove the six bolts and the overdrive oil pan.

CAUTION: *Be careful to avoid spilling hot transmission fluid on the skin.*

4. Remove the bolts which retain the overdrive unit to the transmission intermediate flange. Pull the unit straight to the rear until it clears the transmission mainshaft.

5. Reverse the above procedure to install. Install the overdrive oil pan with a new gasket. After installation of the transmission and overdrive assembly, fill the transmission (which automatically fills the overdrive), to the proper level with the correct lubricant. Check

the lubricant level in the transmission after driving 6–9 miles.

AUTOMATIC TRANSMISSION

Transmission Removal and Installation

1975–76

1. Disconnect fan shroud (if equipped).
2. Disconnect transmission fill tube at upper bracket.
3. Raise car on hoist.

CAUTION: *It is necessary that the hood be open to avoid damage to the hood and air cleaner when the rear crossmember is removed.*

Automatic Transmission Identification

Year	Engine	Transmission
1975–76	6-232	Chrysler 904
	6-258	Chrysler 904 ①
	8-304	Chrysler 998 ①
	8-360	Chrysler 727
	8-401	Chrysler 727
1977–79	4-121	Chrysler 904
	6-232	Chrysler 904
	6-258	Chrysler 904 ①
	8-304	Chrysler 998 ①
	8-360	Chrysler 727
	8-401	Chrysler 727
1980–82	4-151	Chrysler 904 ②
	6-258	Chrysler 904 ③
	6-258 (Eagle)	Chrysler 998

① 727 available as an option on 6-258 and 8-304, except Pacer
② Standard ratio
③ Wide ratio

4. Remove inspection cover from front of converter housing.
5. Rotate torque converter until drain plug is accessible. Remove plug and drain converter.
6. Remove transmission fill tube.
7. Remove starter.
8. Mark rear universal joint and yoke for alignment reference during installation.
9. Remove propeller shaft.
10. Disconnect catalytic converter(s) (if equipped) and front exhaust pipes to provide working clearance.
11. Disconnect front exhaust pipe brace from transmission.
12. Disconnect speedometer cable, throttle and shift linkage, neutral safety, TCS switch wires, fluid cooler lines, and governor pressure oil line from transmission to TCS control switch.
13. Mark converter drive plate and converter for alignment reference during installation.
14. Remove bolts which attach converter to drive plate.
15. Place transmission jack under transmission.
16. Remove crossmember from side sill and rear support cushion.
17. Remove support cushion and adapter from extension housing.
18. Remove bolts which attach transmission to engine.
19. Move transmission and converter a sufficient distance to clear crankshaft.
20. Maintain pressure against converter and lower assembly until transmission housing clears engine.
21. If torque converter is removed, insert Pump Aligning Tool J-24033 (Models 904-998) or J-24045 (Model 727) into pump.
22. Engage pump rotor.
23. Rotate tool until drilled holes in tool are vertical.
24. Remove tool.
25. Rotate converter until pump drive slots are vertical and carefully install converter into pump.
26. Place assembly on transmission jack.
27. Raise transmission assembly and align converter with drive plate. Refer to marks made during removal.
28. Pull transmission forward.
29. Raise, lower, or tilt transmission to align converter housing pilot holes with dowels in engine.
30. Install two lower converter housing attaching bolts and pull housing up snug.

31. Install remaining attaching bolts.

32. Tighten all converter housing attaching bolts to 28 foot-pounds torque.

33. Install rear crossmember, rear support cushion and adapter.

34. Remove transmission jack.

35. Install screws which attach torque converter to drive plate.

36. Install drain plug.

37. Install inspection cover.

38. Install starter.

39. Connect neutral safety, TCS switches, throttle and shift linkages, fluid cooler lines, and speedometer cable.

40. Install transmission filler tube in transmission.

41. Install propeller shaft. Refer to alignment marks made during removal.

42. Connect front exhaust pipes, catalytic converter(s) (if equipped), and lower car.

43. Connect filler tube upper bracket.

44. Fill transmission to correct level.

45. Adjust manual and throttle linkage.

46. Road-test car for proper transmission operation.

1977-79

4-121 Engines

1. Open hood.

CAUTION: *The hood must remain open to avoid damaging the hood and air cleaner when the rear crossmember is removed.*

2. Disconnect fan shroud.

3. Remove bolt attaching transmission filler tube to rear of engine.

4. Place gearshift lever in Neutral.

5. Raise car on hoist.

6. Mark propeller shaft and yoke for assembly alignment reference.

7. Remove propeller shaft.

8. Remove starter motor.

9. Remove speedometer adapter and cable assembly. Cover adapter bore in case after removal.

10. Disconnect gearshift and throttle linkage. On cars with column shift, remove bolt attaching linkage bellcrank bracket to converter housing.

11. Remove cover at front of converter housing.

12. Mark converter drive plate and converter for assembly alignment reference.

13. Remove bolts attaching converter to drive plate. Rotate crankshaft and drive plate using ratchet handle and socket or box-end wrench on crankshaft front pulley bolt to gain access to drive plate-to-converter bolts.

NOTE: *The crankshaft pulley bolt is a metric size and requires a 24 mm socket or wrench. However, a $^{15}/_{16}$ socket or wrench may also be used.*

14. Support transmission using transmission jack. Retain transmission on jack using safety chain.

15. Lower transmission slightly and disconnect oil cooler lines at transmission.

16. Remove bolt attaching rear support cushion to rear support cushion bracket (bracket is attached to transmission extension housing).

17. Remove rear crossmember-to-frame side sill attaching nuts and remove crossmember and support cushion as assembly.

18. Place support stand under front of engine.

19. Remove bolts attaching catalytic converter support bracket to transmission.

20. Remove bolts attaching transmission and filler tube to engine.

NOTE: *The transmission-to-engine block bolts are metric size bolts.*

21. Move transmission and converter rearward until clear of crankshaft.

22. Hold converter in position and lower transmission until converter housing clears engine.

CAUTION: *If the transmission was removed to correct a malfunction that generated sludge or heavy accumulations of metal or friction material particles, the oil cooler and cooler lines must be thoroughly flushed and the torque converter replaced. Do not attempt to flush the converter if it is contaminated.*

23. If torque converter was removed, insert Pump Aligning Tool J-24033 into pump rotor and engage tool slots with pump rotor drive lugs.

24. Rotate aligning tool until hole in tool is vertical then remove tool.

25. Rotate converter until pump drive slots in converter hub are vertical.

26. Carefully insert converter hub into oil pump. Be sure drive lugs of pump inner rotor are completely engaged with drive slots in converter hub.

27. Raise transmission and align converter with drive plate. Refer to alignment marks made during removal.

28. Move transmission forward and raise, lower, or tilt transmission to align converter housing pilot holes with dowels in engine block.

NOTE: *If the downward angle at the rear of the engine is not sufficient to permit transmission installation, raise the front of the engine to increase the downward angle.*

29. Install two, transmission-to-engine lower attaching bolts and tighten bolts to pull transmission to engine.

30. Install drive plate-to-converter attaching bolts. Tighten bolts to 26 ft. lbs. torque.

31. Install remaining transmission-to-engine attaching bolts. Tighten bolts to 54 ft. lbs. torque.

32. Connect oil cooler lines.

33. Raise transmission, position rear crossmember, install crossmember attaching nuts and tighten nuts to 30 ft. lbs. torque.

34. Install rear support cushion-to-support cushion bracket bolt and tighten bolt to 49 ft. lbs. torque.

35. Remove safety chain and transmission jack.

36. Install cover at front of converter housing.

37. Install starter motor.

38. Connect neutral start switch wires to switch terminal.

39. Connect gearshift and throttle linkage. On cars with column shift, position linkage bellcrank, bracket on converter housing and install bracket attaching bolt.

40. Install speedometer cable and adapter assembly. Be sure adapter is correctly indexed.

41. Install catalytic converter support bracket bolts.

42. Lower car.

43. Fill transmission to correct fluid level.

44. Adjust gearshift lever and throttle linkage.

NOTE: *The gearshift lever adjusting trunnion is located on the steering column shift lever.*

45. Road test car to check transmission operation.

6 and V8 Engines

1. Disconnect fan shroud if equipped.

2. Disconnect transmission fill tube at upper bracket.

3. Open hood.

CAUTION: *It is necessary that the hood be open to avoid damaging the hood and air cleaner when the rear crossmember is removed.*

4. Raise car on hoist.

5. Remove inspection cover from converter housing.

6. On six-cylinder cars, remove screw attaching clamp to exhaust pipe support bracket and slide clamp off bracket.

7. Remove transmission fill tube.

8. Mark propeller shaft and rear axle yoke for assembly alignment reference.

10. Remove propeller shaft.

11. On eight-cylinder cars, disconnect exhaust pipes at exhaust manifolds.

12. Remove speedometer adapter and cable assembly. Cover adapter bore in case after adapter removal.

13. Disconnect gearshift and throttle linkage.

14. Disconnect wires at neutral start switch.

15. Disconnect TCS switch oil line at transmission fitting.

16. Mark converter drive plate and converter for assembly alignment reference.

17. Remove bolts attaching converter to drive plate. Rotate crankshaft and drive plate using ratchet handle and socket on crankshaft front pulley bolt to gain access to drive plate bolts.

18. Support transmission using transmission jack. Retain transmission on jack using safety chain.

19. Lower transmission slightly and disconnect oil cooler lines at transmission.

20. Remove bolts attaching rear support cushion to transmission.

21. Remove rear crossmember-to-frame side sill attaching nuts and remove crossmember. On Pacers, remove ground strap.

22. Remove bolts attaching converter support bracket to transmission.

23. Remove bolts attaching transmission to engine.

24. Move transmission and converter rearward to clear crankshaft.

25. Hold converter in position and lower assembly until converter housing clears engine.

CAUTION: *If the transmission was removed to correct a malfunction that generated sludge or heavy accumulations of metal particles or friction material, the oil cooler and cooler lines must be flushed thoroughly and the torque converter replaced. Do not attempt to flush the converter if it is contaminated.*

26. If torque converter was removed, insert Pump Aligning Tool J-24033 in pump rotor until rotor drive lugs engage slots in tool.

27. Rotate tool until drilled hole in tool is vertical and remove tool.

28. Rotate converter until pump drive slots in converter hub are vertical and carefully insert converter hub into pump. Be sure drive lugs of lump inner rotor are properly engaged in drive slots of converter hub.

29. Raise transmission and align converter with drive plate. Refer to assembly alignment marks.

30. Pull transmission forward.

31. Raise, lower, or tilt transmission to align converter housing pilot holes with dowels in engine.

32. Install two converter housing lower attaching bolts and tighten bolts to pull housing to engine.

33. Install drive plate-to-converter attaching bolts.

34. Install remaining converter housing-to-engine attaching bolts and tighten all bolts to 28 ft. lbs. torque.

35. Connect oil cooler lines.

36. Install rear support cushion on transmission.

37. Raise transmission, position rear crossmember, and install crossmember attaching nuts. On Pacers, install ground strap.

38. Remove safety chain and transmission jack.

39. Install inspection cover.

40. On six-cylinder cars, install exhaust pipe support bracket.

41. Install starter.

42. Connect wires to neutral switch.

43. Connect gearshift and throttle linkage.

44. Install speedometer cable and adapter assembly. Be sure adapter is correctly indexed.

45. Install propeller shaft. Refer to alignment marks made during removal.

46. On eight-cylinder cars, connect front exhaust pipes and catalytic converter support bracket bolts.

47. Lower car.

48. Fill transmission to correct level.

49. Adjust gearshift selector lever linkage.

50. Road-test car to check transmission operation.

1980–81

4-151

1. Open hood.

CAUTION: *The hood must remain open to avoid damaging the hood and air cleaner when the rear crossmember is removed.*

2. Disconnect fan shroud.

3. Remove bolt attaching transmission fill tube to engine.

4. Place gearshift lever in Neutral.

5. Raise automobile on hoist.

6. Mark propeller shaft and yoke for assembly alignment reference. On Eagle models, also remove skid plate.

7. Remove propeller shafts.

8. Remove starter motor. On Eagle models, also remove stiffening braces.

9. Remove speedometer adapter and cable assembly. Cover adapter bore after removal.

10. Disconnect gearshift and throttle linkage. On automobiles with column shift, remove bolt attaching linkage bellcrank bracket to converter housing.

11. Remove cover at front of converter housing.

12. Mark converter drive plate and converter for assembly alignment reference.

13. Remove bolts attaching converter to drive plate. Rotate crankshaft and drive plate using ratchet handle and socket or box-end wrench on crankshaft front pulley bolt to gain access to drive plate-to-converter bolts.

NOTE: *The crankshaft pulley bolt is a metric size bolt.*

14. Support transmission using transmission jack. Retain transmission on jack using safety chain.

NOTE: *On Eagle models, both the transmission and transfer case must be properly supported on the transmission jack and retained with safety chain.*

15. Disconnect oil cooler lines at transmission.

16. Remove bolt attaching rear support cushion to rear support cushion bracket (bracket is attached to transmission extension housing).

17. Remove rear crossmember attaching nuts and remove crossmember and support cushion as assembly.

18. Place support stand under front of engine.

19. Remove bolts attaching catalytic converter support bracket to transmission, if equipped.

20. Remove fill tube.

21. Remove bolts attaching transmission to engine.

NOTE: *The transmission-to-engine block bolts are metric size bolts.*

22. Move transmission (and transfer case, if equipped) and converter rearward until clear of crankshaft.

23. Hold converter in position and lower transmission until transmission converter housing clears engine.

CAUTION: *If the transmission was removed to correct a malfunction that generated sludge or heavy accumulations of metal or friction material particles, the oil cooler and cooler lines must be thoroughly flushed and the torque converter replaced. Do not attempt to flush the converter if it is contaminated.*

24. If torque converter was removed, insert Pump Aligning Tool J-24033 into pump rotor and engage tool slots with pump rotor drive lugs.

25. Rotate aligning tool until hole in tool is vertical then remove tool.

26. Rotate converter until pump drive slots in converter hub are vertical.

27. Carefully insert converter hub into oil pump. Be sure drive lugs of pump inner rotor are completely engaged with drive slots in converter hub.

28. Raise transmission and align converter with drive plate. Refer to alignment marks made during removal.

29. Move transmission forward and raise, lower, or tilt transmission to align transmission converter housing dowel holes with dowels in engine block.

NOTE: *If the downward angle at the rear of the engine is not sufficient to permit transmission installation, raise the front of the engine to increase the downward angle.*

30. Install two transmission-to-engine lower attaching bolts and tighten bolts evenly to pull transmission to engine.

31. Install drive plate-to-converter attaching bolts. Tighten bolts to 40 ft. lbs. torque.

NOTE: *Coat threads of drive plate-to-converter attaching bolts with Loctite 271 or equivalent.*

32. Install remaining transmission-to-engine attaching bolts. Tighten bolts to 54 ft. lbs. torque.

33. Connect oil cooler lines.

34. Install rear crossmember and support cushion. Tighten attaching nuts to 30 ft. lbs. torque.

35. Install rear support nushion-to-support cushion bracket bolt. Tighten bolt to 48 ft. lbs. torque.

36. Remove safety chain and transmission jack.

37. Install converter housing inspection cover.

38. Install starter motor. On Eagle models also install stiffening brace and skid plate.

39. Connect neutral start switch wires to switch terminal.

40. Connect gearshift and throttle linkage. On automobiles with column shift, position linkage bellcrank bracket on converter housing and install bracket attaching bolt.

41. Install speedometer cable and adapter assembly. Be sure adapter is correctly indexed.

42. Connect catalytic converter, if equipped. On Eagle models, add correct quantity of transfer case lubricant.

43. Lower automobile.

44. Fill transmission to correct fluid level.

45. Check and adjust gearshift lever and throttle linkage if necessary.

NOTE: *The gearshift lever adjusting trunnion is located at the lower end of the steering column.*

46. Road test automobile to check transmission operation.

6-258

1. Disconnect fan shroud, if equipped.

2. Disconnect transmission fill tube at upper bracket.

3. Open hood.

CAUTION: *It is necessary that the hood be open to avoid damaging the hood and air cleaner when the rear crossmember is removed.*

4. Raise automobile on hoist.

5. Remove inspection cover from converter housing.

6. On Spirit and Concord, remove screw attaching exhaust pipe clamp to exhaust pipe support bracket and slide clamp off bracket.

7. Remove transmission fill tube.

8. Remove starter. On Eagle models, also remove stiffening braces.

9. Mark propeller shaft(s) and yoke(s) for assembly alignment reference.

10. Remove propeller shaft(s).

11. On Eagle models, disconnect the exhaust pipe and move it aside for working clearance.

12. Remove speedometer adapter and cable assembly. Discard adapter and cable seals, they are not reuseable. Cover adapter bore after removal.

13. Disconnect gearshift and throttle linkage.

14. Disconnect wires at neutral start switch.

15. Mark converter drive plate and converter for assembly alignment reference.

16. Remove bolts attaching converter to drive plate. Rotate crankshaft and drive plate using ratchet handle and socket on crankshaft front pulley bolt to gain access to drive plate bolts.

17. On Eagle models, remove skid plate and stiffening brace.

18. Support transmission (and transfer case on Eagle models) using transmission jack. Retain transmission on jack using safety chain.

19. Disconnect oil cooler lines at transmission.

20. Remove bolts attaching rear support cushion to transmission.

21. Remove rear crossmember.

22. Remove bolts attaching transmission to engine.

23. Move transmission and converter rearward to clear crankshaft.

24. Hold converter in position and lower transmission assembly until converter housing clears engine.

CAUTION: *If the transmission was removed to correct a malfunction that generated sludge or heavy accumulations of metal particles or friction material, the oil cooler and cooler lines must be flushed thoroughly and the torque converter replaced. Do not attempt to flush the converter if it is contaminated.*

25. If torque converter was removed, insert Pump Aligning Tool J-24033 in pump rotor until rotor drive lugs engage slots in tool.

26. Rotate tool until drilled hole in tool is vertical and remove tool.

27. Rotate converter until pump drive slots in converter hub are vertical and carefully insert converter hub into pump. Be sure drive lugs of pump inner rotor are properly engaged in drive slots of converter hub.

28. Raise transmission (and transfer case on Eagle models) and align converter with drive plate. Refer to assembly alignment marks.

29. Move transmission forward.

30. Raise, lower, or tilt transmission to align converter housing pilot holes with dowels in engine block.

31. Install two transmission lower attaching bolts and tighten bolts evenly to pull transmission to engine.

32. Install drive plate-to-converter attaching bolts.

33. Install remaining transmission attaching bolts and tighten all bolts to 28 ft. lbs. torque.

34. Connect oil cooler lines.

35. Install rear support cushion on transmission, if removed.

36. Install rear crossmember.

37. Remove safety chain and transmission jack.

38. Install inspection cover.

39. On Spirit and Concord, install exhaust pipe clamp on support bracket.

40. Install starter. On Eagle models, also install stiffening braces.

41. Connect wires to neutral switch.

42. Connect gearshift and throttle linkage.

43. Install speedometer cable and adapter assembly. Be sure adapter is correctly indexed.

44. On Eagle models, connect exhaust pipes, attach stiffening brace and install skid plate.

45. Install propeller shaft(s). Refer to alignment marks made during removal. On Eagle models, add correct quantity of transfer case lubricant.

46. Lower automobile.

47. Fill transmission to correct level.

48. Check and adjust gearshift and throttle linkage if necessary.

49. Road-test automobile to check transmission operation.

1982
4-151

1. Open hood.
CAUTION: *The hood must remain open to avoid damaging the hood and air cleaner when the rear crossmember is removed.*

2. Disconnect fan shroud.

3. Remove bolt attaching transmission fill tube to engine.

4. Place gearshift lever in Neutral.

5. Raise automobile on hoist.

6. Mark propeller shaft and yoke for assembly alignment reference. On Eagle models, also remove skid plate.

7. Remove propeller shafts.

8. On Eagle models, disconnect exhaust system at exhaust manifold, loosen exhaust system hangers and move exhaust system as necessary to gain work space.

9. Remove starter motor. On Eagle models, also remove stiffening braces.

10. Remove speedometer adapter and cable assembly. Cover adapter bore after removal.

11. Disconnect gearshift and throttle linkage. On automobiles with column shift, re-

move bolt attaching linkage bellcrank bracket to converter housing.

12. Remove cover at front of converter housing.

13. Mark converter drive plate and converter for assembly alignment reference.

14. Remove bolts attaching converter to drive plate. Rotate crankshaft and drive plate using ratchet handle and socket or box-end wrench on crankshaft front pulley bolt to gain access to drive plate-to-converter bolts.

NOTE: *The crankshaft pulley bolt is a metric size bolt.*

15. Support transmission using transmission jack. Retain transmission on jack using safety chain.

WARNING: *On Eagle models, both the transmission and transfer case must be properly supported on the transmission jack and retained with safety chain.*

16. Disconnect oil cooler lines at transmission.

17. Remove bolt attaching rear support cushion to rear support cushion bracket (bracket is attached to transmission extension housing).

18. Remove rear crossmember attaching nuts and remove crossmember and support cushion as assembly.

19. Place support stand under front of engine.

20. Remove bolts attaching catalytic converter support bracket to transmission, if equipped.

21. Remove fill tube.

22. Remove bolts attaching transmission to engine.

NOTE: *The transmission-to-engine block bolts are metric size bolts.*

23. Move transmission (and transfer case, if equipped) and converter rearward until clear of crankshaft.

24. Hold converter in position and lower transmission until transmission converter housing clears engine.

CAUTION: *If the transmission was removed to correct a malfunction that generated sludge or heavy accumulations of metal or friction material particles, the oil cooler and cooler lines must be thoroughly flushed and the torque converter replaced. Do not attempt to flush the converter if it is contaminated.*

25. If torque converter was removed, insert Pump Aligning Tool J-24033 into pump rotor and engage tool slots with pump rotor drive lugs.

26. Rotate aligning tool until hole in tool is vertical, then remove tool.

27. Rotate converter until pump drive slots in converter hub are vertical.

28. Carefully insert converter hub into oil pump. Be sure drive lugs of pump inner rotor are completely engaged with drive slots in converter hub.

29. Raise transmission and align converter with drive plate. Refer to alignment marks made during removal.

WARNING: *On Eagle models, both the transmission and transfer case must be supported on a transmission jack and retained with safety chain.*

30. Move transmission forward and raise, lower, or tilt transmission to align transmission converter housing dowel holes with dowels in engine block.

NOTE: *If the downward angle at the rear of the engine is not sufficient to permit transmission installation, raise the front of the engine to increase the downward angle.*

31. Install two transmission-to-engine lower attaching bolts and tighten bolts evenly to pull transmission to engine.

32. Install drive plate-to-converter attaching bolts. Tighten bolts to 40 ft. lbs. torque.

NOTE: *Coat threads of drive plate-to-converter attaching bolts with Loctite 271, or equivalent.*

33. Install remaining transmission-to-engine attaching bolts. Tighten bolts to 54 ft. lbs. torque.

34. Connect oil cooler lines.

35. Install propeller shaft using reference marks made during disassembly.

36. Install rear crossmember and support cushion. Tighten attaching nuts to 30 ft. lbs. torque.

37. Install rear support cushion-to-support cushion bracket bolt. Tighten bolt to 48 ft. lbs. torque.

38. Remove safety chain and transmission jack.

39. Install converter housing inspection cover.

40. Install starter motor. On Eagle models also install stiffening brace and skid plate.

41. Connect neutral start switch wires to switch terminal.

42. Connect gearshift and throttle linkage. On automobiles with column shift, position linkage bellcrank bracket on converter housing and install bracket attaching bolt.

43. Install speedometer cable and adapter

assembly. Be sure adapter is correctly indexed.

44. Connect catalytic converter, if equipped. On Eagle models, add correct quantity of transfer case lubricant.

45. Lower automobile.

46. Fill transmission to correct fluid level.

47. Check and adjust gearshift lever and throttle linkage, if necessary.

NOTE: *The gearshift lever adjusting trunnion is located at the lower end of the steering column.*

48. Road test automobile to check transmission operation.

6-258

1. Disconnect fan shroud, if equipped.

2. Disconnect transmission fill tube at upper bracket.

3. Open hood.

CAUTION: *It is necessary that the hood be open to avoid damaging the hood and air cleaner when the rear crossmember is removed.*

4. Raise automobile on hoist.

5. Remove inspection cover from converter housing.

6. On Spirit and Concord, remove screw attaching exhaust pipe clamp to exhaust pipe support bracket and slide clamp off bracket.

7. Remove transmission fill tube.

8. Remove starter. On Eagle models, also remove stiffening braces.

9. Mark propeller shaft(s) and yoke(s) for assembly alignment reference.

10. Remove propeller shaft(s).

11. On Eagle models, disconnect the exhaust pipe and move it aside for working clearance.

12. Remove speedometer adapter and cable assembly. Discard adapter and cable seals, they are not reuseable. Cover adapter bore after removal.

13. Disconnect gearshift and throttle linkage.

14. Disconnect wires at neutral start switch.

15. Mark converter drive plate and converter for assembly alignment reference.

16. Remove bolts attaching converter to drive plate. Rotate crankshaft and drive plate using ratchet handle and socket on crankshaft front pulley bolt to gain access to drive plate bolts.

17. On Eagle models, remove skid plate and stiffening braces.

WARNING: *Support transmission (and*

transfer case on Eagle models) *using transmission jack. Retain transmission on jack using safety chain.*

18. Disconnect oil cooler lines at transmission.

19. Remove bolts attaching rear support cushion to transmission.

20. Remove rear crossmember.

21. Remove bolts attaching transmission to engine.

22. Move transmission and converter rearward to clear crankshaft.

23. Hold converter in position and lower transmission assembly until converter housing clears engine.

24. If torque converter was removed, insert Pump Aligning Tool J-24033 in pump rotor until rotor drive lugs engage slots in tool.

25. Rotate tool until drilled hole in tool is vertical and remove tool.

26. Rotate converter until pump drive slots in converter hub are vertical and carefully insert converter hub into pump. Be sure drive lugs of pump inner rotor are properly engaged in drive slots of converter hub.

27. Raise transmission (and transfer case on Eagle models) and align converter with drive plate. Refer to assembly alignment marks.

28. Move transmission forward.

29. Raise, lower, or tilt transmission to align converter housing pilot holes with dowels in engine block.

30. Install two transmission lower attaching bolts and tighten bolts evenly to pull transmission to engine.

31. Install drive plate-to-converter attaching bolts.

32. Install remaining transmission attaching bolts and tighten all bolts to 28 ft. lbs. torque.

33. Connect oil cooler lines.

34. Install rear support cushion on transmission, if removed.

35. Install rear crossmember.

36. Remove safety chain and transmission jack.

37. Install inspection cover.

38. On Spirit and Concord, install exhaust pipe clamp on support bracket.

39. Install starter. On Eagle models, also install stiffening braces.

40. Connect wires to neutral switch.

41. Connect gearshift and throttle linkage.

42. Install speedometer cable and adapter assembly. Be sure adapter is correctly indexed.

43. On Eagle models, connect exhaust

pipes, attach stiffening brace and install skid plate.

44. Install propeller shaft(s). Refer to alignment marks made during removal. On Eagle models, add correct quantity of transfer case lubricant.

45. Lower automobile.

46. Fill transmission to correct level.

47. Check and adjust gearshift and throttle linkage, if necessary.

48. Road-test automobile to check transmission operation.

Pan Removal, Filter Replacement

These procedures are covered in Chapter 1.

Band Adjustments

The bands should be adjusted at the intervals specified in Chapter 1 or if slippage is noticed.

LOW AND REVERSE BAND, ALL 904 AND 1978 AND LATER 998

1. Drain the fluid and remove the pan.
2. On six-cylinder models:
   a. Remove the adjusting screw locknut.
   b. Tighten the adjusting screw to 41 in. lbs. On some early Pacers, and all 998, torque the screw to 72 in. lb.
   c. Back the adjusting screw out 7 turns. (3¼ turns on early 1975 Pacers.
   d. Hold the adjusting screw, install the locknut, and tighten the locknut to 35 ft. lbs.

NOTE: *Heavy-duty fleet versions of the 258 six and 304 V8 use the same transmission as the 360 and 401 V8. Thus, these models would follow the adjustment procedure for the 360 and 401 V8.*

3. On V8 models:
   a. Loosen the locknut and back it off 5 turns.
   b. Tighten the adjusting screw to 72 in. lbs.
   c. Back the adjusting screw out 4 turns with the 304 V8 and 2 turns with the 360 and 401 V8s.
   d. Hold the adjusting screw and tighten the locknut to 35 ft. lbs.

4. Install the pan with a new gasket. Tighten the screws to 150 in. lbs. Fill the transmission as explained in Chapter 1.

LOW AND REVERSE BAND, ALL 727, 1975–77 998

1. Raise the car, drain the transmission, and remove the pan.
2. Loosen the locknut on the adjusting screw and back off the locknut above five turns. Be sure the adjusting screw is free to turn.
3. Tighten the adjusting screw to exactly 72 in. lbs. of torque.
4. Back off the adjusting screw exactly to specification. Hold the adjusting screw to keep it from turning and tighten the locknut to 30–35 ft. lbs.
   • 998   4 turns
   • 727   2 turns
5. Install the pan using a new gasket.

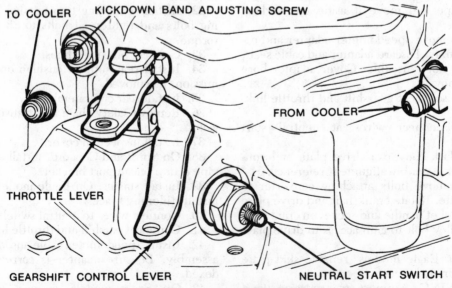

TO COOLER   KICKDOWN BAND ADJUSTING SCREW

FROM COOLER

THROTTLE LEVER

GEARSHIFT CONTROL LEVER   NEUTRAL START SWITCH

Automatic transmission external adjustments and controls

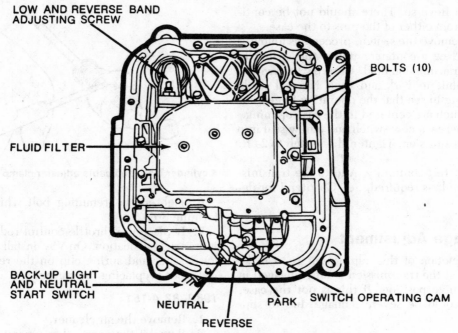

Low and reverse band adjusting screw locations

Tighten the pan bolts to 150 in. lbs. Refill the transmission with DEXRON fluid.

KICK-DOWN BAND

The adjustment screw for the kickdown band is located on the left-side of the transmission, above the throttle and manual linkage levers.

1. Loosen the locknut and back it off 5 turns.

2. Using a torque wrench, tighten the screw to 72 in. lbs.

3. Back off the adjusting screw:
 • 998 and 727, 1972–77   2½ turns
 • 904   2 turns
 • 998, 1978 and later   2 turns
 • 1978   2½ turns

4. Hold the adjusting screw and tighten the locknut to 29 ft. lbs.

Neutral Safety and Backup Light Switch Replacement and Adjustment

This switch prevents the engine from being started in any transmission position other than Neutral or Park. It also operates the backup lights.

On all American Motors cars, a combination backup light/Neutral safety switch is mounted on the left-side of the transmission case. This switch cannot be adjusted; failure requires replacement.

To test the switch, proceed in the following manner:

1. Unfasten the wiring connector from the switch.

2. Use a 12V test lamp to check for continuity between the center pin of the switch and the transmission case. The lamp should light only in Park or Neutral.

3. If the lamp lights in other positions, check the transmission linkage adjustments before replacing the switch.

4. To test the backup light function of the switch repeat Step 2 by bridging the outside pins to test continuity. The lamp should light

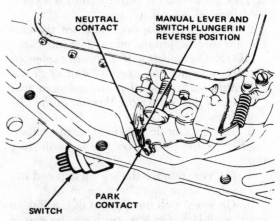

Neutral start and back-up light switch with the pan removed

only in Reverse. There should not be continuity from either of the pins to the case.

To remove the switch, proceed as follows:

1. Place a container under the switch to catch transmission fluid. Unscrew the switch.

2. Shift to Park and then Neutral while checking to see that the operating fingers for the switch are centered in the case opening.

3. Screw a new switch and a new seal into the transmission. Tighten the switch to 24 ft. lbs.

4. Retest continuity. Add to the transmission fluid, as required. See Chapter 1 for details.

Linkage Adjustment

The function of this adjustment is to make sure that the transmission is fully engaged in each range position. If this is not the case, there could be severe damage due to slippage.

ALL MODELS

1. With the engine off, place the selector in Park and the transmission shifting lever in the Park detent.

2. Adjust the shift rod, as necessary, for a free pin fit.

3. See that the steering column lock and the Neutral safety switch operate properly.

Throttle Linkage Adjustment

This adjustment positions a valve which controls shift speed, shift firmness, and part-throttle downshift sensitivity.

ALL EXCEPT 4-151

1. Detach the throttle control rod spring and hook it so that the throttle control lever is held forward against its stop.

2. Block the choke open and set the carburetor throttle linkage off the fast idle cam.

NOTE: *On models with a throttle solenoid valve, energize the solenoid and open the throttle halfway so that the solenoid will lock and then return the throttle to the idle position.*

3. Loosen, but do not remove, the retaining bolt on the throttle control rod adjusting link.

4. On V8s, remove the spring clip and nylon washer; leave them in place on sixes.

5. On sixes, pull on the end of the link to remove all lash. On V8s, push on the end of the link to remove all lash.

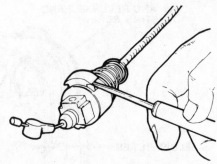

4 cylinder T-shaped cable adjuster clamp

6. Tighten the retaining bolt while performing Step 5.

7. Replace the throttle control rod spring in its original location. On V8s, install the nylon washer and spring clip on the retaining rod before replacing the spring.

1980–82 4-151

1. Remove the air cleaner.

2. Remove the spark plug separator from the throttle cable bracket and move the separator and bracket out of the way.

3. Raise the car and support it on jack stands. Remove the strut rod bushing heat shield from the bottom of the transmission and hold the throttle control lever rearward against its stop using a spring.

4. Lower the car and block the choke open, then set the carburetor linkage completely off the fast idle cam.

5. Turn the ignition key to the ON position to energize the throttle stop solenoid.

6. Unlock the throttle control cable by releasing the T-shaped clamp. Release the clamp by prying it up with a screwdriver.

7. Grasp the cable outer sheath and pull it and the cable forward to remove any load on the throttle cable bellcrank, which is part of the carburetor linkage.

8. Adjust the cable by moving the cable.

TRANSFER CASE

REMOVAL AND INSTALLATION
Manual Transmission

NOTE: *Steps 1 through 6, below, pertain to models with the SR-4 transmission only.*

1. Shift transmission into neutral.

2. Remove screws attaching gearshift lever bezel to floorpan or console, if equipped.

3. Slide bezel and boot upward on gearshift lever to provide access to lever attaching bolts.

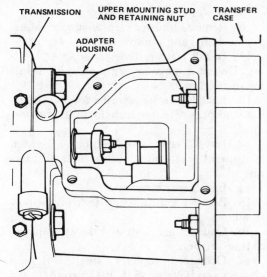

TRANSMISSION   UPPER MOUNTING STUD   TRANSFER
               AND RETAINING NUT   CASE

ADAPTER
HOUSING

Transfer case mounting stud location on models mated to the SR4 transmission

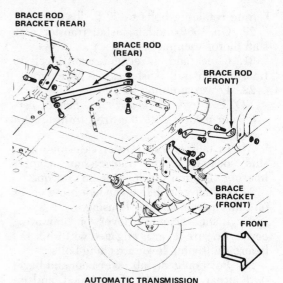

BRACE ROD
BRACKET (REAR)

BRACE ROD
(REAR)

BRACE ROD
(FRONT)

BRACE
BRACKET
(FRONT)

FRONT

AUTOMATIC TRANSMISSION

Automatic transmission brace and bracket

4. Remove bolts attaching gearshift lever to lever mounting cover on transmission adapter housing and remove lever.

5. Remove bolts attaching gearshift lever mounting cover to transmission adapter housing and remove cover.

6. Remove nut from transfer case mounting stud located inside transmission adapter housing.

7. Raise automobile.

8. Remove skid plate and rear brace rod at transfer case.

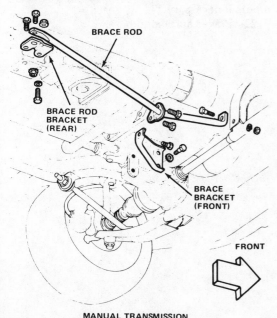

BRACE ROD

BRACE ROD
BRACKET
(REAR)

BRACE
BRACKET
(FRONT)

FRONT

MANUAL TRANSMISSION

Manual transmission brace and bracket

9. Remove speedometer adapter retainer attaching bolt and remove retainer, adapter, and cable. Plug adapter opening in transfer case to prevent excessive oil spillage.

NOTE: *Mark the position of the speedometer adapter for assembly reference before removing it.*

10. Mark propeller shafts and axle yokes for assembly alignment reference and disconnect propeller shafts at transfer case.

11. On 1982 models remove transfer case shift motor vacuum harness.

12. Support transfer case with transmission jack.

13. Remove nuts from transfer case mounting stud nuts to 33 ft. lbs. torque.

14. Align transmission output and transfer case input shafts and install transfer case on transmission adapter housing.

15. Install and tighten transfer case mounting stud nuts to 33 foot-pounds torque.

16. Remove jack used to support transfer case.

17. Align and connect propeller shafts to axle yokes. Tighten clamp strap bolts to 15 ft. lbs. torque.

18. Install replacement O-ring on speedometer adapter and install adapter and cable and retainer. Tighten retainer bolt to 100 in. lbs. torque.

CAUTION: *Do not attempt to reuse the original adapter O-ring. The O-ring is designed to swell in service to improve its sealing qualities and could be cut or torn during installation if reuse is attempted.*

19. Install skid plate and rear brace rod.

Torque retaining bolts to 30 ft. lbs. torque.

20. On 1982 models install transfer case shift motor vacuum harness.

21. Check and correct lubricant levels in transmission and transfer case if necessary.

22. Lower automobile.

NOTE: *Steps 10 through 13, below, pertain to models with the SR-4 transmission only.*

23. Install nut on transfer case mounting stud located inside transmission adapter housing. Tighten nut to 33 ft. lbs. torque.

24. Install gearshift lever mounting cover on transmission adapter housing.

25. Install gearshift lever on mounting cover. Be sure lever is engaged with shift rail before tightening lever attaching bolts.

26. Position gearshift lever boot and bezel on floorpan or console, if equipped, and install bezel attaching screws.

Automatic Transmission

1. Raise automobile.

2. Support engine and transmission with support stand or transmission jack.

3. Disconnect catalytic converter support bracket at adapter housing.

4. Remove skid plate and rear brace rod at transfer case.

5. Remove speedometer cable and adapter from transfer case. Discard adapter O-ring, it is not reusable.

6. Mark propeller shafts and transfer case yokes for assembly reference.

7. Disconnect propeller shafts at yokes. Secure shafts to underside of automobile.

8. Disconnect gearshift and throttle linkage at transmission.

9. Lower rear crossmember.

10. Remove transfer case-to-adapter housing stud nuts and remove transfer case.

11. Install transfer case on adapter housing. Do not damage output shaft splines during installation.

12. Install transfer case-to-adapter housing stud nuts. Tighten nuts to 33 ft. lbs. torque.

13. Install rear crossmember. Tighten crossmember attaching nuts to 30 ft. lbs. torque.

14. Install rear brace rod.

15. Remove transmission jack or support stand.

16. Connect gearshift and throttle linkage to transmission.

17. Connect propeller shafts. Tighten clamp strap bolts to 15 ft. lbs. torque.

18. Install new O-ring on speedometer adapter and install adapter and cable in transfer case.

NOTE: *Do not attempt to reuse the old adapter O-ring. O-ring is designed to "swell" in service to provide improved sealing qualities and could be cut or torn if reinstallation is attempted.*

19. Install skid plate and stiffening brace, if equipped. Tighten retaining bolts to 30 ft. lbs.

20. Connect catalytic converter support bracket to adapter housing.

21. Check and adjust transfer case lubricant level and transmission linkage adjustments if necessary.

22. Lower automobile.

Drive Train

7

DRIVELINE

Driveshaft and U-Joints

Two types of driveshafts are used, designated types 1 and 2, depending on the type of bearing cap retaining ring. See the illustration.

REMOVAL AND INSTALLATION

All Except Eagle

1. Mark the rear universal joint yoke and bearing retainers so that you can reinstall them in their original positions.

2. Remove the U-bolts, being careful not

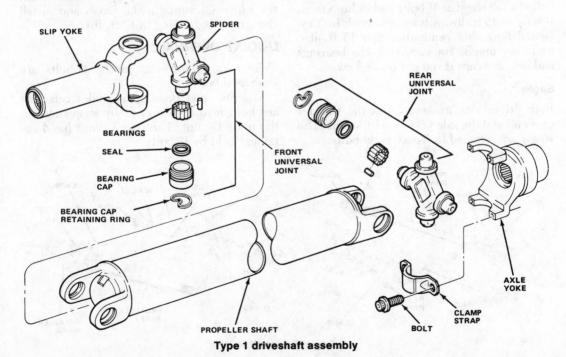

Type 1 driveshaft assembly

SLIP YOKE

SPIDER

BEARINGS

SEAL

BEARING CAP

BEARING CAP RETAINING RING

FRONT UNIVERSAL JOINT

REAR UNIVERSAL JOINT

AXLE YOKE

CLAMP STRAP

BOLT

PROPELLER SHAFT

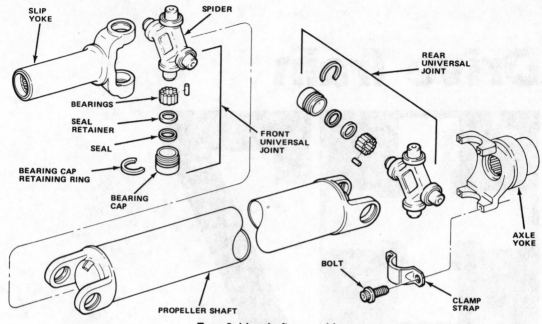

SLIP YOKE

SPIDER

REAR UNIVERSAL JOINT

BEARINGS

SEAL RETAINER

SEAL

FRONT UNIVERSAL JOINT

BEARING CAP RETAINING RING

BEARING CAP

AXLE YOKE

BOLT

CLAMP STRAP

PROPELLER SHAFT

Type 2 driveshaft assembly

to lose the round bearing retainer caps, which are filled with little needle bearings. Don't make any attempt to remove the large nut holding the yoke to the front of the rear axle assembly.

3. Slide the driveshaft back and remove it.

4. On installation, slide the front yoke on the transmission output shaft splines far enough to align the rear universal joint.

5. Align the marks you made in Step 1.

6. Install the rear U-bolts and tighten them evenly to 15 ft. lbs. A torque wrench isn't essential here, but remember that 15 ft. lbs. isn't very much. You can crush the bearings and retainer caps if you get carried away.

Eagle

Both driveshafts are secured at the transfer case end and the axle yoke end by straps. The straps are retained by Torx® head bolts.

1. Shift into Neutral. Raise and support the car.

2. Matchmark the driveshaft(s) at the transfer case and axle yoke for alignment reference.

3. Remove the retaining straps with a Torx® bit tool of the proper size. Remove the driveshaft(s).

4. To install, align the matchmarks made during removal to assure proper balance. Seat the universal joints in the yokes and install the straps, tightening to 17 ft. lbs.

U-JOINT OVERHAUL

U-Joints are Universal joints; U-bolts are U-shaped bolts.

The four end bearings or roller retainers are held in the yoke ends by snap-rings on the front U-joint. The rear U-joint has 4 retainers held by U-bolts.

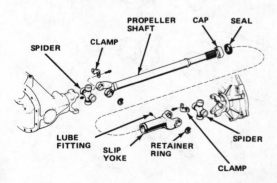

SPIDER

CLAMP

PROPELLER SHAFT

CAP

SEAL

LUBE FITTING

SLIP YOKE

RETAINER RING

SPIDER

CLAMP

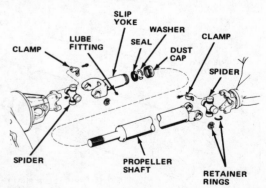

SLIP YOKE

WASHER

CLAMP

LUBE FITTING

SEAL

DUST CAP

CLAMP

SPIDER

SPIDER

PROPELLER SHAFT

RETAINER RINGS

Eagle driveshafts

1. The snap-rings can be pried out with a screwdriver.

2. Place the assembly in a vise with a $^9/_{16}$ in. socket against the bearing retainer on one side and a 1⅛ in. socket against the yoke on the other side.

3. Tighten the vise slowly; the bearing retainer will be forced out into the big socket.

4. Clamp the protruding bearing retainer gently in the vise and remove it. Watch out for the little needle bearings inside.

5. Remove the other bearing retainers in the same way.

6. Wash all the parts in a safe solvent and check carefully for wear. These parts aren't very expensive and aren't serviced often, so replace any doubtful parts. The 4-armed part is called a cross or a spider.

7. Pack enough high-quality grease into each bearing retainer so that you can install the needle bearings without them falling out.

On Installation:

8. Install the cross into the yoke and put the end bearing retainer in place.

9. Place the yoke in a vise and press the bearing retainer, using the $^9/_{16}$ in. socket, past the outside of the yoke.

10. Install the snap-rings, making sure that they are securely seated.

EAGLE FRONT AXLE

Axle, Shaft, Shaft Seal and Bearing
REMOVAL AND INSTALLATION

The procedure for replacing the axle shafts and seals on four-wheel drive models calls for removal of the axle first.

1. Raise and support the front of the car. Install protectors over the halfshaft boots.

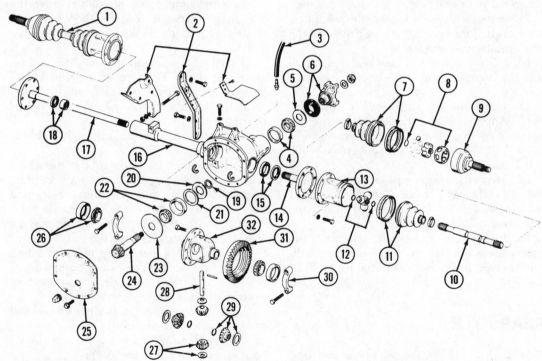

1. Half-shaft assembly	13. Tri-pot housing	25. Cover
2. Axle mounting brackets	14. Axle shaft (short)	26. Differential bearing and cup
3. Vent hose	15. Ball bearing and seal	27. Differential pinion and thrust
4. Pinion and front bearing cup	16. Axle housing	washer
5. Washer	17. Axle shaft (long)	28. Pinion mate shaft
6. Yoke and seal	18. Needle bearing and seal	29. Side gear, thrust washer and
7. Outer boot and retainer	19. Preload shim	lockring
8. Rzeppa joint assembly	20. Washer	30. Bearing cap
9. Spindle	21. Depth shim	31. Ring gear
10. Half-shaft	22. Pinion rear bearing and cup	32. Differential case
11. Inner boot and retainer	23. Slinger	
12. Tri-pot joint assembly	24. Pinion gear	

Eagle front drive axle

Remove the halfshaft-to-axle flange bolts, and tie the halfshafts out of the way.

2. Matchmark the driveshaft and the axle yoke. Remove the driveshaft.

3. Support the axle on stands. Remove the five axle-to-engine mounting bolts.

4. Lower the axle partway and remove the vent hose. Remove the axle.

5. Remove the differential cover and drain the oil. Remove the axle shaft "C" clips.

6. Remove the axle shafts.

7. Carefully remove the shaft seal using a screwdriver.

8. Two different bearings are used; the left side uses a ball bearing, and the right side uses a needle bearing. The ball bearing may be removed using a brass drift and a hammer. The needle bearing should be removed using a needle bearing removal too.

NOTE: *If the proper bearing removal tool is not available, remove the differential and remove the needle bearing using $15/16$ inch socket and a three foot ratchet extension.*

9. Install the bearings, using drivers of the appropriate type and size.

10. Oil the lips of the new seal and install into the housing using a driver of the correct size.

11. Install the axle shafts and "C" clips.

12. Apply a bead of silicone seal to the differential cover and install the cover.

13. Fill the axle with 2.5 pints of 85W–90 GL-5 gear oil.

14. Move the axle into place under the car. Raise it sufficiently to connect the vent hose, then raise it fully into place and install the mounting bolts. Tighten to 50 lbs.

15. Install the driveshaft, aligning the marks made during removal. Install the halfshaft to axle flange bolts, tightening to 45 ft. lbs.

REAR AXLE

Two sizes of differential assemblies are used on American Motors cars; $7\,9/16$ inch and $8\,7/8$ inch ring gear units. A Twin-Grip limited slip differential is available as an option on both units.

A leter code used to identify the axle ratio will be found on most differentials, stamped on the right axle tube housing boss, on the rear side, adjacent to the dowel hole. Some earlier cars have either a metal tag attached to one of the bolts of the differential housing cover or the code letter stamped on the right differential housing cover flange. It may be necessary to remove the cover from the differential to locate the letter. The codes and the axle ratios are listed in dealer parts books and shop manuals.

NOTE: *The $7\,9/16$ inch axle can be identified by the cover mounted filler plug, and the $8\,7/8$ inch axle by the front filler on the housing.*

Axle Shaft, Bearing and Seal
REMOVAL AND INSTALLATION

1. The hub and drum are separate units and are removed after the wheel is removed. The hub and axle shaft are serrated together on the taper. An axle shaft key assures proper alignment during assembly.

2. With the wheel on the ground and the parking brake applied, remove and discard the axle shaft nut cotter pin and remove the nut. Raise the car and remove the wheel. Release the parking brakes and remove the drum.

3. Attach a puller to the rear hub and remove the hub. The use of a "Knock-out" puller should be discouraged, since it may result in damage to the axle shaft or wheel bearings.

4. Disconnect the parking brake cable at the equalizer.

5. Disconnect the brake tube at the wheel cylinder and remove the brake support plate assembly, oil seal, and axle shims. Note that the axle shims are located on the left side only.

6. Using a screw type puller, remove the axle shaft and bearings from the axle housing.

CAUTION: *On Twin-Grip axles, rotating the differential with one shaft removed will misalign the side gear splines, preventing installation of the replacement shaft.*

7. Remove the axle shaft inner oil seal and install new seals at assembly.

8. The bearing is a press fit and should be removed with an arbor press.

9. The axle shaft bearings have no provision for lubrication after assembly. Before installing the bearings, they should be packed with a good quality wheel bearing lubricant.

10. Press the axle shaft bearings onto the axle shaft with the small diameter of the cone toward the outer (tapered) end of the shaft.

11. Soak the inner axle shaft seal in light lubricating oil. Coat the outer surface of the seal retainer with sealant.

12. Install the inner oil seal.

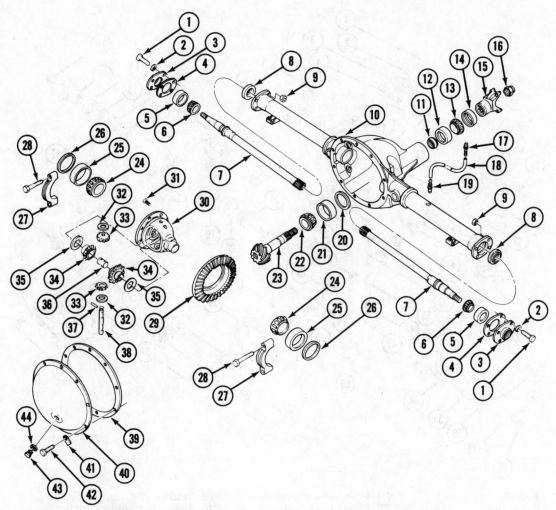

1. Bolt
2. Washer
3. Axle shaft oil seal and retainer assembly
4. Axle shaft bearing shim
5. Axle shaft bearing cup
6. Axle shaft bearing
7. Axle shaft
8. Axle shaft inner oil seal
9. Nut
10. Axle housing
11. Collapsible spacer
12. Pinion bearing cup-front
13. Pinion bearing-front
14. Pinion oil seal
15. Universal joint yoke
16. Pinion nut
17. Breather
18. Breather hose
19. Breather
20. Pinion depth adjusting shim
21. Pinion rear bearing cup
22. Pinion bearing-rear
23. Pinion gear
24. Differential bearing
25. Differential bearing cup
26. Differential bearing shim
27. Differential bearing cap
28. Differential bearing cap bolt
29. Ring gear
30. Differential case
31. Ring gear bolt
32. Differential pinion washer
33. Differential pinion
34. Differential side gear
35. Differential side gear thrust washer
36. Differential pinion shaft thrust block
37. Differential pinion shaft pin
38. Differential pinion shaft
39. Axle housing cover gasket
40. Axle housing cover
41. Axle identification tag
42. Bolt
43. Axle housing cover fill plug
44. Washer

7⁹/₁₆ inch ring gear rear axle with standard differential

13. Install the axle shafts, indexing the splined end with the differential side gears.

14. Install the outer bearing cup.

15. Install the brake support plate. Sealant should be applied to the axle housing flange and brake support mounting plate.

16. Install the original shims, oil seal and brake support plate. Torque the nuts to 30–35 ft. lbs.

NOTE: *The oil seal and retainer go between the axle housing flange and the brake support plate on 9 in. brakes or 7⁹/₁₆ axle. On 10 in. brakes or 8⅞ axle, they go on the outside of the brake support plate.*

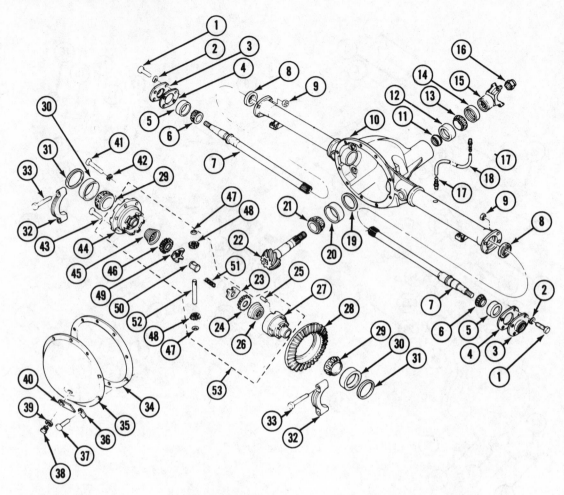

1. Bolt
2. Washer
3. Axle shaft oil seal
4. Axle shaft bearing shim
5. Axle shaft bearing cup
6. Axle shaft bearing
7. Axle shaft
8. Axle shaft inner oil seal
9. Nut
10. Axle housing
11. Collapsible spacer
12. Pinion bearing cup-front
13. Pinion bearing-front
14. Pinion oil seal
15. Universal joint yoke
16. Pinion nut
17. Breather
18. Breather hose
19. Pinion depth
    adjusting shim
20. Pinion bearing cup-rear
21. Pinion bearing-rear
22. Pinion gear
23. Retainer clip
24. Differential side gear
25. Differential pinion shaft pin
26. Clutch cone
27. Differential case
28. Ring gear
29. Differential bearing
30. Differential bearing cup
31. Differential bearing shim
32. Differential bearing cap
33. Differential bearing cap bolt
34. Axle housing cover gasket
35. Axle housing cover
36. Axle identification tag
37. Bolt
38. Axle housing cover fill plug
39. Washer
40. Twin grip identification tag
41. Differential case bolt
42. Washer
43. Ring gear bolt
44. Differential case
45. Clutch cone
46. Differential side gear
47. Differential pinion thrust washer
48. Differential pinion
49. Retainer clip
50. Differential pinion shaft thrust block
51. Spring
52. Differential pinion shaft
53. Differential serviced
    as assembly only

Twin-Grip differential

17. To adjust the axle shaft end-play, strike the axle shafts with a lead mallet to seal the bearings. Install a dial indicator on the brake support plate and check the play while pushing and pulling the axle shaft. End-play should be 0.004–0.008 in., with 0.006 in. desirable. Add shims to the left side only to decrease the play and remove shims to increase the play.

18. Slide the hub onto the axle shafts

Rear Axle Ratios

An axle ratio code is stamped on the differential housing. It is located either at the cover flange or on the axle tube housing boss near the dowel hole. Codes are interpreted as follows:

Code	Ratio	Number of Teeth	Ring Gear Diameter (in.)
A	3.54:1	11/39	8⅞
B	3.15:1	13/41	8⅞
C	2.87:1	15/43	8⅞
D	3.91:1	11/43	8⅞
E	3.58:1	12/43	7⁹/₁₆
F	3.08:1	13/40	7⁹/₁₆
G	3.31:1	13/43	7⁹/₁₆
H	2.73:1	15/41	7⁹/₁₆
J	2.73:1	19/45	7⁹/₁₆
K	2.53:1	17/43	7⁹/₁₆
L	4.10:1	10/41	8⅞
M	4.10:1	10/41	8⅞
N	3.54:1	11/39	8⅞
O	2.87:1	15/43	8⅞
P	3.15:1	13/41	8⅞

Rear Axle Ratios (cont.)

An axle ratio code is stamped on the differential housing. It is located either at the cover flange or on the axle tube housing boss near the dowel hole. Codes are interpreted as follows:

Code	Ratio	Number of Teeth	Ring Gear Diameter (in.)
Q	3.91:1	11/43	8⅞
R	3.58:1	12/43	7⁹/₁₆
S	3.31:1	13/43	7⁹/₁₆
T	3.08:1	13/40	7⁹/₁₆
U	2.73:1	15/41	7⁹/₁₆
V	2.53:1	17/43	7⁹/₁₆
W	2.56:1	16/41	8⅞
X	3.07:1	14/43	8⅞
Y	3.07:1	14/43	8⅞
EE	3.54:1	13/46	7⁹/₁₆
FF	3.54:1	13/46	7⁹/₁₆
JJ	2.73:1	15/41	7⁹/₁₆
LL	2.35:1	17/40	7⁹/₁₆
MM	2.21:1	19/42	7⁹/₁₆

aligning the serrations and the keyway on the hub with the axle shaft key.

19. Replace the hub and drum, install the wheel, lower the car onto the floor and tighten the axle shaft nut to 250 ft. lbs. If the cotter pin hole is not aligned with a castellation on the nut, tighten the nut to the next castellation.

NOTE: *A new hub must be installed whenever a new axle shaft is installed. Install two thrust washers on the shaft. Tighten the new hub onto the shaft until the hub is* 1.19 *in. from the end of the shaft on* 7⁹/₁₆ *in. differentials, and* 1.31 *in. on* 8⅞ *in. models. Remove the nut; remove one thrust washer. Install the nut and torque to 250 ft. lbs. New hubs do not have serrations on the axle shaft mating surface. The serrations are cut when the hub is installed to the axle shaft.*

20. Connect the parking brake cable at the equalizer.

21. Connect the brake tube at the wheel cylinder and bleed the brakes.

Suspension and Steering

FRONT SUSPENSION

The front suspension on all models except Pacer is an independent linked type with the coil springs located between seats in the wheelwell panels and seats in the upper control arms. Rubber insulators between the springs and seats reduce noise transmission to the body.

Direct acting, telescopic shock absorbers are located inside the coil springs and the control arms are attached to the body via rubber bushings.

The suspension system is a double ball joint design, both upper and lower control arms each having one joint.

On all models, strut rods serve to support the lower control arms. Stabilizer bars are used on some models.

The Pacer front suspension is different from all other AMC cars. The coil spring is mounted between the two control arms; seated at the bottom on the lower control arm and at the top in the suspension/engine mount crossmember. The crossmember is isolated from the rest of the body structure by rubber mounting points. The shock absorbers are mounted inside the coil spring. The steering knuckle is attached to the upper and lower control arms by upper and lower ball joints. A front stabilizer bar is optional.

NOTE: *The front end alignment must be checked after any disassembly procedure.*

Shock Absorber
REPLACEMENT

NOTE: *When installing new shock absorbers, purge them of air by extending them in their normal position and compressing them while inverted. Do this several times. It is normal for there to be more resistance to extension than to compression.*

Except Pacer

1. Remove the two lower shock absorber attaching nuts. Remove the washers and the grommets.

2. Remove the upper mounting bracket nuts and bolts.

3. Remove the bracket, complete with shock.

4. Remove the upper attaching nut and separate the shock from the mounting bracket.

5. For adjustable shocks: To adjust the shock, compress the piston completely. Holding the upper part of the shock, turn the shock until the lower arrow is aligned with the desired setting. A click will be heard when the desired setting is reached.

Install the shock as follows:

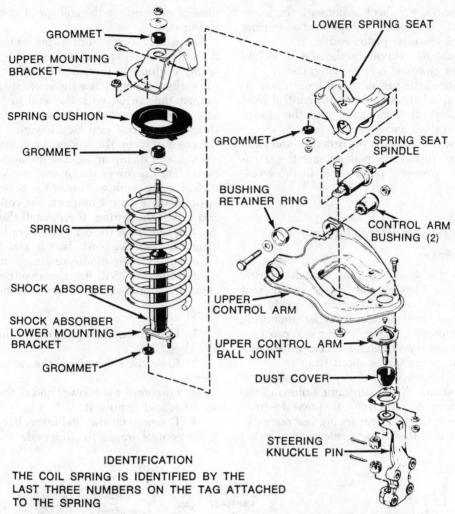

GROMMET

UPPER MOUNTING
BRACKET

SPRING CUSHION

GROMMET

SPRING

SHOCK ABSORBER

SHOCK ABSORBER
LOWER MOUNTING
BRACKET

GROMMET

LOWER SPRING SEAT

GROMMET

SPRING SEAT
SPINDLE

BUSHING
RETAINER RING

CONTROL ARM
BUSHING (2)

UPPER
CONTROL ARM

UPPER CONTROL ARM
BALL JOINT

DUST COVER

STEERING
KNUCKLE PIN

IDENTIFICATION
THE COIL SPRING IS IDENTIFIED BY THE
LAST THREE NUMBERS ON THE TAG ATTACHED
TO THE SPRING

Upper control arm and shock absorber for all except Eagle and Pacer

1. Fit the grommets, washers, upper mounting bracket and nut on the shock, in the reverse order of removal. Tighten the nut to 8 ft. lbs.

2. Fully extend the shock and install two grommets on the lower mounting studs.

3. Lower the shock through the hole in the wheel arch. Fit the lower attachment studs through the lower spring seat.

4. Install the grommets, washers, and nuts. Tighten the nuts to 15 ft. lbs.

5. Secure the upper mounting bracket with its attachment nuts and bolts. Tighten them to 20 ft. lbs.

Pacer

1. Remove the shock absorber upper lock-nut.

2. Raise the car and remove the nuts from the lower shock absorber mounting studs.

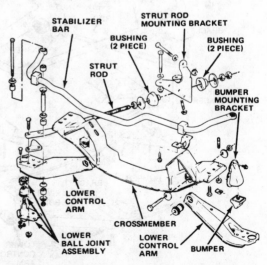

STABILIZER
BAR

STRUT ROD
MOUNTING BRACKET

BUSHING
(2 PIECE)

STRUT
ROD

BUSHING
(2 PIECE)

BUMPER
MOUNTING
BRACKET

LOWER
CONTROL
ARM

LOWER
BALL JOINT
ASSEMBLY

CROSSMEMBER

LOWER
CONTROL
ARM

BUMPER

Lower control arm assembly for all except Eagle and Pacer

3. Remove the shock along with the lower grommet and jounce bumper retainer from the shock absorber piston rod.

4. Install the retainer on the new shock and the lower grommet on the piston rod.

5. Extend the piston to full length and insert the shock through the lower control arm.

6. Install the locknuts on the lower mounting studs and lower the car.

7. Install the grommet, retainer, and locknut on the piston rod, making sure the grommet seats properly in the hole in the crossmember.

Spring

REMOVAL AND INSTALLATION

Except Pacer

Remove the shock absorber. Install a spring compressor through the upper spring seat opening and bolt it to the lower spring seat using the lower shock absorber mounting holes. Remove the lower spring seat pivot retaining nuts, then tighten the compressor tool to compress the spring about 1 in.

Jack up the front of the car and support it on axle stands at the subframe (allowing the control arms to hang free). Remove the front wheel and pull the lower spring seat out away from the car, then slowly release the spring tension and remove the coil spring and lower spring seat.

To install, place the spring compressor through the coil spring and tape the rubber spring cushion to the small-diameter end of the spring (upper). Place the lower spring seat against the spring with the end of the coil against the formed shoulder in the seat. The shoulder and coil end face inwards, toward the engine, when the spring is installed.

Place the spring up against the upper seat, then align the lower spring seat pivot so that the retaining studs will enter the holes in the upper control arm. Compress the coil spring and install the spring, then install the wheel and tire and lower the car to the floor (to place weight on suspension). Install and tighten lower spring seat spindle retaining nuts and tighten them to 35 ft. lbs. Remove the spring compressor and install the shock absorber.

Pacer

1. Disconnect the upper end of the shock absorber.

2. Raise the front end of the car and support it.

3. Disconnect the lower end of the shock absorber and remove it.

4. Disconnect the stabilizer bar at the lower control arm, if so equipped.

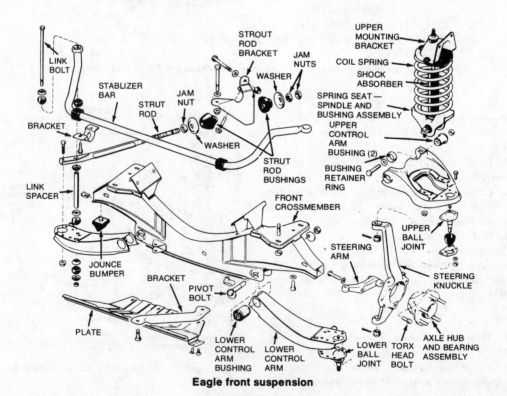

Eagle front suspension

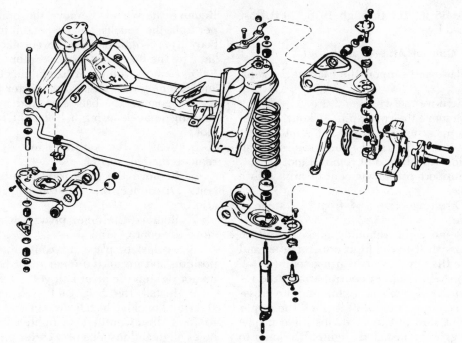

Pacer front suspension

5. Remove the wheel, brake drum, or caliper and rotor. Do not allow the brake hose to support the weight of the caliper; use a length of wire to suspend the caliper from the frame.

6. Remove the two bolts that attach the steering arm to the steering knuckle and move the steering arm aside.

7. Use a spring compressor to compress the coil spring.

8. Remove the cotter pin and nut from the lower ball joint stud and disengage the stud from the steering knuckle with a puller.

9. Move the steering knuckle, steering spindle, and support plate, or anchor plate assembly, aside to provide working clearance. Do not allow the brake hose to support the weight of these components. Use wire to hang the components from the upper control arm.

10. Move the lower control arm aside and remove the spring.

To install the front coil spring:

11. Position the upper end of the spring in the spring seat of the front crossmember. Align the cut-off end of the bottom coil with the formed shoulder in the spring seat. The top coil is flat and does not use an insulator. Use a floor jack or jack stand to support the spring until the spring compressor is installed. Install the spring compressor.

12. Assemble the remaining components of the front suspension in the reverse order of removal. Tighten the ball joint stud nut to 75 ft. lbs., the steering arm-to-knuckle attaching bolts to 80 ft. lbs. through 1976, 55 ft. lbs. 1977 and later, the shock absorber lower mounting nuts to 20 ft. lbs., and the stabilizer bar locknut to 8 ft. lbs.

Control Arm

REMOVAL AND INSTALLATION

Upper Control Arm—Except Pacer

Remove the shock absorber and compress the coil spring approximately 2 in. using the procedure under Front Spring Removal and Installation.

Jack up the front of the car and support the body on jackstands placed under the subframes (allow the control arms to hang free). Remove the wheel and the upper ball joint cotter pin and retaining nut. Separate the ball joint stud from the steering knuckle using a ball joint removal tool. Remove the inner pivot bolts then remove the control arm.

To install, reverse the removal procedure. Do not tighten the pivot bolt nuts until the full weight of the car is on the wheels. The ball joint stud nut must be tightened to 40 ft. lbs., through 1975 and 75 ft. lbs. thereafter, the lower spring seat pivot retaining nuts to 35 ft. lbs., and the control arm inner pivot bolts to 45 ft. lbs. through 1976, 80 ft. lbs. 1977 and later.

Upper Control Arm—Pacer

1. Raise and support the front of the vehicle.
2. Remove the wheel and tire.
3. Remove the cotter pin, locknut, and retaining nuts from the upper ball joint stud.
4. Loosen the stud from the steering knuckle with a ball joint removal tool.
5. Support the lower control arm with a floor jack.
6. Disengage the stud from the steering knuckle.
7. Remove the retaining nuts that attach the cross-shaft to the front crossmember and remove the upper control arm assembly.
8. Install the upper control arm in the reverse order of removal, tightening the cross-shaft retaining nuts to 80 ft. lbs., the upper ball joint stud nut to 75 ft. lbs., and if new bushings were installed, tighten the nuts to 60 ft. lbs. after the car is lowered to the floor.

Lower Control Arm—Except Eagle and Pacer

The inner end of the lower control arm is attached to a removable crossmember. The outer end is attached to the steering knuckle pin and ball joint assembly.

To remove, jack up the car and support it on axle stands under the subframes. Remove the brake drum or caliper and rotor from the spindle, then disconnect the steering arm from the knuckle pin. Remove the lower ball joint stud cotter pin and nut. Separate the ball joint from the knuckle pin using a ball joint removal tool.

Disconnect the sway bar from the control arm, then unbolt the strut rod. Remove the inner pivot bolt and the control arm.

To install, reverse the removal procedure; do not tighten inner pivot bolt until car weight is on wheels. Tighten ball joint retaining nut to 40 ft. lbs. through 1976, 75 ft. lbs. thereafter, strut rod bolts to 75 ft. lbs., sway bar bolts to 8 ft. lbs., steering arm bolts to 65 ft. lbs. through 1979, 55 ft. lbs. thereafter, and control arm inner pivot bolt to 95 ft. lbs. through 1976, 110 ft. lbs. thereafter.

Lower Control Arm—Eagle

1. Remove the wheel cover. Remove and discard the cotter pin. Remove the nut lock and the hub pin.
2. Raise and support the front of the car.

Remove the wheel. Remove the brake caliper from the knuckle and suspend it from the body by a length of wire; do not allow it to hang by the hose. Remove the rotor.
3. Remove the lower ball joint cotter pin and retaining nut. Discard the cotter pin.
4. Separate the ball joint stud from the steering knuckle using a ball joint removal tool.
5. Remove the halfshaft flange bolts and remove the half shaft.
6. Remove the strut rod-to-control arm bolts. Disconnect the stabilizer bar from the arm.
7. Remove the inner pivot bolt and remove the control arm.
8. To install, place the control arm into position and install the inner pivot bolt, but do not tighten the pivot bolt yet.
9. Install the ball joint stud into the steering knuckle. Install the nut and tighten to 75 ft. lbs. Continue to tighten until the holes align and install a new cotter pin.
10. Connect the stabilizer bar to the arm; tighten the bolts to 7 ft. lbs. Install the strut rod; tighten to 45 ft. lbs.
11. Install the halfshaft-to-axle flange bolts; tighten to 45 ft. lbs.
12. Place a jack under the lower control arm. Raise the jack carefully to compress the spring slightly. Tighten the control arm pivot bolt to 110 ft. lbs.
13. Install the rotor, caliper, and hub nut. Tighten the hub nut to 180 ft. lbs. Install the nut lock and a new cotter pin.
14. Install the wheel. Check and adjust the front end alignment as necessary.

Lower Control Arm—Pacer

1. Disconnect the upper end of the shock absorber, raise the front end of the car and disconnect the lower end of the shock absorber and remove the shock absorber.
2. Disconnect the stabilizer bar at the lower control arm, if so equipped.
3. Remove the wheel, brake drum, or caliper and rotor. Do not allow the brake hose to support the weight of the caliper. Use wire to support it from the frame.
4. Remove the two bolts attaching the steering arm to the steering knuckle and move the steering arm aside.
5. Install a spring compressor and compress the spring.
6. Remove the cotter pin and nut from the lower ball joint stud. Remove the ball joint

from the steering knuckle using a ball joint removal tool.

7. Move the steering knuckle assembly out of the way. Support the assembly with wire from the upper control arm.

8. Remove the two pivot bolts that attach the lower arm to the front crossmember and remove the lower control arm.

9. Install the lower control arm in the reverse order of removal, tightening the ball joint stud nut to 75 ft. lbs., the steering arm attaching bolts to 80 ft. lbs. through 1976, 55 ft. lbs. 1977 and later, the shock absorber lower attaching nuts to 20 ft. lbs., the stabilizer bar locknut to 8 ft. lbs., and lastly, after the car has been lowered to the ground with the wheel and tire installed, tighten the lower control arm pivot bolts to 95 ft. lbs. through 1976, and 110 ft. lbs. thereafter.

Ball Joints

INSPECTION

Except Pacer

NOTE: *Be sure that the front wheel bearings are adjusted to specification before checking the upper ball joint.*

1. Jack up the front of the car and place jackstands under the frame side sills.

NOTE: *The control arms must hang free if an accurate reading is to be obtained.*

2. Check the lower ball joints by grasping the lower portion of the wheel and pulling it in and out.

3. If there is noticeable lateral free-play, the lower ball joint is worn and must be replaced.

NOTE: *The lower ball joints and control arms must be replaced as assemblies on Eagles.*

4. To check the condition of the upper ball joint, place a dial indicator with its plunger against the tire scrub bead (just outside the whitewall).

5. Move the upper portion of the wheel and tire toward the car's center, while watching the dial indicator.

6. Move the wheel and tire back out while watching the indicator.

7. The upper ball joint should be replaced if its *total* movement is greater than 0.160 in.

NOTE: *The upper ball joints and control arms must be replaced as assemblies on 1980 Eagles. On 1981 and later Eagles the upper ball joints are replaceable separately.*

Pacer

1. Check that the front wheel bearings are adjusted properly.

2. Remove the lubrication plug from the lower ball joint. Insert a piece of stiff wire until it contacts the ball. Mark the wire even with the edge of the plug hole.

3. Measure from the end of the wire to the mark. If it exceeds 7/16 in., the ball joint should be replaced.

4. Place a jack under the lower control arm and lift the wheel off the floor.

5. Push the top of the tire in and out. If there is any looseness, replace the upper ball joint.

6. Pry the upper control arm up and down. If there is any looseness, replace the upper ball joint.

REMOVAL AND INSTALLATION

NOTE: *On Eagles, do not attempt to replace the ball joints separately. If the ball joints are worn, the control arms and ball joints must be replaced as complete assemblies.*

Lower Ball Joint

1. On all vehicles except Pacer, place a $2 \times 4 \times 5$ in. block of wood on the side sill so that it supports the control arm.

2. Jack up the front end of the car and place jackstands underneath the frame side sills to support the body.

3. Remove the wheel and the brake drum. On cars equipped with disc brakes, remove the caliper and rotor.

4. Disconnect the lower control arm strut rod, on models other than Pacer. Disconnect the stabilizer bar, if so equipped.

5. Separate the steering arm from the steering knuckle.

6. Remove the ball stud retaining nut, after removing its cotter pin.

7. Install a ball joint removal tool then loosen the ball stud in the knuckle pin. Leave the tool in place on the stud.

8. Place a jackstand under the lower control arm.

9. Chisel the heads off the rivets which secure the ball joint to the control arm. Use a punch to remove the rivets.

10. Remove the tool from the ball stud.

11. Remove the ball stud from the knuckle pin and remove the joint from the control arm.

Installation of a new lower ball joint is as follows:

1. Position the new ball joint so that its securing holes align with the rivet holes in the control arm.

2. Install the special $^5/_{16}$ in. bolts, used to secure the ball joint, loosely.

CAUTION: *Use only the hardened $^5/_{16}$ in. bolts supplied with the ball joint replacement kit; standard bolts are not strong enough.*

3. Install the steering strut and stop on the lower control arm. Tighten their bolts to 75 ft. lbs.

4. Tighten the $^5/_{16}$ in. ball joint securing bolts to 25 ft. lbs.

5. Apply chassis grease to the steering stops and fit the knuckle pin and retaining nut on the ball stud; tighten the nut to 40 ft. lbs. through 1976, 75 ft. lbs. through 1976, 75 ft. lbs. thereafter, and 75 ft. lbs. on all Pacers. Install a new cotter pin.

6. Complete the installation procedure in the reverse order of removal and then check front end alignment.

Upper Ball Joint

1. Perform Steps 1–3 of the "Lower Ball Joint Removal" procedure.

NOTE: *It is not necessary to remove the brake drum in Step 3. On 1981 and later Eagle models temporarily reinstall two lug nuts to retain each brake rotor. This eliminates repositioning rotors and calipers prior to reassembly.*

2. Next, perform Steps 6–9 of the "Lower Ball Joint Removal" procedure to the upper ball joint.

3. Separate the upper ball joint from the control arm.

4. Remove the ball joint puller from the knuckle pin.

Installation of a new upper ball joint is as follows:

1. Perform Steps 1–2 of the "Lower Ball Joint Installation" procedure.

2. Skip Step 3 and go on to Steps 4–5 of the "Lower Ball Joint Installation" procedure.

3. Complete the installation in the reverse order of removal and check front end alignment.

Wheel Bearings

Four-wheel drive models have sealed, non-adjustable front hubs and bearings. There are darkened areas surrounding the bearing races in the hubs, which are the result of a heat treatment process; the darkened areas do not signify a defect.

INSPECTION

Check to see that the inner cones of the bearings are free to "creep" on the spindle. Polish and lubricate the spindle to allow "creeping" movement and to keep rust from forming.

ADJUSTMENT

1. With the tire and wheel removed and the car supported by a suitable and safe means, remove the dust cover from the spindle.

2. Remove the cotter pin and nut retainer.

3. Rotate the wheel while tightening the spindle nut to 20–25 ft. lbs.

4. Loosen the spindle nut ⅓ of a turn.

5. Rotate the wheel while tightening the spindle nut to 6 in. lbs.

6. Fit the nut retainer over the spindle and align the slots in it with the cotter pin hole. Insert the cotter pin.

7. Install the dust cover.

REAR SUSPENSION

Shock Absorber

REPLACEMENT

NOTE: *When installing new shocks purge them of air by repeatedly extending them in their normal position and compressing them while inverted. It is normal for there to be more resistance to extension than to compression.*

1. Support the rear axle with jacks or a lift; this allows the weight of the car to compress the rear spring.

2. Remove the lower shock attachment.

3. Remove the access plate on the rear underbody panel and remove the upper securing nut. It may be necessary to hold the top of the shock while unfastening the nut.

NOTE: *Some models do not have an access plate. On these cars, remove the upper attachment plate complete as an assembly from under the car.*

4. Remove the shock from under the car.

5. Installation is the reverse of removal.

Spring

REMOVAL AND INSTALLATION

Leaf Springs

1. Raise the car. Support the rear axle with jacks or a lift to take the load off the rear springs.

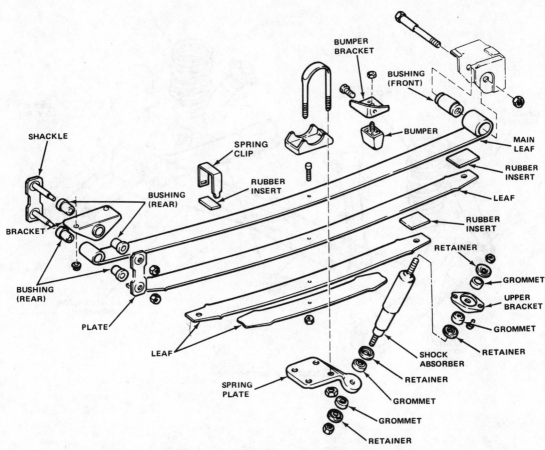

1975–76 rear suspension, except Matador

2. Disconnect the rear shock from the lower mounting stud.

3. Disconnect the axle U-bolts.

4. Remove the nut from the bolt which attaches the eye of the spring to the front mount. Remove the bolt.

5. On all except Pacer, remove the nuts from the rear shackle. Remove the shackle.

6. On the Pacer, remove the nuts from the rear hanger bracket on the frame side sill and remove the spring. Remove the shackle nuts and the shackle after the spring is removed.

7. Installation is the reverse.

Coil Springs

1. Raise the rear of the car and support the rear axle with jacks or a lift to take the load off the rear springs.

2. Disconnect the shock from the axle tube. Lower the axle to the fullest extent of its travel (limited by the control arms). Detach the upper control arms at the axle on 1975 and later models.

3. Pull down the axle tube to completely release the spring.

4. Reverse the above to install the spring. Torque the control arm pivot bolts to 45–80 ft. lbs. with the weight of the car on the springs.

STEERING

A collapsible, energy-absorbing steering column is used. No service operations involving removal or disassembly of the steering column are given here. Such critical and delicate operations should be entrusted to qualified AMC service personnel.

Steering Wheel
REMOVAL AND INSTALLATION

NOTE: *Some steering shafts have metric steering wheel nut threads. Metric shafts are identified by a groove running around the splines, and blue colored threads.*

1. Disconnect the battery ground cable.

2. On wheels with horn button, remove the button by lifting up and pulling out.

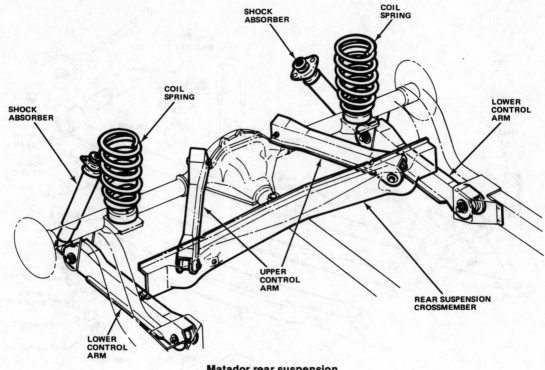

SHOCK
ABSORBER

COIL
SPRING

COIL
SPRING

SHOCK
ABSORBER

LOWER
CONTROL
ARM

UPPER
CONTROL
ARM

REAR SUSPENSION
CROSSMEMBER

LOWER
CONTROL
ARM

Matador rear suspension

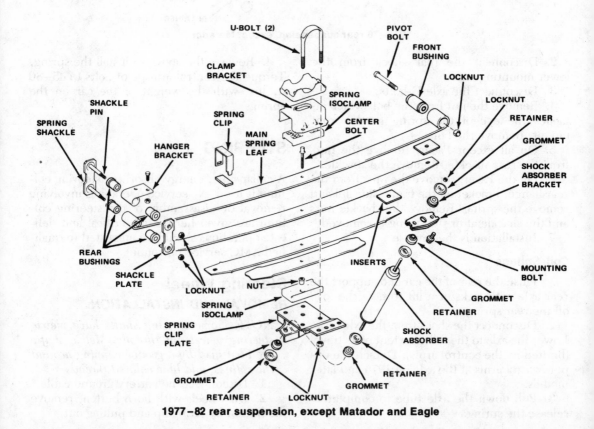

U-BOLT (2)

PIVOT
BOLT

FRONT
BUSHING

LOCKNUT

CLAMP
BRACKET

SPRING
ISOCLAMP

LOCKNUT

SHACKLE
PIN

SPRING
CLIP

CENTER
BOLT

RETAINER

GROMMET

SPRING
SHACKLE

HANGER
BRACKET

MAIN
SPRING
LEAF

SHOCK
ABSORBER
BRACKET

REAR
BUSHINGS

INSERTS

MOUNTING
BOLT

SHACKLE
PLATE

LOCKNUT

NUT

GROMMET

SPRING
ISOCLAMP

RETAINER

SPRING
CLIP
PLATE

SHOCK
ABSORBER

GROMMET

RETAINER

GROMMET

LOCKNUT

RETAINER

1977–82 rear suspension, except Matador and Eagle

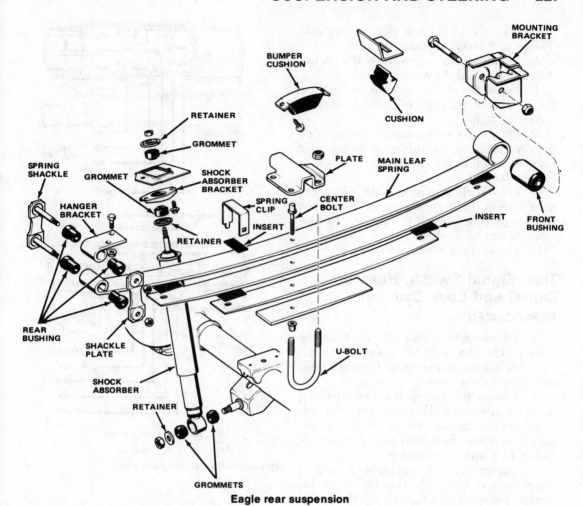

Eagle rear suspension

3. On wheels with a horn bar, remove the screws from the back of the wheel and remove the bar. Do the same on rimblow wheels.

4. On rim-blow wheels, pull the wire out of the center connection.

5. Remove the nut and washer.

6. Install the bolts of a steering wheel puller into the tapped holes in the wheel and pull off the wheel.

CAUTION: *Don't hammer on the steering*

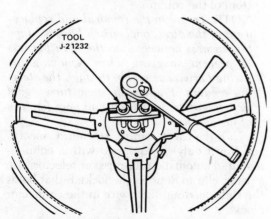

Steering wheel removal

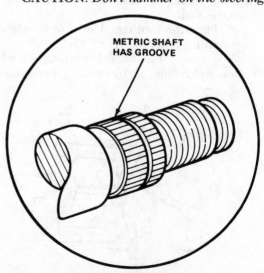

Metric steering shaft identification

wheel or the shaft. You could easily collapse your collapsible steering column.

7. On installation, align the marks on the steering shaft and the wheel at the top.

8. Install the washer and nut and tighten the nut to 20 ft. lbs. This is a critical fastener; it must be torqued.

9. On wheels with a horn button, index the projection on the rubber retaining ring with the notch in the cup and push down to engage the ring.

10. On wheels with a horn bar, place the horn wire in the hole and secure it with the retainer and then install the screws. Do the same for rim-blow wheels.

11. Connect the battery cable.

Turn Signal Switch, Hazard Signal and Lock Cylinder

REPLACEMENT

1. Disconnect the ground cable from the battery. On cars with tilt steering wheels, place the column in the straight position. Remove the steering wheel.

2. Loosen the anti-theft cover attaching screws and remove the cover from the column. Do not hammer on the shaft. Do not move the screws from the cover; they are attached to it with plastic retainers.

3. To remove the lockplate, a special compressor is required. This tool is an inverted U-shape with a hole for the shaft. The shaft nut is used to force it down. Depress the lockplate and pry the snap-ring from the groove in the steering shaft. Remove the tool, snap-ring, plate, turn signal cam, upper bearing preload spring, and thrust washer from the shaft.

4. Place the turn signal lever in the right turn position and remove it.

5. Depress the hazard warning switch button and remove it, by rotating it counter-

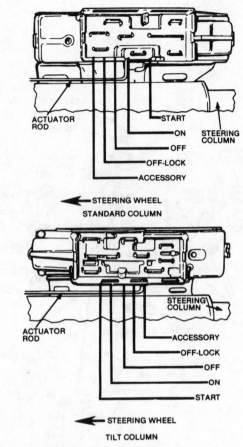

Ignition switch slider positions

clockwise. Remove the package tray (if equipped) and the lower trim panel.

6. Disconnect the wire harness connector block at its mounting bracket, which is located on the right side of the lower column. Remove the steering column mounting bracket attaching bolts. Remove the turn signal switch wiring harness protector from the bottom of the column.

NOTE: *To aid in the removal and replacement of the directional switch harness, tape the harness connector to the wire harness to prevent snagging when removing the wiring harness assembly through the steering column. Prepare the new turn signal switch harness in the same manner for ease of installation.*

7. If the car (Gremlin, Hornet, Concord, and Spirit only) is equipped with a column-mounted automatic transmission selector, use a paper clip to depress the locktab that holds the shift quadrant light wire in the connector block.

8. Remove the switch attaching screws.

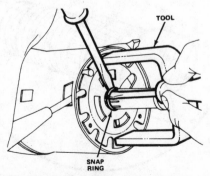

Using the special lockplate remover tool

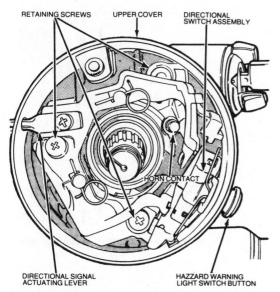

RETAINING SCREWS   UPPER COVER   DIRECTIONAL SWITCH ASSEMBLY

HORN CONTACT

DIRECTIONAL SIGNAL ACTUATING LEVER

HAZZARD WARNING LIGHT SWITCH BUTTON

Turn signal switch

Withdraw the switch and wire harness from the column.

9. Insert the key into the lock cylinder and turn the key to the ON position. Remove the warning buzzer switch and the contacts as an assembly using needlenosed pliers. Take care not to let the contacts fall into the column.

10. Turn the key to the LOCK position and compress the lock cylinder retaining tab. Remove the lock cylinder. If the tab is not visible through the slot, knock the casting flash out of the slot.

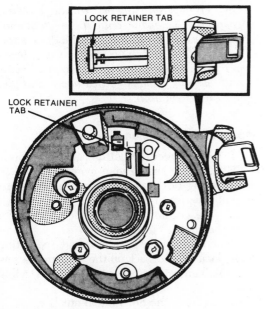

LOCK RETAINER TAB

LOCK RETAINER TAB

Lock cylinder removal

To install:

1. Hold the lock cylinder sleeve and turn the lock cylinder clockwise (counterclockwise 1977 and later) until it contacts the stop.

2. Align the lock cylinder key with the keyway in the housing and slip the cylinder into the housing.

3. Lightly depress the cylinder against the sector, while turning it counterclockwise, until the cylinder and sector are engaged.

4. Depress the cylinder until the retaining tab engages, and the lock cylinder is secured.

5. Install the turn signal switch. Be sure that the actuating lever pivot is properly seated and aligned in the top of the housing boss, before installing it with its screws.

6. Install the turn signal lever and check the operation of the switch.

7. Install the thrust washer, spring and turn signal cancelling cam on the steering shaft.

8. Align the lockplate and steering shaft splines, and position the lockplate so that the turn signal camshaft protrudes from the "dogleg" opening in the lockplate.

9. Use snap-ring pliers to install the snap-ring on the end of the steering shaft.

10. Secure the anti-theft cover with its screws.

11. Install the button on the hazard warning switch. Install the steering wheel, as detailed above.

Ignition Switch
REPLACEMENT

The ignition switch on all models is mounted on the lower steering column tube and is connected to the lock cylinder via a lock rod.

1. Place the key in "OFF-LOCK."

2. Remove switch mounting screws.

3. Disconnect the lock rod, remove harness connector and switch.

4. To install on the standard column, move the switch slide as far as it will go to the left (toward the wheel). On the tilt-column, push the slide to the extreme right.

5. Position the lock rod into the hole on the switch slide.

6. Install the switch on the steering column. Be sure that the slide stays in its detent.

7. On the tilt-column, do not tighten the mounting screws. Instead, push the switch down the column, away from the steering

wheel. This will remove any slack from the lock rod.

8. Tighten the switch mounting screws.

Manual Steering Gear-Except Pacer

REMOVAL

1. Remove flexible coupling bolts.
2. Remove pitman arm, using puller J-5566-04.
3. Remove steering gear mounting screws and lower steering gear.

INSTALLATION

1. Center steering gear with index mark up. Mark on shaft of flange must be aligned at assembly.
2. Insert the flexible coupling bolts into shaft flange. Tighten nuts to 20 ft. lbs. torque and pinch bolt 30 ft. lbs.
3. Tighten gear mounting screws to 65 ft. lbs. and Pitman arm nut to 115 ft. lbs.

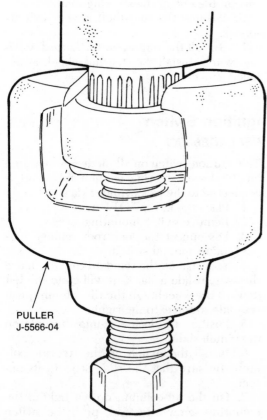

Pitman arm removal

PULLER J-5566-04

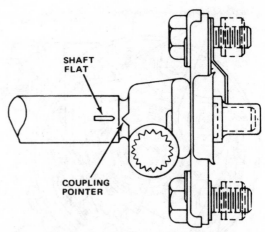

SHAFT FLAT

COUPLING POINTER

Intermediate shaft and flexible coupling alignment

NOTE: *After tightening Pitman shaft nut, stake thread at nut with a center punch to insure nut retention.*

NOTE: *Whenever the steering gear assembly is removed for replacement or overhaul, or the mounting bolts are loosened for any reason, the steering column MUST be realigned to the gear assembly. Slight misalignment of the steering column may cause increased steering effort and additional wear to the steering components.*

ADJUSTMENTS—EXCEPT PACER

All these cars use Saginaw recirculating ball steering gear.

CAUTION: *Adjustments to the steering gear must be made only in the sequence given here or the steering gear will be damaged. That is, you must do the worm bearing preload adjustment before the sector and ball nut backlash adjustment, and you must do them both.*

Worm Bearing Preload Adjustment

1. Disconnect the battery ground cable.
2. Remove the Pitman arm (the arm on the steering box) nut and mark the relationship of the arm to the shaft.
3. Use a puller to remove the pitman arm from the shaft.
4. Loosen the pitman shaft adjusting screw locknut and back off the adjusting screw (the small adjusting screw on the cover) a few turns.
5. Remove the horn button or bar.
6. Gently turn the steering wheel in one

direction until it can't go any further, then turn it back half a turn.

CAUTION: *If you turn the steering wheel hard against the stop with the linkage disconnected, you will damage the steering gear.*

7. Attach a torque wrench with a maximum reading of 50 in. lbs. or less to the steering wheel nut. Turn the wheel through a quarter turn with the wrench. The torque reading should be 5–8 in. lbs.

8. To adjust, loosen the big worm bearing adjuster locknut with a brass drift and hammer. Turn the adjuster plug (viewed from underneath) clockwise to increase the preload.

9. Tighten the locknut to 50 ft. lbs. and recheck the preload.

10. Go on to the next adjustment.

Sector and Ball Nut Backlash Adjustment

1. Turn the wheel gently from full right stop to full left stop and count the total number of turns stop-to-stop.

2. Turn back half the number of turns to the center position, then turn half a turn past the center position.

3. Use the torque wrench on the steering

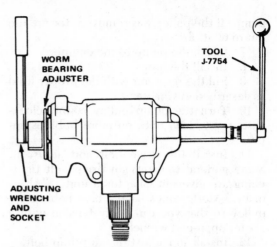

Adjusting worm bearing preload on manual steering gear

wheel nut to turn the gear through the center of travel. The torque required should be 4–10 in. lbs. The sum of this torque and that measured after worm bearing preload adjustment must not exceed 16 in. lbs.

4. To adjust, turn the adjusting screw on the cover. Tighten the locknut and recheck the torque or force required.

5. Replace the pitman arm on the shaft, aligning the marks you made back in Step 2 of "Worm Bearing Preload Adjustment."

6. Tighten the pitman arm nut to 115 ft. lbs. and stake it to the shaft. This is a critical fastener; it must be torqued. To stake the nut means to slightly distort its inner edge by use of a punch or chisel.

7. Replace the horn button or bar and battery ground cable.

Power Steering Pump—Except Pacer

REMOVAL AND INSTALLATION

6 and V8

1. Place a drip pan under the pump.

2. Disconnect both hoses at the pump and plug them.

3. It may be necessary to remove the air pump drive belt. You might also have to remove the steering pump pulley. On cars with A/C, it may be necessary to remove the compressor drivebelt and pulley.

4. Remove the pump mounting nuts and washers from behind.

5. On sixes, loosen the pump bracket pivot bolts. On V8 engines, remove the front pump mounting bracket.

6. Remove the pump drive belt and the

Manual steering gear Pitman shaft over-center torque drag adjustment

pump. If the pulley was removed, torque the nut to 60 ft. lbs.

7. Install the pump to the engine.

8. Install the hoses.

9. Fill the reservoir with the proper fluid as described in Chapter 1.

10. Turn the pump pulley counterclockwise (front view) until no more bubbles appear.

11. Install the drive belt and adjust it. Some general thoughts on drive belt tightening are given in Chapter 3 under "Alternator." Most pumps have a boss behind the pulley so that you can apply tension with a 1⅝ in. open-end wrench.

12. Install and adjust the air pump belt.

13. Bleed the system by raising the front of the car and turning the wheels from side-to-side without hitting the stops for a few minutes. Check the level frequently.

4-121

1. Remove adjuster locknuts and lockwashers retaining pump and pivot bracket to pump mounting bracket. Lower adjuster is accessible from underneath car.

NOTE: *Except for the adjuster locknuts, all of the pump mounting bolts are metric sizes. The adjuster locknuts are loosened and tightened using a* ⁹/₁₆ *box-end wrench having a 45° offset.*

2. Move pump toward engine and remove pump belt.

3. Loosen return hose clamp and slide clamp back along hose.

4. Pull pump forward and disconnect both hoses.

5. Remove bolts attaching pump front mounting bracket to rear mounting bracket and engine block. Remove pump, pivot bracket, and front mounting bracket as assembly.

6. Position pump, front mounting bracket, and pivot bracket on rear mounting bracket and connect pressure and return hoses to pump. Tighten pressure hose fitting to 38 ft. lbs. torque.

7. Install front bracket-to-rear bracket bolts. Tighten bolts to 25 ft. lbs. torque. Tighten front bracket-to-engine block bolt to 16 ft. lbs. torque.

8. Slide return hose clamp into position and tighten hose clamp.

9. Install adjuster locknuts and lockwashers.

10. Adjust pump belt.

4-151

1. Remove ambient air induction hose and remove adjusting bracket nuts/bolts.

2. Move pump toward engine and remove pump belt.

3. Loosen return hose clamp and slide clamp back along hose.

4. Pull pump forward and disconnect both hoses. Pressure hose has 18 mm metric fitting.

5. Remove bolts attaching pump front mounting bracket to rear mounting bracket and engine block. Remove pump, pivot bracket, and front mounting bracket as assembly.

6. Position pump and mounting brackets on engine. Connect pressure and return hoses to pump. Tighten pressure hose fitting to 38 ft. lbs. torque.

7. Install bracket and bracket bolts/nuts. Tighten bolts to 25 ft. lbs. torque.

8. Adjust pump belt tension.

Power Steering Gear—Except Pacer

REMOVAL

1. Place wheels in straight-ahead position.

2. Position drain pan under steering gear.

3. Disconnect hoses at gear. Raise and secure hoses above pump fluid level to prevent excessive oil spillage and cap ends of hoses to prevent entry of dirt.

4. Remove flexible coupling-to-intermediate shaft attaching nuts.

5. Raise automobile on hoist.

NOTE: *On Eagle models, remove:*

a. skid plate, if equipped;

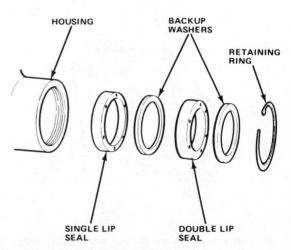

Pitman shaft seal assembly sequence

b. left side crossmember-to-sill support brace;

c. stabilizer bar brackets from frame.

6. Paint alignment marks on pitman arm and pitman shaft for assembly reference.

7. Remove pitman arm using Puller Tool J-5566-04.

8. Remove steering gear mounting bolts and remove steering gear.

INSTALLATION

1. Center steering gear. Turn stub shaft (using flexible coupling) from stop-to-stop and count total number of turns; then turn back from either stop one-half total number of turns to center gear. At this point, flat on stub shaft should be facing upward.

2. Align flexible coupling and intermediate shaft flange.

3. Install gear mounting bolts in gear, install spacer on gear, and mount gear on frame side sill. Tighten gear mounting bolts to 65 ft. lbs. torque.

4. Install and tighten flexible coupling nuts to 25 ft. lbs. torque.

5. Install pitman arm. Index arm to shaft using alignment marks made during removal.

6. Install pitman arm nut. Tighten nut to 115 ft. lbs. torque and stake nut to pitman shaft in one place.

CAUTION: *The pitman arm nut must be staked to the shaft to retain it properly.*

NOTE: *On Eagle models, install:*

a. stabilizer bar brackets;

b. left side crossmember-to-sill support brace;

c. skid plate, if equipped.

7. Lower automobile.

8. Align flexible coupling, if necessary. Refer to Flexible Coupling Adjustment.

9. Connect hoses to gear and tighten fittings to 25 ft. lbs. torque.

10. Fill pump reservoir with power steering fluid and bleed air from system.

ADJUSTMENTS—EXCEPT PACER

Because of the complexity involved in adjusting worm bearing preload and pitman shaft overcenter drag torque plus the friction effect produced by hydraulic fluid, the power steering gear must be adjusted off the automobile only.

The power steering gear requires two adjustments which are: worm bearing preload and pitman shaft overcenter drag torque.

Worm bearing preload is controlled by the amount of compression force exerted on the

conical worm bearing thrust races by the adjuster plug.

Pitman shaft overcenter torque is controlled by the pitman shaft adjuster screw which determines the clearance between the rack piston and pitman shaft sector teeth.

CAUTION: *The following adjustment procedures must be performed exactly as described and in the sequence outlined. Failure to do so can result in damage to the gear internal components and improper steering response. Always adjust worm bearing preload first; then adjust pitman shaft overcenter drag torque.*

Worm Bearing Preload

1. Seat adjuster plug firmly in housing using Spanner Tool J-7624. Approximately 20 ft. lbs. torque is required to seat housing.

2. Place index mark on gear housing opposite one of the holes in adjuster plug.

3. Measure back (counterclockwise) 3/16 to ¼ inch (4.7 to 6.3 mm) from index mark and remark housing.

4. Turn adjuster plug counterclockwise until hole in plug is aligned with second mark on housing.

5. Install adjuster plug locknut and tighten it to 85 ft. lbs. torque. Be sure adjuster plug does not turn when tightening locknut.

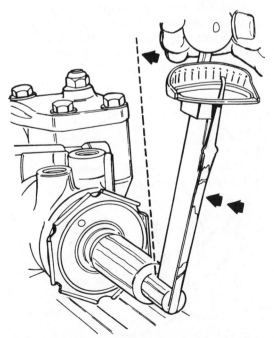

Measuring wormshaft bearing preload on power steering gears

6. Turn stub shaft clockwise to stop, then turn shaft back ¼ turn.

7. Using in. lbs. torque wrench with maximum capacity of 50 in. lbs. and twelve-point deep socket, measure torque required to turn stub shaft. Take reading with beam of torque wrench at, or near, vertical position while turning stub shaft at an even rate.

8. Record torque reading. Torque required to turn stub shaft should be 4 to 10 in. lbs. torque. If reading is above or below indicated torque, adjuster plug may not be tightened properly or may have turned when locknut was tightened, or the gear may be assembled incorrectly, or the thrust bearings and races may be defective.

Pitman Shaft Overcenter Drag Torque

1. Turn pitman shaft adjuster screw counterclockwise until fully extended, then turn it back ½ turn clockwise.

2. Rotate stub shaft from stop-to-stop and count total number of turns.

3. Starting from either stop, turn stub shaft back ½ total number of turns. This is gear center.

NOTE: *When the gear is centered, the flat on the stub shaft should face upward and be parallel with the side cover and the master spline on the pitman shaft should be in line with the adjuster screw.*

4. Install in. lbs. torque wrench with maximum capacity of 50 in. lbs. and twelve-point deep socket on stub shaft. Place torque wrench in vertical position to take reading.

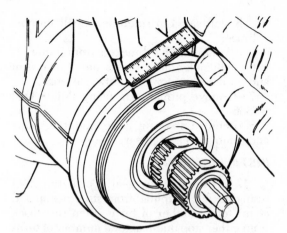

Make a second mark ³/₁₆ to ¼ inch from the first on models through 1979 and ½ inch from the first on 1980–82 models

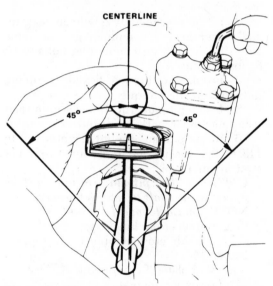

Measuring Pitman shaft over-center torque drag on power steering gears

5. Rotate torque wrench 45 degrees each side of center and record highest drag torque measured on or near center.

6. Adjust overcenter drag torque by turning pitman shaft adjusting screw clockwise until desired drag torque is obtained. Adjust drag torque to following limits:

On new steering gears, add 4 to 8 in. lbs. torque to previously measured worm bearing preload torque but do not exceed a combined total of 18 in. lbs drag torque.

On used steering gears (400 or more miles), add 4 to 5 in. lbs. torque to previously measured worm bearing preload torque but do not exceed a combined total of 14 in. lbs drag torque.

7. Tighten pitman shaft adjusting screw

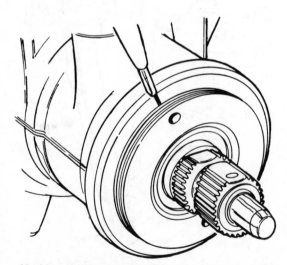

Marking the power steering gear housing adjacent to the hole in the adjuster

locknut to 35 ft. lbs. torque after adjusting overcenter drag torque.

8. Install gear as outlined in Steering Gear Installation.

9. Fill pump reservoir and bleed gear and pump as outlined in Fluid Level and Initial Operation after completing overcenter drag torque adjustment.

FLUID LEVEL AND INITIAL OPERATION

1. Fill pump reservoir.

2. Operate engine until power steering fluid reaches normal operating temperature of approximately 170°F, then stop engine.

3. Turn wheels to full left turn position and add power steering fluid to COLD mark on dipstick.

4. Start engine, operate it at hot idle speed and recheck fluid level. Add fluid, if necessary, to COLD mark on dipstick.

5. Bleed system by turning wheels from side to side without hitting stops. Maintain fluid level just above pump housing. Fluid with air in it will have a milky appearance. Air must be eliminated from fluid before normal steering action can be obtained.

6. Return wheels to center position and operate engine for additional 2 to 3 minutes, then stop engine.

7. Road-test automobile to make sure steering functions normally and is free of noise.

8. Check fluid level. Add fluid as required to raise level to HOT mark on dipstick after system has stabilized at its normal operating temperature.

Tie Rod End

REMOVAL AND INSTALLATION— EXCEPT PACER

1. Raise and support the front of the car.

2. Remove the cotter pin and retaining nut from the tie rod end stud.

3. Mark the position of the tie rod end, adjuster tube, and inner tie rod for reference.

4. Loosen the adjuster tube clamps.

5. Disconnect the tie rod end from the steering arm with a puller.

6. Remove the tie rod end from the adjuster tube.

7. Install the replacement tie rod end in the adjuster tube, and insert the end stud in the steering arm. Tighten the nut to 35 ft. lbs. and install a new cotter pin. Do not loosen the nuts to align. Adjust the toe-in and tighten the clamps.

Pacer Manual Steering

RUBBER BOOT, MOUNTING CLAMP AND GROMMET REPLACEMENT

1. Raise and support front end of car.

2. Cut and remove boot clamps from boot adjacent to mounting clamp.

3. Mark position of adjuster tube and tie rod for assembly reference.

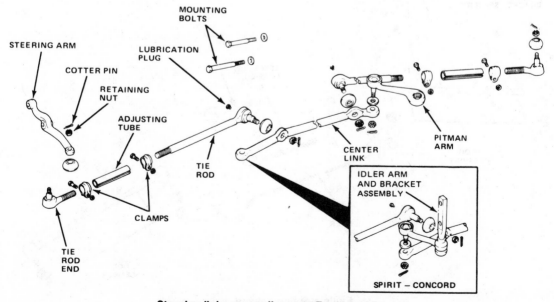

Steering linkage on all except Eagle and Pacer

4. Loosen adjuster tube clamp bolts and unthread tube from tie rod.

5. Remove boot.

CAUTION: *Do not allow the protective boot to become cut or torn during service operations. A damaged boot will expose the gear internal components to dirt, foreign material, and road splash resulting in premature wear.*

6. Remove bolts attaching mounting clamp to front crossmember. Loosen bolts before removing to minimize clamp distortion.

7. Remove clamp and grommet using a twisting, pulling motion.

8. Install replacement clamp and grommet. Align hole in grommet with breather tube.

9. Install mounting clamp attaching bolts. Tighten bolts to 50 ft. lbs. torque.

10. Install boot. Align hole in boot with breather tube.

11. Install boot clamps. Position ear of clamps ¾ inch (19.05 mm) from breather tube. Compress clamps using tool J-22610.

12. Install adjuster tube on tie rod and tighten clamp bolts to 22 ft. lbs. torque.

NOTE: *At least three threads should be visible at each end of adjuster tube. The number of threads per side should not differ by more than three.*

13. Remove supports, lower car, and correct toe-in as necessary.

BREATHER TUBE REPLACEMENT

1. Raise and support front of car.

2. Cut and remove large diameter boot clamps from boots.

3. Slide boots away from breather tube and remove tube.

CAUTION: *Do not allow the protective boots to become cut or torn during service operations. A damaged boot will expose the gear internal components to dirt, foreign material, and road splash resulting in premature wear.*

4. Remove bolts attaching mounting clamp to front crossmember. Loosen bolts before removing to minimize clamp distortion.

5. Remove clamp and grommet using a twisting-pulling motion.

6. Install replacement breather tube. Align holes in boots with tube.

7. Install mounting clamp and grommet. Be sure to align hole in grommet with breather tube.

8. Install and tighten mounting clamp bolts to 50 ft. lbs. torque.

9. Position boots on flanges at each end of tube and housing and install boot clamps. Position ear of clamps ¾ inch (19.05 mm) from breather tube and compress clamps using tool J-22610.

10. Remove supports and lower car.

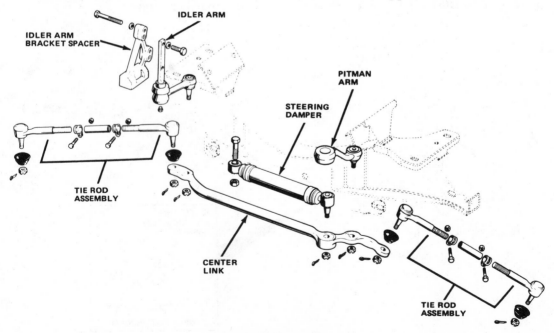

Eagle steering linkage

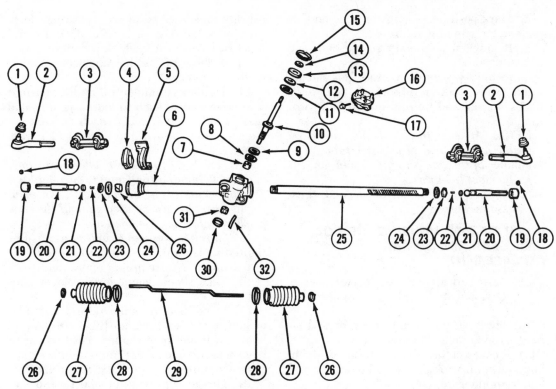

1. Tie rod seal
2. Tie rod end
3. Adjuster tube
4. Mounting grommet
5. Mounting clamp
6. Tube and housing assembly
7. Upper pinion bushing
8. Lower thrust bearing race
9. Lower thrust bearing
10. Pinion shaft
11. Upper thrust bearing

12. Upper thrust bearing race
13. Adjuster plug
14. Pinion shaft seal
15. Adjuster plug locknut
16. Flexible coupling
17. Pinch bolt
18. Set screw
19. Tie rod housing
20. Inner tie rod
21. Ball seat
22. Ball seat spring

23. Jam nut
24. Shock dampener ring
25. Steering rack
26. Boot retainer
27. Boot
28. Boot clamp
29. Breather tube
30. Contraction plug
31. Lower pinion bushing
32. Preload spring

Pacer manual steering

FLEXIBLE COUPLING REPLACEMENT

1. Remove nuts attaching coupling to intermediate shaft flange and compress shaft to provide working clearance.

2. Remove coupling pinch bolt using $7/16$, 12-point socket or box end wrench and remove coupling.

3. Install replacement coupling (flat-to-flat) and install pinch bolt. Tighten bolt to 30 ft. lbs. torque.

4. Connect intermediate shaft to coupling and tighten nuts to 25 ft. lbs. torque.

TIE ROD ENDS AND ADJUSTER TUBE REPLACEMENT

1. Raise and support front of car.
2. Disconnect tie rod end using tool J-26951.

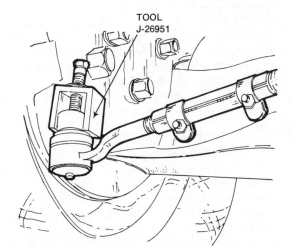

Disconnecting the tie rod end on Pacer manual steering

3. Mark position of adjuster tube and tie rod end for assembly reference.

4. Remove and separate tie rod ends and adjuster tubes.

5. Install replacement tie rod ends and adjuster tubes. Tighten tube clamp bolts to 22 ft. lbs. torque and tie rod nuts to 50 ft. lbs. torque.

NOTE: *At least three threads should be visible at each end of adjuster tubes. The number of threads per side should not differ by more than three.*

6. Remove supports, lower car, and adjust toe-in as necessary.

INNER TIE ROD HOUSING, TIE ROD, BALL SEAT, AND SPRING REPLACEMENT

1. Raise and support front of car.

2. Disconnect tie rod ends using tool J-26951.

3. Mark position of adjuster tube and inner tie rod for assembly reference.

4. Loosen adjuster tube inboard clamp bolt and unthread adjuster tube and tie rod end from inner tie rod assembly.

5. Cut and remove large boot clamp and move boot aside.

CAUTION: *Do not allow the protective boot to become cut or torn during service operations. A damaged boot will expose the gear internal components to dirt, foreign material, and road splash resulting in premature wear.*

6. Slide shock dampener ring off jamnut.

7. Loosen jamnut. Use open end wrench to loosen jamnut and place another open end wrench on rack flat (adjacent to rack teeth) to prevent rack from turning.

CAUTION: *If the rack is allowed to turn when loosening the jamnuts, gear internal components could be damaged. An open end wrench must be used to hold the rack when loosening the jamnut.*

8. Loosen setscrew in tie rod housing, unthread housing from rack and remove inner tie rod, tie rod housing, inner tie rod ball seat, and ball seat spring.

9. Liberally apply a waterproof, EP-type, lithium base chassis lubricant to all replacement inner tie rod assembly wear surfaces. Pack tie rod housing with same lubricant.

10. Install ball seat spring and ball seat in end of rack.

11. Assemble inner tie rod and housing and install on rack.

12. Hand tighten tie rod housing while rocking inner tie rod to prevent grease lock; then back housing off ⅛-turn (45°). Tie rod must rock and turn freely in housing.

13. Tighten tie rod housing setscrew to 9 ft. lbs. torque.

14. Tighten jamnut to 60 ft. lbs. torque. Use open end wrench to loosen jamnut and place another open and wrench on rack flat (adjacent to rack teeth) to prevent rack from turning.

CAUTION: *If the rack is allowed to turn when tightening the jamnut, gear internal components could be damaged. An open end wrench must be used to hold the rack when tightening the jamnut.*

15. Check movement of inner tie rod after tightening jamnut. Tie rod must move freely in housing to ensure proper operation.

16. Slide shock dampener ring over jamnut.

17. Install boot on inner tie rod and tube or housing. Align breather tube with hole in boot and install boot clamps. Position ear of large clamp ¾-inch (19.05 mm) from breather tube. Compress clamps using Tool J-22610.

18. Thread adjuster tube and tie rod end assembly on inner tie rod. Refer to alignment marks made at disassembly.

19. Tighten adjuster tube bolts to 22 ft. lbs. torque.

20. Connect tie rod ends to steering arms. Tighten tie rod end nuts to 50 ft. lbs. torque and install replacement cotter pins.

21. Remove supports, lower car, and adjust toe-in as necessary.

STEERING GEAR REMOVAL

1. Unlock steering column.

2. Raise and support front of car.

3. Remove screws attaching reinforcement brace to front crossmember and left engine support bracket and remove brace.

4. Remove flexible coupling pinch bolt and disengage flexible coupling from steering gear pinion shaft.

5. Remove cotter pins and nuts from tie rod ends.

6. Disconnect tie rod ends using tool J-26951.

7. Remove bolts attaching steering gear mounting clamp to right side of front crossmember.

NOTE: *Before removing bolts, loosen them slightly to minimize clamp distortion.*

8. Remove steering gear housing-to-crossmember nuts. Remove bolts, washers, sleeves, and grommets using blunt punch.

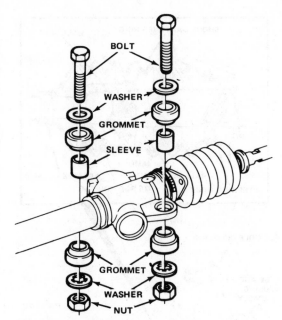

BOLT

WASHER

GROMMET

SLEEVE

GROMMET

WASHER

NUT

Pacer manual steering gear housing attachment

9. Rotate bottom of gear housing toward front of car until pinion shaft is approximately parallel with skid plate. Slide gear assembly toward right side of car until housing and tube clear mounting plate and remove steering gear assembly.

STEERING GEAR INSTALLATION

1. Assemble grommets, sleeves, and washers and install on steering gear. Sleeves will hold grommets in place during assembly.

2. Position steering gear assembly on crossmember. Install tube and housing from right side of car. During installation, keep pinion shaft approximately parallel with mounting plate.

3. Install mounting clamp-to-crossmember attaching bolts. Hand tighten bolts only.

4. Install steering gear housing-to-crossmember attaching bolts, washers, and nuts and tighten to 60 ft. lbs. torque.

5. Tighten mounting clamp-to-crossmember attaching bolts to 50 ft. lbs. torque.

6. Connect tie rod ends to steering arms. Tighten nuts to 50 ft. lbs. torque and install replacement cotter pins.

7. Align flat spline on pinion shaft with flat on flexible coupling and install coupling on shaft. Install pinch bolt and tighten to 30 ft. lbs. torque.

8. Install bolts attaching reinforcement brace to front crossmember and engine support bracket. Tighten bolts to 30 foot-pounds torque.

9. Remove supports and lower car.

10. Check and correct toe-in adjustment if necessary.

Pacer Power Steering
RUBBER BOOT, MOUNTING CLAMP AND GROMMET REPLACEMENT

1. Raise and support front end of car.

2. Cut and remove boot clamps from boot adjacent to mounting clamp.

3. Mark position of adjuster tube on inner tie rod for assembly reference.

4. Loosen adjuster tube inboard clamp bolt and unthread tube from inner tie rod.

5. Remove bolts attaching mounting clamp to front crossmember. Loosen both bolts before removing to minimize clamp distortion.

6. Remove protective boot.

CAUTION: *Do not allow the protective boot to become cut, torn, or damaged during service operations. A damaged boot will expose the gear internal components to dirt, foreign material and road splash resulting in premature wear.*

7. Remove clamp and grommet using twisting, pulling motion.

8. Install replacement clamp and grommet. Align hole in grommet with breather tube.

9. Install boot. Align hole in boot with breather tube.

10. Install boot clamps. Position clamp ear ¾ inch (19.05 mm) from breather tube. Tighten clamps using tool J-22610.

11. Install adjuster tube on tie rod and tighten clamp bolts to 14 ft. lbs. torque.

NOTE: *At least three threads should be visible at each end of adjuster tube. The number of threads per side should not differ by more than three.*

12. Install and tighten mounting clamp bolts to 48 ft. lbs. torque.

13. Remove supports, lower car, and correct toe-in as necessary.

BREATHER TUBE REPLACEMENT

1. Raise and support front of car.

2. Cut and remove large diameter boot clamps from boots.

3. Slide boots away from breather tube and remove tube.

4. Install replacement breather tube. Align holes in boots with tube.

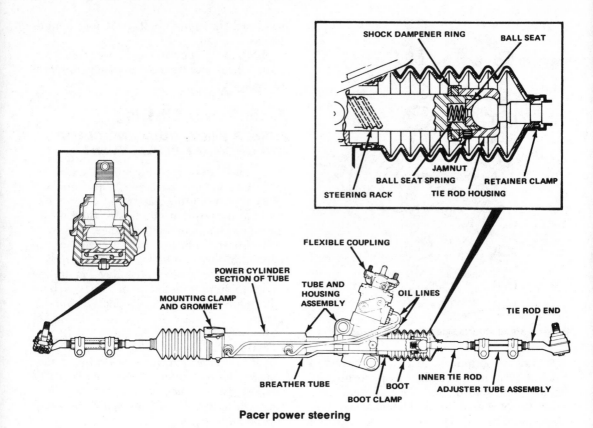

Pacer power steering

5. Position boots on flanges at each end of tube and housing and install boot clamps. Position clamp ear ¾ inch (19.05 mm) from breather tube. Tighten clamps using tool J-22610.

6. Remove supports and lower car.

FLEXIBLE COUPLING REPLACEMENT

1. Remove nuts attaching coupling to intermediate shaft flange and compress shaft to provide working clearance.

2. Remove coupling pinch bolt using $7/16$, 12-point socket or box end wrench and remove coupling.

3. Install replacement coupling (flat-to-flat) and install pinch bolt. Tighten bolt to 30 ft. lbs. torque.

4. Connect intermediate shaft to coupling. Tighten nuts to 25 ft. lbs. torque.

TIE ROD END AND ADJUSTER TUBE REPLACEMENT

1. Raise and support front of car.

2. Disconnect tie rod ends using tool J-26951.

3. Mark position of tie rod end, adjuster tube, and inner tie rod for assembly reference.

4. Loosen adjuster tube inboard clamp bolt.

5. Remove and separate tie rod end and adjuster tube.

6. Install replacement tie rod end and adjuster tube. Tighten adjuster tube clamp bolt to 14 ft. lbs. torque and tie rod end nut to 50 ft. lbs. torque.

NOTE: *At least three threads should be visible at each end of adjuster tubes. The number of threads per side should not differ by more than three.*

7. Remove supports, lower car, and correct toe-in as necessary.

OIL LINE REPLACEMENT

1. Raise and support front of car.

2. Remove oil lines.

3. Install replacement oil lines. Tighten fittings to 30 ft. lbs. torque.

4. Apply parking brake, shift transmission into Park or Neutral (on manual transmission) and start engine. Turn steering wheel right and left several times and check for leaks at oil line fittings. If leaks are not evident, proceed to next step. If leaks are evident, tighten fittings and check again. If leaks persist, remove and replace steering gear assembly.

5. Remove supports and lower car. Add power steering fluid as necessary.

BULKHEAD SEAL REPLACEMENT

1. Raise and support front of car.
2. Disconnect tie rod end connected to tube side of rack from steering arm using tool J-26951.

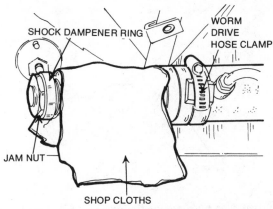

Installing the hose clamp, ribber seal and protective cloths

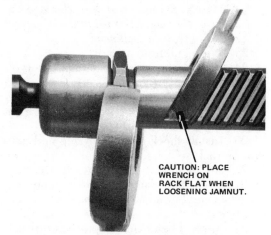

CAUTION: PLACE WRENCH ON RACK FLAT WHEN LOOSENING JAMNUT.

Loosening or tightening the jamnut on Pacer power steering

3. Remove mounting clamp bolts.
4. Remove clamps from boot at tube-end of gear and slide boot away from end of tube.

CAUTION: *Do not allow the protective boot to become cut or torn during service operations. A damaged boot will expose the gear internal components to dirt, foreign material and road splash resulting in premature wear.*

5. Remove large boot clamp at housing end of gear.
6. If flat on rack teeth is not visible, pull back boot at housing end of gear and turn steering wheel (to rotate pinion) and extend rack until rack flat is accessible.
7. Slide shock dampener ring off jamnut.
8. Loosen jamnut using open end wrench. Also use open end wrench on rack flat to prevent rack from turning.

CAUTION: *Do not allow the rack to turn when loosening the jamnut. If the rack turns, gear internal components could be damaged. Place an open end wrench over the flat adjacent to the rack teeth to prevent the rack from turning.*

9. Loosen setscrew in tie rod housing, unthread housing from rack and remove tie rod assembly, inner tie rod ball seat, and ball seat spring.

10. Turn jamnut counterclockwise until it is one thread away from end of rack and reinstall shock dampener ring on jamnut.

CAUTION: *Do not remove the jamnut and shock dampener ring from the rack at this time. The jamnut and shock dampener ring will function as a stop when the bulkhead is removed.*

11. Remove bulkhead retaining ring from end of tube by inserting pin punch through access hole in end of tube to force retaining ring out of its groove. Place screwdriver blade under ring and pry ring from tube.

12. Remove bulkhead assembly as follows:

a. Clean rack and bulkhead area of tube with shop cloth.

b. Position small piece of rubber over access hole in tube and secure rubber with wormdrive-type hose clamp.

c. Position drain pan under tube end of gear and wrap shop cloths around rack and tube to prevent excessive oil spillage.

d. Start engine and turn steering wheel to left until stop is contacted. Oil pressure will force outer bulkhead out of tube. Stop engine immediately when oil pressure forces bulkhead out of tube.

13. Remove jamnut and shock dampener ring.

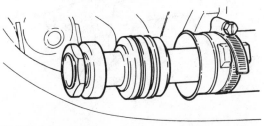

Bulkhead removal

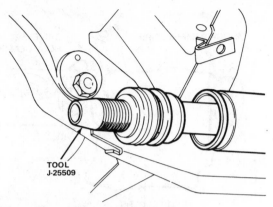

TOOL
J-25509

Installing bulkhead on the rack

14. Remove and discard outer bulkhead.

NOTE: *Do not remove the inner bulkhead and do not remove the seals from the outer bulkhead. The outer bulkhead, bulkhead seal, and O-ring are serviced as an assembly only.*

15. Remove hose clamp and small piece of rubber from tube.

16. Inspect tube bore and bulkhead snap ring groove area in tube for nicks and scratches. Remove nicks and scratches using crocus cloth or 600-grit emery cloth. Remove burrs and sharp edges from shoulder at threaded end of rack, using emery cloth, crocus cloth, or small fine-tooth file. Burrs must be removed to avoid damaging bulkhead seal during installation.

17. Lubricate replacement outer bulkhead and bulkhead seal with power steering fluid.

18. Lubricate replacement outer bulkhead O-ring seal with power steering fluid and install seal on bulkhead.

19. Place Seal Protector Tool J-25509 over rack threads and install outer bulkhead on rack.

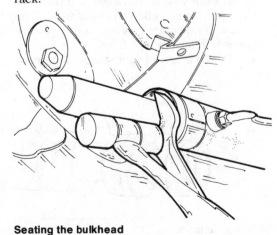

Seating the bulkhead

20. Install outer bulkhead in tube using 1¼-inch open end wrench and plastic hammer.

21. Seat outer bulkhead in tube using brass drift.

22. Install bulkhead retaining ring. Position gap in retaining ring ½ inch (12.7 mm) away from access hole in tube.

CAUTION: *Do not scratch or damage the surface of the rack when using the open end wrench to seat the bulkhead.*

23. Wipe bulkhead area dry.

24. Fill power steering pump reservoir with fluid and start engine.

25. Turn steering wheel left and right several times and check for leaks. If leaks are not evident, proceed to next step.

26. Install shock dampener ring and jamnut on rack.

27. Install mounting clamp and grommet on tube. Position clamp on crossmember and install clamp but do not tighten clamp attaching bolts.

28. Apply liberal quantity of waterproof, EP-type, lithium-base chassis lubricant to inner tie rod ball seat and ball end of inner tie rod. Pack tie rod housing with same lubricant and apply heavy coat of lubricant to rack teeth.

29. Install ball seat spring in end of rack and install ball seat.

30. Assemble inner tie rod and tie rod housing and install on rack.

31. Hand tighten tie rod housing on rack while rocking tie rod to prevent grease lock.

32. Back tie rod housing off approximately ⅛-turn.

33. Tighten tie rod housing setscrew to 9 ft. lbs. torque.

34. Tighten jamnut to 60 ft. lbs. torque. Use open end wrench on rack flat to prevent rack from turning.

CAUTION: *Do not allow the rack to turn when tightening the jamnut. If the rack turns, gear internal components could be damaged. Place an open wrench over the flat adjacent to the rack teeth to prevent the rack from turning.*

35. Check inner tie rod movement. Tie rod must rock and turn freely in housing to ensure proper operation.

36. Install shock dampener ring over jamnut.

37. Position breather tube in mounting grommet.

38. Install protective boot over end of tube. Be sure boot is fully seated in tube undercut

and that hole in boot is aligned with breather tube.

39. Install boot clamps. Tighten clamps using tool J-22610.

40. Tighten mounting clamp bolts to 48 ft. lbs. torque.

41. Connect tie rod end to steering arm and install tie rod end nut. Tighten nut to 50 ft. lbs. torque and install replacement cotter pin.

42. Remove supports and lower car.

43. Check and correct power steering system fluid level as necessary. Refer to Fluid Level and Initial Operation.

TIE ROD HOUSING, INNER TIE ROD, AND BALL SEAT AND SPRING REPLACEMENT

1. Raise and support front of car.

2. Mark position of tie rod end, adjuster tube and inner tie rod for assembly reference.

3. Disconnect tie rod end using tool J-26951 if tie rod end is to be replaced.

4. Loosen adjuster tube inboard clamp bolts and unthread adjuster tube and tie rod end from inner tie rod.

5. Remove boot clamps and move boot aside.

CAUTION: *Do not allow the protective boot to become cut or torn during service operations. A damaged boot will expose the gear internal components to dirt, foreign material and road splash resulting in premature wear.*

6. Remove large boot clamp at housing end of gear.

7. Slide shock dampener ring off jamnut.

8. If flat on rack teeth is not visible, pull back boot and turn steering wheel (to rotate pinion) and extend rack until rack flat is accessible.

9. Loosen jamnut using open end wrench. Also install open end wrench on rack flat to prevent rack from turning.

CAUTION: *Do not allow the rack to turn when loosening the jamnut. If the rack turns, gear internal components could be damaged. Place an open end wrench over the flat adjacent to the rack teeth to prevent the rack from turning.*

10. Loosen setscrew in tie rod housing, unthread housing from rack and remove inner tie rod, tie rod housing, inner tie rod ball seat, and ball seat spring.

11. Apply liberal quantity of waterproof, EP-type, lithium-base chassis lubricant to re-

placement inner tie rod assembly wear surfaces. Pack tie rod housing with same lubricant.

12. Install ball seat spring and ball seat in end of rack.

13. Assemble inner tie rod and housing and install on rack.

14. Hand tighten tie rod housing while rocking inner tie rod to prevent grease lock.

15. Back housing off approximately ⅛-turn.

16. Tighten tie rod housing setscrew to 9 ft. lbs. torque.

17. Tighten jamnut to 60 ft. lbs. torque. Use open end wrench on rack flat to prevent rack from turning.

CAUTION: *Do not allow the rack to turn when tightening the jamnut. If the rack turns, gear internal components could be damaged. Place an open end wrench over the flat adjacent to the rack teeth to prevent the rack from turning.*

18. Check inner tie rod movement after tightening jamnut. Tie rod must rock and turn freely in housing to ensure proper operation.

19. Install shock dampener ring over jamnut.

20. Install protective boot.

21. Align breather tube with hole in boot and install boot clamps. Position ear of large clamp ¾ inch (19.05 mm) from breather tube. Tighten clamp using tool J-22610.

22. Thread adjuster tube and tie rod end assembly on inner tie rod. Refer to alignment mark made at disassembly.

23. Connect tie rod end to steering arm, if removed. Tighten tie rod end nut to 50 ft. lbs. torque and install replacement cotter pin.

24. Remove supports, lower car, and adjust toe-in as necessary.

STEERING GEAR REMOVAL

1. Unlock steering column.

2. Raise and support front of car.

3. Remove screws attaching reinforcement brace to front crossmember and left engine support bracket and remove brace.

4. Disconnect stabilizer bar at left-side lower control arm, if equipped.

5. Remove bolts attaching stabilizer bar mounting clamps to frame rail brackets and move bar away from front crossmember.

6. Place support under stabilizer bar to prevent damaging bolt attaching bar to right-side lower control arm.

7. Remove left-side frame rail clamp brackets.

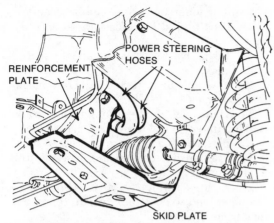

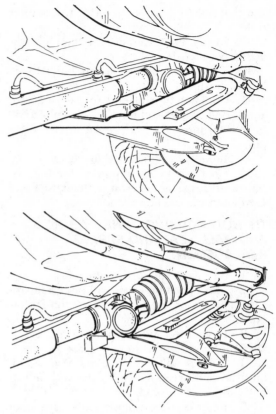

Pacer power steering gear mounting

8. Position drain pan under steering gear housing and disconnect power steering hoses at gear housing. Cap hoses and plug gear to prevent entry of dirt.

9. Remove flexible coupling pinch bolt and disengage flexible coupling from steering gear pinion shaft.

10. Remove and discard cotter pins from tie rod end retaining nuts.

11. Disconnect tie rod ends using tool J-26951.

12. Remove bolts attaching steering gear mounting clamp to crossmember.

CAUTION: *Before removing the bolts, loosen them slightly to minimize clamp distortion.*

13. Remove steering gear housing-to-crossmember attaching bolt nuts.

14. Remove bolts, washers, sleeves and grommets from steering gear housing using blunt punch.

15. Rotate bottom of gear housing toward front of car until pinion shaft is approximately parallel with skid plate. Slide gear assembly toward right side of car until housing and tube clear mounting plate and remove steering gear assembly.

STEERING GEAR INSTALLATION

1. Assemble and install grommets, sleeves, and washers on steering gear. Sleeves will hold grommets in place during assembly.

2. Position steering gear assembly on crossmember. Install gear from drivers side of car.

NOTE: *When installing the gear, keep the pinion shaft approximately parallel with the mounting plate.*

3. Install mounting clamp bolts. Hand-tighten bolts only.

Pacer power steering gear removal

4. Install steering gear housing-to-crossmember attaching bolts, washers, and nuts and tighten to 60 ft. lbs. torque.

5. Tighten mounting clamp bolts to 48 ft. lbs. torque.

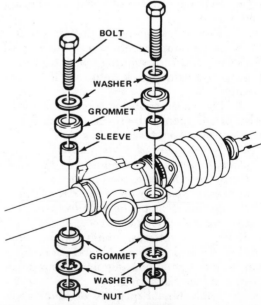

Pacer power steering gear attachment

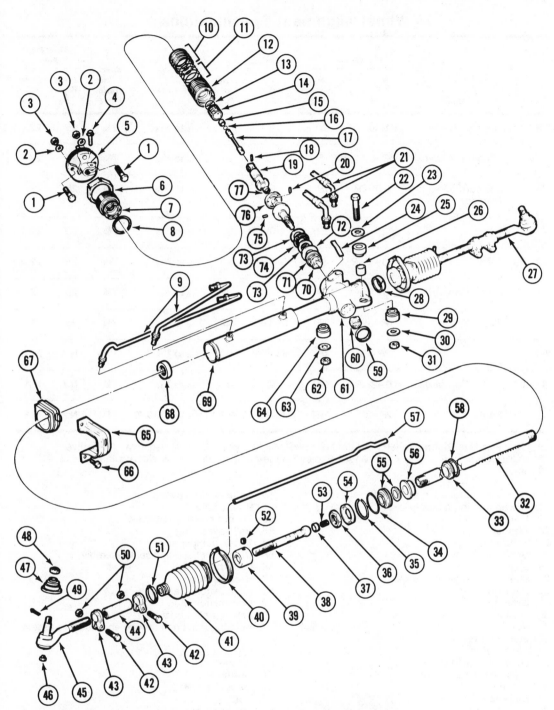

1. Flexible coupling-to-intermediate shaft attaching bolt
2. Lockwasher
3. Nut
4. Pinch bolt
5. Flexible coupling
6. Adjuster plug locknut
7. Adjuster plug assembly
8. Adjuster plug O-ring
9. Oil lines
10. Valve body seal rings
11. Valve body O-rings
12. Valve body
13. Spool valve damper O-ring
14. Spool valve
15. Torsion bar bushing (included in stub shaft)
16. Torsion bar seal ring (included in stub shaft)
17. Torsion bar (included in stub shaft)
18. Drive pin (included in stub shaft)
19. Stub shaft

Pacer power steering gear assembly exploded view

Wheel Alignment Specifications

Year	Model	Caster Range (deg)	Caster Pref Setting (deg)	Camber Range (deg)	Camber Pref Setting (deg)	Toe-in (in.)	Steering Axis Inclin. (deg)	Wheel Pivot Ratio Inner Wheel (deg)	Outer Wheel (deg)
'75–'77	Hornet, Gremlin	½N to ½P	0	①	②	1/16 to 3/16	7¾	25	22
	Matador, Pacer	½P to 1½P	1P	①	②	1/16 to 3/16	7¾	25	22
'78	Concord, Gremlin, Matador	0–2P	1P	①	②	1/16 to 3/16	7¾	25	22
	Pacer	1P–3P	2P	①	②	1/16 to 3/16	7¾	25	22
'79–'80	AMX	0–2½P	1P	0–¾P	¼P	1/16 to 3/16	7¾	25	22
	Spirit, Concord	0–2½P	1P	0–¾P	¼P	1/16 to 3/16	7¾	25	22
	Pacer	1P–3½P	2P	0–¾P	¼P	1/16 to 3/16	7¾	25	22
'80	Eagle	3P–5P	4P	⅜N–⅜P	0	1/16 to 3/16 ③	11½	N.A.	N.A.
'81–'82	Spirit, Concord	0–2½P	1P	④	②	1/16 to 3/16	7¾	N.A.	N.A.
	Eagle	2P–3P	2½P	⅛N–⅝P	⅜P	1/16 to 3/16 ③⑤	11½	N.A.	N.A.

① Left: ⅛P to ⅝P; Right: 0 to ½P   ④ Left: ¾P to ⅛P; Right: ½P to ⅛P   N Negative   P Positive
② Left: ⅜P; Right: ⅛P   ⑤ 1982 Eagles ¹/₁₆ toe-out, ¹/₁₆ toe in   N.A. Not Available
③ Toe-out

20. Drive pin (included in stub shaft)
21. Power steering hoses
22. Mounting bolt
23. Washer
24. Preload spring
25. Grommet
26. Bushing
27. Steering linkage (assembled)
28. Rack bushing
29. Grommet
30. Washer
31. Nut
32. Steering rack
33. Rack piston
34. Outer bulkhead O-ring
35. Bulkhead retaining ring
36. Jam nut
37. Ball seat
38. Inner tie rod
39. Inner tie rod housing
40. Boot clamp
41. Boot
42. Adjuster tube clamp bolt
43. Adjuster tube clamp
44. Adjuster tube
45. Tie rod end
46. Lube plug
47. Tie rod end seal
48. Tie rod end-nut
49. Cotter pin
50. Adjuster tube clamp nut
51. Boot clamp
52. Tie rod housing setscrew
53. Ball seat spring
54. Shock dampener ring
55. Outer bulkhead and seal assembly
56. Inner bulkhead
57. Breather tube
58. Rack piston seal ring
59. Contraction plug
60. Lower pinion bushing
61. Housing (included in tube and housing assembly)
62. Nut
63. Washer
64. Grommet
65. Mounting clamp
66. Bolt
67. Mounting grommet
68. Inner rack seal
69. Tube and power cylinder (included in tube and housing assembly)
70. Upper pinion bushing
71. Pinion shaft seal (lip type)
72. Support washer
73. Conical thrust bearing race
74. Thrust bearing
75. Drive pin (included in stub shaft)
76. Shaft cap (included in stub shaft)
77. Torsion bar bushing (included in stub shaft)

6. Connect tie rod ends to steering arms. Tighten tie rod end retaining nuts to 50 ft. lbs. torque and install replacement cotter pins.

7. Align flat spline of steering gear pinion shaft with index flat of flexible coupling and install coupling on pinion shaft. Install pinch bolt and tighten to 30 ft. lbs. torque.

8. Install bolts attaching reinforcement brace to front crossmember and engine support bracket. Tighten bolts to 30 ft. lbs torque.

9. Connect power steering hoses to gear housing. be sure that hoses do not touch brace or crossmember.

10. Install left-side frame rail clamp brackets.

11. Position stabilizer bar on frame rail brackets and install mounting clamp bolts. Hand tighten bolts only.

12. Install bolts, washers, and grommets attaching stabilizer bar to left-side lower control arm.

13. Tighten stabilizer bar mounting clamp bolts to 18 ft. lbs. torque.

14. Remove supports and lower car.

15. Fill power steering pump reservoir with power steering fluid.

16. Operate engine until fluid reaches normal operating temperature. Turn wheel right and left several times (do not hold wheel against steering stops). Stop engine and check fluid level. Add fluid as necessary.

Brakes

HYDRAULIC SYSTEM

Master Cylinder

REMOVAL AND INSTALLATION

1. Detach the front and rear brake lines from the master cylinder. On cars with drum brakes, the check valves will keep the fluid from draining out of the cylinder. If the car has disc brakes, one or both of the outlets must be plugged, to prevent fluid loss.

2. Remove the nuts which attach the master cylinder to the firewall or the power brake booster.

3. On cars that don't have power brakes, detach the pedal pushrod from the brake pedal.

4. Remove the master cylinder from the car.

5. Installation is the reverse of removal. Bleed the brake system once the master cylinder has been installed.

OVERHAUL

If the master cylinder leaks externally, or if the pedal sinks while being held down, the master cylinder is worn. There are three possible solutions:

    a. Buy a new master cylinder.

    b. Trade the old one in on a rebuilt unit.

    c. Rebuild the old one with a rebuilding kit.

1. Remove the cylinder from the car and drain the brake fluid.

2. Mount the cylinder in a vise so that the outlets are up and remove the seal from the hub.

3. Remove the stop screw from the bottom of the front reservoir.

4. Remove the snap-ring from the front of the bore and remove the primary piston assembly.

5. Remove the secondary piston assembly using compressed air or a piece of wire. Cover the bore opening with a cloth to prevent damage to the piston.

6. Clean the metal parts in brake fluid and discard all rubber parts.

7. Inspect the bore for damage or wear, and check the pistons for damage and proper clearance in the bore.

8. If the bore is only slightly scored or pitted it may be honed. Always use hones that are in good condition and completely clean the cylinder with brake fluid when honing is completed. If there is any evidence of contamination in the master cylinder, the entire hydraulic system should be flushed and refilled with clean brake fluid. Blow out all passages with compressed air.

9. Install new secondary seals in the two

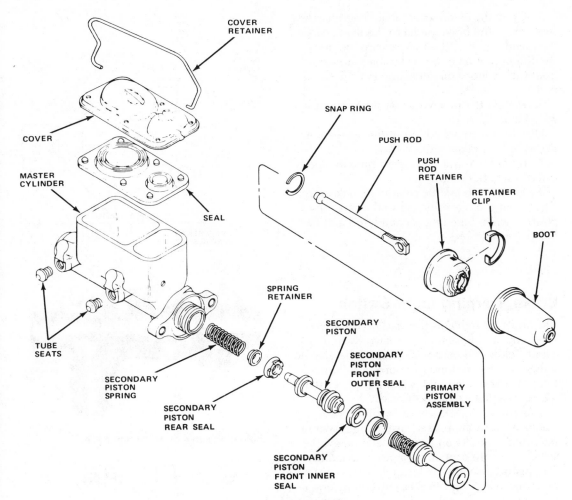

Typical master cylinder

grooves in the flat end of the front piston. The lips of the seals will be facing away from each other.

10. Install a new primary seal and the seal protector on the opposite end of the front piston with the lips of the seal facing outward.

11. Coat the seals with brake fluid. Install the spring on the front piston with the spring retainer in the primary seal.

12. Insert the piston assembly, spring end first, into the bore and use a wooden rod to seat it.

13. Coat the rear piston seals with brake fluid and install them into the piston grooves with the lips facing the spring end.

14. Assemble the spring onto the piston and install the assembly into the bore spring first. Install the snap-ring.

15. Hold the piston assembly at the bottom of the bore and install the stop screw. Install a new seal on the hub. Bleed the cyl-

inder as shown, before installation. Install the cylinder on the car. Bleed the system of air.

BLEEDING

The purpose of bleeding brakes is to expel air trapped in the hydraulic system. The system must be bled whenever the pedal feels spongy, indicating that compressible air has entered the system. It must also be bled whenever the system has been opened or leaking. You will need a helper for this job.

NOTE: *When bleeding brakes the stem on the front of the brake combination valve must be held out 0.060 in.*

1. Clean the bleed screw at each wheel.

2. Attach a small rubber hose to one of the bleed screws and place the end in a container of brake fluid.

3. Fill the master cylinder with brake fluid. Check the level often during bleeding. Pump up the brake pedal and hold it.

4. Open the bleed screw about one-quarter turn, press the brake pedal to the floor, close the bleed screw, and slowly release the pedal. Continue until no more air bubbles are forced from the cylinder on application of the brake pedal.

5. Repeat the procedure on the remaining wheel cylinders.

Disc brakes may be bled in the same manner as drum brakes, except that:

1. It usually requires a longer time to bleed a disc brake thoroughly.

2. The disc should be rotated to make sure that the piston has returned to the unapplied position when bleeding is completed and the bleed screw closed.

Brake Warning Light Switch

The warning light on the dashboard is activated by a differential pressure switch located below the master cylinder. The signal indicates a loss of fluid pressure in either the front or rear brakes, and warns the driver that a hydraulic failure has occurred.

The pressure differential warning valve is a housing with the brake warning light switch mounted centrally on top. Directly below the switch is a bore containing a piston assembly. The piston assembly is located in the center of the bore and kept in that position by equal fluid pressure on either side. Fluid pressure is provided by two brake lines, one coming from the rear brake system and one from the front brakes. If a leak develops in either system (front or rear), fluid pressure to that side of the piston will decrease or stop causing the piston to move in that direction. The plunger on the end of the switch engages with the piston. When the piston moves off center, the plunger moves and triggers the switch to activate the warning light on the dash.

After repairing and bleeding any part of the hydraulic system the warning light may remain on due to the pressure differential valve remaining in the off-center position. All models have a self-centering valve. After repairs or bleeding have been performed, center the valve by applying moderate pressure on the brake pedal. This will turn out the light.

NOTE: *Front wheel balancing, on the car, of cars equipped with disc brakes may also cause a pressure differential in the front branch of the system.*

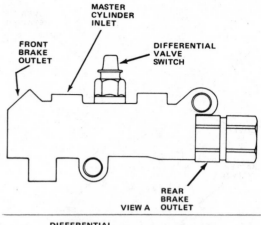

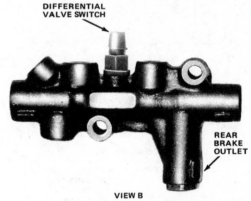

Combination valve on all except Pacer

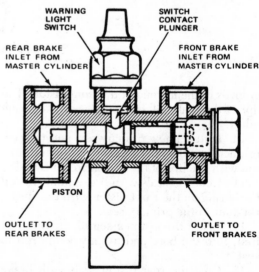

Pacer pressure differential valve

Adjustments
DRUM BRAKES

The drum brakes are self-adjusting and do not normally require attention. However, if the brakes are disassembled, they must be ad-

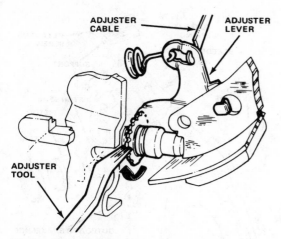

ADJUSTER CABLE

ADJUSTER LEVER

ADJUSTER TOOL

Brake shoe adjustment

justed upon assembly; or, if necessary, the brakes may be manually adjusted during the course of normal service.

1. Remove the rubber plug from the access slot on the backing plate.

NOTE: *It may be easier to perform Step 1 with the drum removed; however, be sure that the drum is installed properly before beginning adjustment.*

2. Rotate the starwheel with a screwdriver or an adjoining tool until the wheel will not rotate.

3. Mark the starwheel and back it off one complete revolution.

NOTE: *In order to back off the starwheel, it may be necessary to use a piece of ⅛ in. welding rod to hold the adjusting lever off the adjusting screw.*

4. Install the rubber plug in the access slot.

5. Make 10–15 hard applications of the brakes while backing the car up and then road-test the car.

FRONT DISC BRAKES

The optimal front disc brakes require no adjustment as hydraulic pressure maintains the proper brake pad-to-disc contact at all times.

NOTE: *Because of this, the brake fluid level should be checked regularly (see Chapter 1).*

FRONT DISC BRAKES

Disc Brake Pads

REMOVAL AND INSTALLATION

CAUTION: *To prevent paint damage from brake fluid, be sure to remove part of the brake fluid (don't re-use it) from the master cylinder and to keep the master cylinder covered. Do not allow the cylinder to drain too low or air will be pumped into the system.*

All 1975–82 Except Pacer

1. Raise the front of the car and remove the front wheels.

2. Working on only one brake at a time, remove the caliper guide pins and positioners which attach the caliper to the adapter. Lift the caliper away from the disc.

3. Remove (and discard) the positioners

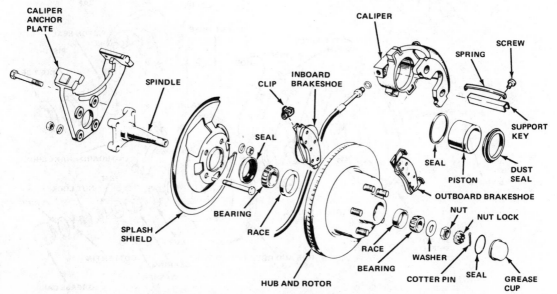

CALIPER ANCHOR PLATE

SPINDLE

CLIP

INBOARD BRAKESHOE

CALIPER

SPRING

SCREW

SUPPORT KEY

SEAL

SEAL

PISTON

DUST SEAL

OUTBOARD BRAKESHOE

NUT

NUT LOCK

BEARING

SPLASH SHIELD

RACE

RACE

BEARING

WASHER

COTTER PIN

SEAL

GREASE CUP

HUB AND ROTOR

1975–76 disc brake components for all models

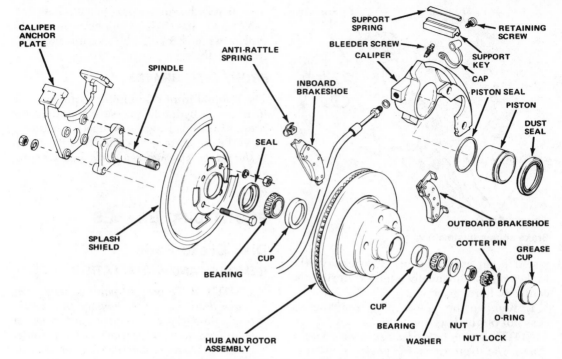

1977 and later Matador disc brake components

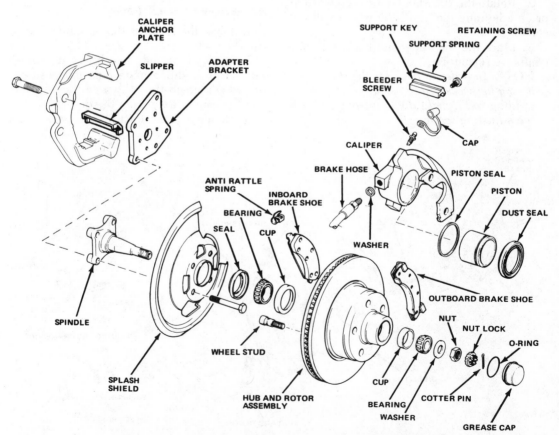

1977−81 disc brake components for all except Matador and Eagle

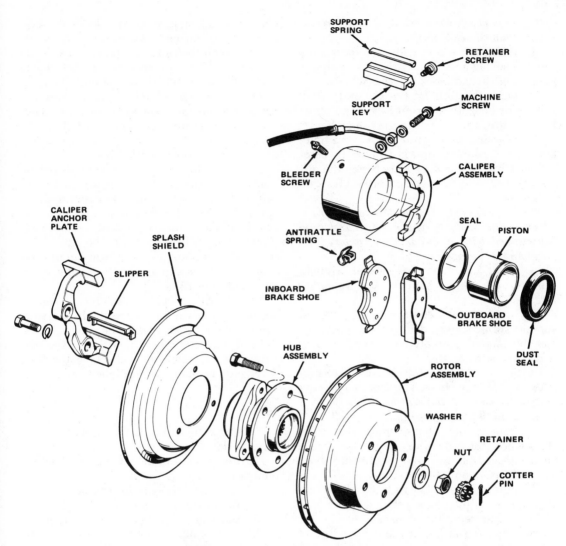

1980–81 Eagle disc brake components

and inner bushings from the guide pins, and the outboard bushings from the caliper.

4. Slide the disc pads out of the caliper, and carefully push the piston back into the bore. Later models have antirattle clips. Note their positions before removing them.

5. Lubricate the new outboard bushings and work them into position from the outboard side of the caliper.

6. Slide the new disc pads into position (outboard pad in the retaining spring) and carefully slide the caliper assembly over the rotor.

7. Lubricate and install the new inner bushings in the caliper. Install the new positioners on the guide pins with the open ends toward the outside.

8. Install the assembled guide pins from the inboard side and press in while threading

the pin into the adapter. *Use extreme care to avoid crossing the threads.* Tighten the caliper guide pins to 26 ft. lbs. Be sure that the tabs of the positioners are over the machined surfaces of the caliper.

9. Check the brake fluid level and pump the brake pedal to seat the linings against the disc. Replace the wheels and road test the car.

Pacer

CAUTION: *To prevent paint damage from leaking brake fluid, remove about ⅔ of the brake fluid from the larger reservoir (supplying the front brakes), in the master cylinder and keep the cylinder reservoir covered. Do not allow the reservoir level to get too low or air will enter the hydraulic sys-*

tem, *necessitating bleeding. Do not reuse the removed brake fluid.*

1. Remove the hub caps and loosen the front wheel lug nuts slightly. Firmly apply the parking brake and block the rear wheels.

2. Raise the front of the car and install jackstands beneath the front jacking points or lower control arms. Remove the front wheels.

3. Working on only one caliper at a time, bottom the caliper piston in its bore by carefully inserting a screwdriver between the piston and the inboard shoe and prying back on the piston.

NOTE: *Take care not to damage the rubber piston seals. If the piston cannot be bottomed with a screwdriver, a large C-clamp will suffice.*

4. Using a ¼ in. hex key or allen wrench, remove the caliper support key retaining screw.

5. Remove the caliper support key and support spring using a drift pin and hammer. Lift the caliper assembly off its anchor plate and over the rotor (disc.).

NOTE: *Do not allow the caliper to hang by its flexible brake hose. Use a piece of heavy wire to suspend the caliper from the coil spring until you are ready to reinstall it.*

6. Remove the inboard brake shoe from the anchor plate. Remove the inboard brake shoe anti-rattle spring from the inboard shoe, noting its position for reassembly.

7. Remove the outboard brake shoe from the caliper, rapping lightly with a hammer, if necessary, to free it from the caliper.

8. Wipe the inside of the caliper free of all accumulated brake pad dust, road dirt and other foreign material with a clean, dry rag.

NOTE: *Do not blow the caliper clean with compressed air as this may dislodge the rubber dust cover.*

Check the piston seals for evidence of leakage from the piston bore, and overhaul the caliper if necessary. Clean all rust and dirt from the abutment (sliding), surfaces of the caliper and caliper anchor plate using a wire brush and crocus cloth. Then, lightly grease the sliding surfaces with white grease to ensure that the sliding motion of the caliper is not impaired.

9. Install the inboard brake shoe antirattle spring on the rear flange of the inboard brake shoe, making sure that the looped section of the clip is facing away from the rotor.

10. Install the assembled inboard brake shoe and anti-rattle spring in the caliper an-chor plate, taking care not to dislodge the anti-rattle spring during installation.

11. Install the outboard brake shoe in the caliper, making sure to seat the shoe flange fully into the outboard arms of the caliper.

12. Install the caliper assembly over the rotor and into position in the anchor plate. Exercise extreme care when installing the caliper not to tear or dislodge the piston dust cover on the inboard brake shoe.

13. Align the caliper assembly with the abutment surfaces of the anchor plate and insert the caliper support key and support spring between the abutment surfaces at the rearward end of the caliper and anchor plate. Then, using a hammer and drift pin, drive the caliper support key and spring into position. Install the support key retaining screw and tighten to 15 ft. lbs.

14. Fill the master cylinder reservoir to within ¼ in. of the rim. Press the brake pedal firmly several times to seat the shoes.

15. Install the wheels and lower the car. Road-test the car after rechecking the fluid level and checking for firm brake pedal.

1982

1. Drain about ½ the fluid from the master cylinder.

2. Remove hub cap and loosen wheel retaining nuts.

3. Raise and support automobile.

4. Remove front wheels.

5. Work on one caliper at a time only.

6. Press caliper piston to bottom of piston bore using screwdriver. If piston cannot be bottomed using screwdriver, use C-clamp.

7. Remove caliper mounting pins using 7 mm hex or Allen wrench.

8. Lift caliper assembly out of anchor plate and off rotor.

9. Suspend caliper from coil spring using heavy wire. Do not let brake hose support weight of caliper.

10. Remove outboard brakeshoe from anchor plate while holding anti-rattle clip against caliper anchor plate. Note position of anti-rattle clip for assembly reference.

11. Remove inboard brakeshoe from anchor plate and remove anti-rattle clip.

CAUTION: *The abutment surfaces of the caliper and anchor plate must be clean, smooth, and lightly-lubricated with moly-disulfide grease before brakeshoe and caliper installation. Rust, corrosion, or foreign*

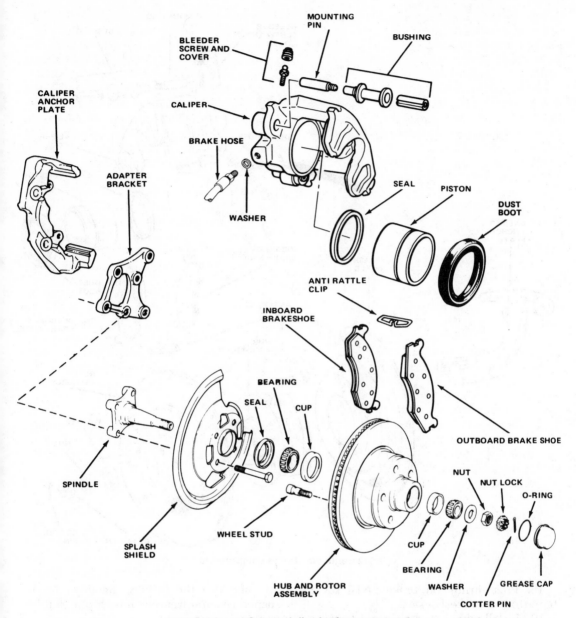

1982 Spirit and Concord disc brake components

material on the abutment surfaces will impair the sliding action of the brakeshoes in the anchor plate.

12. Install anti-rattle clip on trailing end of anchor plate being sure split end of clip faces away from rotor.

13. Install inboard brakeshoe in caliper anchor plate while holding anti-rattle clip in place.

14. Install outboard brakeshoe in caliper anchor plate while holding anti-rattle clip in place.

15. Install caliper over rotor and into position in anchor plate.

16. Install caliper mounting pins and tighten to 26 ft. lbs. torque.

CAUTION: *Be very careful to avoid tearing or dislodging the dust boot when installing the caliper. A damaged boot will expose the caliper piston to road splash resulting in corrosion and eventual piston seizure.*

17. Fill both master cylinder reservoirs to within ¼ inch (6.3 mm) of rim.

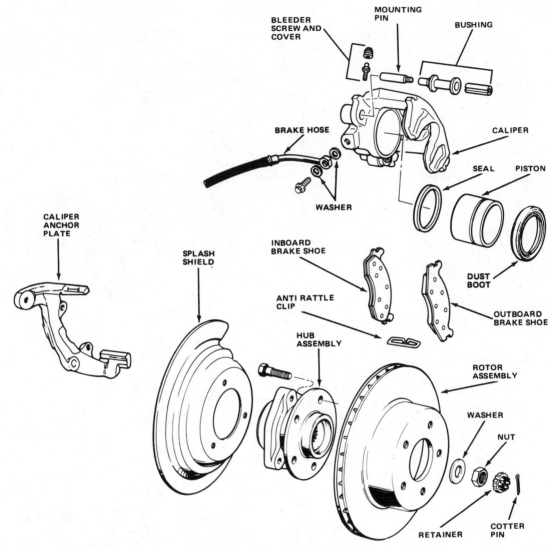

1982 Eagle disc brake components

18. Press firmly on brake pedal several times to seat brakeshoes.

19. Install wheels and tires and lower automobile.

20. Check fluid level in master cylinder and correct if necessary.

CAUTION: *Check for firm brake pedal and proper brake operation before moving the automobile.*

Disc Brake Calipers

REMOVAL, INSTALLATION, OVERHAUL

1975–81 Except Pacer

1. Raise the front of the car and remove the front wheels.

2. Working on one side at a time only, disconnect the brake hose from the steel brake line and cap the fittings. Remove the U-shaped retainer from the hose fitting (if it has one).

3. Remove the caliper mounting bolts (locating pins) and positioners and lift the caliper away from the disc.

4. Clean the holes in the caliper ears, and wipe all dirt from the mounting bolts. If the bolts are corroded or damaged they should be replaced.

5. Remove the shoe support springs from the piston.

6. Remove the rubber bushings from the grooves in the caliper ears.

7. Remove the brake hose, drain the brake fluid, and clean the outside of the caliper.

8. Pad the inside of the caliper with tow-

els and direct compressed air into the brake fluid inlet hole to remove the piston.

CAUTION: *To prevent damage to the piston use just enough air pressure to ease it out of the bore. Do not attempt to catch or protect the piston with your hand since this may cause serious injury.*

9. Use a screwdriver to pry the boot out of the caliper. Avoid scratching the bore.

10. Remove the piston seal from its groove in the caliper bore. *Do not use a metal tool of any type for this operation.*

11. Blow out all passages in the caliper and bleeder valve. Clean the piston and piston bore with fresh brake fluid.

12. Examine the piston for scoring, scratches, or corrosion. If any of these conditions exist the piston must be replaced, as it is plated and cannot be refinished.

13. Examine the bore for the same defects. Light rough spots may be removed by rotating crocus cloth, using finger pressure, in the bore. Do not polish with an in and out motion or use any other abrasive. Piston-to-bore clearance should be 0.002–0.006 in.

14. Lubricate the piston bore and the new rubber parts with fresh brake fluid. Position the seal in the piston bore groove.

15. Lubricate the piston with brake fluid and assemble the boot into the piston groove so that the fold faces the open end of the piston.

16. Insert the piston into the bore, taking care not to unseat the seal.

17. Force the piston to the bottom of the bore. (This will require a force of 50–100 lbs.). Seat the boot lip around the caliper counterbore. Proper seating of the boot is very important for sealing out contaminants.

18. Install the brake hose into the caliper using a new copper gasket.

19. Lubricate the rubber bushings. Install the bushings in the caliper ears.

NOTE: *Lubrication of the bushings is essential to ensure the proper operation of the sliding caliper design.*

20. Install the shoe support spring in the piston.

21. Install the disc pads in the caliper and remount the caliper on the hub (see "Disc Pad Installation").

22. Reconnect the brake hose to the steel brake line. Install the retainer clip. Bleed the brakes.

23. Replace the wheels, check the brake fluid level, check the brake pedal travel, and road test the vehicle.

Pacer

1. Remove the caliper as outlined under Steps 1–7 of "Brake Pad Replacement."

2. Place a clean piece of paper on your work area to put the parts of the caliper on while it is being disassembled.

3. Drain the brake fluid from the caliper by opening the bleeder plug.

4. Place the caliper assembly in a vise with padded jaws.

CAUTION: *Do not overtighten the vise; too much pressure will cause distortion of the caliper bore.*

5. Using compressed air, remove the piston from the caliper bore. Be careful not to damage the piston or the bore. Leave the dust boot in the caliper groove while the piston is being removed.

6. Take the caliper out of the vise and withdraw the dust boot.

7. Work the piston seal out of its groove in the piston bore with a small, pointed wooden or plastic stick. Do not use a screwdriver or other metallic tool to remove the seal as it could damage the bore. Throw the old seal away.

8. Unscrew the bleeder plug.

9. Clean all of the parts in brake fluid (*do not use solvent*) and wipe them dry with a clean, lint-free cloth. Dry the passages and bores with compressed air.

Check the cylinder bore for scoring, pitting, and/or corrosion. If the caliper bore is deeply scored or corroded, replace the entire caliper.

If it is only lightly scored or stained, polish with crocus cloth. Use finger-pressure to rotate the crocus cloth in the cylinder bore. Any black stains found in the bore are caused by seals and are harmless.

CAUTION: *Do not slide the crocus cloth in and out of the bore. Do not use any other type of abrasive material.*

Check the piston. If it is pitted, scored, or worn, it should be replaced with a new one.

Check the piston-to-bore clearance with a feeler gauge. It should be 0.002–0.006 in. If it is more than this, replace the caliper assembly.

Assembly and installation are performed in the following order:

1. Dip a new piston seal in clean brake fluid. Position the seal in one area of the groove in the cylinder bore and gently work it into place around the groove until it is seated. Be sure that your fingers are clean before touching the seal.

CAUTION: *Never reuse an old piston seal.*

2. Coat a new piston boot with clean brake fluid. Work it into the outer groove of the bore with your fingers until it snaps into place. Don't worry if the boot seems too large for the groove; once seated, it will fit properly. Check the boot, by running your forefinger around the inside of it, to be sure that it is correctly installed.

3. Coat the piston with plenty of brake fluid. Spread the boot with your fingers and insert the piston into it.

4. Depress the piston until it bottoms in the bore.

CAUTION: *Apply uniform force to the piston or it will crack.*

5. Unstall the caliper assembly as outlined under Steps 9–15 of "Brake Pad Replacement."

1982

1. Drain and discard two-thirds of brake fluid from master cylinder reservoir serving front disc brakes. Do not drain reservoir completely.

2. Remove hub cap and loosen wheel retaining nuts.

3. Raise and support automobile.

4. Remove front wheels.

5. Work on one caliper at a time.

6. Wipe all dirt and grease from caliper brake hose fitting using shop cloth.

7. Disconnect brake line at caliper and discard hose fitting washer. Cover open end of hose with tape or clean shop cloth.

8. Remove caliper and brakeshoes as outlined in Brakeshoe Replacement.

9. Clean caliper exterior with brake cleaning solvent.

10. Drain remaining fluid from caliper and place caliper on clean work surface.

11. Pad caliper interior with clean shop cloths.

WARNING: *Do not, under any circumstances, place fingers in front of the piston in an attempt to catch or protect it. In addition, use only enough air pressure to ease the piston out of the bore. Excessive air pressure can eject the piston with enough force to cause damage or injury.*

12. Insert air nozzle into caliper fluid inlet hole and slowly apply just enough air pressure to ease piston out of bore.

13. Remove and discard dust boot. Use screwdriver to pry boot from bore. Do not scratch piston bore during boot removal.

14. Remove and discard piston seal. Use pencil or similar wood implement to remove seal.

CAUTION: *Remove the seal using a pencil, wooden stick, piece of plastic, or similar tool only. Do not use a metal tool or similar object to remove the seal as the bore could be scored.*

15. Remove bleeder screw.

16. Remove and discard plastic sleeves and rubber bushings from caliper mounting ears.

Inspect the caliper piston. Replace the piston if nicked, scratched, corroded, or if the protective plating has worn off.

CAUTION: *Do not attempt to refinish the piston in any way. The outside diameter is the sealing surface and is manufactured to very close tolerances. Removal of the nickel-chrome protective plating will lead to pitting, corrosion, and eventual piston seizure.*

Inspect the piston bore. Replace the caliper if the bore is nicked, scratched, worn, cracked, or badly corroded. However, minor stains or corrosion can be removed using crocus cloth.

CAUTION: *Do not use emery cloth or similar abrasives on the piston bore. If the bore*

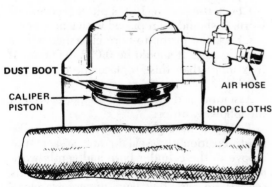

Caliper piston removal

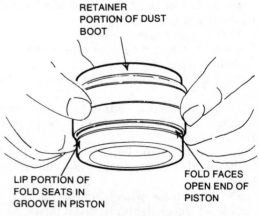

Installing the dust boot on the piston

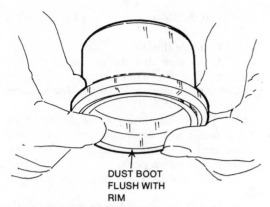

DUST BOOT
FLUSH WITH
RIM

Positioning the dust boot fold

does not clean up with crocus cloth, re-place the caliper. Clean the caliper thor-oughly with brake fluid or brake cleaning solvent if the bore was polished.

17. Lubricate piston bore and replace-ment seal with brake fluid.

18. Install seal in bore groove. Work seal into groove using fingers only.

19. Lubricate piston with brake fluid.

20. Install replacement dust boot on pis-ton. Slide metal retainer portion of seal over open end of piston and pull seal rearward un-til rubber boot lip seats in piston groove.

21. Push metal retainer portion of boot forward until retainer is flush with rim at open end of piston and seal fold snaps into place.

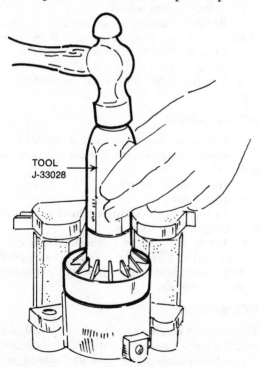

TOOL
J-33028

Seating the dust boot in the counterbore

22. Insert piston into bore and into piston seal. Do not unseat seal.

23. Press piston to bottom of bore using hammer handle.

24. Seat metal retainer portion of dust boot in counterbore at upper end of piston bore using Tool J-33028.

CAUTION: *The metal portion of the dust boot must be seated evenly and below the face of the caliper.*

25. Install bleeder screw. Tighten screw securely but not to required torque until brakes have been bled.

26. Install replacement plastic sleeves and rubber bushings in caliper mounting ears.

27. Check rotor for face runout, thickness variation, deep scores, cracks, and broken ventilating ribs.

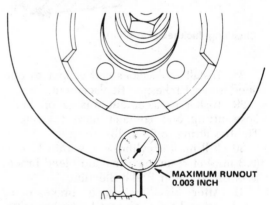

MAXIMUM RUNOUT
0.003 INCH

Checking lateral runout

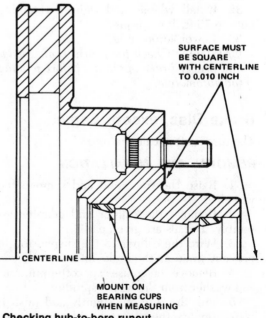

SURFACE MUST
BE SQUARE
WITH CENTERLINE
TO 0.010 INCH

CENTERLINE

MOUNT ON
BEARING CUPS
WHEN MEASURING

Checking hub-to-bore runout

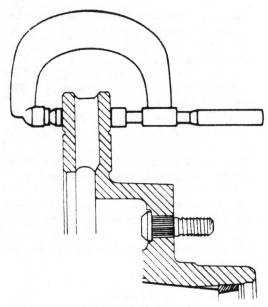

Checking thickness variation

28. Install brakeshoes and caliper as outlined under Brakeshoe Replacement.

29. Install replacement washer on brake hose fitting and connect hose to caliper. Tighten fitting to 25 ft. lbs. torque.

30. Fill master cylinder to within ¼ inch (6.3 mm) of reservoir rims and bleed brakes as outlined under Brake Bleeding.

31. After bleeding, press brake pedal firmly several times to seat brakeshoes. Recheck master cylinder fluid level and correct if necessary.

32. Install wheels and tighten retaining nuts to 75 ft. lbs. torque.

33. Lower automobile.

CAUTION: *Check for a firm brake pedal and proper brake operation before moving the automobile.*

Brake Disc, except Eagle

The disc is often called a rotor.

REMOVAL AND INSTALLATION

1. Raise the front end and remove the wheel.

2. Remove the caliper and adapter assembly. Details are given earlier.

3. Wire the caliper to the suspension to prevent straining the brake line.

4. Remove the grease cap, cotter pin, nut, and washer from the wheel spindle.

5. Pull the disc out slightly and push it back. Remove the outer wheel bearing.

CAUTION: *Keep your greasy hands off the disc surface!*

6. Remove the hub and disc.

7. Make sure that the grease in the hub is clean, that the wheel bearings are both packed with grease, and that the disc surfaces are clean.

CAUTION: *Use only grease specified for disc brake use. Ordinary grease will melt and ooze all over the braking surfaces, ruining the friction pads.*

8. Slide the hub and disc onto the spindle.

9. Install the outer bearing, washer, and nut. Adjust the wheel bearings as described later in this Section. Install the cotter pin.

10. Clean the grease cap and coat the inside with grease. Don't pack it full. Install it.

11. Replace the caliper.

12. On replacing the wheel, torque the nuts to 75 ft. lbs.

NOTE: *You may feel a little silly torquing wheel nuts, but this is important to prevent distorting the disc.*

Brake Disc, Eagle

REMOVAL

1. Remove hubcap and loosen wheel retaining nuts.

2. Raise and support automobile.

3. Remove front wheels.

4. Remove caliper assembly but do not disconnect brake line. Suspend caliper from wire hook attached to front spring. Do not let brake hose support weight of caliper.

5. Remove rotor. Pull rotor straight off of hub.

INSTALLATION

1. Clean hub and rotor mating surfaces.

2. Clean rotor braking surfaces, if necessary.

3. Install rotor on hub.

4. Install caliper.

5. Install wheel. Tighten wheel retaining nuts to 75 ft. lbs. torque.

6. Lower automobile and install hubcap.

CAUTION: *Check for a firm brake pedal and proper brake operation before moving the automobile.*

INSPECTION

The disc can be checked for run-out (wobble) and thickness variations with a dial indicator and a micrometer while mounted on the car or in a lathe. Run-out should not exceed 0.005

in. and thickness variation should not exceed 0.001 in. The disc can be machined to correct, but the final thickness must be at least 0.940 in.

NOTE: *These are the factory's specifications; some state inspection laws aren't this lenient.*

Wheel Bearings

REMOVAL, PACKING, AND INSTALLATION

1. Use the "Brake Disc Removal and Installation" procedure to remove the bearings.

2. Remove the inner bearing.

3. Clean the bearings thoroughly in a safe solvent. Check their condition, but don't spin them any more than is absolutely necessary.

4. Replace the seal on assembly.

5. Make sure that the inner cones of the bearings are free to creep (move slowly) on the spindle. This adds to the life of the bearings.

6. Pack both wheel bearings using wheel bearing grease made for disc brakes. Ordinary grease will melt and ooze out, ruining the pads. Place a healthy glob of grease in the palm of one hand and force the edge of the bearing into it so that the grease fills the

bearing. Do this until the whole bearing is packed. Grease packing tools are available which make this job a lot less messy.

7. Install the inner bearing and seal.

8. Use the Brake Disc Removal and Installation procedure to replace the bearings and disc.

ADJUSTMENT

1. Raise the front wheel off the floor.

2. Remove the grease cap and cotter pin.

3. To seat the bearings, tighten the wheel spindle nut to 20–25 ft. lbs. while turning the wheel.

4. Loosen the nut ⅓ turn. Tighten the nut to 2–10 in. lbs.

5. If there is a nut retainer, place it on the nut with the slots of the retainer aligned with the spindle cotter pin hole. Install a new cotter pin and the dust cap.

FRONT DRUM BRAKES

Brake Drums

REMOVAL AND INSTALLATION

1. Remove the wheel cover, except on models with styled wheels which have the lug nuts exposed, and loosen the lug nuts.

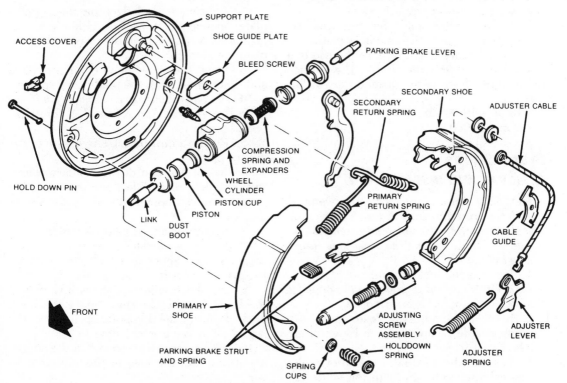

Self-adjusting front drum brake components

ACCESS COVER

SUPPORT PLATE

SHOE GUIDE PLATE

BLEED SCREW

PARKING BRAKE LEVER

SECONDARY SHOE

SECONDARY RETURN SPRING

ADJUSTER CABLE

HOLD DOWN PIN

COMPRESSION SPRING AND EXPANDERS

WHEEL CYLINDER

PISTON CUP

PISTON

LINK

DUST BOOT

PRIMARY RETURN SPRING

CABLE GUIDE

FRONT

PRIMARY SHOE

ADJUSTING SCREW ASSEMBLY

HOLDDOWN SPRING

ADJUSTER LEVER

PARKING BRAKE STRUT AND SPRING

SPRING CUPS

ADJUSTER SPRING

2. Set the parking brake, block the rear wheels, and raise the front of the car, supporting it with jackstands.

CAUTION: *Be sure that the car is securely supported.*

3. Remove the lug nuts and the wheel.

4. Loosen the brake adjusting starwheel by removing the plug from the adjusting slot and inserting a thin screwdriver into the hole to push the adjusting lever away from the wheel.

5. Insert a brake adjusting tool into the hole and rotate the starwheel so that the shoes contract.

NOTE: *It may not always be necessary to back off on the adjuster in order to remove the drum.*

6. Remove the dust cover, grease cap, cotter pin, nut retainer, nut and the outer wheel bearing.

7. Remove the drum from the spindle.

Installation is performed in the reverse order of removal. Pack and adjust the wheel bearing as indicated in "Wheel Bearings," following. Adjust the brakes, as outlined at the beginning of this chapter, after completing the drum installation.

INSPECTION

1. Clean the drum.

2. Inspect the drum for scoring, grooves, cracks, and out-of-roundness.

3. Light scoring may be removed by dressing the drum with *fine* emery cloth.

4. Heavy scoring will require the use of a brake lathe to turn the drum. The service limits of the drum inside diameter are as follows:

- 10 in.—10.060 in.
- 9 in.—9.060 in.

Brake Shoes

REMOVAL AND INSTALLATION

NOTE: *If you are not thoroughly familiar with the procedure involved with brake shoe replacement, disassemble and assemble one side at a time, leaving the other side intact as a reference.*

1. Remove the brake drum.

CAUTION: *Do not depress the brake pedal once the drum has been removed.*

2. Remove the adjusting lever tang from the hole in the secondary shoe by grabbing the lever with a pair of pliers.

3. Place a wheel cylinder clamp over the wheel cylinder to retain its piston while the brake shoes are removed.

4. Unfasten the return springs with a brake spring removal tool by twisting them off the anchor pin.

5. Carefully remove the secondary shoe return spring, the adjusting cable, primary shoe return spring, the cable guide, the adjusting lever and spring in that order.

CAUTION: *Be careful that all of the components of the brake do not fly out at once when the spring tension is being released.*

6. Unfasten the hold-down springs and withdraw the shoes. Be careful not to get grease on the lining surfaces of the shoes.

Shoe installation is performed in the following order:

NOTE: *Always replace the shoes and linings on both wheels of the same axle; do not replace the shoes and linings on one side only.*

1. If there is any grease contamination, clean all of the parts, except the drums, with mineral spirits. If there is brake fluid contamination, use alcohol to clean the parts. Then clean all parts, including the drums with soap and water.

2. Polish the ledges on the brake support plate with *fine* emery cloth. If there are any grooves on the support plate which limit shoe movement, the plate *must* be replaced (do not attempt to regrind).

3. Lubricate the ledges on the support plate, anchor pin, adjusting cable guide, adjusting screw threads and the pivot with moly-disulfide grease.

4. Place the shoes on the support plate and retain them with the hold-down springs.

NOTE: *The following sequence is for 10 in. brakes; reverse Steps 5 and 6 for 9 in. brakes.*

5. Fit the adjusting cable eyelet over the anchor pin.

6. Install one end of the primary return spring in the primary shoe and the other end over the anchor pin with the brake spring tool.

7. Install the adjusting cable guide.

8. Fit the secondary shoe return spring in the same manner in which you installed the primary spring.

9. Install the adjusting screw assembly at the base of the brake shoe. Place the *small* hooked end of the adjusting spring into the large hole in the primary shoe.

10. Fit the *large* hooked end of the adjusting spring into the hole in the adjusting lever.

11. Engage the hooked end of the adjust-

ing cable with the adjusting lever and place the cable over the cable guide.

CAUTION: *Be sure that the adjusting cable is not twisted and that it cannot ride out of the guide.*

12. Hook the tang on the adjusting lever into the large hole at the base of the secondary shoe by grasping the lever with pliers and pulling it into place.

13. Adjust the brakes and install the drums, as detailed elsewhere in this chapter.

Wheel Cylinders

SERVICING

1. Raise the vehicle on a hoist and remove the wheel and drum from the brake to be serviced.

2. Remove the brake shoes and clean the backing plate and wheel cylinder.

3. Disconnect the brake line from the brake hose. Remove the brake hose retainer clip at the frame bracket and remove the hose from the wheel cylinder. (On the rear brakes it will only be necessary to remove the line from the cylinder.)

4. Remove the cylinder mounting bolts and remove the cylinder.

5. Remove the boots from the cylinder ends and discard. Remove the pistons, remove and discard the seal cups, and remove the expanders and spring.

6. Inspect the bore and pistons for damage or wear. Damaged pistons should be discarded, as they cannot be reconditioned. Slight bore roughness can be removed using a brake cylinder hone or crocus cloth. (Cloth should be rotated in the bore under finger pressure. Do not slide lengthwise). Use only lint-free cloth for cleaning.

7. Clean the cylinder and internal parts *using only brake fluid or denatured alcohol.*

8. Insert the spring expander assembly. Lubricate all rubber parts using only fresh brake fluid.

9. Install new cups with the seal lips facing inward.

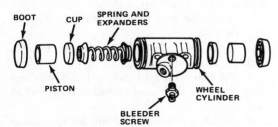

BOOT   CUP   SPRING AND EXPANDERS

PISTON   WHEEL CYLINDER

BLEEDER SCREW

Typical wheel cylinder

10. Install the pistons and rubber boots. Install the cylinder on the car in reverse order of removal. Bleed the cylinder (see the preceding "Bleeding" section).

Wheel Bearings

REMOVAL AND INSTALLATION (PACKING)

1. The outer bearing is removed as part of the brake drum removal procedure.

2. Use a brass drift to remove the inner bearing and cup from the hub.

3. For installation and packing procedures, see "Wheel Bearings" in the "Front Disc Brake" section.

ADJUSTMENT

The bearing adjustment procedure for models equipped with front drum brakes is the same as for the disc brake-equipped models. See "Wheel Bearings" in the "Front Disc Brake" section for the correct procedure.

REAR DRUM BRAKES

Brake Drums

REMOVAL AND INSTALLATION

NOTE: *Release the parking brake before attempting rear drum removal.*

1. Remove the wheel cover and loosen the lug nuts. Remove the cotter key and the axle shaft nut.

NOTE: *If the car is equipped with styled wheels, it will be necessary to raise the car and remove the wheel first.*

2. Block the front wheels, raise the car, and support it with jackstands.

CAUTION: *Be sure that the car is securely supported.*

3. Remove the wheel.

4. Unfasten the three screws which secure the brake drum and withdraw the drum.

CAUTION: *Do not depress the brake pedal once the drum has been removed.*

Installation is performed in the reverse order of removal.

INSPECTION

Rear drum inspection procedures and specifications are identical to those given in the preceding "Front Drum Brake Inspection" section.

Brake Shoes
REMOVAL AND INSTALLATION

The removal and installation procedure for the rear brake shoes is similar to that for the front shoes. The only differences are: the parking brake lever must be removed from (and installed on) the secondary shoe and the parking brake strut spring assembly must be removed from (and installed), between the shoes.

Wheel Cylinders
SERVICING

The servicing procedures for the rear wheel cylinders are identical to those for the front cylinders previously described.

Hubs and Bearings
REMOVAL AND INSTALLATION

The rear axle splines cut serrations into the inner diameter of the rear wheel hub. If the hub is to be removed, matchmark the hub to the axle so that the job of aligning the serrations and splines will be easier. If this is not done, the axle will cut new splines which may

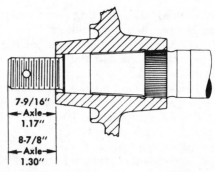

Proper installation of a new rear hub and drum assembly

be so near the old that the hub will move on the axle with resultant damage to the hub, axle, and differential gears.

When a new hub is installed, the serrations will be cut in the hub as it is installed on the shaft.

If a new axle shaft is installed, a new hub, without serrations, must be installed. And old shaft with a new hub also is an allowable combination.

1. Remove the wheel and brake drum as detailed above.

2. Matchmark the hub and axle shaft.

3. Attach a suitable puller to the wheel hub and remove it.

CAUTION: *Do not use a "knock-out" type puller on the end of the axle shaft, as this could damage the wheel bearings or the thrust blocks. Use a screw type puller.*

4. Inspect the hub for faulty lug studs, a worn keyway or center bore, and damaged serrations. Replace the hub and drum if any of these are present or if it is cracked.

NOTE: *The hub and drum must both be replaced if either one is defective.*

Installation, if the *old* hub and drum are being replaced, is performed in the reverse order of removal. Tighten the axle shaft nut to 250 ft. lbs. with the weight of the car resting on the rear wheels.

CAUTION: *Be sure to align the matchmarks made during removal.*

A *new* hub and drum assembly must be installed in the following order:

1. Align the hub keyway with the key on the axle shaft.

2. Slide the hub and drum onto the axle shaft as far as they will go.

3. Fit *two* well-lubricated thrust washers over the axle shaft and install the axle shaft nut.

4. Install the wheel and lug nuts, remove the jackstands, and lower the car.

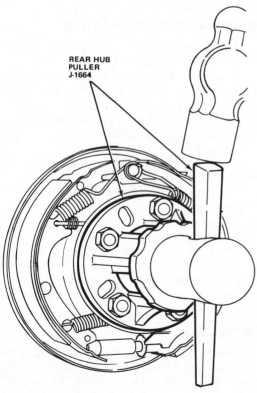

REAR HUB
PULLER
J-1664

Rear hub removal

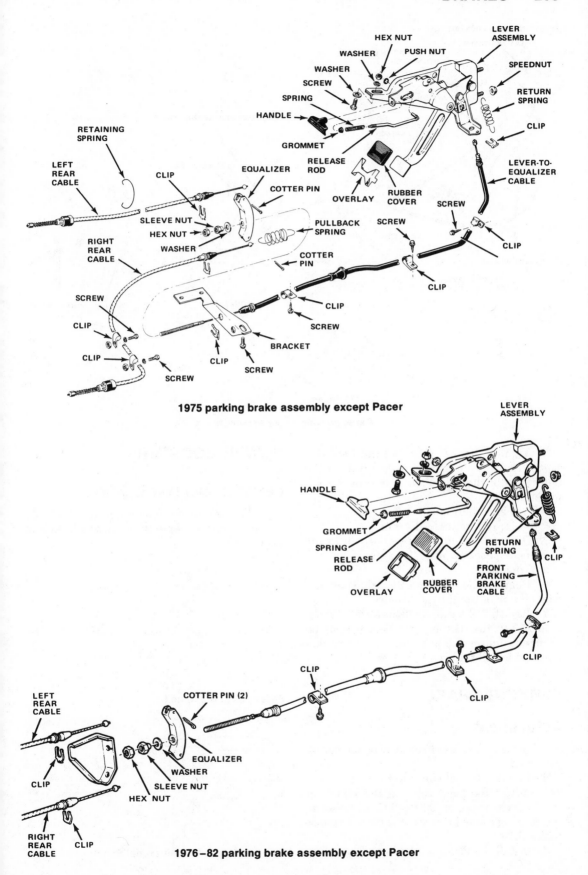

1975 parking brake assembly except Pacer

1976–82 parking brake assembly except Pacer

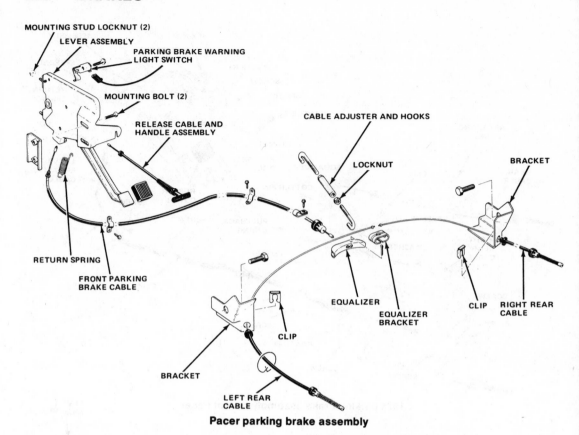

MOUNTING STUD LOCKNUT (2)

LEVER ASSEMBLY

PARKING BRAKE WARNING
LIGHT SWITCH

MOUNTING BOLT (2)

RELEASE CABLE AND
HANDLE ASSEMBLY

CABLE ADJUSTER AND HOOKS

LOCKNUT

BRACKET

RETURN SPRING

FRONT PARKING
BRAKE CABLE

EQUALIZER

EQUALIZER
BRACKET

CLIP

RIGHT REAR
CABLE

CLIP

BRACKET

LEFT REAR
CABLE

Pacer parking brake assembly

5. Tighten the axle shaft nut until the distance from the outer face of the hub to the outer end of the axle shaft is one of the following:

- $7^9/_{16}$ in. differential—1.7 in.
- $8^5/_8$ in. differential—1.30 in.

NOTE: *If the hub is not pressed-in to the proper specifications, the splines will be improperly cut.*

6. Remove the nut from the axle shaft and take off one of the thrust washers.

7. Reinstall the axle shaft nut and tighten it to 250 ft. lbs. If the cotter key cannot be inserted, tighten the nut to the next castellation and install the key.

PARKING BRAKE

Adjustment

1. Raise and support the rear of the car on jackstands.

2. Remove the wheels and brake drums.

3. Adjust the front cable at the equalizer to give a clearance of .0001–.005 in. between the parking brake lever strut and the primary brake shoe.

4. Install the drums and wheels.

POWER BOOSTER

REMOVAL AND INSTALLATION

1. Disconnect the power booster clevis pin or the pushrod, depending on which type of unit is used.

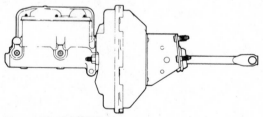

Pacer power brake unit

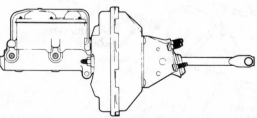

Power brake unit for all except Pacer

2. Remove the vacuum hose from the power unit.

3. Unbolt and remove the master cylinder from the booster. It is not necessary to disconnect the brake lines from the master cylinder. There should be enough play in the lines to move the cylinder aside.

4. Unbolt and remove the booster from the firewall.

5. Installation is the reverse of removal. Torque the booster-to-dash nuts to 30 ft. lbs.

CAUTION: *Some cars have two holes in the brake pedal for the pushrod. On cars with power brakes, use the lower hole.*

Brake Specifications

Year	Model	Caliper Piston Diameter	Rotor Hub-to-Bore Runout (in.)	Rotor Lateral Runout (in.)	Rotor Replacement Thickness (in.)	Rotor Thickness Variation (in.)	Drum Original Diameter	Drum Maximum Diameter
1975	All	2.60 ③	.010	.003	1.12	.0005	9.000 ②	9.060 ②
1976	All	2.60 ③	.010	.003	1.12	.0005	9.000 ②	9.060 ②
1977	All	2.60 ③	.010	.003	.810 ④	.0005	9.000 ②	9.060 ②
1978	All	2.60 ③	.010	.003	.810 ④	.0005	9.000 ②	9.060 ②
1979	All	2.60	.010	.003	.810	.0005	9.000 ②	9.060 ②
1980	All	2.60	.010	.003	.815	.0005	9.000 ②	9.060 ②
1981	All	2.60	.010	.003 ①	.815	.0005	9.000 ②	9.060 ②
1982	All	2.60	.010	.003 ①	.815	.0005	9.000 ②	9.060 ②

① Eagle: .004
② Optional: 10.000 with a 10.060 max.
③ Matador: 3.10
④ Matador: 1.120

Body

10

You can repair most minor auto body damage yourself. Minor damage usually falls into one of several categories: (1) small scratches and dings in the paint that can be repaired without the use of body filler, (2) deep scratches and dents that require body filler, but do not require pulling, or hammering metal back into shape and (3) rust-out repairs. The repair sequences illustrated in this chapter are typical of these types of repairs. If you want to get involved in more complicated repairs including pulling or hammering sheet metal back into shape, you will probably need more detailed instructions. Chilton's *Minor Auto Body Repair, 2nd Edition* is a comprehensive guide to repairing auto body damage yourself.

TOOLS AND SUPPLIES

The list of tools and equipment you may need to fix minor body damage ranges from very basic hand tools to a wide assortment of specialized body tools. Most minor scratches, dings and rust holes can be fixed using an electric drill, wire wheel or grinder attachment, half-round plastic file, sanding block, various grades of sandpaper (#36, which is coarse through #600, which is fine) in both wet and dry types, auto body plastic,

primer, touch-up paint, spreaders, newspaper and masking tape.

Most manufacturers of auto body repair products began supplying materials to professionals. Their knowledge of the best, most-used products has been translated into body repair kits for the do-it-yourselfer. Kits are available from a number of manufacturers and contain the necessary materials in the required amounts for the repair identified on the package.

Kits are available for a wide variety of uses, including:

- Rusted out metal
- All purpose kit for dents and holes
- Dents and deep scratches
- Fiberglass repair kit
- Epoxy kit for restyling.

Kits offer the advantage of buying what you need for the job. There is little waste and little chance of materials going bad from not being used. The same manufacturers also merchandise all of the individual products used—spreaders, dent pullers, fiberglass cloth, polyester resin, cream hardener, body filler, body files, sandpaper, sanding discs and holders, primer, spray paint, etc.

CAUTION: *Most of the products you will be using contain harmful chemicals, so be extremely careful. Always read the complete label before opening the containers. When* *you put them away for future use, be sure they are out of children's reach!*

Most auto body repair kits contain all the materials you need to do the job right in the kit. So, if you have a small rust spot or dent you want to fix, check the contents of the kit before you run out and buy any additional tools.

ALIGNING BODY PANELS

Doors

There are several methods of adjusting doors. Your vehicle will probably use one of those illustrated.

Whenever a door is removed and is to be reinstalled, you should matchmark the position of the hinges on the door pillars. The holes of the hinges and/or the hinge attaching points are usually oversize to permit alignment of doors. The striker plate is also moveable, through oversize holes, permitting up-and-down, in-and-out and fore-and-aft movement. Fore-and-aft movement is made by adding or subtracting shims from behind the striker and pillar post. The striker should be adjusted so that the door closes fully and remains closed, yet enters the lock freely.

DOOR HINGES

Don't try to cover up poor door adjustment with a striker plate adjustment. The gap on each side of the door should be equal and uniform and there should be no metal-to-metal contact as the door is opened or closed.

1. Determine which hinge bolts must be loosened to move the door in the desired direction.

2. Loosen the hinge bolt(s) just enough to allow the door to be moved with a padded pry bar.

3. Move the door a small amount and check the fit, after tightening the bolts. Be sure that there is no bind or interference with adjacent panels.

4. Repeat this until the door is properly positioned, and tighten all the bolts securely.

Hood, Trunk or Tailgate

As with doors, the outline of hinges should be scribed before removal. The hood and trunk can be aligned by loosening the hinge bolts in their slotted mounting holes and moving the hood or trunk lid as necessary.

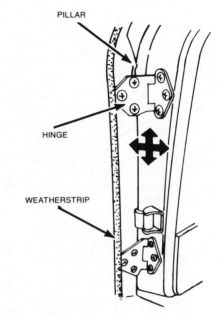

Door hinge adjustment

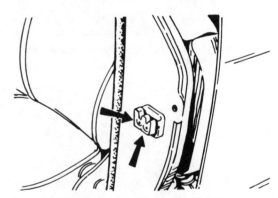

Move the door striker as indicated by arrows

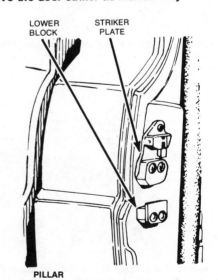

Striker plate and lower block

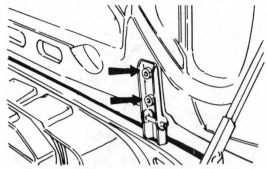

Loosen the hinge boots to permit fore-and-aft and horizontal adjustment

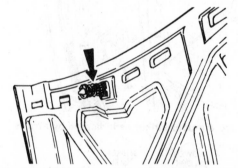

The hood is adjusted vertically by stop-screws at the front and/or rear

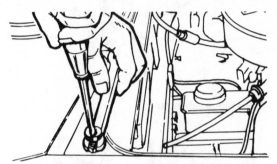

The hood pin can be adjusted for proper lock engagement

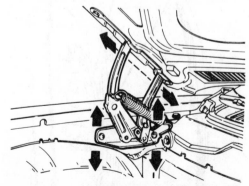

The height of the hood at the rear is adjusted by loosening the bolts that attach the hinge to the body and moving the hood up or down

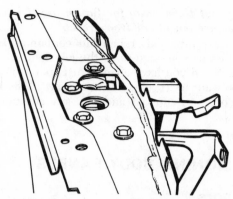

The base of the hood lock can also be repositioned slightly to give more positive lock engagement

The hood and trunk have adjustable catch locations to regulate lock engagement. Bumpers at the front and/or rear of the hood provide a vertical adjustment and the hood lockpin can be adjusted for proper engagement.

The tailgate on the station wagon can be adjusted by loosening the hinge bolts in their slotted mounting holes and moving the tailgate on its hinges. The latchplate and latch striker at the bottom of the tailgate opening can be adjusted to stop rattle. An adjustable bumper is located on each side.

RUST, UNDERCOATING, AND RUSTPROOFING

Rust

Rust is an electrochemical process. It works on ferrous metals (iron and steel) from the inside out due to exposure of unprotected surfaces to air and moisture. The possibility of rust exists practically nationwide—anywhere humidity, industrial pollution or chemical salts are present, rust can form. In coastal areas, the problem is high humidity and salt air; in snowy areas, the problem is chemical salt (de-icer) used to keep the roads clear, and in industrial areas, sulphur dioxide is present in the air from industrial pollution and is changed to sulphuric acid when it rains. The rusting process is accelerated by high temperatures, especially in snowy areas, when vehicles are driven over slushy roads and then left overnight in a heated garage.

Automotive styling also can be a contributor to rust formation. Spot welding of panels creates small pockets that trap moisture and form an environment for rust formation. Fortunately, auto manufacturers have been working hard to increase the corrosion protection of their products. Galvanized sheet metal enjoys much wider use, along with the increased use of plastic and various rust retardant coatings. Manufacturers are also designing out areas in the body where rust-forming moisture can collect.

To prevent rust, you must stop it before it gets started. On new vehicles, there are two ways to accomplish this.

First, the car or truck should be treated with a commercial rustproofing compound. There are many different brands of franchised rustproofers, but most processes involve spraying a waxy "self-healing" compound under the chassis, inside rocker panels, inside doors and fender liners and similar places where rust is likely to form. Prices for a quality rustproofing job range from $100–$250, depending on the area, the brand name and the size of the vehicle.

Ideally, the vehicle should be rustproofed as soon as possible following the purchase. The surfaces of the car or truck have begun to oxidize and deteriorate during shipping. In addition, the car may have sat on a dealer's lot or on a lot at the factory, and once the rust has progressed past the stage of light, powdery surface oxidation rustproofing is not likely to be worthwhile. Professional rustproofers feel that once rust has formed, rustproofing will simply seal in moisture already present. Most franchised rustproofing operations offer a 3–5 year warranty against rust-through, but will not support that warranty if the rustproofing is not applied within three months of the date of manufacture.

Undercoating should not be mistaken for rustproofing. Undercoating is a black, tar-like substance that is applied to the underside of a vehicle. Its basic function is to deaden noises that are transmitted from under the car. It simply cannot get into the crevices and seams where moisture tends to collect. In fact, it may clog up drainage holes and ventilation passages. Some undercoatings also tend to crack or peel with age and only create more moisture and corrosion attracting pockets.

The second thing you should do immediately after purchasing the car is apply a paint sealant. A sealant is a petroleum based product marketed under a wide variety of brand names. It has the same protective properties as a good wax, but bonds to the paint with a chemically inert layer that seals it from the air. If air can't get at the surface, oxidation cannot start.

The paint sealant kit consists of a base coat and a conditioning coat that should be applied every 6–8 months, depending on the manufacturer. The base coat must be applied before waxing, or the wax must first be removed.

Third, keep a garden hose handy for your car in winter. Use it a few times on nice days during the winter for underneath areas, and it will pay big dividends when spring arrives. Spraying under the fenders and other areas which even car washes don't reach will help remove road salt, dirt and other build-ups which help breed rust. Adjust the nozzle to a high-force spray. An old brush will help break up residue, permitting it to be washed away more easily.

It's a somewhat messy job, but worth it in the long run because rust often starts in those hidden areas.

At the same time, wash grime off the door sills and, more importantly, the under portions of the doors, plus the tailgate if you have a station wagon or truck. Applying a coat of wax to those areas at least once before and once during winter will help fend off rust.

When applying the wax to the under parts of the doors, you will note small drain holes. These holes often are plugged with undercoating or dirt. Make sure they are cleaned out to prevent water build-up inside the doors. A small punch or penknife will do the job.

Water from the high-pressure sprays in car washes sometimes can get into the housings for parking and taillights, so take a close look. If they contain water merely loosen the retaining screws and the water should run out.

Repairing Scratches and Small Dents

Step 1. This dent (arrow) is typical of a deep scratch or minor dent. If deep enough, the dent or scratch can be pulled out or hammered out from behind. In this case no straightening is necessary

Step 2. Using an 80-grit grinding disc on an electric drill grind the paint from the surrounding area down to bare metal. This will provide a rough surface for the body filler to grab

Step 3. The area should look like this when you're finished grinding

Step 4. Mix the body filler and cream hardener according to the directions

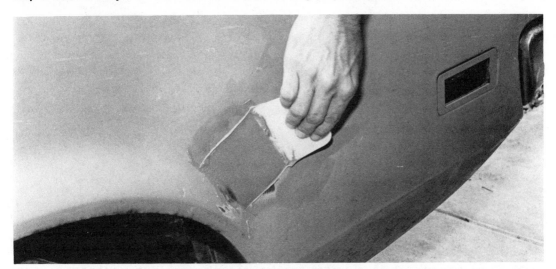

Step 5. Spread the body filler evenly over the entire area. Be sure to cover the area completely

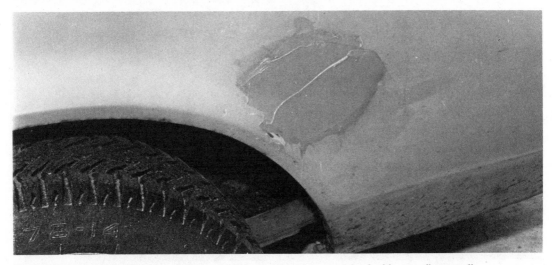

Step 6. Let the body filler dry until the surface can just be scratched with your fingernail

Step 7. Knock the high spots from the body filler with a body file

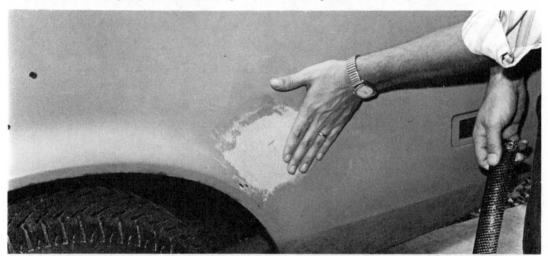

Step 8. Check frequently with the palm of your hand for high and low spots. If you wind up with low spots, you may have to apply another layer of filler

Step 9. Block sand the entire area with 320 grit paper

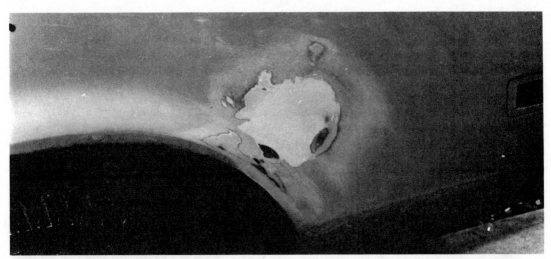

Step 10. When you're finished, the repair should look like this. Note the sand marks extending 2—3 inches out from the repaired area

Step 11. Prime the entire area with automotive primer

Step 12. The finished repair ready for the final paint coat. Note that the primer has covered the sanding marks (see Step 10). A repair of this size should be able to be spotpainted with good results

REPAIRING RUST HOLES

One thing you have to remember about rust: even if you grind away all the rusted metal in a panel, and repair the area with any of the kits available, *eventually* the rust will return. There are two reasons for this. One, rust is a chemical reaction that causes pressure under the repair from the inside out. That's how the blisters form. Two, the back side of the panel (and the repair) is wide open to moisture, and unpainted body filler acts like a sponge. That's why the best solution to rust problems is to remove the rusted panel and install a new one or have the rusted area cut out and a new piece of sheet metal welded in its place. The trouble with welding is the expense; sometimes it will cost more than the car or truck is worth.

One of the better solutions to do-it-yourself rust repair is the process using a fiberglass cloth repair kit (shown here). This will give a strong repair that resists cracking and moisture and is relatively easy to use. It can be used on large or small holes and also can be applied over contoured surfaces.

Step 1. Rust areas such as this are common and are easily fixed

Step 2. Grind away all traces of rust with a 24-grit grinding disc. Be sure to grind back 3—4 inches from the edge of the hole down to bare metal and be sure all traces of rust are removed

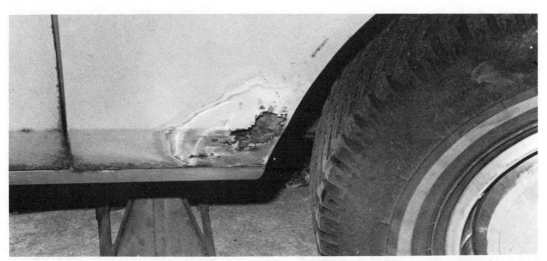

Step 3. Be sure all rust is removed from the edges of the metal. The edges must be ground back to un-rusted metal

Step 4. If you are going to use release film, cut a piece about 2″ larger than the area you have sanded. Place the film over the repair and mark the sanded area on the film. Avoid any unnecessary wrinkling of the film

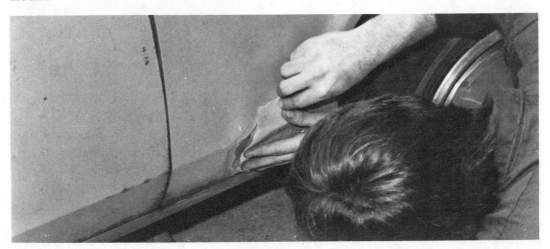

Step 5. Cut 2 pieces of fiberglass matte. One piece should be about 1″ smaller than the sanded area and the second piece should be 1″ smaller than the first. Use sharp scissors to avoid loose ends

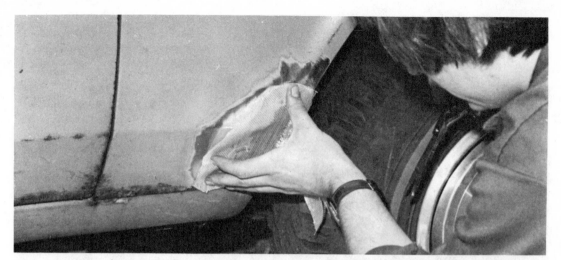

Step 6. Check the dimensions of the release film and cloth by holding them up to the repair area

Step 7. Mix enough repair jelly and cream hardener in the mixing tray to saturate the fiberglass material or fill the repair area. Follow the directions on the container

Step 8. Lay the release sheet on a flat surface and spread an even layer of filler, large enough to cover the repair. Lay the smaller piece of fiberglass cloth in the center of the sheet and spread another layer of repair jelly over the fiberglass cloth. Repeat the operation for the larger piece of cloth. If the fiberglass cloth is not used, spread the repair jelly on the release film, concentrated in the middle of the repair

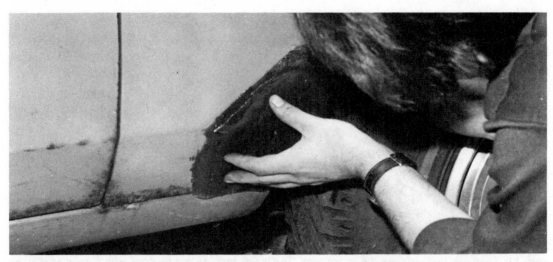

Step 9. Place the repair material over the repair area, with the release film facing outward

Step 10. Use a spreader and work from the center outward to smooth the material, following the body contours. Be sure to remove all air bubbles

Step 11. Wait until the repair has dried tack-free and peel off the release sheet. The ideal working temperature is 65—90° F. Cooler or warmer temperatures or high humidity may require additional curing time

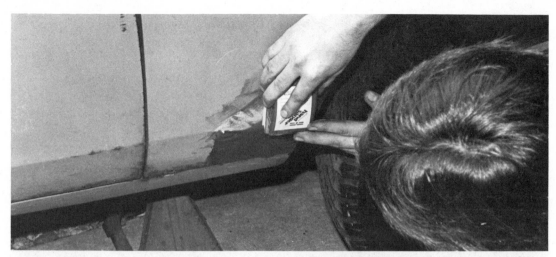

Step 12. Sand and feather-edge the entire area. The initial sanding can be done with a sanding disc on an electric drill if care is used. Finish the sanding with a block sander

Step 13. When the area is sanded smooth, mix some topcoat and hardener and apply it directly with a spreader. This will give a smooth finish and prevent the glass matte from showing through the paint

Step 14. Block sand the topcoat with finishing sandpaper

Step 15. To finish this repair, grind out the surface rust along the top edge of the rocker panel

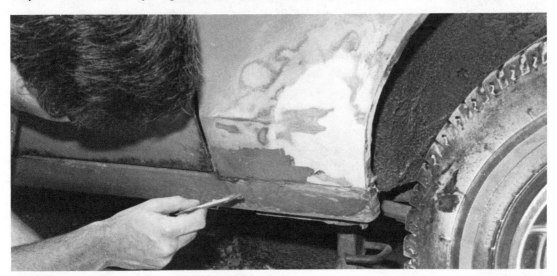

Step 16. Mix some more repair jelly and cream hardener and apply it directly over the surface

Step 17. When it dries tack-free, block sand the surface smooth

Step 18. If necessary, mask off adjacent panels and spray the entire repair with primer. You are now ready for a color coat

AUTO BODY CARE

There are hundreds—maybe thousands—of products on the market, all designed to protect or aid your car's finish in some manner. There are as many different products as there are ways to use them, but they all have one thing in common—the surface must be clean.

Washing

The primary ingredient for washing your car is water, preferably "soft" water. In many areas of the country, the local water supply is "hard" containing many minerals. The little rings or film that is left on your car's surface after it has dried is the result of "hard" water.

Since you usually can't change the local water supply, the next best thing is to dry the surface before it has a chance to dry itself.

Into the water you usually add soap. Don't use detergents or common, coarse soaps. Your car's paint never truly dries out, but is always evaporating residual oils into the air. Harsh detergents will remove these oils, causing the paint to dry faster than normal. Instead use warm water and a non-detergent soap made especially for waxed surfaces or a liquid soap made for waxed surfaces or a liquid soap made for washing dishes by hand.

Other products that can be used on painted surfaces include baking soda or plain soda water for stubborn dirt.

Wash the car completely, starting at the top, and rinse it completely clean. Abrasive grit should be loaded off under water pressure; scrubbing grit off will scratch the finish. The best washing tool is a sponge, cleaning mitt or soft towel. Whichever you choose, replace it often as each tends to absorb grease and dirt.

Other ways to get a better wash include:

• Don't wash your car in the sun or when the finish is hot.

• Use water pressure to remove caked-on dirt.

• Remove tree-sap and bird effluence immediately. Such substances will eat through wax, polish and paint.

One of the best implements to dry your car is a turkish towel or an old, soft bath towel. Anything with a deep nap will hold any dirt in suspension and not grind it into the paint.

Harder cloths will only grind the grit into the paint making more scratches. Always start drying at the top, followed by the hood and trunk and sides. You'll find there's always more dirt near the rocker panels and wheelwells which will wind up on the rest of the car if you dry these areas first.

Cleaners, Waxes and Polishes

Before going any farther you should know the function of various products.

Cleaners—remove the top layer of dead pigment or paint.

Rubbing or polishing compounds—used to remove stubborn dirt, get rid of minor scratches, smooth away imperfections and partially restore badly weathered paint.

Polishes—contain no abrasives or waxes; they shine the paint by adding oils to the paint.

Waxes—are a protective coating for the polish.

CLEANERS AND COMPOUNDS

Before you apply any wax, you'll have to remove oxidation, road film and other types of pollutants that washing alone will not remove.

The paint on your car never dries completely. There are always residual oils evaporating from the paint into the air. When enough oils are present in the paint, it has a healthy shine (gloss). When too many oils evaporate the paint takes on a whitish cast known as oxidation. The idea of polishing and waxing is to keep enough oil present in the painted surface to prevent oxidation; but when it occurs, the only recourse is to remove the top layer of "dead" paint, exposing the healthy paint underneath.

Products to remove oxidation and road film are sold under a variety of generic names—polishes, cleaner, rubbing compound, cleaner/polish, polish/cleaner, self-polishing wax, pre-wax cleaner, finish restorer and many more. Regardless of name there are two types of cleaners—abrasive cleaners (sometimes called polishing or rubbing compounds) that remove oxidation by grinding away the top layer of "dead" paint, or chemical cleaners that dissolve the "dead" pigment, allowing it to be wiped away.

Abrasive cleaners, by their nature, leave thousands of minute scratches in the finish, which must be polished out later. These should only be used in extreme cases, but are usually the only thing to use on badly oxidized paint finishes. Chemical cleaners are much milder but are not strong enough for severe cases of oxidation or weathered paint.

The most popular cleaners are liquid or paste abrasive polishing and rubbing compounds. Polishing compounds have a finer abrasive grit for medium duty work. Rubbing compounds are a coarser abrasive and for heavy duty work. Unless you are familiar with how to use compounds, be very careful. Excessive rubbing with any type of compound or cleaner can grind right through the paint to primer or bare metal. Follow the directions on the container—depending on type, the cleaner may or may not be OK for your paint. For example, some cleaners are not formulated for acrylic lacquer finishes.

When a small area needs compounding or heavy polishing, it's best to do the job by hand. Some people prefer a powered buffer for large areas. Avoid cutting through the paint along styling edges on the body. Small, hand operations where the compound is applied and rubbed using cloth folded into a thick ball allow you to work in straight lines along such edges.

To avoid cutting through on the edges when using a power buffer, try masking tape. Just cover the edge with tape while using power. Then finish the job by hand with the tape removed. Even then work carefully. The paint tends to be a lot thinner along the sharp ridges stamped into the panels.

Whether compounding by machine or by hand, only work on a small area and apply the compound sparingly. If the materials are spread too thin, or allowed to sit too long, they dry out. Once dry they lose the ability to deliver a smooth, clean finish. Also, dried out polish tends to cause the buffer to stick in one spot. This in turn can burn or cut through the finish.

WAXES AND POLISHES

Your car's finish can be protected in a number of ways. A cleaner/wax or polish/cleaner followed by wax or variations of each all provide good results. The two-step approach (polish followed by wax) is probably slightly better but consumes more time and effort. Properly fed with oils, your paint should never need cleaning, but despite the best polishing job, it won't last unless it's protected with wax. Without wax, polish must be renewed at least once a month to prevent oxidation. Years ago (some still swear by it today), the best wax was made from the Brazilian palm, the Carnuba, favored for its vegetable base and high melting point. However, modern synthetic waxes are harder, which means they protect against moisture better, and chemically inert silicone is used for a long lasting protection. The only problem with silicone wax is that it penetrates all layers of paint. To repaint or touch up a panel or car protected by silicone wax, you have to completely strip the finish to avoid "fish-eyes."

Under normal conditions, silicone waxes will last 4–6 months, but you have to be careful of wax build-up from too much waxing. Too thick a coat of wax is just as bad as no wax at all; it stops the paint from breathing.

Combination cleaners/waxes have become popular lately because they remove the old layer of wax plus light oxidation, while putting on a fresh coat of wax at the same time. Some cleaners/waxes contain abrasive cleaners which require caution, although many cleaner/waxes use a chemical cleaner.

Applying Wax or Polish

You may view polishing and waxing your car as a pleasant way to spend an afternoon, or as a boring chore, but it has to be done to keep the paint on your car. Caring for the paint doesn't require special tools, but you should follow a few rules.

1. Use a good quality wax.

2. Before applying any wax or polish, be sure the surface is completely clean. Just because the car looks clean, doesn't mean it's ready for polish or wax.

3. If the finish on your car is weathered, dull, or oxidized, it will probably have to be compounded to remove the old or oxidized paint. If the paint is simply dulled from lack of care, one of the non-abrasive cleaners known as polishing compounds will do the trick. If the paint is severely scratched or really dull, you'll probably have to use a rubbing compound to prepare the finish for waxing. If you're not sure which one to use, use the polishing compound, since you can easily ruin the finish by using too strong a compound.

4. Don't apply wax, polish or compound in direct sunlight, even if the directions on the can say you can. Most waxes will not cure properly in bright sunlight and you'll probably end up with a blotchy looking finish.

5. Don't rub the wax off too soon. The result will be a wet, dull looking finish. Let the wax dry thoroughly before buffing it off.

6. A constant debate among car enthusiasts is how wax should be applied. Some maintain pastes or liquids should be applied in a circular motion, but body shop experts have long thought that this approach results in barely detectable circular abrasions, especially on cars that are waxed frequently. They advise rubbing in straight lines, especially if any kind of cleaner is involved.

7. If an applicator is not supplied with the wax, use a piece of soft cheesecloth or very soft lint-free material. The same applies to buffing the surface.

SPECIAL SURFACES

One-step combination cleaner and wax formulas shouldn't be used on many of the special surfaces which abound on cars. The one-step materials contain abrasives to achieve a clean surface under the wax top coat. The abrasives are so mild that you could clean a car every week for a couple of years without fear of rubbing through the paint. But this same level of abrasiveness might, through repeated use, damage decals used for special trim effects. This includes wide stripes, wood-grain trim and other appliques.

Painted plastics must be cleaned with care. If a cleaner is too aggressive it will cut through the paint and expose the primer. If bright trim such as polished aluminum or chrome is painted, cleaning must be performed with even greater care. If rubbing compound is being used, it will cut faster than polish.

Abrasive cleaners will dull an acrylic finish. The best way to clean these newer finishes is with a non-abrasive liquid polish. Only dirt and oxidation, not paint, will be removed.

Taking a few minutes to read the instructions on the can of polish or wax will help prevent making serious mistakes. Not all preparations will work on all surfaces. And some are intended for power application while others will only work when applied by hand.

Don't get the idea that just pouring on some polish and then hitting it with a buffer will suffice. Power equipment speeds the operation. But it also adds a measure of risk. It's very easy to damage the finish if you use the wrong methods or materials.

Caring for Chrome

Read the label on the container. Many products are formulated specifically for chrome, but others contain abrasives that will scratch the chrome finish. If it isn't recommended for chrome, don't use it.

Never use steel wool or kitchen soap pads to clean chrome. Be careful not to get chrome cleaner on paint or interior vinyl surfaces. If you do, get it off immediately.

Troubleshooting

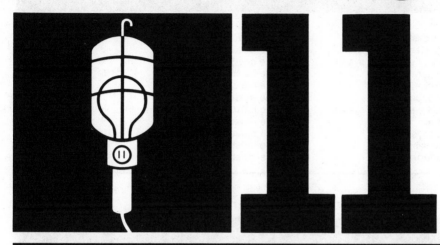

This section is designed to aid in the quick, accurate diagnosis of automotive problems. While automotive repairs can be made by many people, accurate troubleshooting is a rare skill for the amateur and professional alike.

In its simplest state, troubleshooting is an exercise in logic. It is essential to realize that an automobile is really composed of a series of systems. Some of these systems are interrelated; others are not. Automobiles operate within a framework of logical rules and physical laws, and the key to troubleshooting is a good understanding of all the automotive systems.

This section breaks the car or truck down into its component systems, allowing the problem to be isolated. The charts and diagnostic road maps list the most common problems and the most probable causes of trouble. Obviously it would be impossible to list every possible problem that could happen along with every possible cause, but it will locate MOST problems and eliminate a lot of unnecessary guesswork. The systematic format will locate problems within a given system, but, because many automotive systems are interrelated, the solution to your particular problem may be found in a number of systems on the car or truck.

USING THE TROUBLESHOOTING CHARTS

This book contains all of the specific information that the average do-it-yourself mechanic needs to repair and maintain his or her car or truck. The troubleshooting charts are designed to be used in conjunction with the specific procedures and information in the text. For instance, troubleshooting a point-type ignition system is fairly standard for all models, but you may be directed to the text to find procedures for troubleshooting an individual type of electronic ignition. You will also have to refer to the specification charts throughout the book for specifications applicable to your car or truck.

TOOLS AND EQUIPMENT

The tools illustrated in Chapter 1 (plus two more diagnostic pieces) will be adequate to troubleshoot most problems. The two other tools needed are a voltmeter and an ohmmeter. These can be purchased separately or in combination, known as a VOM meter.

In the event that other tools are required, they will be noted in the procedures.

Troubleshooting Engine Problems

See Chapters 2, 3, 4 for more information and service procedures.

Index to Systems

System	To Test	Group
Battery	Engine need not be running	1
Starting system	Engine need not be running	2
Primary electrical system	Engine need not be running	3
Secondary electrical system	Engine need not be running	4
Fuel system	Engine need not be running	5
Engine compression	Engine need not be running	6
Engine vacuum	Engine must be running	7
Secondary electrical system	Engine must be running	8
Valve train	Engine must be running	9
Exhaust system	Engine must be running	10
Cooling system	Engine must be running	11
Engine lubrication	Engine must be running	12

Index to Problems

Problem: Symptom	, Begin at Specific Diagnosis, Number ____
Engine Won't Start:	
Starter doesn't turn	1.1, 2.1
Starter turns, engine doesn't	2.1
Starter turns engine very slowly	1.1, 2.4
Starter turns engine normally	3.1, 4.1
Starter turns engine very quickly	6.1
Engine fires intermittently	4.1
Engine fires consistently	5.1, 6.1
Engine Runs Poorly:	
Hard starting	3.1, 4.1, 5.1, 8.1
Rough idle	4.1, 5.1, 8.1
Stalling	3.1, 4.1, 5.1, 8.1
Engine dies at high speeds	4.1, 5.1
Hesitation (on acceleration from standing stop)	5.1, 8.1
Poor pickup	4.1, 5.1, 8.1
Lack of power	3.1, 4.1, 5.1, 8.1
Backfire through the carburetor	4.1, 8.1, 9.1
Backfire through the exhaust	4.1, 8.1, 9.1
Blue exhaust gases	6.1, 7.1
Black exhaust gases	5.1
Running on (after the ignition is shut off)	3.1, 8.1
Susceptible to moisture	4.1
Engine misfires under load	4.1, 7.1, 8.4, 9.1
Engine misfires at speed	4.1, 8.4
Engine misfires at idle	3.1, 4.1, 5.1, 7.1, 8.4

Sample Section

Test and Procedure	Results and Indications	Proceed to
4.1—Check for spark: Hold each spark plug wire approximately ¼" from ground with gloves or a heavy, dry rag. Crank the engine and observe the spark.	→ If no spark is evident: ——————— → If spark is good in some cases: ———— → If spark is good in all cases: ———————	→**4.2** →**4.3** →**4.6**

Specific Diagnosis

This section is arranged so that following each test, instructions are given to proceed to another, until a problem is diagnosed.

Section 1—Battery

Test and Procedure	Results and Indications	Proceed to
1.1—Inspect the battery visually for case condition (corrosion, cracks) and water level.	If case is cracked, replace battery:	**1.4**
	If the case is intact, remove corrosion with a solution of baking soda and water (**CAUTION**: *do not get the solution into the battery*), and fill with water:	**1.2**

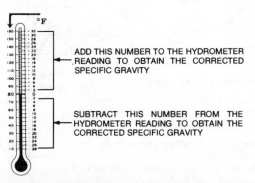

DIRT ON TOP OF BATTERY   PLUGGED VENT
CORROSION
LOOSE CABLE OR POSTS
CRACKS
LOW WATER LEVEL

Inspect the battery case

Test and Procedure	Results and Indications	Proceed to
1.2—Check the battery cable connections: Insert a screwdriver between the battery post and the cable clamp. Turn the headlights on high beam, and observe them as the screwdriver is gently twisted to ensure good metal to metal contact.	If the lights brighten, remove and clean the clamp and post; coat the post with petroleum jelly, install and tighten the clamp:	**1.4**
	If no improvement is noted:	**1.3**

TESTING BATTERY CABLE CONNECTIONS USING A SCREWDRIVER

Test and Procedure	Results and Indications	Proceed to
1.3—Test the state of charge of the battery using an individual cell tester or hydrometer.	If indicated, charge the battery. **NOTE:** *If no obvious reason exists for the low state of charge (i.e., battery age, prolonged storage), proceed to:*	**1.4**

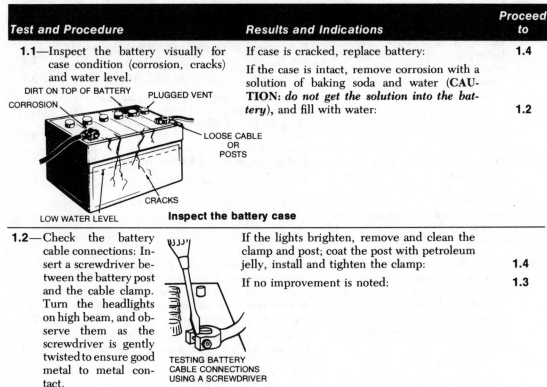

°F

ADD THIS NUMBER TO THE HYDROMETER READING TO OBTAIN THE CORRECTED SPECIFIC GRAVITY

SUBTRACT THIS NUMBER FROM THE HYDROMETER READING TO OBTAIN THE CORRECTED SPECIFIC GRAVITY

Specific Gravity (@ 80° F.)

Minimum	Battery Charge
1.260	100% Charged
1.230	75% Charged
1.200	50% Charged
1.170	25% Charged
1.140	Very Little Power Left
1.110	Completely Discharged

The effects of temperature on battery specific gravity (left) and amount of battery charge in relation to specific gravity (right)

Test and Procedure	Results and Indications	Proceed to
1.4—Visually inspect battery cables for cracking, bad connection to ground, or bad connection to starter.	If necessary, tighten connections or replace the cables:	**2.1**

Section 2—Starting System
See Chapter 3 for service procedures

Test and Procedure	Results and Indications	Proceed to
Note: Tests in Group 2 are performed with coil high tension lead disconnected to prevent accidental starting.		
2.1—Test the starter motor and solenoid: Connect a jumper from the battery post of the solenoid (or relay) to the starter post of the solenoid (or relay).	If starter turns the engine normally:	**2.2**
	If the starter buzzes, or turns the engine very slowly:	**2.4**
	If no response, replace the solenoid (or relay).	**3.1**
	If the starter turns, but the engine doesn't, ensure that the flywheel ring gear is intact. If the gear is undamaged, replace the starter drive.	**3.1**
2.2—Determine whether ignition override switches are functioning properly (clutch start switch, neutral safety switch), by connecting a jumper across the switch(es), and turning the ignition switch to "start".	If starter operates, adjust or replace switch:	**3.1**
	If the starter doesn't operate:	**2.3**
2.3—Check the ignition switch "start" position: Connect a 12V test lamp or voltmeter between the starter post of the solenoid (or relay) and ground. Turn the ignition switch to the "start" position, and jiggle the key.	If the lamp doesn't light or the meter needle doesn't move when the switch is turned, check the ignition switch for loose connections, cracked insulation, or broken wires. Repair or replace as necessary:	**3.1**
	If the lamp flickers or needle moves when the key is jiggled, replace the ignition switch.	**3.3**

Checking the ignition switch "start" position

STARTER RELAY (IF EQUIPPED)

Test and Procedure	Results and Indications	Proceed to
2.4—Remove and bench test the starter, according to specifications in the engine electrical section.	If the starter does not meet specifications, repair or replace as needed:	**3.1**
	If the starter is operating properly:	**2.5**
2.5—Determine whether the engine can turn freely: Remove the spark plugs, and check for water in the cylinders. Check for water on the dipstick, or oil in the radiator. Attempt to turn the engine using an 18″ flex drive and socket on the crankshaft pulley nut or bolt.	If the engine will turn freely only with the spark plugs out, and hydrostatic lock (water in the cylinders) is ruled out, check valve timing:	**9.2**
	If engine will not turn freely, and it is known that the clutch and transmission are free, the engine must be disassembled for further evaluation:	**Chapter 3**

Section 3—Primary Electrical System

Test and Procedure	Results and Indications	Proceed to
3.1—Check the ignition switch "on" position: Connect a jumper wire between the distributor side of the coil and ground, and a 12V test lamp between the switch side of the coil and ground. Remove the high tension lead from the coil. Turn the ignition switch on and jiggle the key.	If the lamp lights:	**3.2**
	If the lamp flickers when the key is jiggled, replace the ignition switch:	**3.3**
	If the lamp doesn't light, check for loose or open connections. If none are found, remove the ignition switch and check for continuity. If the switch is faulty, replace it:	**3.3**

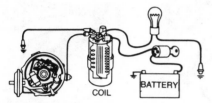

Checking the ignition switch "on" position

3.2—Check the ballast resistor or resistance wire for an open circuit, using an ohmmeter. See Chapter 3 for specific tests.	Replace the resistor or resistance wire if the resistance is zero. **NOTE:** *Some ignition systems have no ballast resistor.*	**3.3**

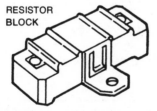

RESISTOR BLOCK

CALIBRATED RESISTANCE LEAD

Two types of resistors

3.3—On point-type ignition systems, visually inspect the breaker points for burning, pitting or excessive wear. Gray coloring of the point contact surfaces is normal. Rotate the crankshaft until the contact heel rests on a high point of the distributor cam and adjust the point gap to specifications. On electronic ignition models, remove the distributor cap and visually inspect the armature. Ensure that the armature pin is in place, and that the armature is on tight and rotates when the engine is cranked. Make sure there are no cracks, chips or rounded edges on the armature.	If the breaker points are intact, clean the contact surfaces with fine emery cloth, and adjust the point gap to specifications. If the points are worn, replace them. On electronic systems, replace any parts which appear defective. If condition persists:	**3.4**

Test and Procedure	Results and Indications	Proceed to
3.4—On point-type ignition systems, connect a dwell-meter between the distributor primary lead and ground. Crank the engine and observe the point dwell angle. On electronic ignition systems, conduct a stator (magnetic pickup assembly) test. See Chapter 3.	On point-type systems, adjust the dwell angle if necessary. **NOTE:** *Increasing the point gap decreases the dwell angle and vice-versa.*	**3.6**
	If the dwell meter shows little or no reading;	**3.5**
	On electronic ignition systems, if the stator is bad, replace the stator. If the stator is good, proceed to the other tests in Chapter 3.	

CLOSE   OPEN

NORMAL DWELL

WIDE GAP

SMALL DWELL

INSUFFICIENT DWELL

NARROW GAP

LARGE DWELL

EXCESSIVE DWELL

Dwell is a function of point gap

3.5—On the point-type ignition systems, check the condenser for short: connect an ohmmeter across the condenser body and the pigtail lead.	If any reading other than infinite is noted, replace the condenser	**3.6**

OHMMETER

Checking the condenser for short

3.6—Test the coil primary resistance: On point-type ignition systems, connect an ohmmeter across the coil primary terminals, and read the resistance on the low scale. Note whether an external ballast resistor or resistance wire is used. On electronic ignition systems, test the coil primary resistance as in Chapter 3.	Point-type ignition coils utilizing ballast resistors or resistance wires should have approximately 1.0 ohms resistance. Coils with internal resistors should have approximately 4.0 ohms resistance. If values far from the above are noted, replace the coil.	**4.1**

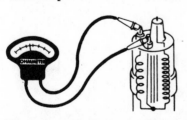

Check the coil primary resistance

Section 4—Secondary Electrical System
See Chapters 2–3 for service procedures

Test and Procedure	Results and Indications	Proceed to
4.1—Check for spark: Hold each spark plug wire approximately ¼″ from ground with gloves or a heavy, dry rag. Crank the engine, and observe the spark.	If no spark is evident:	**4.2**
	If spark is good in some cylinders:	**4.3**
	If spark is good in all cylinders:	**4.6**

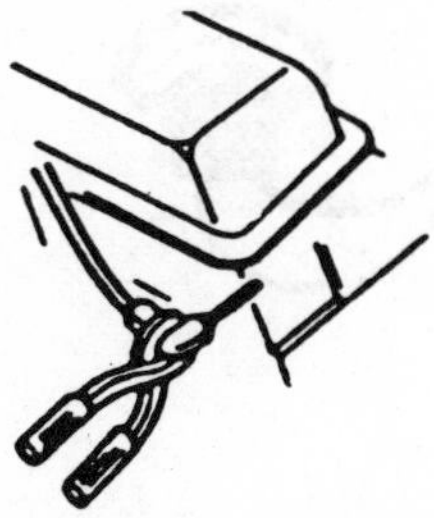

Check for spark at the plugs

4.2—Check for spark at the coil high tension lead: Remove the coil high tension lead from the distributor and position it approximately ¼″ from ground. Crank the engine and observe spark. **CAUTION:** *This test should not be performed on engines equipped with electronic ignition.*	If the spark is good and consistent:	**4.3**
	If the spark is good but intermittent, test the primary electrical system starting at 3.3:	**3.3**
	If the spark is weak or non-existent, replace the coil high tension lead, clean and tighten all connections and retest. If no improvement is noted:	**4.4**
4.3—Visually inspect the distributor cap and rotor for burned or corroded contacts, cracks, carbon tracks, or moisture. Also check the fit of the rotor on the distributor shaft (where applicable).	If moisture is present, dry thoroughly, and retest per 4.1:	**4.1**
	If burned or excessively corroded contacts, cracks, or carbon tracks are noted, replace the defective part(s) and retest per 4.1:	**4.1**
	If the rotor and cap appear intact, or are only slightly corroded, clean the contacts thoroughly (including the cap towers and spark plug wire ends) and retest per 4.1: If the spark is good in all cases:	**4.6**
	If the spark is poor in all cases:	**4.5**

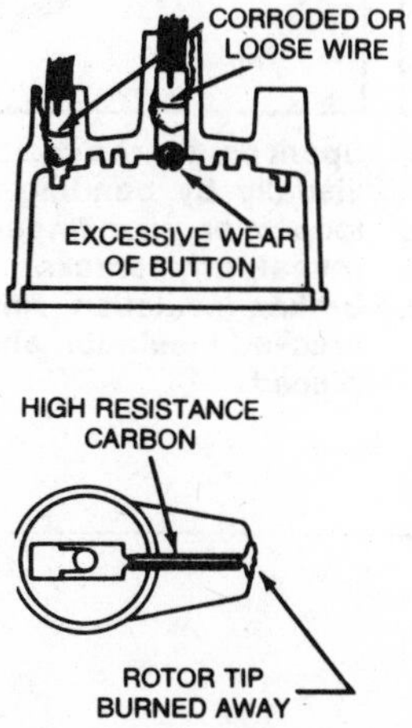

CORRODED OR LOOSE WIRE

EXCESSIVE WEAR OF BUTTON

HIGH RESISTANCE CARBON

ROTOR TIP BURNED AWAY

Inspect the distributor cap and rotor

Test and Procedure	*Results and Indications*	*Proceed to*

4.4—Check the coil secondary resistance: On point-type systems connect an ohmmeter across the distributor side of the coil and the coil tower. Read the resistance on the high scale of the ohmmeter. On electronic ignition systems, see Chapter 3 for specific tests.

The resistance of a satisfactory coil should be between 4,000 and 10,000 ohms. If resistance is considerably higher (i.e., 40,000 ohms) replace the coil and retest per 4.1. **NOTE:** *This does not apply to high performance coils.*

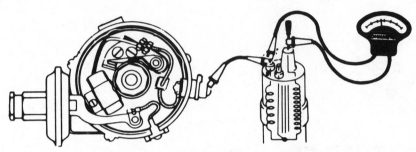

Testing the coil secondary resistance

4.5—Visually inspect the spark plug wires for cracking or brittleness. Ensure that no two wires are positioned so as to cause induction firing (adjacent and parallel). Remove each wire, one by one, and check resistance with an ohmmeter.

Replace any cracked or brittle wires. If any of the wires are defective, replace the entire set. Replace any wires with excessive resistance (over $8000\,\Omega$ per foot for suppression wire), and separate any wires that might cause induction firing.

4.6

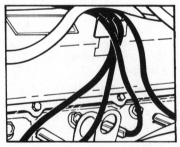

Misfiring can be the result of spark plug leads to adjacent, consecutively firing cylinders running parallel and too close together

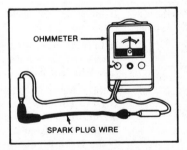

On point-type ignition systems, check the spark plug wires as shown. On electronic ignitions, do not remove the wire from the distributor cap terminal; instead, test through the cap

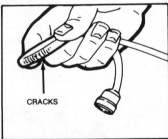

Spark plug wires can be checked visually by bending them in a loop over your finger. This will reveal any cracks, burned or broken insulation. Any wire with cracked insulation should be replaced

4.6—Remove the spark plugs, noting the cylinders from which they were removed, and evaluate according to the color photos in the middle of this book.

See following.

See following.

Test and Procedure	Results and Indications	Proceed to
4.7—Examine the location of all the plugs.	The following diagrams illustrate some of the conditions that the location of plugs will reveal.	**4.8**

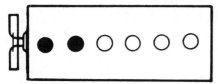

Two adjacent plugs are fouled in a 6-cylinder engine, 4-cylinder engine or either bank of a V-8. This is probably due to a blown head gasket between the two cylinders

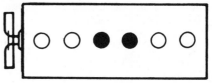

The two center plugs in a 6-cylinder engine are fouled. Raw fuel may be "boiled" out of the carburetor into the intake manifold after the engine is shut-off. Stop-start driving can also foul the center plugs, due to overly rich mixture. Proper float level, a new float needle and seat or use of an insulating spacer may help this problem

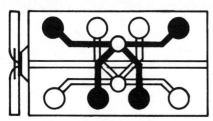

An unbalanced carburetor is indicated. Following the fuel flow on this particular design shows that the cylinders fed by the right-hand barrel are fouled from overly rich mixture, while the cylinders fed by the left-hand barrel are normal

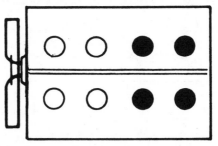

If the four rear plugs are overheated, a cooling system problem is suggested. A thorough cleaning of the cooling system may restore coolant circulation and cure the problem

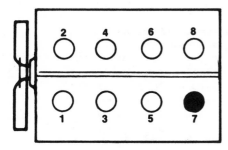

Finding one plug overheated may indicate an intake manifold leak near the affected cylinder. If the overheated plug is the second of two adjacent, consecutively firing plugs, it could be the result of ignition cross-firing. Separating the leads to these two plugs will eliminate cross-fire

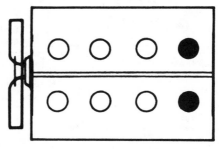

Occasionally, the two rear plugs in large, lightly used V-8's will become oil fouled. High oil consumption and smoky exhaust may also be noticed. It is probably due to plugged oil drain holes in the rear of the cylinder head, causing oil to be sucked in around the valve stems. This usually occurs in the rear cylinders first, because the engine slants that way

Test and Procedure	Results and Indications	Proceed to
4.8—Determine the static ignition timing. Using the crankshaft pulley timing marks as a guide, locate top dead center on the compression stroke of the number one cylinder.	The rotor should be pointing toward the No. 1 tower in the distributor cap, and, on electronic ignitions, the armature spoke for that cylinder should be lined up with the stator.	**4.8**
4.9—Check coil polarity: Connect a voltmeter negative lead to the coil high tension lead, and the positive lead to ground (**NOTE:** *Reverse the hook-up for positive ground systems*). Crank the engine momentarily. **Checking coil polarity**	If the voltmeter reads up-scale, the polarity is correct: If the voltmeter reads down-scale, reverse the coil polarity (switch the primary leads):	**5.1** **5.1**

Section 5—Fuel System
See Chapter 4 for service procedures

Test and Procedure	Results and Indications	Proceed to
5.1—Determine that the air filter is functioning efficiently: Hold paper elements up to a strong light, and attempt to see light through the filter.	Clean permanent air filters in solvent (or manufacturer's recommendation), and allow to dry. Replace paper elements through which light cannot be seen:	**5.2**
5.2—Determine whether a flooding condition exists: Flooding is identified by a strong gasoline odor, and excessive gasoline present in the throttle bore(s) of the carburetor.	If flooding is not evident: If flooding is evident, permit the gasoline to dry for a few moments and restart. If flooding doesn't recur: If flooding is persistent:	**5.3** **5.7** **5.5**

If the engine floods repeatedly, check the choke butterfly flap

Test and Procedure	Results and Indications	Proceed to
5.3—Check that fuel is reaching the carburetor: Detach the fuel line at the carburetor inlet. Hold the end of the line in a cup (not styrofoam), and crank the engine.	If fuel flows smoothly: If fuel doesn't flow (**NOTE:** *Make sure that there is fuel in the tank*), or flows erratically:	**5.7** **5.4**

Check the fuel pump by disconnecting the output line (fuel pump-to-carburetor) at the carburetor and operating the starter briefly

Test and Procedure	Results and Indications	Proceed to
5.4—Test the fuel pump: Disconnect all fuel lines from the fuel pump. Hold a finger over the input fitting, crank the engine (with electric pump, turn the ignition or pump on); and feel for suction.	If suction is evident, blow out the fuel line to the tank with low pressure compressed air until bubbling is heard from the fuel filler neck. Also blow out the carburetor fuel line (both ends disconnected):	**5.7**
	If no suction is evident, replace or repair the fuel pump: **NOTE:** *Repeated oil fouling of the spark plugs, or a no-start condition, could be the result of a ruptured vacuum booster pump diaphragm, through which oil or gasoline is being drawn into the intake manifold (where applicable).*	**5.7**
5.5—Occasionally, small specks of dirt will clog the small jets and orifices in the carburetor. With the engine cold, hold a flat piece of wood or similar material over the carburetor, where possible, and crank the engine.	If the engine starts, but runs roughly the engine is probably not run enough. If the engine won't start:	**5.9**
5.6—Check the needle and seat: Tap the carburetor in the area of the needle and seat.	If flooding stops, a gasoline additive (e.g., Gumout) will often cure the problem:	**5.7**
	If flooding continues, check the fuel pump for excessive pressure at the carburetor (according to specifications). If the pressure is normal, the needle and seat must be removed and checked, and/or the float level adjusted:	**5.7**
5.7—Test the accelerator pump by looking into the throttle bores while operating the throttle.	If the accelerator pump appears to be operating normally:	**5.8**
	If the accelerator pump is not operating, the pump must be reconditioned. Where possible, service the pump with the carburetor(s) installed on the engine. If necessary, remove the carburetor. Prior to removal:	**5.8**
Check for gas at the carburetor by looking down the carburetor throat while someone moves the accelerator		
5.8—Determine whether the carburetor main fuel system is functioning: Spray a commercial starting fluid into the carburetor while attempting to start the engine.	If the engine starts, runs for a few seconds, and dies:	**5.9**
	If the engine doesn't start:	**6.1**

Test and Procedure	Results and Indications	Proceed to
5.9—Uncommon fuel system malfunctions: See below:	If the problem is solved: If the problem remains, remove and recondition the carburetor.	6.1

Condition	Indication	Test	Prevailing Weather Conditions	Remedy
Vapor lock	Engine will not restart shortly after running.	Cool the components of the fuel system until the engine starts. Vapor lock can be cured faster by draping a wet cloth over a mechanical fuel pump.	Hot to very hot	Ensure that the exhaust manifold heat control valve is operating. Check with the vehicle manufacturer for the recommended solution to vapor lock on the model in question.
Carburetor icing	Engine will not idle, stalls at low speeds.	Visually inspect the throttle plate area of the throttle bores for frost.	High humidity, 32–40° F.	Ensure that the exhaust manifold heat control valve is operating, and that the intake manifold heat riser is not blocked.
Water in the fuel	Engine sputters and stalls; may not start.	Pump a small amount of fuel into a glass jar. Allow to stand, and inspect for droplets or a layer of water.	High humidity, extreme temperature changes.	For droplets, use one or two cans of commercial gas line anti-freeze. For a layer of water, the tank must be drained, and the fuel lines blown out with compressed air.

Section 6—Engine Compression
See Chapter 3 for service procedures

6.1—Test engine compression: Remove all spark plugs. Block the throttle wide open. Insert a compression gauge into a spark plug port, crank the engine to obtain the maximum reading, and record.	If compression is within limits on all cylinders:	7.1
	If gauge reading is extremely low on all cylinders:	6.2
	If gauge reading is low on one or two cylinders: (If gauge readings are identical and low on two or more adjacent cylinders, the head gasket must be replaced.)	6.2

Checking compression

6.2—Test engine compression (wet): Squirt approximately 30 cc. of engine oil into each cylinder, and retest per 6.1.	If the readings improve, worn or cracked rings or broken pistons are indicated:	See Chapter 3
	If the readings do not improve, burned or excessively carboned valves or a jumped timing chain are indicated: NOTE: *A jumped timing chain is often indicated by difficult cranking.*	7.1

Section 7—Engine Vacuum
See Chapter 3 for service procedures

Test and Procedure	Results and Indications	Proceed to
7.1—Attach a vacuum gauge to the intake manifold beyond the throttle plate. Start the engine, and observe the action of the needle over the range of engine speeds.	See below.	See below

INDICATION: normal engine in good condition

Proceed to: 8.1

Normal engine
Gauge reading: steady, from 17–22 in./Hg.

INDICATION: sticking valves or ignition miss

Proceed to: 9.1, 8.3

Sticking valves
Gauge reading: intermittent fluctuation at idle

INDICATION: late ignition or valve timing, low compression, stuck throttle valve, leaking carburetor or manifold gasket

Proceed to: 6.1

Incorrect valve timing
Gauge reading: low (10–15 in./Hg) but steady

INDICATION: improper carburetor adjustment or minor intake leak.

Proceed to: 7.2

Carburetor requires adjustment
Gauge reading: drifting needle

INDICATION: ignition miss, blown cylinder head gasket, leaking valve or weak valve spring

Proceed to: 8.3, 6.1

Blown head gasket
Gauge reading: needle fluctuates as engine speed increases

INDICATION: burnt valve or faulty valve clearance. Needle will fall when defective valve operates

Proceed to: 9.1

Burnt or leaking valves
Gauge reading: steady needle, but drops regularly

INDICATION: choked muffler, excessive back pressure in system

Proceed to: 10.1

Clogged exhaust system
Gauge reading: gradual drop in reading at idle

INDICATION: worn valve guides

Proceed to: 9.1

Worn valve guides
Gauge reading: needle vibrates excessively at idle, but steadies as engine speed increases

White pointer = steady gauge hand   Black pointer = fluctuating gauge hand

Test and Procedure	Results and Indications	Proceed to
7.2—Attach a vacuum gauge per 7.1, and test for an intake manifold leak. Squirt a small amount of oil around the intake manifold gaskets, carburetor gaskets, plugs and fittings. Observe the action of the vacuum gauge.	If the reading improves, replace the indicated gasket, or seal the indicated fitting or plug: If the reading remains low:	**8.1** **7.3**
7.3—Test all vacuum hoses and accessories for leaks as described in 7.2. Also check the carburetor body (dashpots, automatic choke mechanism, throttle shafts) for leaks in the same manner.	If the reading improves, service or replace the offending part(s): If the reading remains low:	**8.1** **6.1**

Section 8—Secondary Electrical System
See Chapter 2 for service procedures

Test and Procedure	Results and Indications	Proceed to
8.1—Remove the distributor cap and check to make sure that the rotor turns when the engine is cranked. Visually inspect the distributor components.	Clean, tighten or replace any components which appear defective.	**8.2**
8.2—Connect a timing light (per manufacturer's recommendation) and check the dynamic ignition timing. Disconnect and plug the vacuum hose(s) to the distributor if specified, start the engine, and observe the timing marks at the specified engine speed.	If the timing is not correct, adjust to specifications by rotating the distributor in the engine: (Advance timing by rotating distributor opposite normal direction of rotor rotation, retard timing by rotating distributor in same direction as rotor rotation.)	**8.3**
8.3—Check the operation of the distributor advance mechanism(s): To test the mechanical advance, disconnect the vacuum lines from the distributor advance unit and observe the timing marks with a timing light as the engine speed is increased from idle. If the mark moves smoothly, without hesitation, it may be assumed that the mechanical advance is functioning properly. To test vacuum advance and/or retard systems, alternately crimp and release the vacuum line, and observe the timing mark for movement. If movement is noted, the system is operating.	If the systems are functioning: If the systems are not functioning, remove the distributor, and test on a distributor tester:	**8.4** **8.4**
8.4—Locate an ignition miss: With the engine running, remove each spark plug wire, one at a time, until one is found that doesn't cause the engine to roughen and slow down.	When the missing cylinder is identified:	**4.1**

Section 9—Valve Train
See Chapter 3 for service procedures

Test and Procedure	Results and Indications	Proceed to
9.1—Evaluate the valve train: Remove the valve cover, and ensure that the valves are adjusted to specifications. A mechanic's stethoscope may be used to aid in the diagnosis of the valve train. By pushing the probe on or near push rods or rockers, valve noise often can be isolated. A timing light also may be used to diagnose valve problems. Connect the light according to manufacturer's recommendations, and start the engine. Vary the firing moment of the light by increasing the engine speed (and therefore the ignition advance), and moving the trigger from cylinder to cylinder. Observe the movement of each valve.	Sticking valves or erratic valve train motion can be observed with the timing light. The cylinder head must be disassembled for repairs.	**See Chapter 3**
9.2—Check the valve timing: Locate top dead center of the No. 1 piston, and install a degree wheel or tape on the crankshaft pulley or damper with zero corresponding to an index mark on the engine. Rotate the crankshaft in its direction of rotation, and observe the opening of the No. 1 cylinder intake valve. The opening should correspond with the correct mark on the degree wheel according to specifications.	If the timing is not correct, the timing cover must be removed for further investigation.	**See Chapter 3**

Section 10—Exhaust System

Test and Procedure	Results and Indications	Proceed to
10.1—Determine whether the exhaust manifold heat control valve is operating: Operate the valve by hand to determine whether it is free to move. If the valve is free, run the engine to operating temperature and observe the action of the valve, to ensure that it is opening.	If the valve sticks, spray it with a suitable solvent, open and close the valve to free it, and retest. If the valve functions properly: If the valve does not free, or does not operate, replace the valve:	**10.2** **10.2**
10.2—Ensure that there are no exhaust restrictions: Visually inspect the exhaust system for kinks, dents, or crushing. Also note that gases are flowing freely from the tailpipe at all engine speeds, indicating no restriction in the muffler or resonator.	Replace any damaged portion of the system:	**11.1**

Section 11—Cooling System
See Chapter 3 for service procedures

Test and Procedure	Results and Indications	Proceed to
11.1—Visually inspect the fan belt for glazing, cracks, and fraying, and replace if necessary. Tighten the belt so that the longest span has approximately ½″ play at its midpoint under thumb pressure (see Chapter 1).	Replace or tighten the fan belt as necessary:	11.2

Checking belt tension

Test and Procedure	Results and Indications	Proceed to
11.2—Check the fluid level of the cooling system.	If full or slightly low, fill as necessary:	11.5
	If extremely low:	11.3
11.3—Visually inspect the external portions of the cooling system (radiator, radiator hoses, thermostat elbow, water pump seals, heater hoses, etc.) for leaks. If none are found, pressurize the cooling system to 14–15 psi.	If cooling system holds the pressure:	11.5
	If cooling system loses pressure rapidly, reinspect external parts of the system for leaks under pressure. If none are found, check dipstick for coolant in crankcase. If no coolant is present, but pressure loss continues:	11.4
	If coolant is evident in crankcase, remove cylinder head(s), and check gasket(s). If gaskets are intact, block and cylinder head(s) should be checked for cracks or holes. If the gasket(s) is blown, replace, and purge the crankcase of coolant:	12.6
	NOTE: *Occasionally, due to atmospheric and driving conditions, condensation of water can occur in the crankcase. This causes the oil to appear milky white. To remedy, run the engine until hot, and change the oil and oil filter.*	
11.4—Check for combustion leaks into the cooling system: Pressurize the cooling system as above. Start the engine, and observe the pressure gauge. If the needle fluctuates, remove each spark plug wire, one at a time, noting which cylinder(s) reduce or eliminate the fluctuation.	Cylinders which reduce or eliminate the fluctuation, when the spark plug wire is removed, are leaking into the cooling system. Replace the head gasket on the affected cylinder bank(s).	

Pressurizing the cooling system

Test and Procedure	Results and Indications	Proceed to
11.5—Check the radiator pressure cap: Attach a radiator pressure tester to the radiator cap (wet the seal prior to installation). Quickly pump up the pressure, noting the point at which the cap releases.	If the cap releases within ± 1 psi of the specified rating, it is operating properly:	**11.6**
	If the cap releases at more than ± 1 psi of the specified rating, it should be replaced:	**11.6**

Checking radiator pressure cap

Test and Procedure	Results and Indications	Proceed to
11.6—Test the thermostat: Start the engine cold, remove the radiator cap, and insert a thermometer into the radiator. Allow the engine to idle. After a short while, there will be a sudden, rapid increase in coolant temperature. The temperature at which this sharp rise stops is the thermostat opening temperature.	If the thermostat opens at or about the specified temperature:	**11.7**
	If the temperature doesn't increase: (If the temperature increases slowly and gradually, replace the thermostat.)	**11.7**
11.7—Check the water pump: Remove the thermostat elbow and the thermostat, disconnect the coil high tension lead (to prevent starting), and crank the engine momentarily.	If coolant flows, replace the thermostat and retest per 11.6:	**11.6**
	If coolant doesn't flow, reverse flush the cooling system to alleviate any blockage that might exist. If system is not blocked, and coolant will not flow, replace the water pump.	

Section 12—Lubrication
See Chapter 3 for service procedures

Test and Procedure	Results and Indications	Proceed to
12.1—Check the oil pressure gauge or warning light: If the gauge shows low pressure, or the light is on for no obvious reason, remove the oil pressure sender. Install an accurate oil pressure gauge and run the engine momentarily.	If oil pressure builds normally, run engine for a few moments to determine that it is functioning normally, and replace the sender.	—
	If the pressure remains low:	**12.2**
	If the pressure surges:	**12.3**
	If the oil pressure is zero:	**12.3**
12.2—Visually inspect the oil: If the oil is watery or very thin, milky, or foamy, replace the oil and oil filter.	If the oil is normal:	**12.3**
	If after replacing oil the pressure remains low:	**12.3**
	If after replacing oil the pressure becomes normal:	—

Test and Procedure	Results and Indications	Proceed to
12.3—Inspect the oil pressure relief valve and spring, to ensure that it is not sticking or stuck. Remove and thoroughly clean the valve, spring, and the valve body.	If the oil pressure improves: If no improvement is noted:	— **12.4**
12.4—Check to ensure that the oil pump is not cavitating (sucking air instead of oil): See that the crankcase is neither over nor underfull, and that the pickup in the sump is in the proper position and free from sludge.	Fill or drain the crankcase to the proper capacity, and clean the pickup screen in solvent if necessary. If no improvement is noted:	**12.5**
12.5—Inspect the oil pump drive and the oil pump:	If the pump drive or the oil pump appear to be defective, service as necessary and retest per 12.1: If the pump drive and pump appear to be operating normally, the engine should be disassembled to determine where blockage exists:	**12.1** **See Chapter 3**
12.6—Purge the engine of ethylene glycol coolant: Completely drain the crankcase and the oil filter. Obtain a commercial butyl cellosolve base solvent, designated for this purpose, and follow the instructions precisely. Following this, install a new oil filter and refill the crankcase with the proper weight oil. The next oil and filter change should follow shortly thereafter (1000 miles).		

TROUBLESHOOTING EMISSION CONTROL SYSTEMS

See Chapter 4 for procedures applicable to individual emission control systems used on specific combinations of engine/transmission/ model.

TROUBLESHOOTING THE CARBURETOR

See Chapter 4 for service procedures

Carburetor problems cannot be effectively isolated unless all other engine systems (particularly ignition and emission) are functioning properly and the engine is properly tuned.

Condition	Possible Cause
Engine cranks, but does not start	1. Improper starting procedure 2. No fuel in tank 3. Clogged fuel line or filter 4. Defective fuel pump 5. Choke valve not closing properly 6. Engine flooded 7. Choke valve not unloading 8. Throttle linkage not making full travel 9. Stuck needle or float 10. Leaking float needle or seat 11. Improper float adjustment
Engine stalls	1. Improperly adjusted idle speed or mixture **Engine hot** 2. Improperly adjusted dashpot 3. Defective or improperly adjusted solenoid 4. Incorrect fuel level in fuel bowl 5. Fuel pump pressure too high 6. Leaking float needle seat 7. Secondary throttle valve stuck open 8. Air or fuel leaks 9. Idle air bleeds plugged or missing 10. Idle passages plugged **Engine Cold** 11. Incorrectly adjusted choke 12. Improperly adjusted fast idle speed 13. Air leaks 14. Plugged idle or idle air passages 15. Stuck choke valve or binding linkage 16. Stuck secondary throttle valves 17. Engine flooding—high fuel level 18. Leaking or misaligned float
Engine hesitates on acceleration	1. Clogged fuel filter 2. Leaking fuel pump diaphragm 3. Low fuel pump pressure 4. Secondary throttle valves stuck, bent or misadjusted 5. Sticking or binding air valve 6. Defective accelerator pump 7. Vacuum leaks 8. Clogged air filter 9. Incorrect choke adjustment (engine cold)
Engine feels sluggish or flat on acceleration	1. Improperly adjusted idle speed or mixture 2. Clogged fuel filter 3. Defective accelerator pump 4. Dirty, plugged or incorrect main metering jets 5. Bent or sticking main metering rods 6. Sticking throttle valves 7. Stuck heat riser 8. Binding or stuck air valve 9. Dirty, plugged or incorrect secondary jets 10. Bent or sticking secondary metering rods. 11. Throttle body or manifold heat passages plugged 12. Improperly adjusted choke or choke vacuum break.
Carburetor floods	1. Defective fuel pump. Pressure too high. 2. Stuck choke valve 3. Dirty, worn or damaged float or needle valve/seat 4. Incorrect float/fuel level 5. Leaking float bowl

Condition	Possible Cause
Engine idles roughly and stalls	1. Incorrect idle speed 2. Clogged fuel filter 3. Dirt in fuel system or carburetor ' 4. Loose carburetor screws or attaching bolts 5. Broken carburetor gaskets 6. Air leaks 7. Dirty carburetor 8. Worn idle mixture needles 9. Throttle valves stuck open 10. Incorrectly adjusted float or fuel level 11. Clogged air filter
Engine runs unevenly or surges	1. Defective fuel pump 2. Dirty or clogged fuel filter 3. Plugged, loose or incorrect main metering jets or rods 4. Air leaks 5. Bent or sticking main metering rods 6. Stuck power piston 7. Incorrect float adjustment 8. Incorrect idle speed or mixture 9. Dirty or plugged idle system passages 10. Hard, brittle or broken gaskets 11. Loose attaching or mounting screws 12. Stuck or misaligned secondary throttle valves
Poor fuel economy	1. Poor driving habits 2. Stuck choke valve 3. Binding choke linkage 4. Stuck heat riser 5. Incorrect idle mixture 6. Defective accelerator pump 7. Air leaks 8. Plugged, loose or incorrect main metering jets 9. Improperly adjusted float or fuel level 10. Bent, misaligned or fuel-clogged float 11. Leaking float needle seat 12. Fuel leak 13. Accelerator pump discharge ball not seating properly 14. Incorrect main jets
Engine lacks high speed performance or power	1. Incorrect throttle linkage adjustment 2. Stuck or binding power piston 3. Defective accelerator pump 4. Air leaks 5. Incorrect float setting or fuel level 6. Dirty, plugged, worn or incorrect main metering jets or rods 7. Binding or sticking air valve 8. Brittle or cracked gaskets 9. Bent, incorrect or improperly adjusted secondary metering rods 10. Clogged fuel filter 11. Clogged air filter 12. Defective fuel pump

TROUBLESHOOTING FUEL INJECTION PROBLEMS

Each fuel injection system has its own unique components and test procedures, for which it is impossible to generalize. Refer to Chapter 4 of this Repair & Tune-Up Guide for specific test and repair procedures, if the vehicle is equipped with fuel injection.

TROUBLESHOOTING ELECTRICAL PROBLEMS

See Chapter 5 for service procedures

For any electrical system to operate, it must make a complete circuit. This simply means that the power flow from the battery must make a complete circle. When an electrical component is operating, power flows from the battery to the component, passes through the component causing it to perform its function (lighting a light bulb), and then returns to the battery through the ground of the circuit. This ground is usually (but not always) the metal part of the car or truck on which the electrical component is mounted.

Perhaps the easiest way to visualize this is to think of connecting a light bulb with two wires attached to it to the battery. If one of the two wires attached to the light bulb were attached to the negative post of the battery and the other were attached to the positive post of the battery, you would have a complete circuit. Current from the battery would flow to the light bulb, causing it to light, and return to the negative post of the battery.

The normal automotive circuit differs from this simple example in two ways. First, instead of having a return wire from the bulb to the battery, the light bulb returns the current to the battery through the chassis of the vehicle. Since the negative battery cable is attached to the chassis and the chassis is made of electrically conductive metal, the chassis of the vehicle can serve as a ground wire to complete the circuit. Secondly, most automotive circuits contain switches to turn components on and off as required.

Every complete circuit from a power source must include a component which is using the power from the power source. If you were to disconnect the light bulb from the wires and touch the two wires together (don't do this) the power supply wire to the component would be grounded before the normal ground connection for the circuit.

Because grounding a wire from a power source makes a complete circuit—less the required component to use the power—this phenomenon is called a short circuit. Common causes are: broken insulation (exposing the metal wire to a metal part of the car or truck), or a shorted switch.

Some electrical components which require a large amount of current to operate also have a relay in their circuit. Since these circuits carry a large amount of current, the thickness of the wire in the circuit (gauge size) is also greater. If this large wire were connected from the component to the control switch on the instrument panel, and then back to the component, a voltage drop would occur in the circuit. To prevent this potential drop in voltage, an electromagnetic switch (relay) is used. The large wires in the circuit are connected from the battery to one side of the relay, and from the opposite side of the relay to the component. The relay is normally open, preventing current from passing through the circuit. An additional, smaller, wire is connected from the relay to the control switch for the circuit. When the control switch is turned on, it grounds the smaller wire from the relay and completes the circuit. This closes the relay and allows current to flow from the battery to the component. The horn, headlight, and starter circuits are three which use relays.

It is possible for larger surges of current to pass through the electrical system of your car or truck. If this surge of current were to reach an electrical component, it could burn it out. To prevent this, fuses, circuit breakers or fusible links are connected into the current supply wires of most of the major electrical systems. When an electrical current of excessive power passes through the component's fuse, the fuse blows out and breaks the circuit, saving the component from destruction.

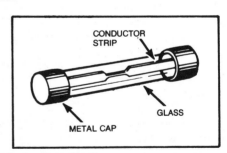

Typical automotive fuse

A circuit breaker is basically a self-repairing fuse. The circuit breaker opens the circuit the same way a fuse does. However, when either the short is removed from the circuit or the surge subsides, the circuit breaker resets itself and does not have to be replaced as a fuse does.

A fuse link is a wire that acts as a fuse. It is normally connected between the starter relay and the main wiring harness. This connection is usually under the hood. The fuse link (if installed) protects all the

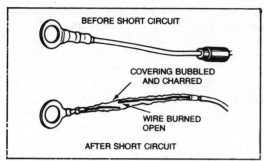

Most fusible links show a charred, melted insulation when they burn out

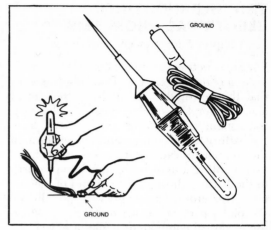

The test light will show the presence of current when touched to a hot wire and grounded at the other end

chassis electrical components, and is the probable cause of trouble when none of the electrical components function, unless the battery is disconnected or dead.

Electrical problems generally fall into one of three areas:

1. The component that is not functioning is not receiving current.

2. The component itself is not functioning.

3. The component is not properly grounded.

The electrical system can be checked with a test light and a jumper wire. A test light is a device that looks like a pointed screwdriver with a wire attached to it and has a light bulb in its handle. A jumper wire is a piece of insulated wire with an alligator clip attached to each end.

If a component is not working, you must follow a systematic plan to determine which of the three causes is the villain.

1. Turn on the switch that controls the inoperable component.

2. Disconnect the power supply wire from the component.

3. Attach the ground wire on the test light to a good metal ground.

4. Touch the probe end of the test light to the end of the power supply wire that was disconnected from the component. If the component is receiving current, the test light will go on.

NOTE: *Some components work only when the ignition switch is turned on.*

If the test light does not go on, then the problem is in the circuit between the battery and the component. This includes all the switches, fuses, and relays in the system. Follow the wire that runs back to the battery. The problem is an open circuit between the

battery and the component. If the fuse is blown and, when replaced, immediately blows again, there is a short circuit in the system which must be located and repaired. If there is a switch in the system, bypass it with a jumper wire. This is done by connecting one end of the jumper wire to the power supply wire into the switch and the other end of the jumper wire to the wire coming out of the switch. If the test light lights with the jumper wire installed, the switch or whatever was bypassed is defective.

NOTE: *Never substitute the jumper wire for the component, since it is required to use the power from the power source.*

5. If the bulb in the test light goes on, then the current is getting to the component that is not working. This eliminates the first of the three possible causes. Connect the power supply wire and connect a jumper wire from the component to a good metal ground. Do this with the switch which controls the component turned on, and also the ignition switch turned on if it is required for the component to work. If the component works with the jumper wire installed, then it has a bad ground. This is usually caused by the metal area on which the component mounts to the chassis being coated with some type of foreign matter.

6. If neither test located the source of the trouble, then the component itself is defective. Remember that for any electrical system to work, all connections must be clean and tight.

Troubleshooting Basic Turn Signal and Flasher Problems

See Chapter 5 for service procedures

Most problems in the turn signals or flasher system can be reduced to defective flashers or bulbs, which are easily replaced. Occasionally, the turn signal switch will prove defective.

F = Front   R = Rear   ● = Lights off   ○ = Lights on

Condition		Possible Cause
Turn signals light, but do not flash	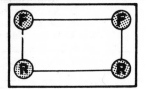	Defective flasher
No turn signals light on either side	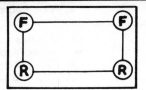	Blown fuse. Replace if defective. Defective flasher. Check by substitution. Open circuit, short circuit or poor ground.
Both turn signals on one side don't work	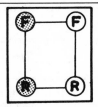	Bad bulbs. Bad ground in both (or either) housings.
One turn signal light on one side doesn't work	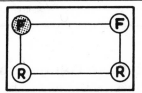	Defective bulb. Corrosion in socket. Clean contacts. Poor ground at socket.
Turn signal flashes too fast or too slowly	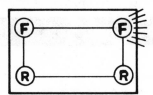	Check any bulb on the side flashing too fast. A heavy-duty bulb is probably installed in place of a regular bulb. Check the bulb flashing too slowly. A standard bulb was probably installed in place of a heavy-duty bulb. Loose connections or corrosion at the bulb socket.
Indicator lights don't work in either direction		Check if the turn signals are working. Check the dash indicator lights. Check the flasher by substitution.
One indicator light doesn't light		On systems with one dash indicator: See if the lights work on the same side. Often the filaments have been reversed in systems combining stoplights with taillights and turn signals. Check the flasher by substitution. On systems with two indicators: Check the bulbs on the same side. Check the indicator light bulb. Check the flasher by substitution.

Troubleshooting Lighting Problems

See Chapter 5 for service procedures

Condition	Possible Cause
One or more lights don't work, but others do	1. Defective bulb(s) 2. Blown fuse(s) 3. Dirty fuse clips or light sockets 4. Poor ground circuit
Lights burn out quickly	1. Incorrect voltage regulator setting or defective regulator 2. Poor battery/alternator connections
Lights go dim	1. Low/discharged battery 2. Alternator not charging 3. Corroded sockets or connections 4. Low voltage output
Lights flicker	1. Loose connection 2. Poor ground. (Run ground wire from light housing to frame) 3. Circuit breaker operating (short circuit)
Lights "flare"—Some flare is normal on acceleration—If excessive, see "Lights Burn Out Quickly"	High voltage setting
Lights glare—approaching drivers are blinded	1. Lights adjusted too high 2. Rear springs or shocks sagging 3. Rear tires soft

Troubleshooting Dash Gauge Problems

Most problems can be traced to a defective sending unit or faulty wiring. Occasionally, the gauge itself is at fault. See Chapter 5 for service procedures.

Condition	Possible Cause
COOLANT TEMPERATURE GAUGE	
Gauge reads erratically or not at all	1. Loose or dirty connections 2. Defective sending unit. 3. Defective gauge. To test a bi-metal gauge, remove the wire from the sending unit. Ground the wire for an instant. If the gauge registers, replace the sending unit. To test a magnetic gauge, disconnect the wire at the sending unit. With ignition ON gauge should register COLD. Ground the wire; gauge should register HOT.
AMMETER GAUGE—TURN HEADLIGHTS ON (DO NOT START ENGINE). NOTE REACTION	
Ammeter shows charge Ammeter shows discharge Ammeter does not move	1. Connections reversed on gauge 2. Ammeter is OK 3. Loose connections or faulty wiring 4. Defective gauge

Condition	Possible Cause

OIL PRESSURE GAUGE

Condition	Possible Cause
Gauge does not register or is inaccurate	1. On mechanical gauge, Bourdon tube may be bent or kinked. 2. Low oil pressure. Remove sending unit. Idle the engine briefly. If no oil flows from sending unit hole, problem is in engine. 3. Defective gauge. Remove the wire from the sending unit and ground it for an instant with the ignition ON. A good gauge will go to the top of the scale. 4. Defective wiring. Check the wiring to the gauge. If it's OK and the gauge doesn't register when grounded, replace the gauge. 5. Defective sending unit.

ALL GAUGES

Condition	Possible Cause
All gauges do not operate	1. Blown fuse 2. Defective instrument regulator
All gauges read low or erratically All gauges pegged	3. Defective or dirty instrument voltage regulator 4. Loss of ground between instrument voltage regulator and frame 5. Defective instrument regulator

WARNING LIGHTS

Condition	Possible Cause
Light(s) do not come on when ignition is ON, but engine is not started	1. Defective bulb 2. Defective wire 3. Defective sending unit. Disconnect the wire from the sending unit and ground it. Replace the sending unit if the light comes on with the ignition ON.
Light comes on with engine running	4. Problem in individual system 5. Defective sending unit

Troubleshooting Clutch Problems

It is false economy to replace individual clutch components. The pressure plate, clutch plate and throwout bearing should be replaced as a set, and the flywheel face inspected, whenever the clutch is overhauled. See Chapter 6 for service procedures.

Condition	Possible Cause
Clutch chatter	1. Grease on driven plate (disc) facing 2. Binding clutch linkage or cable 3. Loose, damaged facings on driven plate (disc) 4. Engine mounts loose 5. Incorrect height adjustment of pressure plate release levers 6. Clutch housing or housing to transmission adapter misalignment 7. Loose driven plate hub
Clutch grabbing	1. Oil, grease on driven plate (disc) facing 2. Broken pressure plate 3. Warped or binding driven plate. Driven plate binding on clutch shaft
Clutch slips	1. Lack of lubrication in clutch linkage or cable (linkage or cable binds, causes incomplete engagement) 2. Incorrect pedal, or linkage adjustment 3. Broken pressure plate springs 4. Weak pressure plate springs 5. Grease on driven plate facings (disc)

Troubleshooting Clutch Problems (cont.)

Condition	Possible Cause
Incomplete clutch release	1. Incorrect pedal or linkage adjustment or linkage or cable binding 2. Incorrect height adjustment on pressure plate release levers 3. Loose, broken facings on driven plate (disc) 4. Bent, dished, warped driven plate caused by overheating
Grinding, whirring grating noise when pedal is depressed	1. Worn or defective throwout bearing 2. Starter drive teeth contacting flywheel ring gear teeth. Look for milled or polished teeth on ring gear.
Squeal, howl, trumpeting noise when pedal is being released (occurs during first inch to inch and one-half of pedal travel)	Pilot bushing worn or lack of lubricant. If bushing appears OK, polish bushing with emery cloth, soak lube wick in oil, lube bushing with oil, apply film of chassis grease to clutch shaft pilot hub, reassemble. NOTE: Bushing wear may be due to misalignment of clutch housing or housing to transmission adapter
Vibration or clutch pedal pulsation with clutch disengaged (pedal fully depressed)	1. Worn or defective engine transmission mounts 2. Flywheel run out. (Flywheel run out at face not to exceed 0.005") 3. Damaged or defective clutch components

Troubleshooting Manual Transmission Problems
See Chapter 6 for service procedures

Condition	Possible Cause
Transmission jumps out of gear	1. Misalignment of transmission case or clutch housing. 2. Worn pilot bearing in crankshaft. 3. Bent transmission shaft. 4. Worn high speed sliding gear. 5. Worn teeth or end-play in clutch shaft. 6. Insufficient spring tension on shifter rail plunger. 7. Bent or loose shifter fork. 8. Gears not engaging completely. 9. Loose or worn bearings on clutch shaft or mainshaft. 10. Worn gear teeth. 11. Worn or damaged detent balls.
Transmission sticks in gear	1. Clutch not releasing fully. 2. Burred or battered teeth on clutch shaft, or sliding sleeve. 3. Burred or battered transmission mainshaft. 4. Frozen synchronizing clutch. 5. Stuck shifter rail plunger. 6. Gearshift lever twisting and binding shifter rail. 7. Battered teeth on high speed sliding gear or on sleeve. 8. Improper lubrication, or lack of lubrication. 9. Corroded transmission parts. 10. Defective mainshaft pilot bearing. 11. Locked gear bearings will give same effect as stuck in gear.
Transmission gears will not synchronize	1. Binding pilot bearing on mainshaft, will synchronize in high gear only. 2. Clutch not releasing fully. 3. Detent spring weak or broken. 4. Weak or broken springs under balls in sliding gear sleeve. 5. Binding bearing on clutch shaft, or binding countershaft. 6. Binding pilot bearing in crankshaft. 7. Badly worn gear teeth. 8. Improper lubrication. 9. Constant mesh gear not turning freely on transmission mainshaft. Will synchronize in that gear only.

Condition	Possible Cause
Gears spinning when shifting into gear from neutral	1. Clutch not releasing fully. 2. In some cases an extremely light lubricant in transmission will cause gears to continue to spin for a short time after clutch is released. 3. Binding pilot bearing in crankshaft.
Transmission noisy in all gears	1. Insufficient lubricant, or improper lubricant. 2. Worn countergear bearings. 3. Worn or damaged main drive gear or countergear. 4. Damaged main drive gear or mainshaft bearings. 5. Worn or damaged countergear anti-lash plate.
Transmission noisy in neutral only	1. Damaged main drive gear bearing. 2. Damaged or loose mainshaft pilot bearing. 3. Worn or damaged countergear anti-lash plate. 4. Worn countergear bearings.
Transmission noisy in one gear only	1. Damaged or worn constant mesh gears. 2. Worn or damaged countergear bearings. 3. Damaged or worn synchronizer.
Transmission noisy in reverse only	1. Worn or damaged reverse idler gear or idler bushing. 2. Worn or damaged mainshaft reverse gear. 3. Worn or damaged reverse countergear. 4. Damaged shift mechanism.

TROUBLESHOOTING AUTOMATIC TRANSMISSION PROBLEMS

Keeping alert to changes in the operating characteristics of the transmission (changing shift points, noises, etc.) can prevent small problems from becoming large ones. If the problem cannot be traced to loose bolts, fluid level, misadjusted linkage, clogged filters or similar problems, you should probably seek professional service.

Transmission Fluid Indications

The appearance and odor of the transmission fluid can give valuable clues to the overall condition of the transmission. Always note the appearance of the fluid when you check the fluid level or change the fluid. Rub a small amount of fluid between your fingers to feel for grit and smell the fluid on the dipstick.

If the fluid appears:	It indicates:
Clear and red colored	Normal operation
Discolored (extremely dark red or brownish) or smells burned	Band or clutch pack failure, usually caused by an overheated transmission. Hauling very heavy loads with insufficient power or failure to change the fluid often result in overheating. Do not confuse this appearance with newer fluids that have a darker red color and a strong odor (though not a burned odor).
Foamy or aerated (light in color and full of bubbles)	1. The level is too high (gear train is churning oil) 2. An internal air leak (air is mixing with the fluid). Have the transmission checked professionally.
Solid residue in the fluid	Defective bands, clutch pack or bearings. Bits of band material or metal abrasives are clinging to the dipstick. Have the transmission checked professionally.
Varnish coating on the dipstick	The transmission fluid is overheating

TROUBLESHOOTING DRIVE AXLE PROBLEMS

First, determine when the noise is most noticeable.

Drive Noise: Produced under vehicle acceleration.

Coast Noise: Produced while coasting with a closed throttle.

Float Noise: Occurs while maintaining constant speed (just enough to keep speed constant) on a level road.

External Noise Elimination

It is advisable to make a thorough road test to determine whether the noise originates in the rear axle or whether it originates from the tires, engine, transmission, wheel bearings or road surface. Noise originating from other places cannot be corrected by servicing the rear axle.

ROAD NOISE

Brick or rough surfaced concrete roads produce noises that seem to come from the rear axle. Road noise is usually identical in Drive or Coast and driving on a different type of road will tell whether the road is the problem.

TIRE NOISE

Tire noise can be mistaken as rear axle noise, even though the tires on the front are at fault. Snow tread and mud tread tires or tires worn unevenly will frequently cause vibrations which seem to originate elsewhere; *temporarily, and for test purposes only*, inflate the tires to 40–50 lbs. This will significantly alter the noise produced by the tires, but will not alter noise from the rear axle. Noises from the rear axle will normally cease at speeds below 30 mph on coast, while tire noise will continue at lower tone as speed is decreased. The rear axle noise will usually change from drive conditions to coast conditions, while tire noise will not. Do not forget to lower the tire pressure to normal after the test is complete.

ENGINE/TRANSMISSION NOISE

Determine at what speed the noise is most pronounced, then stop in a quiet place. With the transmission in Neutral, run the engine through speeds corresponding to road speeds where the noise was noticed. Noises produced with the vehicle standing still are coming from the engine or transmission.

FRONT WHEEL BEARINGS

Front wheel bearing noises, sometimes confused with rear axle noises, will not change when comparing drive and coast conditions. While holding the speed steady, lightly apply the footbrake. This will often cause wheel bearing noise to lessen, as some of the weight is taken off the bearing. Front wheel bearings are easily checked by jacking up the wheels and spinning the wheels. Shaking the wheels will also determine if the wheel bearings are excessively loose.

REAR AXLE NOISES

Eliminating other possible sources can narrow the cause to the rear axle, which normally produces noise from worn gears or bearings. Gear noises tend to peak in a narrow speed range, while bearing noises will usually vary in pitch with engine speeds.

Noise Diagnosis

The Noise Is:	Most Probably Produced By:
1. Identical under Drive or Coast	Road surface, tires or front wheel bearings
2. Different depending on road surface	Road surface or tires
3. Lower as speed is lowered	Tires
4. Similar when standing or moving	Engine or transmission
5. A vibration	Unbalanced tires, rear wheel bearing, unbalanced driveshaft or worn U-joint
6. A knock or click about every two tire revolutions	Rear wheel bearing
7. Most pronounced on turns	Damaged differential gears
8. A steady low-pitched whirring or scraping, starting at low speeds	Damaged or worn pinion bearing
9. A chattering vibration on turns	Wrong differential lubricant or worn clutch plates (limited slip rear axle)
10. Noticed only in Drive, Coast or Float conditions	Worn ring gear and/or pinion gear

Troubleshooting Steering & Suspension Problems

Condition	Possible Cause
Hard steering (wheel is hard to turn)	1. Improper tire pressure 2. Loose or glazed pump drive belt 3. Low or incorrect fluid 4. Loose, bent or poorly lubricated front end parts 5. Improper front end alignment (excessive caster) 6. Bind in steering column or linkage 7. Kinked hydraulic hose 8. Air in hydraulic system 9. Low pump output or leaks in system 10. Obstruction in lines 11. Pump valves sticking or out of adjustment 12. Incorrect wheel alignment
Loose steering (too much play in steering wheel)	1. Loose wheel bearings 2. Faulty shocks 3. Worn linkage or suspension components 4. Loose steering gear mounting or linkage points 5. Steering mechanism worn or improperly adjusted 6. Valve spool improperly adjusted 7. Worn ball joints, tie-rod ends, etc.
Veers or wanders (pulls to one side with hands off steering wheel)	1. Improper tire pressure 2. Improper front end alignment 3. Dragging or improperly adjusted brakes 4. Bent frame 5. Improper rear end alignment 6. Faulty shocks or springs 7. Loose or bent front end components 8. Play in Pitman arm 9. Steering gear mountings loose 10. Loose wheel bearings 11. Binding Pitman arm 12. Spool valve sticking or improperly adjusted 13. Worn ball joints
Wheel oscillation or vibration transmitted through steering wheel	1. Low or uneven tire pressure 2. Loose wheel bearings 3. Improper front end alignment 4. Bent spindle 5. Worn, bent or broken front end components 6. Tires out of round or out of balance 7. Excessive lateral runout in disc brake rotor 8. Loose or bent shock absorber or strut
Noises (see also "Troubleshooting Drive Axle Problems")	1. Loose belts 2. Low fluid, air in system 3. Foreign matter in system 4. Improper lubrication 5. Interference or chafing in linkage 6. Steering gear mountings loose 7. Incorrect adjustment or wear in gear box 8. Faulty valves or wear in pump 9. Kinked hydraulic lines 10. Worn wheel bearings
Poor return of steering	1. Over-inflated tires 2. Improperly aligned front end (excessive caster) 3. Binding in steering column 4. No lubrication in front end 5. Steering gear adjusted too tight
Uneven tire wear (see "How To Read Tire Wear")	1. Incorrect tire pressure 2. Improperly aligned front end 3. Tires out-of-balance 4. Bent or worn suspension parts

HOW TO READ TIRE WEAR

The way your tires wear is a good indicator of other parts of the suspension. Abnormal wear patterns are often caused by the need for simple tire maintenance, or for front end alignment.

Excessive wear at the center of the tread indicates that the air pressure in the tire is consistently too high. The tire is riding on the center of the tread and wearing it prematurely. Occasionally, this wear pattern can result from outrageously wide tires on narrow rims. The cure for this is to replace either the tires or the wheels.

This type of wear usually results from consistent under-inflation. When a tire is under-inflated, there is too much contact with the road by the outer treads, which wear prematurely. When this type of wear occurs, and the tire pressure is known to be consistently correct, a bent or worn steering component or the need for wheel alignment could be indicated.

Feathering is a condition when the edge of each tread rib develops a slightly rounded edge on one side and a sharp edge on the other. By running your hand over the tire, you can usually feel the sharper edges before you'll be able to see them. The most common causes of feathering are incorrect toe-in setting or deteriorated bushings in the front suspension.

When an inner or outer rib wears faster than the rest of the tire, the need for wheel alignment is indicated. There is excessive camber in the front suspension, causing the wheel to lean too much putting excessive load on one side of the tire. Misalignment could also be due to sagging springs, worn ball joints, or worn control arm bushings. Be sure the vehicle is loaded the way it's normally driven when you have the wheels aligned.

Cups or scalloped dips appearing around the edge of the tread almost always indicate worn (sometimes bent) suspension parts. Adjustment of wheel alignment alone will seldom cure the problem. Any worn component that connects the wheel to the suspension can cause this type of wear. Occasionally, wheels that are out of balance will wear like this, but wheel imbalance usually shows up as bald spots between the outside edges and center of the tread.

Second-rib wear is usually found only in radial tires, and appears where the steel belts end in relation to the tread. It can be kept to a minimum by paying careful attention to tire pressure and frequently rotating the tires. This is often considered normal wear but excessive amounts indicate that the tires are too wide for the wheels.

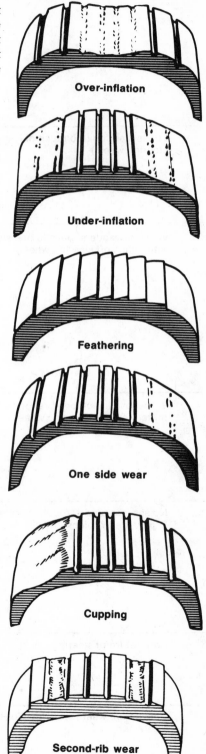

Over-inflation

Under-inflation

Feathering

One side wear

Cupping

Second-rib wear

Troubleshooting Disc Brake Problems

Condition	Possible Cause
Noise—groan—brake noise emanating when slowly releasing brakes (creep-groan)	Not detrimental to function of disc brakes—no corrective action required. (This noise may be eliminated by slightly increasing or decreasing brake pedal efforts.)
Rattle—brake noise or rattle emanating at low speeds on rough roads, (front wheels only).	1. Shoe anti-rattle spring missing or not properly positioned. 2. Excessive clearance between shoe and caliper. 3. Soft or broken caliper seals. 4. Deformed or misaligned disc. 5. Loose caliper.
Scraping	1. Mounting bolts too long. 2. Loose wheel bearings. 3. Bent, loose, or misaligned splash shield.
Front brakes heat up during driving and fail to release	1. Operator riding brake pedal. 2. Stop light switch improperly adjusted. 3. Sticking pedal linkage. 4. Frozen or seized piston. 5. Residual pressure valve in master cylinder. 6. Power brake malfunction. 7. Proportioning valve malfunction.
Leaky brake caliper	1. Damaged or worn caliper piston seal. 2. Scores or corrosion on surface of cylinder bore.
Grabbing or uneven brake action—Brakes pull to one side	1. Causes listed under "Brakes Pull". 2. Power brake malfunction. 3. Low fluid level in master cylinder. 4. Air in hydraulic system. 5. Brake fluid, oil or grease on linings. 6. Unmatched linings. 7. Distorted brake pads. 8. Frozen or seized pistons. 9. Incorrect tire pressure. 10. Front end out of alignment. 11. Broken rear spring. 12. Brake caliper pistons sticking. 13. Restricted hose or line. 14. Caliper not in proper alignment to braking disc. 15. Stuck or malfunctioning metering valve. 16. Soft or broken caliper seals. 17. Loose caliper.
Brake pedal can be depressed without braking effect	1. Air in hydraulic system or improper bleeding procedure. 2. Leak past primary cup in master cylinder. 3. Leak in system. 4. Rear brakes out of adjustment. 5. Bleeder screw open.
Excessive pedal travel	1. Air, leak, or insufficient fluid in system or caliper. 2. Warped or excessively tapered shoe and lining assembly. 3. Excessive disc runout. 4. Rear brake adjustment required. 5. Loose wheel bearing adjustment. 6. Damaged caliper piston seal. 7. Improper brake fluid (boil). 8. Power brake malfunction. 9. Weak or soft hoses.

Troubleshooting Disc Brake Problems (cont.)

Condition	Possible Cause
Brake roughness or chatter (pedal pumping)	1. Excessive thickness variation of braking disc. 2. Excessive lateral runout of braking disc. 3. Rear brake drums out-of-round. 4. Excessive front bearing clearance.
Excessive pedal effort	1. Brake fluid, oil or grease on linings. 2. Incorrect lining. 3. Frozen or seized pistons. 4. Power brake malfunction. 5. Kinked or collapsed hose or line. 6. Stuck metering valve. 7. Scored caliper or master cylinder bore. 8. Seized caliper pistons.
Brake pedal fades (pedal travel increases with foot on brake)	1. Rough master cylinder or caliper bore. 2. Loose or broken hydraulic lines/connections. 3. Air in hydraulic system. 4. Fluid level low. 5. Weak or soft hoses. 6. Inferior quality brake shoes or fluid. 7. Worn master cylinder piston cups or seals.

Troubleshooting Drum Brakes

Condition	Possible Cause
Pedal goes to floor	1. Fluid low in reservoir. 2. Air in hydraulic system. 3. Improperly adjusted brake. 4. Leaking wheel cylinders. 5. Loose or broken brake lines. 6. Leaking or worn master cylinder. 7. Excessively worn brake lining.
Spongy brake pedal	1. Air in hydraulic system. 2. Improper brake fluid (low boiling point). 3. Excessively worn or cracked brake drums. 4. Broken pedal pivot bushing.
Brakes pulling	1. Contaminated lining. 2. Front end out of alignment. 3. Incorrect brake adjustment. 4. Unmatched brake lining. 5. Brake drums out of round. 6. Brake shoes distorted. 7. Restricted brake hose or line. 8. Broken rear spring. 9. Worn brake linings. 10. Uneven lining wear. 11. Glazed brake lining. 12. Excessive brake lining dust. 13. Heat spotted brake drums. 14. Weak brake return springs. 15. Faulty automatic adjusters. 16. Low or incorrect tire pressure.

Condition	Possible Cause
Squealing brakes	1. Glazed brake lining. 2. Saturated brake lining. 3. Weak or broken brake shoe retaining spring. 4. Broken or weak brake shoe return spring. 5. Incorrect brake lining. 6. Distorted brake shoes. 7. Bent support plate. 8. Dust in brakes or scored brake drums. 9. Linings worn below limit. 10. Uneven brake lining wear. 11. Heat spotted brake drums.
Chirping brakes	1. Out of round drum or eccentric axle flange pilot.
Dragging brakes	1. Incorrect wheel or parking brake adjustment. 2. Parking brakes engaged or improperly adjusted. 3. Weak or broken brake shoe return spring. 4. Brake pedal binding. 5. Master cylinder cup sticking. 6. Obstructed master cylinder relief port. 7. Saturated brake lining. 8. Bent or out of round brake drum. 9. Contaminated or improper brake fluid. 10. Sticking wheel cylinder pistons. 11. Driver riding brake pedal. 12. Defective proportioning valve. 13. Insufficient brake shoe lubricant.
Hard pedal	1. Brake booster inoperative. 2. Incorrect brake lining. 3. Restricted brake line or hose. 4. Frozen brake pedal linkage. 5. Stuck wheel cylinder. 6. Binding pedal linkage. 7. Faulty proportioning valve.
Wheel locks	1. Contaminated brake lining. 2. Loose or torn brake lining. 3. Wheel cylinder cups sticking. 4. Incorrect wheel bearing adjustment. 5. Faulty proportioning valve.
Brakes fade (high speed)	1. Incorrect lining. 2. Overheated brake drums. 3. Incorrect brake fluid (low boiling temperature). 4. Saturated brake lining. 5. Leak in hydraulic system. 6. Faulty automatic adjusters.
Pedal pulsates	1. Bent or out of round brake drum.
Brake chatter and shoe knock	1. Out of round brake drum. 2. Loose support plate. 3. Bent support plate. 4. Distorted brake shoes. 5. Machine grooves in contact face of brake drum (Shoe Knock). 6. Contaminated brake lining. 7. Missing or loose components. 8. Incorrect lining material. 9. Out-of-round brake drums. 10. Heat spotted or scored brake drums. 11. Out-of-balance wheels.

Troubleshooting Drum Brakes (cont.)

Condition	Possible Cause
Brakes do not self adjust	1. Adjuster screw frozen in thread. 2. Adjuster screw corroded at thrust washer. 3. Adjuster lever does not engage star wheel. 4. Adjuster installed on wrong wheel.
Brake light glows	1. Leak in the hydraulic system. 2. Air in the system. 3. Improperly adjusted master cylinder pushrod. 4. Uneven lining wear. 5. Failure to center combination valve or proportioning valve.

Appendix

General Conversion Table

Multiply by	To convert	To	
2.54	Inches	Centimeters	.3937
30.48	Feet	Centimeters	.0328
.914	Yards	Meters	1.094
1.609	Miles	Kilometers	.621
6.45	Square inches	Square cm.	.155
.836	Square yards	Square meters	1.196
16.39	Cubic inches	Cubic cm.	.061
28.3	Cubic feet	Liters	.0353
.4536	Pounds	Kilograms	2.2045
3.785	Gallons	Liters	.264
.068	Lbs./sq. in. (psi)	Atmospheres	14.7
.138	Foot pounds	Kg. m.	7.23
1.014	H.P. (DIN)	H.P. (SAE)	.9861
—	To obtain	From	Multiply by

Note: 1 cm. equals 10 mm.; 1 mm. equals .0394".

Conversion—Common Fractions to Decimals and Millimeters

Common Fractions	Decimal Fractions	Millimeters (approx.)	Common Fractions	Decimal Fractions	Millimeters (approx.)	Common Fractions	Decimal Fractions	Millimeters (approx.)
1/128	.008	0.20	11/32	.344	8.73	43/64	.672	17.07
1/64	.016	0.40	23/64	.359	9.13	11/16	.688	17.46
1/32	.031	0.79	3/8	.375	9.53	45/64	.703	17.86
3/64	.047	1.19	25/64	.391	9.92	23/32	.719	18.26
1/16	.063	1.59	13/32	.406	10.32	47/64	.734	18.65
5/64	.078	1.98	27/64	.422	10.72	3/4	.750	19.05
3/32	.094	2.38	7/16	.438	11.11	49/64	.766	19.45
7/64	.109	2.78	29/64	.453	11.51	25/32	.781	19.84
1/8	.125	3.18	15/32	.469	11.91	51/64	.797	20.24
9/64	.141	3.57	31/64	.484	12.30	13/16	.813	20.64
5/32	.156	3.97	1/2	.500	12.70	53/64	.828	21.03
11/64	.172	4.37	33/64	.516	13.10	27/32	.844	21.43
3/16	.188	4.76	17/32	.531	13.49	55/64	.859	21.83
13/64	.203	5.16	35/64	.547	13.89	7/8	.875	22.23
7/32	.219	5.56	9/16	.563	14.29	57/64	.891	22.62
15/64	.234	5.95	37/64	.578	14.68	29/32	.906	23.02
1/4	.250	6.35	19/32	.594	15.08	59/64	.922	23.42
17/64	.266	6.75	39/64	.609	15.48	15/16	.938	23.81
9/32	.281	7.14	5/8	.625	15.88	61/64	.953	24.21
19/64	.297	7.54	41/64	.641	16.27	31/32	.969	24.61
5/16	.313	7.94	21/32	.656	16.67	63/64	.984	25.00
21/64	.328	8.33						

Conversion—Millimeters to Decimal Inches

mm	inches	mm	inches	mm	inches	mm	inches	mm	inches
1	.039 370	31	1.220 470	61	2.401 570	91	3.582 670	210	8.267 700
2	.078 740	32	1.259 840	62	2.440 940	92	3.622 040	220	8.661 400
3	.118 110	33	1.299 210	63	2.480 310	93	3.661 410	230	9.055 100
4	.157 480	34	1.338 580	64	2.519 680	94	3.700 780	240	9.448 800
5	.196 850	35	1.377 949	65	2.559 050	95	3.740 150	250	9.842 500
6	.236 220	36	1.417 319	66	2.598 420	96	3.779 520	260	10.236 200
7	.275 590	37	1.456 689	67	2.637 790	97	3.818 890	270	10.629 900
8	.314 960	38	1.496 050	68	2.677 160	98	3.858 260	280	11.032 600
9	.354 330	39	1.535 430	69	2.716 530	99	3.897 630	290	11.417 300
10	.393 700	40	1.574 800	70	2.755 900	100	3.937 000	300	11.811 000
11	.433 070	41	1.614 170	71	2.795 270	105	4.133 848	310	12.204 700
12	.472 440	42	1.653 540	72	2.834 640	110	4.330 700	320	12.598 400
13	.511 810	43	1.692 910	73	2.874 010	115	4.527 550	330	12.992 100
14	.551 180	44	1.732 280	74	2.913 380	120	4.724 400	340	13.385 800
15	.590 550	45	1.771 650	75	2.952 750	125	4.921 250	350	13.779 500
16	.629 920	46	1.811 020	76	2.992 120	130	5.118 100	360	14.173 200
17	.669 290	47	1.850 390	77	3.031 490	135	5.314 950	370	14.566 900
18	.708 660	48	1.889 760	78	3.070 860	140	5.511 800	380	14.960 600
19	.748 030	49	1.929 130	79	3.110 230	145	5.708 650	390	15.354 300
20	.787 400	50	1.968 500	80	3.149 600	150	5.905 500	400	15.748 000
21	.826 770	51	2.007 870	81	3.188 970	155	6.102 350	500	19.685 000
22	.866 140	52	2.047 240	82	3.228 340	160	6.299 200	600	23.622 000
23	.905 510	53	2.086 610	83	3.267 710	165	6.496 050	700	27.559 000
24	.944 880	54	2.125 980	84	3.307 080	170	6.692 900	800	31.496 000
25	.984 250	55	2.165 350	85	3.346 450	175	6.889 750	900	35.433 000
26	1.023 620	56	2.204 720	86	3.385 820	180	7.086 600	1000	39.370 000
27	1.062 990	57	2.244 090	87	3.425 190	185	7.283 450	2000	78.740 000
28	1.102 360	58	2.283 460	88	3.464 560	190	7.480 300	3000	118.110 000
29	1.141 730	59	2.322 830	89	3.503 903	195	7.677 150	4000	157.480 000
30	1.181 100	60	2.362 200	90	3.543 300	200	7.874 000	5000	196.850 000

To change decimal millimeters to decimal inches, position the decimal point where desired on either side of the millimeter measurement shown and reset the inches decimal by the same number of digits in the same direction. For example, to convert 0.001 mm to decimal inches, reset the decimal behind the 1 mm (shown on the chart) to 0.001; change the decimal inch equivalent (0.039" shown) to 0.000039".

Tap Drill Sizes

National Fine or S.A.E.

Screw & Tap Size	Threads Per Inch	Use Drill Number
No. 5	44	37
No. 6	40	33
No. 8	36	29
No. 10	32	21
No. 12	28	15
1/4	28	3
5/16	24	1
3/8	24	Q
7/16	20	W
1/2	20	29/64
9/16	18	33/64
5/8	18	37/64
3/4	16	11/16
7/8	14	13/16
1 1/8	12	1 3/64
1 1/4	12	1 11/64
1 1/2	12	1 27/64

Tap Drill Sizes

National Coarse or U.S.S.

Screw & Tap Size	Threads Per Inch	Use Drill Number
No. 5	40	39
No. 6	32	36
No. 8	32	29
No. 10	24	25
No. 12	24	17
1/4	20	8
5/16	18	F
3/8	16	5/16
7/16	14	U
1/2	13	27/64
9/16	12	31/64
5/8	11	17/32
3/4	10	21/32
7/8	9	49/64
1	8	7/8
1 1/8	7	63/64
1 1/4	7	1 7/64
1 1/2	6	1 11/32

Decimal Equivalent Size of the Number Drills

Drill No.	Decimal Equivalent	Drill No.	Decimal Equivalent	Drill No.	Decimal Equivalent
80	.0135	53	.0595	26	.1470
79	.0145	52	.0635	25	.1495
78	.0160	51	.0670	24	.1520
77	.0180	50	.0700	23	.1540
76	.0200	49	.0730	22	.1570
75	.0210	48	.0760	21	.1590
74	.0225	47	.0785	20	.1610
73	.0240	46	.0810	19	.1660
72	.0250	45	.0820	18	.1695
71	.0260	44	.0860	17	.1730
70	.0280	43	.0890	16	.1770
69	.0292	42	.0935	15	.1800
68	.0310	41	.0960	14	.1820
67	.0320	40	.0980	13	.1850
66	.0330	39	.0995	12	.1890
65	.0350	38	.1015	11	.1910
64	.0360	37	.1040	10	.1935
63	.0370	36	.1065	9	.1960
62	.0380	35	.1100	8	.1990
61	.0390	34	.1110	7	.2010
60	.0400	33	.1130	6	.2040
59	.0410	32	.1160	5	.2055
58	.0420	31	.1200	4	.2090
57	.0430	30	.1285	3	.2130
56	.0465	29	.1360	2	.2210
55	.0520	28	.1405	1	.2280
54	.0550	27	.1440		

Decimal Equivalent Size of the Letter Drills

Letter Drill	Decimal Equivalent	Letter Drill	Decimal Equivalent	Letter Drill	Decimal Equivalent
A	.234	J	.277	S	.348
B	.238	K	.281	T	.358
C	.242	L	.290	U	.368
D	.246	M	.295	V	.377
E	.250	N	.302	W	.386
F	.257	O	.316	X	.397
G	.261	P	.323	Y	.404
H	.266	Q	.332	Z	.413
I	.272	R	.339		

Index